Culture and
Customs of
Costa Rica

D0002570

Recent Titles in
Culture and Customs of Latin America and the Caribbean

Culture and Customs of Argentina
David William Foster, Melissa Fitch Lockhart, and Darrell B. Lockhart

Culture and Customs of Colombia
Raymond Leslie Williams and Kevin G. Guerrieri

Culture and Customs of the Dominican Republic
Isabel Z. Brown

Culture and Customs of Ecuador
Michael Handelsman

Culture and Customs of Costa Rica

Chalene Helmuth

Culture and Customs of Latin America
and the Caribbean
Peter Standish, Series Editor

GREENWOOD PRESS
Westport, Connecticut • London

Library of Congress Cataloging-in-Publication Data

Helmuth, Chalene, 1965–
  Culture and customs of Costa Rica / Chalene Helmuth.
    p. cm.—(Culture and customs of Latin America and the Caribbean, ISSN 1521–8856)
  Includes bibliographical references and index.
  ISBN 0–313–30492–0 (alk. paper)
    1. Costa Rica—Civilization—20th century. 2. Costa Rica—Social life and
  customs. I. Title. II. Series.
  F1548.H45 2000
  972.8605—dc21   99–089161

British Library Cataloguing in Publication Data is available.

Library of Congress Catalog Card Number: 99–089161
ISBN: 0–313–30492–0
ISSN: 1521–8856

First published in 2000

Greenwood Press, 88 Post Road West, Westport, CT 06881
An imprint of Greenwood Publishing Group, Inc.
www.greenwood.com

Printed in the United States of America

The paper used in this book complies with the
Permanent Paper Standard issued by the National
Information Standards Organization (Z39.48–1984).

10 9 8 7 6 5 4 3 2 1

To Carmen Naranjo,
who embodies Costa Rican hospitality

Contents

Illustrations   ix

Series Foreword   xi

Acknowledgments   xiii

Introduction   xv

Chronology   xix

1   **Unique in Latin America**   1

2   **The Legacy of Social Reform: What Makes Costa Rica So Different**   27

3   **Religion**   43

4   **Social Customs**   59

5   **Broadcasting and Print Media**   77

6   **Literature**   85

7   **Performing Arts**   99

8 Art   111

Appendix A: Internet Resources   119

Appendix B: Presidential Elections 1953–Present   121

Appendix C: Costa Rica at a Glance   123

Glossary   125

Selected Bibliography   129

Index   131

Illustrations

Map of Costa Rica   xiv

National Post Office   3

Coffee tree   13

Children line up to "vote"   33

A mother walks home with her schoolchildren   35

Metropolitan Cathedral   51

Neighborhood *pulpería*   60

Soda Tapia   62

Farmer's market   65

Women's soccer match   68

City park   69

Preparing for the holidays   72

Fruit market   75

Urban landscape   79

Carmen Naranjo and friends   92

Grupo de Cámara Surá   100

Street performer   103

An artist at work   112

Series Foreword

"CULTURE" is a problematic word. In everyday language we tend to use it in at least two senses. On the one hand, we speak of cultured people and places full of culture, uses that imply a knowledge or presence of certain forms of behavior or of artistic expression that are socially prestigious. In this sense large cities and prosperous people tend to be seen as the most cultured. On the other hand, there is an interpretation of "culture" that is broader and more anthropological; culture in this broader sense refers to whatever traditions, beliefs, customs, and creative activities characterize a given community—in short, it refers to what makes that community different from others. In this second sense, everyone has culture; indeed, it is impossible to be without culture.

The problems associated with the idea of culture have been exacerbated in recent years by two trends: less respectful use of language and a greater blurring of cultural differences. Nowadays, "culture" often means little more than behavior, attitude, or atmosphere. We hear about the culture of the boardroom, of the football team, of the marketplace; there are books with titles like *The Culture of War* by Richard Gabriel (Greenwood, 1990) or *The Culture of Narcissism* by Christopher Lasch (1979). In fact, as Christopher Clausen points out in a recent article published in the *American Scholar* (Summer 1996), we have gotten ourselves into trouble by using the term so sloppily.

People who study culture generally assume that culture (in the anthropological sense) is learned, not genetically determined. Another general assumption made in these days of multiculturalism has been that cultural differences should be respected rather than put under pressure to change. But these assumptions, too, have sometimes proved to be problematic. For instance, multiculturalism is a fine ideal, but in practice it is not always easy to reconcile it with the beliefs of the very people who advocate it: for example, is female circumcision an issue of human rights or just a different cultural practice?

The blurring of cultural differences is a process that began with the steamship, increased with radio, and is now racing ahead with the Internet. We are becoming globally homogenized. Since the English-speaking world (and the United States in particular) is the dominant force behind this process of homogenization, it behooves us to make efforts to understand the sensibilities of members of other cultures.

This series of books, a contribution toward that greater understanding, deals with the neighbors of the United States, with people who have just as much right to call themselves Americans. What are the historical, institutional, religious, and artistic features that make up the modern culture of such peoples as the Haitians, the Chileans, the Jamaicans, and the Guatemalans? How are their habits and assumptions different from our own? What can we learn from them? As we familiarize ourselves with the ways of other countries, we come to see our own from a new perspective.

Each volume in the series focuses on a single country. With slight variations to accommodate national differences, each begins by outlining the historical, political, ethnic, geographical, and linguistic context, as well as the religious and social customs, and then proceeds to a discussion of a variety of artistic activities, including the press, the media, the cinema, music, literature, and the visual and performing arts. The authors are all intimately acquainted with the countries concerned: some were born or brought up in them, and each has a professional commitment to enhancing the understanding of the culture in question.

We are inclined to suppose that our ways of thinking and behaving are normal. And so they are . . . for us. We all need to realize that ours is only one culture among many, and that it is hard to establish by any rational criteria that ours as a whole is any better (or worse) than any other. As individual members of our immediate community, we know that we must learn to respect our differences from one another. Respect for differences between cultures is no less vital. This is particularly true of the United States, a nation of immigrants, but one that sometimes seems to be bent on destroying variety at home, and, worse still, on having others follow suit. By learning about other people's cultures, we come to understand and respect them; we earn their respect for us; and, not least, we see ourselves in a new light.

Peter Standish
East Carolina University

Acknowledgments

I WOULD LIKE to thank all of those who helped me during the course of this project, especially my family and friends here and in Costa Rica. Wendi Schnaufer at Greenwood Press and Peter Standish provided valuable guidelines for the project's focus, and sent helpful comments along the way. Centre College provided support at key junctures in the preparation of this manuscript. My colleague Phyllis Bellver read the manuscript and provided useful feedback, and Elmer Lehman and Henry Helmuth took the time to reminisce about their experiences as missionaries in Costa Rica. David R. Mullins' expertise in film developing enhanced the book's final presentation, and Marcela Moya's timely assistance was the push needed to get the final version done. Last but by no means least, Christy Halbert took photographs that helped focus my writing. I am grateful to her for her joyful companionship, resilient patience, and genuine interest in Costa Rica.

Map of Costa Rica. Reprinted from DEMANDING DEMOCRACY: REFORM AND RE-ACTION IN COSTA RICA AND GUATEMALA, 1870S–1950S, by Deborah J. Yashar with the permission of the publishers, Stanford University Press. © 1997 by the Board of Trustees of the Leland Stanford Junior University.

Introduction

MOST COSTA RICANS are instilled with the sense that theirs is a unique place in the world. This attitude stems from the traits that set Costa Rica apart from other nations in the region: ethnic makeup; a large middle class; a relatively long and certainly productive tradition of democracy; a historically positive relationship with its bordering nations and with the United States. Indeed, Costa Rica often benefits from comparisons with its Latin American neighbors in terms of political climate, economic stability, and social progressiveness. For the foreign visitor particularly, Costa Rica is the regular winner in ratings of hospitality, physical beauty, ease of travel, and—for better or worse—similarity to the United States.

Divided into seven provinces that vary widely in terrain, flora and fauna, folklore, and cuisine, Costa Rica has long been called *la Suiza centroamericana* (the Switzerland of Central America), in a telling identification with the nation known for its spectacular landscapes and pacifism. Nearly 1.8 million people—over half of Costa Rica's population—live in the Central Valley, nestled within an impressive mountain range that is topped with volcanoes. Most tourists are familiar with Costa Rica's vast array of beaches, and all the world knows of its lush rain and cloud forests. Conscious of its wealth of natural resources, this country has an international reputation in conservation efforts that is well deserved.

Costa Rica boasts a long-standing pacifist stance: the army was abolished in 1948 and since then the government has employed only a civilian police force. In 1987, former president Oscar Arias was awarded the Nobel Peace Prize for his leadership in Central American peace initiatives. Costa Rica also serves as the site of the Latin American headquarters for many international companies and non-profit organizations, as well as a base for foreign-study programs for U.S. colleges and universities. These institutions often cite the nation's peaceful politics, the warm reception from its citizens, and a relatively stable economic environment as reasons for their choice of Costa Rica.

This nation is also proud of its liberal social programs. While not without violence, Costa Rican history gives evidence of conscious choices, at critical junctures, for peace. Following a brief civil war in 1948, the resulting governing coalition based its reforms on a moderate socialist agenda. Citizens witnessed a redirection of funds into education, health, and social security, including generous pension plans. In the 1960s and 1970s, efforts were made to equalize the availability of medical treatment, opportunities for education, and economic development in rural areas. Costa Ricans highly value education (which is free from age six to 12, and compulsory through age 14), and teachers and professors enjoy great social status.

The results of reforms initiated in the late 1940s and early 1950s are impressive: at 97 percent, Costa Rica's literacy rate is one of the highest in the Western Hemisphere; and its voting rate (at nearly 80 percent) puts other democracies in the world to shame.

For these reasons at least, Costa Rica sees itself in the same category as so-called first-world nations like the United States. It espouses democratic ideals and has an impressive economic and educational legacy to substantiate this claim of advanced development. Its government is stable; there is a regular turnover of state officials and delegates who are elected peacefully; and the country's citizens enjoy a wide range of government-funded social and health programs.

It is also noteworthy that many Costa Ricans identify with the whiteness of the United States. Some like to point out that most Ticos (a term derived from the ubiquitous habit of using the diminutive suffix "-tico") look more like their European ancestors than like their native indigenous ones. Although this attitude is representative of many Latin Americans, racism in Costa Rica reveals itself in sometimes surprising contexts in this otherwise progressive culture. The segment of the population of African-Caribbean descent resides mostly on the eastern coast where, typically, educational programs and social services are neglected and underfunded.

The situation among indigenous peoples is similarly discouraging. At less than 1 percent, they comprise a small minority of the population, which is concentrated in rather remote locations in the southern region of the country. Indigenous Costa Ricans have only had local voting booths available since the 1994 presidential elections. Their communities, too, typically suffer from neglect under otherwise generous national programs in health, social services, and education. There is, however, a growing awareness of the disparity in these programs, and a consequent support for the implementation of equalizing measures. The University of Costa Rica and the Instituto Nacional de Turismo (National Tourism Institute) are two organizations spearheading efforts to revaluate the native indigenous contribution to the country's history and culture.

The last two decades have witnessed other changes as well. Costa Rica experienced a significant economic downturn in the 1980s, due particularly to worldwide changes in the coffee and banana export markets. The *colón* (Costa Rica's currency, named after Christopher Columbus, or Cristóbal Colón in Spanish) suffered significant devaluation, and inflation rose sharply during this period. As a result, many families have seen their economic assets shrink severely and poverty is on the rise.

But during the 1980s, tourism—always a steady source of national income—saw massive growth. The spectacular popularity of ecotourism took hold in Costa Rica. Unfortunately, this nation, so well known for its vast network of national parks and reserves, has witnessed an intensified rate of deforestation. While laws protecting the environment are very good, they are not always enforced. An influx of investors (many of them foreigners) have sought to develop—with varying degrees of commitment to maintaining the integrity of natural resources—beachfront zones and forested areas. Not only have property prices skyrocketed, but this trend, matched for years by industrial development, has resulted in massive losses of forests, an alarming rate of soil erosion, a rise in the number of endangered species (like the golden toad and the leatherback sea turtle), and accelerated pollution of waterways.

In the midst of these fluctuations in natural and economic resources, Costa Rican culture remains vibrant and progressive, taking leadership again in areas of debt reduction and conservation efforts. The seven provinces supply a rich cultural legacy, and Costa Ricans still look to the brighter side of life, stubborn in their optimism.

Costa Ricans exhibit great pride in their traditions and in their country's exceptional qualities. Yet they readily acknowledge their shortcomings and are eager to *quedar bien*, to make a good impression and keep the peace at all costs. They are extraordinarily hospitable, devoted to family, and scrupulously neat about their appearance. The Costa Ricans' enthusiastic appreciation of humor is evident in their inclination to make jokes about every conceivable event or attitude, and in their colorful and colloquial sayings, or *dichos ticos*.

Their observation of ritual is formalized, as Costa Ricans enjoy marking special occasions, from *quinceañeras* (a 15-year-old girl's formal birthday celebration), to trips abroad, to weddings. Traditions of celebration are venerated, calling for fairs, parades, dancing, and serenades throughout the year. At the end of every December the Avenida Central, a main thoroughfare in downtown San José, is blocked off to traffic so pedestrians can meander around in the midst of swirling confetti, intent on seeing and being seen.

Both the warmth and frequency of social interactions are legendary. It is not uncommon for a simple invitation to an afternoon *café* (coffee) to extend for hours into the evening, and to include all of the family and other acquaintances who happen to stop by. The Costa Rican psyche is loath to offend by leaving anyone out; in fact, a party is not a party without both family and friends present.

This nation of contrasts inspires affectionate praise from visitors and residents alike. Costa Rica merits a closer look at the factors shaping its vision of itself and the outside world. This book intends to address these and other questions of cultural relevance.

Chronology

11,000 B.C.E.	Evidence suggests that by this time, nomadic peoples are inhabiting the region now known as Costa Rica.
1,000 B.C.E.	The indigenous populations are largely agrarian, cultivating cassava, sweet potatoes, corn, and beans.
500 A.C.E.	Extensive trade routes have been established with other groups as far south as what today is Ecuador, and as far north as Mexico, distributing salt, cacao, quetzal feathers, and dyes extracted from shells. Artisans work with jade and gold.
1500	Various indigenous groups—among them the Corobicí, Chorotega, and Talamanca—populate what is now Costa Rica. At the time of the Europeans' arrival, they number an estimated 400,000.
1502	Christopher Columbus arrives at what is now Limón, on September 25, marking the first recorded European sighting of Costa Rica.
1510–70	The local Indian populations are decimated, mostly through slave labor and disease brought by the Spaniards.
1522	The Spanish forces, led by Gil González, begin a sporadic exploration of the Pacific coast. Costa Rica becomes the colony's official name in 1539.

1562	Juan Vázquez de Coronado, who later becomes the Costa Rican colony's first governor, leads Spanish explorations of the Central Valley.
1564	Cartago becomes the first permanent Spanish settlement in the region, under the dominion of the Viceroyalty of New Spain.
1635	Alleged appearance of *La negrita* (the Dark-Skinned One) at the site on which the Basilica of Our Lady of the Angels is constructed in 1926. She later becomes the patron saint of Costa Rica.
1706	Founding of Heredia, the City of Flowers.
1710	After years of struggle between the Spanish and the local Indians, the *cacique* (warrior chieftain) Pablo Presbere is captured and executed; the Talamanca region is finally wrested from Indian control.
1711	Eruption of Irazú Volcano and destruction of the city of Cartago.
1736	Founding of San José.
1782	The city of Alajuela is founded.
1817	The University of Santo Tomás is established; it closes in 1888 but will eventually reopen as the University of Costa Rica in 1940.
1821	Mexico declares its independence from Spain; the news takes six months to reach the southern areas of the colony (which included what is now Costa Rica). Costa Ricans celebrate Independence Day on September 15.
1821–23	Costa Rica joins the four other Central American territories in the United Provinces of Central America.
1823	Costa Rica declares itself a separate nation and writes its own constitution. San José is named the capital.
1824	The northern region of Guanacaste is annexed to Costa Rica on July 25, following Guanacaste's secession from Nicaragua.

1840s	Coffee production begins to grow exponentially.
1847	The law states that government should provide equal education for both sexes.
1852	The Concordat establishes Catholicism as the official religion of Costa Rica.
1856	William Walker invades Costa Rica, but is defeated by forces who rally against this common threat. A sense of nationhood is galvanized by this event; Juan Santamaría is immortalized as a national hero for setting fire to an enemy barricade.
1869	Education becomes free and obligatory.
1870–82	President Tomás Guardia levies taxes on coffee exports, and makes important initiatives in education and transportation.
1871	Construction of the railroad from San José to the Atlantic coast begins; it is completed in 1890.
1884	Bishop Thiel is expelled from the country for his support of liberal goals.
1888	Date for which the Generation of 1888 is named; this group of leaders helps create a social infrastructure that supports market development and the expansion of social programs. It also promotes the separation of church and state.
1880s	Thousands of West Indians and hundreds of Chinese arrive in Limón to work on construction of the railroad.
1890	Coffee is in production on a third of the Central Valley's land.
1897	The National Theater is inaugurated, funded by the government and the coffee-growing oligarchy.
1897–1910	Construction of the Pacific Railroad.
1908	Banana exports total $5 million, and the industry reaches its peak 10 years later.

1913   First celebration of Día del trabajador (Labor Day).

1927   Public Health Department is established.

1931   Founding of the Communist party.

1932   Creation of the National Association of Coffee Pro-
                ducers.

1934   In a landmark event for labor rights, banana workers
                strike against the United Fruit Company in the At-
                lantic region. The company eventually relocates to the
                southern Pacific region.

1940   President Rafael Angel Calderón Guardia initiates an
                aggressive period of social reform, establishing the cur-
                rent program of social security (in 1941), welfare
                (1942), and a labor code (1943), among others.

1942   A law is signed forbidding Black foreigners to enter
                the country; it is later repealed.

1943   An unusual coalition is formed by President Calderón,
                the Communist party, and the Catholic church. The
                coalition clears the path for widespread support of im-
                portant reforms.

1948   Charges of fraudulent elections escalate into a six-week
                civil war. Costa Rica's standing army is abolished soon
                after.

1948–49   The victorious National Liberation junta rules by de-
                cree for 18 months, led by José (Pepe) Figueres. A
                new constitution is adopted in 1949, declaring full
                citizenship rights to all who are born in Costa Rica
                (this affects Black and indigenous residents, primar-
                ily). After decades of struggle, women are granted the
                right to vote.

1949   President-elect Otilio Ulate becomes president after
                18 months under the junta.

1951   Alabama Quakers arrive and settle in Monteverde; to-
                day, this protected cloud forest attracts scientists and
                tourists from around the world. The government

	funds an institute that provides free instruction in painting and sculpture. Founding of the Partido Liberación Nacional (National Liberation party).
1953	Pepe Figueres is elected president; his government enacts numerous social reforms that eventually result in achieving the region's highest rates of literacy and health. The Castella Conservatory, offering free training in the arts for children, is founded by President Figueres.
1959	Founding of the Editorial Costa Rica, a government-subsidized publishing house.
1960	Date of first television transmission; by 1995, television sets can be found in over 90 percent of Costa Rican households.
1961	Arrival of Mennonite missionaries.
1962	Costa Rica becomes a member of the Central American Common Market; Costa Rican industry is dominated by foreign capital.
1968	Eruption of Arenal Volcano on July 29.
1970s	Creation of the National Youth Symphony Orchestra; influx of Chilean immigrants revitalizes the theater scene.
1976–86	Protestant membership triples; it is estimated that 20 percent of Costa Ricans will identify themselves as Protestant by 2010.
1978	Nicaraguan forces—both *sandinista* and contra sides— violate national boundaries, establishing covert training camps and gun-trading routes. Armed conflict in neighboring countries leads to a huge influx in immigration to Costa Rica, primarily from Nicaragua and El Salvador.
1980	Beginning of economic crisis; the *colón* plunges in value.
1983	La Amistad Biosphere Reserve is declared a World Heritage Site; 12 percent of the national territory is contained in this protected area. Founding of the Partido Unidad Social Christian (Social Christian Unity party.

1987	The Nobel Peace Prize is awarded to President Oscar Arias for his leadership in promoting Central American peace initiatives.
1989	Coffee prices plunge.
1990	Passage of the Bill for Women's True Equality.
1990s	*Maquiladoras* (textile companies' assembly plants moved from the United States) begin operation in Costa Rica.
1990	Tremendous growth in tourism, particularly ecotourism.
1994	The nationalized bank, Banco Anglo Costarricense, is forced to close due to corruption. Bribrí Indians are able to vote in the presidential elections within their own communities for the first time.
1996	The national electric company, Instituto Costarricence de Electricidad (ICE), begins its privatization process; today, cell phone usage appears to match that of standard phones. (Incidentally, the number of Internet accounts per capita in Costa Rica is second only to Chile's.) Private banks begin operations.
1997	Intel, the U.S.-owned information technology company, opens its regional headquarters in San José, reflecting a trend among transnational companies to open branches in Costa Rica, drawn by its political stability, level of education and English-speaking skills of the labor force, and investor-friendly laws.
1998	Writer Carmen Naranjo is nominated for the Nobel Prize in Literature.
1999	An influx of Colombian immigrants—13,000 during the first half of 1999—is telling of the economic pressures and political turmoil in Latin America; as in previous years, the stability of Costa Rica attracts citizens of nearby nations.

1

Unique in Latin America

ENVIRONMENT

OFTEN WHAT first draws people to Costa Rica is its natural beauty. Indeed, this country is endowed with an extraordinary diversity: two coastlines of white-, brown-, and black-sand beaches; rain forests and dry forests; rivers, marshes, forested swamps, and lagoons; banana, cacao, and palm plantations; pastures, savannas, volcanoes (three of ten are active). Four mountain ranges form a backbone that runs north to south through the middle of the country, broken only by the Central Plateau—an area approximately 15 by 40 miles in size—where two-thirds of the population resides. There are two seasons: the dry season (which in the Central Valley runs from December to March) and the rainy season (from April to November). At an altitude of 4,000 feet, San José maintains an ideal climate in the 70° Fahrenheit range. Along the coastline, the temperature oscillates between 80° and 90°, although in the mountains, the night air can be quite cool.

The variety of plant and animal life is incredible, and bird lovers flock to Costa Rica in hopes of seeing a quetzal or a macaw. In this country, which is the size of West Virginia, there are 850 bird species, more than in all of the United States and Canada combined (theirs total 350). In one biological research station alone (*La selva* or "the Jungle," located in northeastern Costa Rica), there are 1,200 species of flora (400 of them trees), over 400 species of birds, and more than 4,000 species of moths and butterflies in a 3,700-acre area.

Costa Ricans are very proud of their country's biodiversity, and regularly take advantage of the easy accessibility to spectacular outdoor spots during weekend trips to the beach, or a day trip to the cool mountains. In many ways, Costa Rica has become a model for conservation: at 29 percent, over a quarter of its land is within a protected area or is a national park. Tens of thousands of visitors visit these parks every year, as ecotourism has fostered huge growth in the Costa Rican tourist industry.

Ecotourism combines the lush and exotic quality of nature with the profitability, and sometimes the threat to nature, of traditional tourism. Ecotourist agencies offer three-day rafting trips down Class VI white water; travelers can stroll through a national park next to the beach at Manuel Antonio, where they are sure to spot several kinds of monkeys. Visitors can ride horses through the rain forest, watch giant sea turtles lay their eggs, and go scuba diving off the extensive coral reef near Cahuita on the Atlantic Ocean. One of the most popular activities that brings tourists to Costa Rica is the canopy tour: small cable cars transport people through the treetops of the forest, where tree sloths and many varieties of birds are easily spotted.

In recent decades, Costa Rica's numerous national parks have brought high praise from international conservation groups. The largest park, declared a World Heritage Site in 1983, is La Amistad (Friendship) Biosphere Reserve, located in the southern area of the country. Managed by the Costa Rican National Park Service, this reserve covers 1.5 million acres (12 percent of the national territory), and includes two national parks, one biological reserve, five Indian reserves, and a botanical garden equipped with a classroom and a laboratory.

It is paradoxical, then, that Costa Rica's rate of deforestation is higher than Brazil's. Environmentalists and park rangers continually face setbacks because they often lack the resources to enforce the integrity of the borders of these protected areas. While the laws are stringent (for instance, a permit must be obtained to cut a tree larger than 10 centimeters in diameter), local wardens with limited budgets have great difficulty in enforcing these enlightened measures. Several factors contribute to deforestation: hardwoods that are increasingly scarce are cut and sold at a high profit; and Costa Rica's longstanding tradition that allows enterprising individuals to secure the use of a piece of land simply by clearing it is deep-seated and difficult to change.

This alarming deforestation trend corroborates worries about population growth rates. In 1990 it was projected that, at present growth rates, Costa Rica's population would double in the next 28 years (by 2018). Efforts are being made continuously, both within the private sector and in the government, to educate Costa Ricans and visitors alike about the benefits of conservation. However, the financial benefits of development continue to hold

The National Post Office was built in 1914. Because the postal service does not offer home delivery, Costa Ricans go to a local post office to collect their mail. Photograph courtesy of Christy Halbert.

great appeal, so Costa Rica enters the twenty-first century both blessed and burdened with prime natural reserves within a rapidly developing world.

PROVINCES

Costa Rica's territory is divided into seven provinces, each named after its capital (except for Guanacaste, whose capital is Liberia). The provinces are subdivided into *cantones* that are governed locally by a Municipal Board. On the official national shield, the seven provinces are represented by the seven stars above the mountains and coastlines of Costa Rica. The Caño and Coco islands are also part of the national territory.

The provinces of San José and Cartago share the Central Plateau. Cartago is considered the repository of traditional Costa Rican values: the city of Cartago was Costa Rica's first capital, and many citizens can trace their lineage back to the founding families of this settlement. In addition, *cartagineses* (those from Cartago) are seen as more traditional than other Costa Ricans. With its urban sprawl, San José is definitely the center of Costa Rican business, technology, and cultural activity.

San José is bordered on the north by Alajuela and Heredia. The capital of Heredia is known as the City of Flowers; the province ends at the San Juan River on Costa Rica's northern border. Similarly, Alajuela stretches north to Nicaragua, but in the area closest to San José, the province is famous for its fertile lands and gentle climate. Much of the nation's coffee and fruit (mangoes, especially) are produced in this region.

The northern Pacific coast lies within the Guanacaste province. Although it was annexed from Nicaragua 34 years after Costa Rica's independence, Guanacaste is considered the cradle of Costa Rican culture, and many songs pay tribute to romanticized aspects of its ranching lifestyle. Two-thirds of the Pacific coast belong to Puntarenas. Its port capital has long been an important stop for freighters along the Pacific seaboard; Golfito, in the southern sector, is site of the banana plantations that are in operation today.

The province of Limón encompasses most of the Atlantic coastline, and is the home of the majority of Black Costa Ricans, the descendants of Jamaicans who came to build the railroad in the 1880s. The banana plantations of the early twentieth century have largely been replaced by the harvesting of cacao, palm, macadamia nuts, and teak. The port city of Limón is the site of the annual Carnavales de Limón (Limón Carnival), and the area's Black and Caribbean culture adds an important dimension to Costa Rican life. Bribrí Indians still live in the Talamanca region to the south. Historically, indigenous groups were concentrated also in the Nicoya area of Guanacaste and the Golfito region of Puntarenas.

AN ACCOUNT OF NATIVE POPULATIONS

Remains of the area's original inhabitants have been found that date back to 11,000 B.C.E. However, archaeological studies of these cultures, as well as the preservation of artifacts, have been hampered in part by the rainy seasons. The historical marginalization of native populations within Costa Rican society has also slowed recovery efforts. A glaring gap in Costa Rica's impressive path toward democracy is marked by the fact that citizens of Bribrí ethnicity have been able to vote in their place of residence only since the 1994 presidential elections. In recent decades, however, awareness of this situation has grown steadily, and more and more attempts—such as those spearheaded by the Art Department of the University of Costa Rica—are being made to support the recovery of Indian material cultures.

We do know that the earliest settlers, who may have arrived as early as 12,000 B.C.E., were nomadic hunters who fashioned a variety of objects of wood, hide, and bone. Four thousand years later, they were settling in permanent sites and subsisting on planted crops of cassava, sweet potatoes, corn, and beans. Recently recovered artifacts reveal the use of grinding stones, nutcrackers, axes, and cooking utensils made from materials such as clay, bamboo, shells, wood, and stone.

By 500 C.E., the social structure of the various indigenous groups was fixed in a hierarchy with the *cacique* (warrior chieftain) at the top; family ties formed the basis of tribal identity. Various commercial and political alliances were formed with other tribes, and trade routes were eventually established with more distant groups. The Atlantic Indian groups began trading with others as far south as what today is Ecuador, and those on the Pacific with peoples as far north as Mexico, distributing salt, cacao, quetzal feathers, and dyes extracted from shells. Jade pieces, reflecting Mayan patterns, were the basis for artwork until they were replaced by metalwork, following the *chibcha* influence from the south. Costa Rican gold pieces have been found in the Yucatán; the Costa Rican population also chewed coca. Thus, the influence of groups from both the north and the south is evident.

Recent scholarly research has yielded new information about the indigenous groups in Costa Rica, revealing a varied landscape of cultures. Although many languages were spoken, it appears that Huetar—the language of the Central Valley inhabitants—was used universally. They shared an animist worldview, believing that people, animals, and natural phenomena were spiritual entities that could bring good, harm, or danger. They also believed in the possibility of immortality, so that funerary rights treated the bodies of the deceased—especially those who were among the elite—with great care. In the case of the death of members of the nobility, their slaves were sacrificed in order to accompany them in the next life, and objects of value were buried alongside their bodies.

The *cacique* leadership structure flourished between 800 and 1500 C.E.; at this time, an agricultural economy was supplemented by hunting and fishing, as well as by the gathering of honey, salt, and fruit. Artisans produced a greater variety of functional and artistic objects, and today the remains of bridges, aqueducts, and drainage systems evidence the increasing urbanization of Indian groups during this period. Housing varied regionally, with groups in the northwest preferring buildings rectangular in shape; in the Atlantic region, enormous round structures with thatched roofs were built that could house as many as 300 people.

The indigenous population of the area that is now Costa Rica was estimated to be 400,000 in the early sixteenth century, and the people were concentrated in the northern Pacific area and in the Central Valley. While the relative proximity of some groups led to the establishment of alliances, in Costa Rica as well as the Guatemalan highlands and El Salvador, indigenous societies were not at all part of a centralized empire like that of the Maya in the lowlands of the Yucatán and Honduras. Rather, the groups in what is now Costa Rica were fragmented and very much localized; this factor contributed to the difficulties later encountered by the Spanish as they attempted to dominate the indigenous population. In addition, there is evidence that these tribes frequently engaged in war. For example, one statue recovered from the Atlantic region shows a warrior with an ax in one hand and an enemy's head in the other.

It seems that violent conflict among the differing groups was widespread and constant. Taking prisoners, particularly adolescent women, was a common tactic of domination; and slavery was common among indigenous groups. In addition, the Indians of the Pacific northwest were known to practice human sacrifice during certain ceremonies held three times a year. When the Spanish arrived, the bucolic nature of the indigenous groups, and the long-held practice of forming local alliances, both aided and hampered the European agenda to dominate the region.

ARRIVAL OF EUROPEANS

The first European sighting of Costa Rica is attributed to Christopher Columbus on September 25, 1502, at what is now the site of the port city of Limón. Making his way down the Central American coastline from Honduras, Columbus came upon a native settlement and was captivated by the sight of gold jewelry in the form of eagles' heads that many of the indigenous people wore. Fernández de Córdoba, who explored the territory several years later, impulsively named it *Costa Rica* (Rich Coast). Upon his arrival, Columbus wrote that he "had seen more signs of gold there in two days than in four years in Spain" (Bird 21). Anxious to justify to King Ferdinand the crown's investment in this fourth venture to the "New World," Columbus precipitously reported that he had found a potential treasure trove of wealth for the Spanish crown. Ironically, it seems that all the gold to be found in this region had already been mined, and that the native population was wearing it.

The absence of gold, the difficult terrain, the small native population (compared to the other areas of conquest), and the distance from the established centers of colonial rule in Mexico and Guatemala contributed to Costa Rica's unique development during the period of early colonization. The effects of this isolation from regional development are evident today and have distinguished Costa Rica's historical trajectory from that of other Central American nations.

At the time of the arrival of the Spanish fleet, the estimated population of

400,000 in Costa Rica flourished in tribes throughout the country. Groups like the Talamanca, Chorotega, Quepo, and Nicoya were decentralized, although the larger groups had developed a thriving trade route in the region of the Gulf of Nicoya, on the Pacific coastline.

While these indigenous groups were present at the time of the Spanish arrival, their numbers were relatively small and their population bases were spread out, in sharp contrast to Mexico's Central Valley, for instance. This made the establishment of colonial rule in Costa Rica difficult, but it did not keep the Spanish from seizing the opportunity to dominate the entire native population. Between 1536 and 1540, many native inhabitants were captured and sent as slave labor to Perú as well as other regions in the Spanish colonies.

The decimation of the Indian populations may be attributed primarily to the diseases they suffered as a result of the European presence. Smallpox, typhoid fever, measles, and other illnesses ravaged the locals. Those who survived disease or escaped capture retreated to remote areas, particularly to the Talamanca mountains in the south. Thus, the Spanish soon depleted the supply of native labor, and they found little else to exploit or develop in the region. One hundred years after Columbus had arrived, the population of Spaniards in Costa Rica had shrunk to 600.

EARLY COLONIAL PERIOD

Columbus remained in the Limón area only 18 days while he repaired his ships, and other explorers were slow to follow to this region. In fact, the Spanish conquest of the Costa Rican territory was not initiated from the Pacific until several years later. In 1522 the Spanish forces, led by Captain Gil González, began a sporadic exploration of the Pacific coast, and mainly engaged in trade with the Indians. González and the other explorers who came at this time were swayed as Columbus was by all the gold they saw. Costa Rica became the territory's official name in 1539.

The first attempts by the Spanish to establish settlements were met with significant resistance by the indigenous groups, who, as mentioned earlier, were prone to engage in armed conflict. Although several Spanish settlements were founded in the 1520s, the invaders were soon forced to abandon them due to relentless attacks by the indigenous population. It was not until 1562 that Juan Vázquez de Coronado, who later became the Costa Rican colony's first governor, led successful Spanish explorations of the Pacific coast. Eventually reaching the Central Valley, in 1564 he founded Cartago, Spain's first permanent settlement and part of the Viceroyalty of New Spain.

In the Atlantic region, the Spanish met with less success. From 1510 to

1542, at least seven expeditions were made with the intent of establishing settlements. None of these succeeded, and it would be a long time before anyone would settle in the area. In the course of defending their territory, many of the Indians fled deep into the Talamanca mountains. Even today, the Atlantic coast is much less populated than the rest of the country.

During the early period of colonization, the Spanish who remained in the area were left largely to themselves. The surviving native population continued to be practically enslaved through the system of *encomiendas*, a form of indentured servanthood in which individuals were tied indefinitely to the landowner whose land they worked. The native servants were deceived by the promise of eventually working off their debt and then owning the land and gaining autonomy; in reality, they were never allowed to buy property. Due to this diminishing work force, it became obvious that the *encomienda* type of labor was not profitable. Even the Spanish governors of Costa Rica had to work their own land in order to survive.

The Costa Rican territory was eventually included in a loose federation with other Central American regional territories under the auspices of a body called the Audiencia de las Fronteras (literally, Audience of the Outposts, also translated as High Court or Tribunal), which reached from Panama to southern Mexico. Then, in 1570, a new governing body—the Audiencia de Guatemala—was established with its headquarters far north of Costa Rica, in what is now southern Mexico. For the next 250 years, the Spanish crown dispensed laws that trickled down the political ranks and over dense and difficult terrain to distant population centers. Being far removed from the colonial seat, these imperial laws were nearly impossible to enforce in Costa Rica, and local governors went largely unmonitored. Cartago, the first Costa Rican capital, was established in 1564. Located in the northern sector of the Central Plateau, Cartago was the single Spanish settlement in the region until the late 1600s. (In Cartago today, the Basílica de los Angeles, or the Basilica of the Angels, still bears witness to the Spanish presence in its Baroque architecture.) The fact that there was only a small Spanish settlement so far from the imperial centers of governance led to an independently functioning, albeit isolated, colonial presence. Indeed, as has been mentioned, the inhabitants of Costa Rica were busy working their own land to survive, thereby fashioning an agricultural industry that relied on a composite of smaller, independently owned farms.

When its independence was obtained in 1821, Costa Rica's population numbered an estimated 57,000 people, most of them living in the Central Valley. During this period, the Spanish territories in the Americas had been undergoing the transition to independence. Each colony varied in its rate of change and breadth of departure from imperial rule. Changes in Spain itself were partly responsible for this: the Napoleonic invasion in 1820 and the ensuing liberal revolution brought instability to the monarchical government, and this weakening of control was felt an ocean away. In addition, the liberal philosophy of Rousseau was capturing the minds of Latin American intellectuals. The succession of Latin American independence took place rapidly, although from country to country it did not always follow the same steps to autonomy, and the resulting democracy in Costa Rica stands in sharp contrast to other governments in the continent: it has the longest-standing democracy in Latin America, while its closest neighbors all have suffered turbulent and violent histories of military rule. Costa Rican society has had a long and largely peaceful trajectory; there has generally been a place for the voicing of dissent and for agreement through compromise.

In spite of parallel developments with other Latin American countries to achieve independence from Spain, since that time Costa Rica has followed a different path. The factors shaping this reality are put forth in the following pages. The early reform period of the 1940s in particular demonstrates the story of Costa Rica's uniqueness. However, a description of the social, economic, and political background to this period is essential to understanding the uniquely democratic development of this country.

THE CENTRAL AMERICAN UNION

Mexico declared its independence from Spain in April 1821. On September 15, 1821, what are now the Central American nations of Costa Rica, Nicaragua, El Salvador, Honduras, and Guatemala declared themselves not only independent from Spain but separate from Mexico—and from the Mexican leader, Agustín Iturbide, who envisioned an empire that would include in its territory the entire isthmus reaching to Panama. An attempt was then made to form a union comprising the five Central American states. This initiative, called the United Provinces of Central America, eventually failed and was dissolved in 1839.

The short-lived Central American federation did, however, provide an early model of democratic rule. Its 1823 constitution structured a federal system, led by an elected president who would coordinate the five member states, and a federal congress; each state would elect its own chief or head. The states were to be independent in governance; the congress would legislate matters of interest to the general populace, and impose taxes to support the federal government. The economic clout of the burgeoning coffee-growing elite was influential in determining many political and social policies. The voice of the civilian sector was thereby beginning to be heard. It is important to note, however, that at this time suffrage was limited to white males of certain social and economic standing.

Meanwhile in South America, Simón Bolívar was attempting to forge a similar continental federation with little success. In Central America this fledgling political unification gave rise to significant adjustments to colonial patterns of governance. In each state a president, senate, and supreme court were elected; slavery was abolished, as were the special privileges of the nobility and the clergy; and Roman Catholicism was declared the only form of public worship, although this decree was subsequently changed to allow freedom of worship. A proposal to build a canal through Nicaragua was also part of the federation's economic plan: the existing waterways of the San Juan River and Lake Nicaragua left only 18 miles of dry land between the Atlantic and Pacific oceans. This plan was of course eventually discarded in favor of a passage through Panama.

Costa Rica was not a part of this Central American union for long, but its reforms helped shape Costa Rica's first constitution, written in December of 1823. That same year, after the Republicans, who favored independence from Spain, defeated the Monarchists centered in Cartago, the capital was moved to San José. Costa Rican territory now included the northern province of Guanacaste as well, which was annexed in 1824 following Guanacaste's secession from Nicaragua.

THE BEGINNINGS OF A NATION (1823–70)

As this newly consolidated nation began to define itself, Costa Rica's first 40 years of nationhood were tumultuous. Between 1824 and 1870, 22 men held power. The country was in need of national focus and an identity. Oddly enough, this sense of nationhood and patriotism came by way of a U.S. citizen, William Walker, who invaded the country in 1856.

Due in part to its policy of Manifest Destiny, the United States considered the territories south of its border accessible and easily acquirable. In 1856, American industrialist Cornelius Vanderbilt helped fund Walker's invasion of Nicaragua and Costa Rica, ostensibly in order to build an east-west canal along the border of the two countries. It seems, however, that the underlying motivation was the possibility of continuing the practice of slavery in these territories, once they were annexed to the United States.

By taking advantage of internal conflict between existing political factions within the country, Walker and his *filibusteros* (mercenaries)—including reinforcements from California—were able to advance into Costa Rica with their superior weaponry. Once the North American invaders had crossed the national border and reached Santa Rosa, Costa Rican President Juan Rafael Mora rallied volunteer troops, who forced Walker's retreat north to Rivas, Nicaragua.

The heroic adventures of individual soldiers in that conflict have survived for many years and have found a permanent place in Costa Rican historical lore. There is evidence that among the Costa Rican troops was a woman named Pancha Carrasco, who had volunteered as a cook, but who later filled her apron pockets with bullets and joined the men on the battlefield. Another example occurred on April 11, 1856, when the Costa Rican volunteers once again defeated Walker's trained troops. During this battle, a young fighter, named Juan Santamaría, was forever immortalized in the national consciousness when he was shot while setting fire to an enemy barricade. The international airport in San José is named after this hero, and many statues capture his moment of braveness on behalf of his country.

The ousting of a foreign invader caused the Costa Rican citizens to rally around the common goal of national defense. Their victory consolidated patriotic sentiment among Costa Ricans and created in them a sense of national identity. However, another important catalyst for growth as a nation came not from the military but from the economic sector, from the coffee industry in particular.

THE COFFEE INDUSTRY

Coffee first arrived in Costa Rica from Jamaica in 1808, and today, exports of Costa Rican Arabica beans account for a substantial amount of the world's supply. The fertility of the soil (enhanced by volcanic activity) and the ideal climate, along with an early government program to distribute seedlings to coffee growers, resulted in a boom in coffee production. By 1890, coffee was being produced on a third of the land in Costa Rica's Central Valley, where the majority (80 percent) of the population resided. Income increased and the boom created an elite of coffee-growing barons, German immigrants among them. The coffee barons' wealth gave rise to an economic oligarchy that permanently contributed to the shaping of the political and social institutions of this country. Distinct from its counterparts in neighboring countries, this prosperous group developed a sense of independence from the government. Unlike those in other Central American nations at the time, government-controlled labor markets were absent in Costa Rica. Thus, in Costa Rica the economic sector, and the general society by extension, was granted a place to develop, and it flourished.

The production of coffee was undertaken by both the coffee barons and smallholders, or laborers who owned the land they worked and who sold the coffee to larger producers for processing. (Even today, an estimated 130,000 farmers cultivate coffee and sell it to large processing plants and exporters.) Therefore in Costa Rica the agricultural economy was based on a network of producers, with both large and small land holdings. Earlier, Costa Rica had escaped the stamp of the feudal *encomienda* system of other Spanish colonies, and it was now able to avoid some of the problems confronted by neighboring countries. In Guatemala, Nicaragua, and El Salvador, for example, coffee production was still limited to a few landholders with vast territories who relied on landless rural workers, whose indebtedness to them was not far from the *encomiendas* of colonial rule. These neighboring countries also relied on government force to maintain and control the labor base, giving rise to repressive markets.

In Costa Rica, in contrast, a combination of factors merged to create a state that allowed its citizens to address the conflicts that arose during its early industrial and social development. Agricultural production was carried out by thousands of independent farmers who owned the land on which they cultivated coffee; through the boom in coffee exportation, Costa Rica entered the international sphere; the profits from this boom benefited individual farmers as well as the larger coffee producers who actually exported the goods. The economic prowess of this oligarchy opened doors to citizen involvement in matters of public policy, and eventually facilitated a reciprocal exchange in the sociopolitical arena between the government and the people. This was to set the tone for the goals of the next generation that ushered in the twentieth century.

THE LIBERAL PERIOD (1870–1940)

During the latter decades of the nineteenth century, the role of the members of the oligarchy had become increasingly participatory. In the early years of the twentieth century, the popular sector too began to make its voice heard, setting in place multiple venues for public expression in governmental affairs. Unfortunately, by the end of the liberal period in the 1940s, Costa Rican politics were characterized by "oligarchic collusion, ephemeral political parties, and fraudulent electoral politics" (Yashar 53).

Interestingly the seven decades of the liberal period began under an authoritarian government. General Tomás Guardia—whose descendants would figure prominently in the Costa Rican political scene—was elected president in 1870. At the time, individuals came to power less through public support

Coffee has long been a fixture of Costa Rican economic and cultural life. Outside of the urban areas in the Central Valley, the bright red beans and dark green leaves of coffee trees—which reach a height of five feet—are a common sight on personal property as well as on commercial farms. Photograph courtesy of Christy Halbert.

than by the design of the coffee-baron oligarchy and its military allies. As a result of their growing economic clout, the alliance between these two institutions had become enmeshed, and politics had become a matter of favoritism. When Guardia came to power, he enforced his rule through 12 years of mild militarism. Guardia did, however, make steady progress toward improving the lives of the average Costa Rican citizen by curbing the power of coffee barons, and levying taxes (affecting mostly this oligarchy) in order to put in place several important initiatives in public welfare programs—including education, public health, and transportation. After the death of Tomás Guardia in 1882, members of the Generation of 1888 took his place. These were leaders of Guardia's generation who brought further progressive measures to Costa Rican governance, and won the support of both the oligarchy and other social classes. They were able to create an infrastructure that would support expanding social programs, as well as market development. The Generation of 1888 was also committed to the separation of church and state.

At the turn of the century, however, things got worse before they improved. The economy depended entirely on one crop—coffee—and at the time 70 percent of the small coffee producers did not own the land on which they cultivated their crops, a result of the machinations of the enterprising coffee barons. The country's leadership entered an era of turmoil as the result of fraudulent elections. In 1889 the duly elected candidate was ignored and another candidate's rule imposed. In 1902, when members of the oligarchy and the government reached an agreement, a compromise candidate was named. During the following presidential term, Cleto González Víquez was appointed to the presidency by the outgoing head of state after three of the five contenders had been exiled.

In spite of this inauspicious beginning, González Víquez is revered today as one of Costa Rica's greatest leaders. He showed himself receptive to public opinion, and promoted public works and health care. His successor, Ricardo Jiménez, changed the voting system from an electoral college to a direct-vote policy. Congress would then choose between the two candidates with the most votes. During the subsequent elections and after a legitimate campaign, however, Congress did not follow the newly established rules: after two of the presidential candidates resigned, Congress declared the third one ineligible and chose the outgoing vice president instead.

Matters deteriorated as World War I brought a decline in exports and a rise in debts, and President Alfredo González Flores responded by levying high income taxes. In 1917 he was ousted in a coup led by his minister of war, Federico Tinoco. The Tinoco government was a dark blot on Costa Rica's record, as it threatened for the first time the basic rights of its citizens, filling jails with political prisoners and imposing rigorous control of the press.

The seeds of democratic protest had been sown much earlier, by Costa Rica's unusual colonial past and, ironically, by the participation of coffee barons in political affairs since the 1870s. This civilian involvement in the process of governance had allowed social reforms to take place, if only intermittently. Under Tinoco's increasingly repressive reign, these seeds bore fruit in a historical moment rich with symbolism. School teachers—mostly women—and high school students organized a demonstration and set fire to the pro-Tinoco newspaper plant. The government reacted by sending troops and firing into the U.S. Consulate where some demonstrators had fled. The Costa Rican Congress intervened: it gave Tinoco permission to resign, and in August of 1918, he went into exile in Europe.

By the end of the liberal period, the Costa Rican government had begun to function as a facilitator of significant social and civic programs. Education was free and compulsory through the sixth grade. By 1937 "workers had benefited from legislation that mandated a maximum workday (1920), accident insurance (1925), a minimum wage (1933), protection of mothers and children (1933), a commission to establish salaries (1934), and industrial hygiene (1937)" (Yashar 110).

The reforms listed above were brought about by somewhat fitful negotiations as this young democracy sought to establish itself. By the fourth decade of the twentieth century, Costa Rica's policy of internal compromise stood in stark contrast to other Central American nations, where authoritarian regimes were supported by regular, violent military intervention, and divided social classes were without an arena in which to address mutual concerns. Costa Rica was different from its Central American counterparts then as it is now, and in the years that followed the liberal period, even more impressive progress was made toward building an equitable society.

THE BANANA INDUSTRY

Today, Costa Rica is the world's second largest exporter of bananas, after Ecuador. But the banana industry in Costa Rica, as in most other Latin American areas, has had a troubled past. This industry's structure is rather insular and sustains few ties with other economic sectors; banana companies have a history of exploiting labor and local resources, of deal-making with governments, and of contributing little to local development. The same is true in Costa Rica, with U.S.-based companies that began their activities in Costa Rica in the late nineteenth century.

It was President Tomás Guardia who had approached the American John Meiggs for the purpose of building a railroad that would connect San José to the Atlantic. The railroad was built to provide a more efficient mode of transportation of coffee exports (which had previously been shipped from Puntarenas, on the western coast, to Europe via Cape Horn, the southern tip of South America), but it also made way for another pivotal development in the country's agricultural economy: the banana industry. The economic consequences of this new crop are widely documented, but the social and cultural toll is remarkable as well.

Construction of the railroad had been financed in the early 1870s by British bankers, but the bulk of the loans went to commissions, and the difficulty in crossing the terrain was such that a decade later, the Costa Rican government was in debt and still without a railroad. It is a fascinating story of how Meiggs' nephew, Minor Cooper Keith, came to play a significant role in the development of the banana industry. Keith had made a fortune from bananas a few years earlier, reportedly by planting bananas alongside the clearings made for the railroad tracks while he supervised the initial railroad construction, financed by his uncle's company. In 1883, Keith negotiated an incredible contract with Secretary of State Bernardo Soto to take over the completion of the railroad: in return for Keith's renegotiation of the British loans, the Costa Rican government would grant him nearly 7 percent of the nation's territory. Keith would cultivate the land and with the revenue, he would finance the railroad, which would in turn eventually become his private property as well.

Construction of the railroad began once again. However, the conditions of working in the humid lowlands proved unbearable for Costa Ricans, and Keith had to resort to imported labor, bringing in many Chinese workers and thousands of West Indians, mostly Jamaicans, to Costa Rica's southeastern coast. This influx of labor introduced an important cultural and racial diversity to Costa Rican society. With his vast resources, Keith and his work crew pushed through the grueling terrain, barely surviving the onslaught of disease and loss of workers (5,000 total) to build a railroad that now extends from San José to Limón. By the time the railroad was completed in 1890, seven years after Keith's infamous contract, banana exports had multiplied tenfold and had drawn the attention of other foreign investors. With sales of $5 million in 1908, the banana export industry soon outpaced coffee, reaching a peak in the second decade of the twentieth century. (In 1930, the United Fruit Company's assets totaled more than $400 million.) The growth of the banana industry was unprecedented, but not without questionable means of achieving such growth.

After its arrival in 1888, the Boston-based United Fruit Company had been left alone to manage the vast plantations it had established on the rather isolated Atlantic coast. The company was responsible for the housing, health care, and food supplies of its workers. In a classic case of worker exploitation, the housing was substandard, health care unavailable, and basic provisions were scarce, sold at inflated prices through the company's own commissaries. Wages were very low, and requests for improved conditions were denied, sometimes violently. Within the workers' barracks, in fact, the strictly hierarchical system was based on gradations of skin color. The company actually incited racial conflict among the workers: it operated on the premise that if workers blamed each other for harsh working conditions, they would be less likely to demand concessions from the company itself. Mistreatment on the plantations continued for years; it appeared as though the Limón province had become the personal possession of the United Fruit Company, and workers seemed to have no advocates.

In 1934, however, a historic event took place: 10,000 individuals participated in the banana workers' strike, one of the largest strikes in Latin America against a U.S. company. The two-week strike was successful, as the government eventually negotiated on behalf of the workers. This event became a rallying point for organized labor in Costa Rica. But rather than comply with new regulations on the banana industry, the United Fruit Company soon after pulled out its operations in the area, and relocated to the southern Pacific coast of Costa Rica, to an equally remote location near Golfito.

Certain other factors contributed to the closure of the United Fruit Company operations in the Atlantic region. The world at large suffered the effects of World War I and of the depression; leaf spot disease damaged crops; and racial tensions between workers escalated. The ensuing chain of events permanently marred Costa Rica's history. Faced with the potential loss of this major investor, the government capitulated to the demands of the United Fruit Company, and a law was signed that did not permit former employees to follow the relocation of the company's operations from the Atlantic coast to the Pacific coast. The company ostensibly wanted to ensure that the same striking workers did not make trouble in its new location; however, the law unmistakably based its specifications on skin color. In the late 1930s, President León Cortés imposed travel restrictions on Blacks, so that they could not go beyond Turrialba, an intermediary point between the Central Valley and the Atlantic region. Some individuals still recount the changing of railroad crews from Black to white workers at the Turrialba stop.

By 1942, banana shipments from Limón stopped, since the United Fruit Company had established its operations on the southern Pacific region. The Costa Rican government had allocated a sizable portion of land to the company, which replicated the production model and hierarchical social structure developed earlier in the Atlantic location. The barracks housing the workers had only minimal sanitary facilities, and the supervisors' dwellings reflected their status: these homes were air-conditioned bungalows, and a private country club complete with golf course was available to those in management, who tended to be either from the United States or Germany. By all accounts, the presence of the United Fruit Company in Costa Rica has been at the very least problematic.

BLACKS IN COSTA RICA

While Black immigrants arrived in Costa Rica as early as 1824, the majority of Black Costa Ricans are descendants of West Indians who came to build the railroad in the late nineteenth century. Black residents have historically lived apart from white Costa Ricans, separated by language, geography, and race; the relations between the two groups have often been strained. During the past hundred years, Blacks have arguably suffered at the hand of the law, experiencing prejudice and neglect. In turn, Blacks have been reticent to assimilate into the dominant culture, contributing to a sense of suspicion on both sides. In recent years, however, the Black community has gained increased visibility as tourism has developed an interest in exploiting this minority culture, and as the general Costa Rican population has begun to acknowledge its multiethnic heritage.

An overview of the legal status of Blacks may be helpful in considering the history of their communities in Costa Rica. West Indians who arrived in the 1880s did not intend to permanently settle in Costa Rica; rather, they planned to return to Jamaica with their earnings from work on the railroad and later on the banana plantations. Although many stayed in the Limón province for generations, Black descendants of the railroad workers were not granted rights to full citizenship until 1949.

For many years, then, Black residents were not considered true Costa Ricans. Adding to this sentiment was the fact that the Black community kept itself separate: they spoke English; they were not Catholic; they had their own Anglican and Episcopalian churches; and they established their own schools. The heavy hand of the United Fruit Company in the area led to governmental restrictions on travel within the country; preferential treatment was given to Costa Ricans in the company (since Blacks had no access to citizenship, they were excluded from these protections); and in 1942, Black immigrants were forbidden to enter the country. In spite of these conditions, Black culture in Costa Rica managed to flourish; it was not until after the social reforms of the late 1940s that the legal status of Black Costa Ricans improved.

In 1949, President Figueres was the first to acknowledge the Black presence in his country; Blacks had fought for the revolution he led, and during his visits to the Atlantic region, he reciprocated support as he spoke English with them. His declaration that anyone born in Costa Rica had all the rights of citizenship paved the way for the gradual inclusion of Blacks in the broader sphere of Costa Rican life.

While the city of Limón has remained the center of Black population in the country, today only 29 percent of the population is Black. The cacao boom financed a large migration from Limón to San José in the 1950s. The graduating class of 1957 at the University of Costa Rica was the first to include Black graduates, and Black professionals began to enter the urban work force. The first Black cabinet member, Maureen Clarke, was perhaps fittingly named minister of justice by Pepe Figueres' son, President José Maria Figueres, during his presidency in 1994–98.

The granting of full citizenship rights for Blacks brought a host of changes to the Black community, as those living in Limón seemed to be merely the recipients of changes determined far off in the capital, rather than possessing participatory voices in local change. The recent loss of banana industry–funded jobs and a lack of understanding of the laws (the language barrier was not a small factor) fueled a migration to Limón from rural areas within the Atlantic region. Many sold family-owned land to get there, as Black citizens became increasingly economically disenfranchised.

The educational system changed dramatically for Black children. Many English-speaking schoolchildren had been taught in schools that followed the British tradition common in Jamaica, in spite of repeated attempts by the Costa Rican government to standardize them. In 1910, for instance, a law imposed a fine on each day a Black schoolchild did not attend public school. After 1950, schools in Limón were told to adapt to the public system in place throughout the country, although this has not always been a smooth transition. As late as the 1970s, students who spoke English in class were punished.

Since 1950, intermarriage has increased and it is now fairly common. However, progress toward full equality for Blacks has been slow. The legacy of a racially based hierarchy—with lighter complexion bringing higher status—remains firmly in place, although white Costa Ricans are loath to admit this and certainly take issue with any charge of racism. Even so, Blacks continue to be portrayed in the media as not quite as Costa Rican as the rest of the country.

In order to accurately assess current conditions of life for Black Costa Ricans, since this segment of history has not been regularly incorporated into written accounts, it is best to listen to those voices from within that community. Local residents of the coastal Atlantic area are a good source of information regarding their fairly recent history; Quince Duncan and Eulalia Bernard are two writers who portray the Black Costa Rican experience in their novels and poetry. It is also important to acknowledge the role of tourism in bringing national and international attention to the preservation of Black communities in Costa Rica.

At the center of the recovery of Black culture is the town of Puerto Viejo, an hour's drive south of the city of Limón. This once-sleepy town has survived on harvesting fish and turtles, and on cultivating cacao, breadfruit, and coconut palms. It has developed a vibrant cultural legacy that is evident here as in few other places. Whereas white Costa Ricans would come in contact with their Black counterparts mostly on travels to Limón (the annual carnival has always been a popular event), today they are likely to go instead further south. While some of Puerto Viejo exhibits the trivialization of local culture that inevitably accompanies tourist development, the town—with its lagoon encircled by a coral reef, black-sand beach, reggae and *salsa* music, and the opportunity to sample a cuisine different from anywhere else in the country—has become a sort of Black cultural Mecca. The view of a particular spot encapsulating one's culture is certainly artificial, and it may further the sense of otherness sustained for so long by the Black community in Costa Rica. The gaze of Costa Ricans has, however, irrevocably been turned onto this section of the country, clearing the path toward recognition of its place on the cultural landscape.

THE SOCIAL REFORM PERIOD (1940–50)

The social and political reforms of the 1940s were made possible due to an extraordinary coalition that was formed between the ruling party, the Communist party, and the Catholic church. In 1940 Dr. Rafael Angel Calderón was elected president with 85 percent of the vote. As a member of the oligarchy, he was expected to support the monied interests. He surprised everyone, however, when he championed the rights of the working class, and he set in motion several initiatives to rally support from this fiscally important group.

During his tenure, President Calderón advanced social programs targeting urban labor, such as the creation of the Social Insurance Fund, which gave maternity and disability benefits. He promoted a national wage increase and recognized the right to strike. But Calderón would eventually require the support of other factions besides the working class in order to counter the opposition from the oligarchy.

In spite of progress made in the 1930s in labor laws, the workers' movement in Costa Rica grew in strength. This was due to two factors: economic hardships—brought about by falling coffee prices, the global impact of World War I, and the depression—as well as Communist party reform proposals that were gaining worldwide support. Together these factors gave impetus to the goals of the workers' movement that often conflicted with the interests of the oligarchy, and things came to a head during the reform period. It is within this polarized environment that the three disparate and influential entities already mentioned formed a coalition that made possible several important reforms.

The entities of this coalition supported an antifascist platform and relief efforts for the current economic crisis. The coalition was formed through compromise. First, seeking the support of the anticommunist church, Manuel Mora Valverde, leader of the Communist party, changed the party's name to the Partido Vanguardia Popular (PVP). During a key speech, Mora stated, "We are not trying to make a socialist revolution at this moment, but to find a practical [way of putting] a brake on the economic crisis" (Yashar 86). This nonradical stance triggered public concessions that in turn facilitated the new coalition.

In response, Archbishop Sanabria of San José made public his support for the PVP. On September 22, 1943, President Calderón and Mora signed a seven-point accord that included initiatives to protect the poor and the workers' movements, to eradicate corruption, and to ensure the election of Teodoro Picado as the next president. In effect, the coalition established important reforms in labor rights, going further than Calderón had been able to go on his own. In 1943, for instance, the government backed the banana workers' strike against the United Fruit Company and ordered the company to negotiate with the union.

This coalition also provided an opportunity for other social legislation to take place. When Picado assumed the presidency in 1944, he continued Calderón's reforms that once again favored the popular sector over the oligarchy. However, some consider Picado merely a puppet of Calderón, who had designs on returning to the presidency in 1948. Near the end of his term, Picado seemed to adopt a less aggressive agenda of reform and showed himself less willing to cooperate with the PVP, whose support had assured his earlier victory. Moreover, the clamor of the oligarchy was increasing, and Picado began to waver in his political distance from them.

During this time, a leader of the conservative opposition offered the nation a reason to shift party alliances. León Cortés, a former president (1936–40), led a coalition of the oligarchy that was critical of the liberal regime and agrarian capitalism. Taking advantage of anticommunist sentiment as well, this conservative coalition had garnered the support of a Catholic faction opposed to Archbishop Sanabria's earlier endorsement of the PVP. Before this time, these right-wing groups had not been able to consolidate sufficient popular support to counter the reform coalition of the *calderonistas*. Cortés therefore offered to support Picado with votes and funding in the next elections, in exchange for Picado's break with the Communist party. However, Cortés died before a conservative-coalition compromise could be achieved. What happened next eventually led to the country's only civil war.

In 1947, during the last year of his presidency, Picado had implemented new taxation laws to deal with a large budget deficit. The oligarchy, as the sector most affected by these laws, looked forward to dominating the upcoming elections. They staged a demonstration, ostensibly to protest both new taxes and electoral fraud, that succeeded in polarizing the government and the conservative opposition. During the commercial strike that came to be known as the *huelga de brazos caídos* (the strike of the crossed arms), businesses were closed for a month, violent acts were committed in the name of both parties, and the government increased its strength by means of a makeshift militia of armed banana workers as general unrest escalated.

It was during the process of civil unrest that Costa Ricans witnessed the de facto participation of women in the political process. Though legally unacknowledged in the political arena and negatively sanctioned by a deeply conservative society, women's participation in the strike was representative of their historic defense of what were then exclusively male rights in Costa Rica.[1] Throughout the development of political parties in the late nineteenth and early twentieth centuries, women had consistently lent their support and physical presence to political demonstrations of all kinds. Yet they were only explicitly included in the electoral process in 1949 when they won the right to vote, and women were only able to vote for the first time during the 1953 presidential elections.

At the height of the unrest of 1947, however, women once again made their voices heard as members of the citizenry. On August 2 of that year, thousands of women took to the streets as part of a demonstration calling for an end to violence and electoral corruption. They had sent a letter to the press on August 1, telling the president of their intent to camp out on the steps of the presidential estate. The next day, while they stood outside, a defiant President Picado came out to confront the demonstrators and refused to sign any agreement as long as the women were present. The women chose to leave, not wanting to give him an opportunity to blame them for stalling negotiations. As they started to leave, government forces began shooting at the unarmed women. The demonstration was ultimately successful, as the following day, President Picado signed an agreement with the opposition. This pivotal confrontation resulted in several concessions; central to them was that Otilio Ulate Blanco, the opposition's presidential candidate, would be allowed to name the Electoral Tribunal. The government thus capitulated to the demonstrators' demands for a change in the electoral process.

THE CIVIL WAR (MARCH–APRIL 1948)

The presidential elections held on February 8, 1948, triggered enormous changes in Costa Rican government, politics, and society. The vote count showed the conservative Ulate as the victor, while the Reform party won the majority of legislative seats. Calderón demanded a recount; the opposition declared electoral fraud. In the tumultuous weeks that followed, the cacophony of voices from different factions rose to a frenzied pitch. The legislature annulled the presidential electoral results but accepted the legislative ones. This set off a series of events that culminated in armed conflict. President-elect Ulate took refuge in the U.S. Embassy, and two weeks later a charismatic leader emerged who would initiate Costa Rica's civil war.

THE LEADERSHIP OF JOSÉ FIGUERES FERRER

José Figueres Ferrer (1906–87) was a maverick, and he was twice elected president, serving in 1953–58 and 1970–74. A member of the oligarchy, he had lived in the United States during the 1920s and was largely self-educated. He had spent most of his time in the Boston Public Library reading the works of Charles Fourier, Leo Tolstoy, and Thomas Jefferson. Figueres became fascinated with the cultural, economic, social, and governmental structures of the United States during this time, believing that he witnessed there "a capacity for social justice within the framework of free enterprise" (Rolbein 88). Upon his return to Costa Rica, Figueres set out to develop a utopian enclave on his farm that he named La lucha sin fin (The Endless Struggle).

This farm was located 35 miles from San José. There, Figueres began growing sisal, a plant whose fibers were used for the production of rope and coffee bags. He also put in place a reforestation program, an act now considered truly visionary. The farm's factory ran on water-generated power, and families on the farm had electricity before many citizens of San José did. Residents had access to health care and schools and later developed specialized technical training programs. In short, Figueres utilized his farm as the site of social experiments that he would later implement on a larger scale.[2]

Although Figueres kept largely to his own interests at La lucha, he became involved in the political arena in the early 1940s. After a radio broadcast in which he criticized the government, Figueres was exiled for two years to Mexico. It was here that he garnered the support of the Caribbean League and various Central American leaders. Linking Calderón to communism, he preyed on U.S. anticommunist fears. His political views were published from exile by his ally Ulate in Ulate's newspaper; Figueres was also busy at work preparing for an armed offensive.

On March 12, 1948, Figueres instigated civil war; 2,000 Costa Ricans died during the next month of skirmishes. A peace treaty was negotiated in April. President Picado had curtailed his own involvement significantly; Figueres was winning the skirmishes and he proclaimed from Cartago with bravado that San José would be next. Nicaragua's forces—tacitly supportive of Calderón's counteroffensive—were already across the border, while U.S. forces in Panamá were rumored to be ready to join Figueres' side.

The peace accord proclaimed general amnesty and included a clause drafted by Mora on behalf of the workers. However, Figueres did not honor the amnesty: not only was Calderón exiled, but many goods were confiscated, and many employees were fired due to their "incorrect" political allegiance. Instead of honoring the election of Ulate, Figueres and the president-elect signed an agreement on May 1, 1948, establishing a revolutionary junta to be led by Figueres and set to rule for 18 months. Indeed, Ulate took office in November of 1949.

During the 18 months of the junta's rule, 834 decrees were passed that established a legacy for decades to come:

> In short order, the Social Security system was bolstered and institutionalized to make sure it would not be ignored. Full voting rights for women were enacted. Minimum wage, low-cost health care, child support—all were realized . . . every bank in the country was nationalized; the flow of money, said Figueres, should be in the public's control like the flow of water and mail. A 10 percent tax surcharge was levied, but only on the wealthiest Costa Ricans—a crude form of graduated income tax. An independent Supreme Tribunal was established with sole authority to run elections. Another tribunal dispersed compensation for all those who had been financially damaged by the war. Public education was bolstered with more funding [and] the Communist party was outlawed. (Rolbein 99)

In addition, a new constitution was adopted in 1949, declaring full citizenship rights to all those born in Costa Rica (this affected Black, Chinese, and indigenous residents, primarily). After decades of struggle, women were granted the right to vote, and the reelection of a president was prohibited. Most significantly, the army was abolished.

Although not a pacifist himself, Figueres sought to preserve the democratic process in his country by removing the power base of the military. The absence of a military force would also exempt Costa Rica from blame of provocation of international conflicts; in turn, funds earmarked for the maintenance of an army could be redirected into social programs. All in all, doing away with the army was a brilliant and simple solution.

Figueres was not without controversy nor did he escape accusations of doing things for personal gain, but he undeniably led the country into a new era, establishing many programs of parity in the distribution of wealth. He ushered in a period of political stability and economic growth. He championed the rights of the middle class along the way. Some say it is precisely this for which he is at fault; others criticize his controversial and active support of revolutionary movements in Cuba and Nicaragua (he was thought to have been linked to several assassination attempts on the dictator Anastasio Somoza).

Still, Figueres is impossible to pigeonhole into any single ideological position. While the changes he implemented required at times the heavy hand of the government, he only continued along a previously established path of social justice. He embodied Costa Rica's unique merging of socialist and capitalist thought, formalized ten years earlier by the coalition of Calderón, Mora, and Archbishop Sanabria. It is evident that the joining of reform ideology and pragmatism go far in defining twentieth-century Costa Rican history.

NOTES

1. For further discussion of women's role in Costa Rican history, see Ilse Abshagen Leitinger, ed. and trans., *The Costa Rican Women's Movement: A Reader* (Pittsburgh: University of Pittsburgh Press, 1997); see also Carmen Naranjo's collection of essays entitled *Mujer y cultura* (San José, Costa Rica: EDUCA, 1989).

2. For an amplified description of La lucha farm and Figueres, see Seth Rolbein, *Nobel Costa Rica: A Timely Report on Our Peaceful Pro-Yankee, Central American Neighbor* (New York: St. Martin's Press, 1989); Deborah J. Yashar, *Demanding Democracy: Reform and Reaction in Costa Rica and Guatemala, 1870's–1950's* (Stanford, Calif.: Stanford University Press, 1997); and Kyle Longley, *The Sparrow and the Hawk: Costa Rica and the United States during the Rise of José Figueres* (Tuscaloosa: University of Alabama Press, 1997).

REFERENCES

Bell, John Patrick. *Crisis in Costa Rica: The 1948 Revolution*. Austin: University of Texas Press, 1971.

Biesanz, Richard, Karen Zubris Biesanz, and Mavis Hiltunen Biesanz. *The Costa Ricans*. Prospect Heights, Ill.: Waveland Press, 1988.

Bird, Leonard. *Costa Rica: The Unarmed Democracy*. London: Shephard Press, 1984.

Fallas, Carlos Luis. *Mamita Yunai*. San José, Costa Rica: Editorial Costa Rica, 1986.

Gradwohl, Judith, and Russell Greenberg. *Saving the Tropical Forests*. Washington, D.C.: Island Press, 1988.

Lara, Silvia, Tom Barry, and Peter Simonson. *Inside Costa Rica.* Albuquerque: Resource Center Press, 1995.

Locher, Uli. "Migration and Environmental Change in Costa Rica since 1950." In *Demographic Diversity and Change in the Central American Isthmus,* edited by Anne R. Pebley and Luis Rosero-Bixby. Santa Monica, Calif.: RAND, 1997. 667–705.

Longley, Kyle. *The Sparrow and the Hawk: Costa Rica and the United States during the Rise of José Figueres.* Tuscaloosa: University of Alabama Press, 1997.

McDade, Lucinda A., Kamaljit S. Bawa, Henry A. Hespenheide, and Gary S. Hartshortn. *La Selva: Ecology and Natural History of a Neotropical Rain Forest.* Chicago: University of Chicago Press, 1994.

Meléndez, Carlos, and Quince Duncan. *El negro en Costa Rica.* 5th ed. San José, Costa Rica: Editorial Costa Rica, 1978.

Palmer, Paula. *"What Happen": A Folk-History of Costa Rica's Talamanca Coast.* San José, Costa Rica: Ecodesarrollos, 1977.

Purcell, Trevor W. *Banana Fallout: Class, Color, and Culture among West Indians in Costa Rica.* Los Angeles: Center for Afro-American Studies Publications, 1993.

Rolbein, Seth. *Nobel Costa Rica: A Timely Report on Our Peaceful Pro-Yankee, Central American Neighbor.* New York: St. Martin's, 1989.

Roseberry, William, Lowell Gudmundson, and Mario Samper Kutschbach, eds. *Coffee, Society, and Power in Latin America.* Baltimore: Johns Hopkins University Press, 1995.

Stiles, F. Gary, and Alexander F. Skutch. *A Guide to the Birds of Costa Rica.* Ithaca, N.Y.: Comstock Publishing Associates, 1990.

Yashar, Deborah J. *Demanding Democracy: Reform and Reaction in Costa Rica and Guatemala, 1870's–1950's.* Stanford, Calif.: Stanford University Press, 1997.

2

The Legacy of Social Reform: What Makes Costa Rica So Different

COSTA RICA POST-1948

IN THE DECADES since the seminal events of 1948, many changes have occurred in Costa Rica. The abolition of the army, election reform, and a climate encouraging social progress and civic participation fostered a healthy political environment that in later decades has been able to withstand the pressures, at times severe, associated with growing internationalization of markets and an increasing debt. Many contemporary observers point to the uniquely Costa Rican context of peace and democracy, and easily trace back the seeds of such stability to the reforms enacted during its mid-century convulsive history.

The junta of 1948–49, led by Figueres, set the stage not only for Ulate's presidency, but for the political trajectory of following decades as well. Figueres nationalized banking and insurance, supported the labor codes and social security initiatives led by Calderón in the 1940s, and in honoring the passing of power to the elected candidate, set Costa Rica on a course that it has not deviated from since: in ten of the last 12 elections, the incumbent party has lost, effectively establishing a peaceful pattern of party alternation.

In addition, during the reform era of Figueres, social services were expanded, and the results were remarkable: the literacy rate, life expectancy, and social security coverage became the highest in the region. As a side note, Costa Rica has been a leader for decades in health care, offering substantial services that surpass that of many communities in the United States, and that are in Latin America second only to Cuba. In fact, since the 1980s,

Costa Rica has been regarded as a desirable vacation spot where one can undergo plastic surgery; at the same time, several tourist packages appeal to visitors from around the world who recognize the high quality and low cost of these medical services.

Continuing the optimism that flourished under Figueres' leadership after World War II, economic prosperity increased in Costa Rica, as it did in other areas of the globe. Demand for both coffee and banana exports rose considerably. Costa Rica benefited from its participation in the Central American Common Market, subsidized services continued to expand, and wages grew at a healthy pace.

By the early 1970s, the government's lengthy prioritization of public social services had resulted in remarkable increases in health and education, and in widespread social mobility. During the second administration of Don Pepe Figueres (1970–74), the Social Assistance Institute was established to extend affordable health care to all its citizens. Hospitals were nationalized and medical personnel were integrated into a national system that for the first time reached rural areas; health coverage was greatly expanded; work-force training programs proliferated; and numerous low-income housing programs were created. By 1981, one-third of the budget was devoted to education, and 46 percent to health. Indeed, since the 1960s, Costa Rica has been touted as an exception within Latin America because of its large middle class. While Costa Ricans have historically been prosperous, especially in comparison to much of Latin America, the economic crisis of 1979–81 plunged the country into a period of financial difficulty from which it has not yet fully recovered.

THE ECONOMIC CRISIS

Several factors account for the economic crisis in Costa Rica that began during the late 1970s and reached its crisis point in the 1980s. In hindsight, the reasons seem clear: after the abolition of the army, Costa Rica began an era of unprecedented prosperity coupled with political and social peace and a sense of well-being. Tourism, today the largest generator of income in the country, had begun its ascent. Development led to foreign investments and foreign debt, continuing a pattern that Costa Rica had sustained since borrowing funds to build the Atlantic railroad in the late nineteenth century. In fact, Costa Rica has been in debt for much of its modern history.

The nation was also affected by the general Latin American economic crisis in the early 1980s; certainly, the escalation of violence in neighboring countries had a profound impact on the region's economy. Also, Costa Rica's economy relied heavily on income generated by its two primary exports, coffee and bananas, both of which experienced drastic drops in price during this period in the early 1980s. In combination with the pressures caused by rising oil prices worldwide, this period spurred heavy borrowing and deficit spending; the last straw was the devaluation of the *colón*. From 1980 to 1982, annual inflation rose from 18 to 82 percent: although the exchange rate had remained steady at eight *colones* per U.S. dollar for nearly 30 years, in late 1999, the exchange rate hovered around 290 *colones* per dollar.

Changes in the banking system, too, have contributed to Costa Rica's financial woes. The Partido Liberación Nacional (PLN, Figueres' party) had nationalized the banking system in the late 1940s, and for many years banks were able to offer low-interest loans, helping fund education, transportation, small farmers, rural development, and so forth. The PLN later took steps toward privatizing banking during Luis Alberto Monge's presidential term (1982–86). Over the years, however, the national banking system had developed into a weighty bureaucracy; and political favoritism governed its operations, from employment to credit approval. This precarious situation came to a halt in 1994, with the collapse of the Banco Anglo-Costarricense. The bank's directors had made so many enormous unsecured loans that the national treasury was left with a deficit of $136 million.

Another significant factor shaping much of modern Costa Rican life is how it has managed its foreign debt. After the government's request for assistance, Costa Rican economic policy has been overseen by the World Bank since 1985. In a relatively standard practice in its dealing with developing countries, the World Bank imposes certain guidelines that must be met in order for loans to be approved and grant funds disbursed. To comply with structural-adjustment guidelines imposed by these foreign lending institutions, then, neoliberal policies have been stressed. In compliance with World Bank requirements, severe budget cuts have strained social service programs that are already in need of refurbishment and increased funding, which reverses a trend that had lent great benefit to the country for nearly 50 years. In vital areas such as education, these cuts have begun to take their toll.

EDUCATION

Education became the cornerstone of the radical reforms of the post-1948 era. It represented universal opportunity and became for many Costa Ricans the shining example of their country's highly developed culture and of their government's achievements; indeed, the statistics are impressive. For 50 years, the government devoted a significant portion—nearly 30 percent—of its budget to education. While sources of funding for education have come under intense pressure lately, the culture of reverence for education in Costa Rica remains strong.[1]

Costa Rica has a long tradition of placing great priority on education: one of its first acts after gaining independence was to establish the University of Santo Tomás, which provided secondary and some professional education; an 1825 law mandated the formation of public schools in all municipalities; and in the years that followed, the state repeatedly made a commitment to education, providing for equal instruction for both sexes in 1847, and making education free and obligatory in 1869. During various periods of fiscal and political instability, some schools were closed but as soon as the government was on its feet again it reopened and expanded them.

The mid-century reforms of Calderón and Figueres, particularly, further solidified education as a primary responsibility of the state. From the early 1950s through the 1970s, spending on education remained steady, with generous pension packages offered to teachers as well. Schools eventually reached the great majority of rural areas, and the national cliché of Costa Rica boasting more teachers than soldiers prevailed. Since 1949, education has been free from grades one to twelve, and compulsory from age six through fourteen. The state has declared its commitment to making educational opportunities equal through economic stimuli, and guarantees the autonomy of its universities. Private education is subject to state supervision. In 1992, taking its responsibility one step further, the government declared education a fundamental right, not simply a state's obligation.

Public schools run for nine months, with a summer break during the coffee harvest (November through January), and with a standard two-week break in July. The length of the school year has been shortened considerably in the span of a century, from 240 days to 177; the daily high school schedule generally runs from 7:00 A.M. to 2:30 P.M., including a lunch break, and the primary school runs from three to five hours a day. The curriculum of elementary and general education is divided into four cycles: the first three cycles last a total of nine years, and the last one provides students a choice of topic for two to three years' instruction (an academic track or a vocational track in health, fine arts, industry, media, etc.). In comparison with the public school system in the United States, then, the first two cycles are the equivalent of grades one through six; the third cycle initiates what is termed *colegio*, beginning with the equivalent in the United States of seventh grade, and lasting through ninth grade. The specialized curriculum of the final cycle leads many directly into careers, although Costa Rica has always been a regional leader in higher education.

Beginning in the 1970s, higher education became the focus of intense development. The University of Costa Rica, the nation's flagship institution, was established in 1940, in effect a reopening of the University of Santo Tomás (established in 1817 but closed in 1888 due to a financial crisis). Following several decades of aggressive governmental support, state-funded universities had grown to four, and private universities had appeared on the scene. Today, 70,000 students are enrolled in institutions of higher education, and San José is the site of over 40 private universities.

PUBLIC HIGHER EDUCATION

The government funds the public universities almost entirely, as tuition is charged on a sliding scale based on family income; one-fourth of the students in these schools pay no tuition. The University of Costa Rica, with an enrollment of 30,000 students, offers a liberal-arts core of study that students generally follow throughout their first two years of study (it may take seven years to complete a degree, as many students hold jobs while they are in school). Core courses include math, fine arts, sports, sociology, and a cross-disciplinary course in Spanish, philosophy, and Western history. Many professors do not teach full time, in part because the salaries are so low, and so they must work in other venues, which lends an edge of practical knowledge to the classroom. Many university professors are social activists as well, and are visible participants in current issues and national events.

Established in 1973, the National Autonomous University in Heredia is reputed to have a different approach to course content. Its curriculum includes liberal arts, but it prides itself on having a distinct philosophy, calling itself more practical, making claims that it prepares students better for life in the real world, with added emphasis on practicums and technical training. It is also renown for its musical program.

Two other institutions complete the panorama of public higher education in Costa Rica. Cartago's Institute of Technology, founded in 1975, serves a significant number of agricultural technology students, among others. Finally the State University at a Distance offers basic liberal arts courses, making higher education available to those in outlying or rural communities. The 1980s witnessed a rise in private institutions of higher learning and, increasingly, students from other Central American countries are going to Costa Rica to attend university. The University of Costa Rica Medical School is considered the best by far in all of Central America.

A particularly noteworthy feature of the public university system in Costa Rica is the graduation requirement of 150 hours of community service for the bachelor's degree, and 300 hours for the master's degree. Students select a project that is generally related to their field of study, and learn the lesson about "giving back" to the government what one has received through public education. Interestingly, in 1995 a similar requirement was imposed on high school students, stipulating that they complete 30 hours of community service. Even in times of great financial duress, it seems that Costa Rican civic spirit has manifested itself in extraordinary measures once again.

Facing budget cuts because of the structural adjustments that began in the 1980s, Costa Rican university students, faculty, and administrators launched a campaign (through demonstrations and newspaper coverage in ads and articles) against such measures. The social and political climate has historically encouraged broad-based participation in organizations; Costa Ricans are accustomed to having the right to organize, and to be heard. Therefore, in the mid-1990s, when the government's neoliberal policies sought to reduce the higher-education budget, students and faculty protested, and the cuts were never made. Around the same time, the government announced its plan to change the retirement age and reduce teachers' control over their pensions. Educators from around the country took part in several memorable, peaceful demonstrations in San José, which thousands of citizens witnessed. Unfortunately, these particular changes were eventually approved and enacted.

PRIVATE EDUCATION

In recent years, Costa Rica has witnessed a handful of private schools multiplying into a sizable number of educational alternatives for those who can afford them. This country has a strong tradition of private schooling, primarily parochial, language based, or based on the U.S. or British models: Liceo Francés (French School), Colegio San Francis (an all-boys Catholic school), Colegio Lincoln (one of the first Spanish-English bilingual schools in the country, and still a purveyor of social status among its graduates), Country Day School (a U.S.-modeled college-preparatory school where nearly all classes are taught in English), Escuela Humboldt (bilingual in German and Spanish), Colegio Sión (one of the oldest academic institutions in the country and an all-girls Catholic school), Colegio Metodista (a bilingual, Spanish-English school founded by missionaries).

Today, there are many more private schools as a result of the growth surge in the 1980s. These newly established schools were founded primarily in response to what was perceived as an increasing laxity of the public educa-

Children line up to "vote" at a local public school on election day. The school is decorated with banners representing the candidates' political parties. Photograph by the author.

tional system. Parents and educators were concerned with the lack of technological and linguistic resources, and shrinking budgets—not only for teaching resources but for teachers—that resulted in a reduction in teachers' pensions, and the consequent decrease in the quality of instruction. They saw with increasing urgency the need to give their children an edge to compete in an increasingly technological and international world. As a result, private schools began to appear at a quick pace.

One such case is that of the Instituto de Psicopedagogía Integral (Institute of Holistic Psychopedagogy), founded in 1981 by a licensed psychologist, Annie Blanco. Part of the popularity of the school can be attributed to its mission of matriculating children who are at risk academically; less than 20 years later, the primary and secondary school has grown to 525 students, with long waiting lists for admittance. As one school administrator explains, teachers' salaries often provide the incentive to attract and retain quality instructors; private school salaries tend to be 15 percent to 20 percent higher than those in public schools.[2]

PRIVATE HIGHER EDUCATION

The Central American Autonomous University (UACA), founded in 1976, was the first of its kind in Costa Rica. This institution remains the most prestigious school in the private sector. At its best, the UACA offers a flexible class schedule, exposure to a greater variety of newer careers, and eased entrance requirements in comparison to public institutions. At its worst, this and other private universities are far more expensive than any public university, its lower entrance standards can contribute to a less stimulating intellectual environment, and library facilities may be insufficient to support serious research. There is no question, however, that the newly competitive higher-education environment in Costa Rica has energized its educational institutions. Such energy and growth is also a testament both to Costa Rica's ability to find a path for itself toward greater preparedness for the business environments of the future, and its reaffirmation of the value placed on education. What remains to be seen is the long-term impact of these new private schools on the national educational system.

EDUCATIONAL VALUES

Teachers traditionally inspire great respect in Costa Rica, even though their pay does not reflect their social status. The surrounding culture envisions educators—at the primary and secondary levels, particularly—as the foundation builders of patriotic consciousness: school rituals celebrating state holidays are always highly festive events. At the same time, the school staff takes very seriously its roll of instilling respect for Costa Rica's sociopolitical heritage, and so marks these occasions with a compelling mix of solemnity and enthusiasm. The September 15 celebration of independence is a good example: for weeks previous to the actual date, children are treated to special history lessons in anticipation of the holiday. Everyone is involved in preparing for the celebration, contributing decorations in red, white, and blue, the colors of the Costa Rican flag. Lines are memorized for recitation, and elaborate plans are made for a school-wide party complete with music, food, and drink to mark this occasion.

Costa Ricans see the education of children as a collective priority of any nation, and take very seriously the view of children as the future of their country. It is a great status symbol to send a child abroad to study; for example, presidents Oscar Arias (1986–90) and Miguel Angel Rodríguez (1990–94) earned doctorates at foreign institutions.

In addition, schoolchildren dressed in their blue-and-white uniforms figure

A mother walks home with her schoolchildren on a dusty Guanacaste road after a Christmas party. Since this is the last day of school before summer vacation, the children are not required to wear their uniforms. Photograph courtesy of Christy Halbert.

prominently in all official parades and presidential inaugurations. They serve as an attractive symbol of Costa Rica's tradition of patriotism and peace.

One noteworthy tradition of Costa Rican education has yielded admirable results in Latin America's oldest democracy. On election day, schoolchildren are encouraged to vote in mock presidential elections (the results are published nationally in newspapers), in an effort to instill in them the importance of taking part in this fundamental democratic right. Indeed, regular voter turnout has hovered at 80 percent for 30 years.[3]

The educational scenario is changing, however. The sharp decline in funding (since 1994 particularly) comes at a time when the school-going population is increasing; as a result, many teachers complain of a deplorable lack of material resources. A growing number of individuals without proper certification are teaching, especially in the rural areas. University funding has remained constant, but primary and secondary school budgets have shrunk steadily; while the national high school dropout rate was 7 percent in 1987, today it is much higher. Yet most Costa Ricans continue to see education as the path to prosperity.

Even during the most difficult years of the economic crisis in the 1980s and 1990s, energetic efforts were made to introduce computers into primary school classrooms, and as a result, in 1996 one-third of all schools had computers. In the mid-1990s, foreign languages were introduced in the primary school curriculum, an effort that shows clear commitment to improving the educational preparation of students. Also during this period, the government made large donations of school supplies, uniforms, and even shoes to many children whose families could not afford them.

In spite of the difficulties and challenges that this nation has faced in recent years, Costa Rica is again rising to the occasion, setting forth initiatives that are truly surprising in their inventiveness and success. At its best, Costa Rica looks out for the community good. Responses to continued economic hardship, to regional political pressures and the influx of immigrants, and to ecotourism and deforestation reveal an impressive depth of humanity amidst a rapidly changing world.

IMMIGRATION

Political instability and economic crisis in the region have contributed to a significant influx of immigrants during the past 15 years. Their presence has changed the urban landscape, and has taxed many social services (no woman, for instance, is turned away from a hospital to birth a child, regardless of her legal status). During the 1970s and 1980s, the majority of immigrants came from Nicaragua and other parts of Central America; the 1990s have witnessed large numbers of Colombians coming to Costa Rica to escape violence and an economic recession at home. Despite their social impact, Costa Rica's humanitarian policies toward these refugees are such that undocumented residents have access to most social services. One of the country's recent presidents serves as an exceptional model for the kind of citizenship Costa Rica seeks to develop.

PRESIDENT OSCAR ARIAS

The presidency of Oscar Arias (1986–90) was marked by his commitment to advancing the goals of peace. In 1987 he was awarded the Nobel Peace Prize for his leadership in promoting peace among Central American nations. At the time, the escalation of conflicts in Guatemala, El Salvador, Nicaragua, and Honduras had created a generalized instability in the region. The United States was heavily (though covertly) involved in supporting the contras (counterrevolutionaries) in Nicaragua, and Arias' peace plan revealed his deep disagreements with the policies of the Reagan administration.[4] In spite of the harsh and vocal United States response, Arias' convictions were ultimately honored when his peace accord was signed, and because of it, Arias was awarded the Nobel Prize.

The Arias peace plan called for cease-fires, free elections, restoration of the freedom of the press and other civil liberties, amnesty for political prisoners, the repatriation of refugees, and the initiation of a dialogue between governments and the internal opposition. It was signed on August 7, 1987, and did in fact provide an important catalyst for reaching peace in the region: in Guatemala, for instance, the 30-year civil war came to an end. Since the conclusion of his presidency, Arias has continued his advocacy for peace. An intellectual who has authored several books on the nature of Costa Rican democracy, this former political science professor has lectured extensively around the world.

THE QUAKERS OF MONTEVERDE

Another group that has caught the world's attention are the Quakers of Monteverde. Although they surely did not set out to create a model for conservation, their preservation of a cloud forest in the northern region of Costa Rica has inspired the admiration of naturalists, biologists, ornithologists, butterfly specialists, and environmentally concerned citizens around the globe. Today, in an ecotourist industry that is expanding at a clipping pace, the Monteverde Cloud Forest is the nature reserve that easily draws the most visitors annually.

The Quaker migration to Costa Rica began in response to the activation of the draft in the United States. In 1951, after scouting out various sites throughout Central America, seven Quaker families from Alabama settled in Costa Rica, a country that had recently abolished its standing army. The Quaker settlers purchased 3,000 acres nestled far up in the mountains. Their purpose was to jointly farm the land, although they soon found they needed to supplement this venture, and so founded a cheese factory. By the 1990s, the Monteverde cheese cooperative was producing several tons of dairy products daily, purchasing $100,000 of milk monthly from local dairy farmers, and employing over 50 people in a unique community business venture. Today, Monteverde cheese constitutes a significant portion of Costa Rica's domestic cheese market, and does a thriving export business to other Central American countries.

But the Quakers of this community, located a difficult four hours' drive from San José, have done much more than boost the local economy: their foresight in protecting their water source has led to the establishment of the Monteverde Cloud Forest Preserve, an extravagantly plant-and-animal-rich area, and one of the last remaining cloud forests on the planet. Monteverde has developed a consciousness within Costa Rica of its incredible wealth in natural resources, and has set in motion the national establishment of other protected areas.

The original Quaker settlers kept free from development 1,000 acres of the mountaintop land they had purchased. Eventually, seeing the results of their decision to keep free the rivers that flowed downstream, noting the demise of rapidly developed areas around them, and hearing from visiting naturalists of the incalculable worth of the forest high in the clouds, they resolved to create a 27,000-acre preserve. Over the next years, they purchased additional cloud forest, so that today, the park has reached its goal and annually hosts tens of thousands of visitors a year. They come to catch a glimpse of the quetzal, or of a hummingbird, or of any other of the 400 species of birds in the forest; and they come to see the lush, cloud-draped forest with 2,500 kinds of plants and trees, 100 species of mammals, and nearly 500 species of butterflies.

The phenomenon of increased environmental concern is due in no small part to the vision of these Quaker settlers. The education of one generation of Costa Rican children has been saturated with environmental awareness from a conservationist perspective. In fact, children from around the globe have contributed to the Children's Eternal Forest, a 20,000-acre plot adjacent to the Monteverde Cloud Forest Preserve that was established in 1987. Costa Rica is contributing in remarkable ways to the education of the world community.

Similar educational efforts have yielded results in other areas of the country. In the Tamarindo Beach region of the Pacific coast, sea turtles come to lay their eggs twice a year. They land at night—only when a combination of environmental factors is present—slowly making their way up the beach to dig a three- or four-foot hole with surprising speed and agility, where they lay their rubbery-shelled eggs, sometimes 100 eggs at a time. Because of increasing numbers of visitors to witness this phenomenon, the ensuing development of hotels to accommodate them, the growing population of the area, and the continued poaching of the eggs (a local delicacy, especially before the laws were written to protect the sea turtles), the leatherback sea turtle is in grave danger of extinction.

After intense campaigns to educate the local populace of such conditions and possible extinctions, citizens have taken upon themselves the task of protecting the turtle population. They have garnered private funding from organizations and individuals around the world to establish a park, and have secured protected-area status from the government. The park is operated by a joint venture of European donors and local volunteers. Many of these volunteers are former poachers themselves. The park monitors tourist activity near the turtles, and also coordinates international science research on this endangered species. The park is patrolled 24 hours a day, mostly by local volunteers who take shifts around their normal working hours. Such mobilization is a testament to the potential of education to effect change.

THE STRUGGLE FOR WOMEN'S RIGHTS

Women in Costa Rica find themselves in a better position than women in many other countries in Latin America, yet they still face challenges to equality and opportunity that individually and collectively they are seeking to overcome. The literacy rate is the same for men and women, and women enjoy equal access to education. Yet, while the female work force is on average better educated than their male counterpart, women are paid less than men.

The average life span for women is 76 years; hospitalization during childbirth is free, and maternal leave was made obligatory in 1990; and that same year, Costa Rica's legal system made strides in offering legal protection from domestic violence (between 1995 and 1997, the number of reported cases of domestic abuse increased by 200 percent).

The history of the struggle for equal rights for women in Costa Rica casts a long shadow, and comes as a natural extension, perhaps, of women's participation in civil rights. Angela Acuña, Costa Rica's first woman lawyer, founded the Feminist League in 1923; she spearheaded the lengthy struggle for women's suffrage. After universal suffrage was granted in 1949, she and several women rose to prominence in national and international affairs. Acuña was the first woman on record to be appointed ambassador to the Organization of American States. Emma Gamboa, activist and president of the teacher's union, was named minister of education in 1949, and became the first dean of the Department of Education at the University of Costa Rica. Since the 1970s, Carmen Naranjo and other women have served in various government posts. To date, Costa Rica has had two women vice presidents, Astrid Fischel and Elizabeth Odio, who were elected in 1994 as presidential candidate Miguel Angel Rodriguez's two running mates.

In recent years, major initiatives have been undertaken to bring about gender equality under the legal system. The most significant initiative, perhaps, called the Proyecto de Ley sobre la Igualdad Real de la Mujer (Bill for Women's True Equality), was proposed in 1988 in response to the low participation of women in politics, labor markets, and legal and administrative posts. This bill called attention to the discrepancy between women's legal rights and their actual, or "real," lives. The bill's far-reaching objectives included demands for reform in six areas: the exercise of public office; social and economic rights (establishing mandatory child care and access to credit, for instance); protection of women during litigation in cases of sexual abuse or aggression; the elimination of sexist content from educational materials; advocacy through an office specifically designated for women's rights; and reforms of existing laws as necessary.

The bill, officially presented to the public by First Lady Margarita Penón Góngora, was hotly debated and underwent four versions before it became law in 1990. Some of the original demands were weakened (childcare was not made obligatory), and some provisions were upheld and strengthened: not only were gender-role stereotypes to be eliminated from teaching materials, but the materials were to include women's contributions to history; and, as proposed, women won the right to family inheritance.

Since 1990, several important changes have taken place. Access to public office is taking place slowly: in 1998, for instance, 34 percent of all elected representatives were women, although a huge majority (94 percent) of the Legislative Assembly remains male. While women are gradually filling positions in the government administration and in the legal field, they remain underrepresented in the upper ranks of most institutions, and in private industry as well. Although implementation of this bill's many provisions is not yet complete, the results of this and other initiatives have signaled a renewed commitment to women's real equality in Costa Rica.

CONCLUSION

While Costa Rica's history has not been devoid of violence, at critical junctures Costa Ricans have consistently chosen peace and committed themselves to the process of social reform. As late as 1948, the outcome of its civil war was the abolition of the army and the inauguration of visionary social reforms, so that today, in spite of critical challenges facing this nation, Costa Rica seems well equipped to make right and just choices for its future.

NOTES

1. Much of this section on education is based on information found in two sources, *The Ticos: Culture and Social Change in Costa Rica* (Boulder, Colo.: Lynne Rienner Publishers, 1999), written by Mavis Hiltunen Biesanz, Richard Biesanz, and Karen Zubris Biesanz, and *Costa Rica: Quest for Democracy*, by John A. Booth (Boulder, Colo.: Westview Press, 1998).

2. Victoria Vargas, personal interview with the author.

3. During the most recent presidential elections in 1998, voter turnout dropped dramatically, to 70 percent.

4. In fact, during the Nicaraguan Revolution, Costa Rica had some difficulty keeping contra forces from training in its territory across the northern border. Some say the Costa Rican and U.S. governments were in collusion, allowing Costa Rica to become a covert drop-off site for the United States to send weapons and ammunition to the Nicaraguan counterrevolutionary forces.

REFERENCES

Biesanz, Mavis Hiltunen, Richard Biesanz, and Karen Zubris Biesanz. *The Ticos: Culture and Social Change in Costa Rica*. Boulder, Colo.: Lynne Rienner Publishers, 1999.

Booth, John A. *Costa Rica: Quest for Democracy*. Boulder, Colo.: Westview Press, 1998.

Calvo Fajardo, Yadira. "Different Times, Women, Visions: The Deep Roots of Costa Rican Feminism." In *The Costa Rican Women's Movement: A Reader*, edited and translated by Ilse Abshagen Leitinger. Pittsburgh, Pa.: University of Pittsburgh Press, 1997.

Edelman, Marc, and Joanne Kenen, eds. *The Costa Rica Reader*. New York: Grove Weidenfeld, 1989.

Leitinger, Ilse Abshagen, ed. and trans. *The Costa Rican Women's Movement: A Reader*. Pittsburgh, Pa.: University of Pittsburgh Press, 1997.

Molina, Iván, and Steven Palmer. *Historia de Costa Rica: Breve, actualizada, y con ilustraciones*. San José, Costa Rica: Editorial de la Universidad de Costa Rica, 1997.

Sharratt, Sara. "The Suffragist Movement in Costa Rica, 1889–1949: Centennial of Democracy?" In *The Costa Rican Women's Movement: A Reader*, edited and translated by Ilse Abshagen Leitinger. Pittsburgh, Pa.: University of Pittsburgh Press, 1997.

3

Religion

IN COSTA RICA, the indelible imprint of Catholicism is evident in its historical presence, political power, and cultural traditions. The religious affiliation of the majority of the Costa Rican populace is Roman Catholicism; and consistent with the rest of Latin America, a cathedral dominates the historic center of Costa Rican towns. The clergy has traditionally played an important part in endorsing governmental authority. With few exceptions, however, the clergy has not been actively involved in political activity or government office.

Other religious faiths in Costa Rica do thrive, of course, and Protestants, in particular, represent a large and fast-growing contingency. Although mainstream Christian churches (like those represented by the Latin American Mission have been established in the country for nearly 70 years, only since the 1960s has U.S. missionary activity resulted in significant changes in the cultural landscape of Costa Rica: evangelical Protestants are visible and vocal in politics, the media, and bilingual (English-Spanish) education.[1] The conversion to Protestantism appears to some as an extension of the United States's multidimensional influence over the region, giving evidence of Costa Ricans' pursuit of prosperity and eager adoption of things "American." Others see the growth and visibility of Costa Rican evangelicals as positive evidence of yet another aspect of its "leadership by example" for the rest of Central America. In any case, Costa Rican Protestant churches have taken root in the national consciousness and the fabric of society.

Missionary representatives of the Church of Latter-Day Saints and Jehovah's Witness are also fixtures of Costa Rican religious life. Since the 1970s the B'ahai faith has also made a small but noticeable appearance.

The Jewish community has been a part of Costa Rican society for many years (the majority emigrated from Poland in the 1930s and 1950s), and Eastern European surnames often give evidence of their successful grafting into all sectors of society; currently, Jewish individuals comprise 1 percent of the country's population. Historically, Jewish communities have often remained somewhat sequestered in certain neighborhoods within the capital city, and today Jewish families still maintain strong ties through the Centro Israelita Sionista (Zionist Israelite Center).

In Limón, within the Black populace, Anglican, Baptist, and Methodist churches are part of a long-standing religious heritage, and Black Catholics are in the minority. In rural areas along the southern Atlantic coast, the prevalence of African beliefs is evident in certain ritual celebrations, as in the practice of *Obeah* (or power). As its name suggests, this belief system is based on the supernatural power some individual possesses; in the past, several obeahmen have become community leaders and have established a strong tradition based on the use of medicinal herbs. African in origin, *Obeah* influences the perspective of many *limonenses* who consider themselves Christian. Limón, therefore, provides a particularly visual example of religious convergence at work in Costa Rica, much like the U.S. evangelicals' adoption of local musical styles in worship in other areas of the country.

NATIVE RELIGIOUS TRADITIONS

No comprehensive study of indigenous religious traditions is available to date, although interest in the subject has grown tremendously. Costa Rican anthropologists have been able to study the funerary rites and the music of early Indian groups due to the wealth of related artifacts recovered from various archaeological sites. The most extensive studies of ongoing native religious traditions that can be found today—due in part to the relatively large size of and access to their communities—center on the Bribrí Indians in the Talamanca region.

From present-day Bribrí shaman, scholars have learned that their world consists of eight vertically stacked layers that lie beneath our ninth level. These worlds are also referred to as houses; and they are all contained within Sibo's master-house. Sibo configured the world as it is today, so that it could sustain the existence of souls. Several manifestations of souls have been necessary to perfect the Bribrí of today.

Sula is the creator of souls and lives in the subterranean world. Sula is a composite of four distinct beings: two males create men's souls and two females create women's souls. Following Sibo's instructions, Sula fashions souls in the form of clay dolls and then bathes them in colored waters that assign specific attributes to each individual.

The Bribrí tradition holds that people have more than one soul and these souls do not necessarily depart when a person dies; therefore elaborate funeral rites prepare the body and preserve the bones for future incarnations. When a soul is released, it is sent to a particular house that corresponds to its behavior before death. The Bribrí adherence to a strict code of behavior—condemning specific acts such as cruelty to animals, stinginess, and incest—is the basis for determining the soul's destination.

The renewal of popular and academic interest in indigenous religious traditions promises to yield greater knowledge and aid in our understanding of this integral part of the Costa Rican heritage. The Catholic and Mennonite churches that have come in contact with the Bribrí have contributed to a merging of different beliefs; and, the slow but steady migration into the city to find work has caused significant changes in the Bribrí culture as well.

EARLY CATHOLIC PRESENCE

The arrival of the Catholic church in the early sixteenth century coincided with the arrival of the Spanish forces bent on controlling new territories. God, honor, and glory were the tripartite motivations for the venture of conquest. Spanish soldiers justified their activities: in addition to seeking wealth for themselves and their crown, they were participating in an epic crusade of faith and conversion in service to God.

As God's representative on earth, the Spanish monarchy included in its aims not only the political and economic domination of new subjects in the Americas, but what they considered the civilizing of these territories through conversion to the Catholic faith. Some theologians attribute the growth of the Catholic church in Central America to the spread of colonization. The first Spanish priests to arrive did in fact take part in the often violent domination of the native population, until reformist pressures—critical of the *encomienda* system and the treatment of the indigenous peoples in general—were imposed by religious orders that arrived later.

As in other parts of Latin America, the Church in Costa Rica carried out its "civilizing" ventures in part through the founding of schools; much of the early education was carried out by missionary priests from diverse orders. The arrival of the Dominicans and Franciscans brought a new consciousness of the abuses carried out by the secular priests who had accompanied the soldiers, and provoked these missionary orders to defend the Indians' human rights.

Costa Rica was invaded by Spanish conquistadores and priests on two fronts: the Pacific northwest, and the southern Atlantic coast. Although the invasions occurred simultaneously, they were separate ventures; and from both regions, the campaign to bring the whole territory under Spanish control proved difficult. Founded in 1548 and extending from Chiapas to Costa Rica, this newly claimed Spanish territory was considered remote and Spanish explorers and priests made only intermittent incursions, between 1510 and 1560 via the Atlantic, and between 1522 and 1570 from the Pacific northwest. Not only was this area at the distant fringe of the Audiencia de Guatemala, but the native populations had been decimated by disease brought by the first wave of Spaniards. In addition, local Indian groups were fragmented, passage through the territory was grueling, and the heat in the coastal areas was unrelenting. This first phase of Spain's quest to convert the inhabitants of the "New World" was prolonged and only marginally successful.

The fierce animosity between conquistadores and locals extended to all regions where there was contact between the two groups. In the Atlantic area of Limón, the locals burned their fields to reduce the food supply for the conquistadores, and fled to the nearly impenetrable Talamanca mountain range. The priest Juan de Estrada Rávago arrived in the area near the southern Atlantic coast in 1560, where he established a settlement that was soon abandoned due to lack of food and resistance from the native population. Throughout the country, subsequent efforts by the Spanish clergy to establish outposts came to a similar end.

Historical documentation suggests that Spanish conquistadores and the clergy who initially accompanied them followed a pattern in what is now Costa Rica much like that in other colonized areas: the priests would administer the sacraments and baptize the native peoples en masse. The combined forces of soldiers and secular clergy would mandate that the indigenous group be baptized as a sign of compliance and conversion. Churches were often built in these settlements, and this activity was accompanied by the persecution of the leaders of the pre-Hispanic native religion. At first believing the indigenous people to be savages and their beliefs heretical, priests would seize and burn their codices, or written historical and religious documents. Fray Bartolomé de las Casas would later initiate a revolution from within the Spanish missionary ranks that denounced this treatment, and he spent his life fiercely advocating the humanity and dignity of the indigenous groups.

Some characterize this early Spanish presence, which began with the distribution of *encomiendas* in 1569, as a contest between the colonial administration, the Catholic church, and the *encomenderos* to "despoil" the native populations. The conquerers were successful to such a degree that it was estimated that by 1611 (42 years later), there was a 70 percent decrease in the number of native laborers who worked for free. The lack of Indian manual labor led to a renewed campaign to dominate and virtually enslave the *indios bravos* (uncivilized Indians) remaining in the Talamanca region. These attempts were fitful, uneven, and ended in 1710, when the Indian *cacique* Pablo Presbere was captured and executed. The Spaniards were eventually faced with the consequences of their decimation of the area's population: they had effectively reduced the available work force as well.

THE CHURCH THROUGH THE NINETEENTH CENTURY

The Catholic church and the Spanish crown maintained their close relationship in the so-called New World. The interdependence of these institutions brought the combined financial acumen and political power necessary to create out of these newly conquered lands Spanish colonies that were also Catholic. As a result, colonial government became synonymous with the Church; the rightness of what was preached in the pulpit was underscored by the might of the governing powers and vice versa. Thus, the failure to "settle the natives" was equated with missionary failure. As the Church organization developed, neighboring León in Nicaragua became the first diocese to be established in the region in 1531. It incorporated Costa Rica on March 9, 1545, and was dependent on the archdiocese of Lima until the area was annexed to Guatemala.

The arrival of religious orders—Jesuits, Franciscans, Dominicans, and Carmelites—marked a significant departure from previous Church activities. During the colonial period, the clergy came to be an essential pillar of the social organization of the region. Generally stridently opposed to the poor treatment of native peoples, the religious orders dedicated themselves to promoting education by founding schools throughout Central America. This participation in *criollo* (first-generation Spaniards who resided in the Americas) life paved the way for their intense involvement in the independence movements of the first half of the nineteenth century. *Criollo* priests took active roles in uprisings and university debate. Advocating either independence or continued allegiance to Spain, they were involved in the political dialogue one way or another.

In 1812 a Costa Rican priest, Florencio del Castillo, attended the Courts of Cadiz (in Spain) as a representative of Central American civilian *criollos*. *Criollo* priests also took an active part in the meeting that resulted in the declaration of Central American independence on September 15, 1821. Of the 49 people in attendance, 17 were clergy: their presence was a formal acknowledgment of their former, unofficial involvement in the governance of the colonies. In fact, for several years during this initial period of nationhood, clerical delegates participated in both federal and national assemblies that defined legal policy for the five national states.

After the failed attempt to incorporate Central America into Mexico, the Central American Federation was established in 1824. The five-nation membership shared the goal of modernizing their territories, which in turn resulted in the secularization of the state. The changes brought about by this objective marked a clear separation of church and state, but by no means concluded their collaboration. The state seemed to assert pointedly its authority by instituting the following series of measures: bishops' pastoral letters would be subject to censorship; parish priests would be appointed by the head of state; a poll tax would be imposed on the clergy; illegitimate children, including the children of priests and nuns, had the right to an inheritance even if not included in a will; mandatory tithes were reduced by half; and local religious superiors were forbidden to communicate with their respective superior generals based in Spain.

Throughout Central America, the clergy responded in a variety of ways, from supporting an even greater distance between church and state, to establishing alliances with local politicians in order to further the development of an independent state (as was the case in Honduras, for example). In Costa Rica, a diocese was established in 1825 but no one was found to act as bishop; it was not until 1850 that Pope Pius XI appointed Anselmo Llorente y Fuente as bishop, thereby definitively establishing a diocese within the country. Parish life in those times seems to have followed the pattern of Costa Rican society in general: local communities went about their own affairs undisturbed by neighboring churches and communities.

THE DEVELOPMENT OF MODERN CATHOLICISM

The lack of a country-wide Church hierarchy must not be interpreted as a loss of religious influence in the region: the dominance of Catholicism in early Costa Rican society is unmistakable. During the early days of independence, the 1852 Concordat established Catholicism as the official religion of Costa Rica. The Concordat gave bishops the authority to oversee education and impose censorship, while the state recognized the rights of the Catholic church and formally became its protector. The state was granted the right to present candidates for administrative posts within the Church; the Church, in turn, gave up its claim to property that had been nationalized or confiscated by the state. In the course of the following 20 years, Bishop Llorente fell in and out of grace with the state due to his espousal of unpopular causes (raising tithes during a rise in the price of coffee, for instance). After his death in 1871, President Tomás Guardia and the Holy See were involved in a lengthy conflict as to who Llorente's successor should be, agreeing only in 1880 to appoint Bernardo Augusto Thiel.

Bishop Thiel's appointment began a new chapter in ecclesiastical participation in the affairs of state. He aligned himself with liberal reformers, thereby confronting the government's authority, and presaging Monsignor Sanabria's pivotal role in securing a peaceful era of social reform in the 1940s. In the latter part of the nineteenth century, the goals of the liberals included stimulating agrarian capitalism, strengthening the administrative arm of the state, and making primary education secular, centralized, free, and mandatory. Unable to consolidate support among the clergy who did not recognize the bishop (due to his departure from the Church's traditionally conservative political views), Thiel was expelled from the country in 1884.

It is important to remember that the conquest of the Americas came on the heels of the Spanish Inquisition: the Catholic church extended its enforced prohibitions throughout the Americas, publishing lists of forbidden books and holding trials. This long-distance censure continued throughout the Spanish colonies until the early nineteenth century, when liberal revolutionaries challenged not only the crown's authority, but the Church's power as well. One Catholic theologian explains the interplay between church and state at the turn of the century this way:

> The Church clung to the idea that official recognition and protection were essential. . . . The state, for its part, needed the Church to confer the legitimacy it sought. For these reasons, the separation between Church and state was more one of form than content. Conservative by temperament and anxious to recover its former influence and privileges, the Church . . . became, together with the military, one of the major props of the oligarchic social order imposed by the coffee barons, a state of affairs that lasted till the mid twentieth century. (Cardenal 256)

In Costa Rica, the conservative nature of the population has traditionally expressed itself by giving strong support to a conservative government, and by largely rejecting liberal reforms (with the consistent exception of those that concern themselves with state support of community rights such as health and education). Costa Rica's Catholic church has typically defended the political status quo, as well. Some have labeled this role a "bourgeoisification" of the clergy, a process that is compounded by the Church's promulgation of the myth that Costa Rica is devoid of social problems. A noted exception took place in the 1940s, when Archbishop Sanabria entered into the political process by forming an alliance with President Rafael Angel Calderón Guardia, and with the Communist leader Manuel Mora.

COSTA RICAN CATHOLICISM TODAY

Throughout the development of Costa Rican Catholicism, the centrality of the city of Cartago cannot be underestimated. Founded in 1564, Cartago was the capital of Costa Rica until 1823. It was also the site of the country's first two cathedrals, whose construction produced an important rallying point for Catholicism in early Costa Rican society.

In Cartago today stands the Basílica de Nuestra Señora de los Angeles (Basilica of Our Lady of the Angels), built on the site where a dark-skinned statue of the Virgen de los Angeles reportedly appeared in 1635. The Catholic church consolidated its efforts around developing a cult of the Virgin; *La negrita* (The Dark-Skinned One), as she is known, became the country's patron saint.

The basilica was constructed in 1926 around the large rock on which the Virgin's statue is said to have appeared. A small stream flows nearby, and many worshipers flock to the spot. There are claims that the flowing water has healing powers and the devout pour water into a bottle to carry to the infirm. The underground level of the building contains a veritable museum of miracles attributed to the curative powers of the Virgin, of the water, and of the site itself. Impressive rows of glass cases house many thousands of charms— in the shape of eyes, hands, hearts, and so forth—representing the body parts that have been afflicted but then healed by the power of the Virgin.

Located in the country's oldest city, this striking Baroque cathedral is the symbolic center of Costa Rican Catholicism and the site of an annual pilgrimage. Called *La Romería*, this event celebrates the feast of the Patron Saint. Thousands travel to the site (from all over the country, as well as from Panamá and Nicaragua), and the most devout walk the 14-mile trek from San José. Once they arrive at the sprawling steps of the cathedral, worshipers enter on their knees to pay their respects or make their requests to the Virgin.

Throughout Costa Rican history, the Catholic faith has left its indelible mark on official as well as popular expression. The traditions of a burgeoning society were shaped by the Catholic calendar and its views on social interaction and behavior. Observation of religious life in Costa Rica seems to

The Metropolitan Cathedral in San José's Central Park. Photograph courtesy of Christy Halbert.

indicate that the nation's Catholicism is not so much devout as it is concerned with the maintenance of deep-seated traditions. In fact, in 1985, although 90 percent of the population claimed to be Roman Catholic, only 15 percent reported attending mass once a week.

However nominal the practice of Catholicism, the influence of Catholic traditions runs deep, and the Church provides a significant social network that is the heart of virtually every community. Indeed, one is likely to find in every rural town, suburban center, and bustling city alike, a centrally located square with a church situated on one flank of a park or soccer field. As they do in Spain and elsewhere in Latin America, in Costa Rica travelers come upon astonishing surprises in the form of impressive churches tucked away in the most unassuming spots. These edifices on the town square are the symbolic center of community life, and they provide a familiar image that is replicated across the country.

Just as growth and development can displace the town square from its original geographic center, in some ways the Church has receded into the background, with other social forces thrown into relief in the panorama of cultural life. Historically, the Church was linked to the oligarchy in its opposition to the liberal reforms enacted in the nineteenth century. Today voters cast only a casual glance in the direction of the Church for guidance in elections, as this institution continues a long tradition of positioning itself outside the political sphere.

The official holiday calendar follows a Christian pattern, although it also accommodates the country's six major patriotic highlights: March 19 is Día de San José, marking the founding of this city as the capital in 1823; April 11 commemorates the national hero, Juan Santamaría; May 1 is Día del trabajador, acknowledging the importance of workers to the nation; July 25 celebrates the annexation of the Guanacaste province in 1824; September 15 is Día de la Independencia (Independence Day); and October 12 marks Columbus Day.

Ten state-sanctioned religious holidays outnumber these political holidays, however: three feasts honor the Virgin (April 21, August 1 and 2), one honors the patron saint of San José (mid-March), others celebrate Saints Peter and Paul (June 29), Holy Week (early April), Corpus Christi (May/June), the Feast of the Assumption (August 15, also Mother's Day; Father's Day is celebrated the third Sunday in June), the Immaculate Conception (December 8), and Christmas. These holidays tend to be extravagant and popular affairs.

A description of the Semana Santa (Holy Week) celebration provides an apt illustration. During the entire week preceeding Easter Sunday, all government offices, schools, and many businesses shut down. In fact, the focus of the event is Good Friday, when restaurants, supermarkets, and bars are closed and public transportation comes to a virtual standstill. Many families use this week for an annual vacation to the coast, but the religious backdrop of the holiday is unmistakable.

On Good Friday, religious processions take place all over the country, in commemoration of this centerpiece of Catholic doctrine. Elaborate enactments of the crucifixion involve months of planning, lavish costumes and props, and enthusiastic participation by large numbers of devout individuals. Within communities organizing their own processions, individuals vie for the best roles: Jesus carrying the cross, Roman soldiers, an assortment of biblical personages, some of whom whip themselves as they parade in a show of repentance and penance.

Catholic traditions that are present in the worldwide Hispanic community are evident in Costa Rican customs as well. It is not uncommon to meet men named José María (Joseph Mary), a nod toward the revered parents of Jesus, while a woman's given name may include a sometimes extensive reference to María del Milagro (Mary of the Miracle), or María Purísima (Purest Mary). Parents routinely name their children after saints whose names appear on their birthdate on the Catholic calendar.

Religious tradition is also evident in popular speech: when a light mist sprays in sunny skies, the phrase, *La Virgen se está bañando* (the Virgin is bathing) is often overheard. As will be discussed in the following chapter, Costa Rican speech is peppered with lively sayings and expressions. The common and mild expletives, *¡Dios mío!* (My God!), *¡Santísima Trinidad!* (Holy Trinity!), and *¡Señor de la Gloria!* (Lord have mercy!), point to a substratum of religious beliefs.

If a baby is born Catholic, he or she is baptized as an infant. The child's parents, godparents, and extended family gather to celebrate this event. Many Costa Rican children also experience the rites of their First Communion; it is a common sight in many households to see a photograph of a solemn young eight- or nine-year-old child, dressed formally and holding a small white Bible to mark this important and symbolic event.

Catholicism holds a respected place in Costa Rica, and is seen as fundamental to its culture. Religion in general has been an important part of life in this traditionally conservative society. Nevertheless, other groups have flourished, as well, including Protestants, Jews, Mormons, and Jehovah's Witnesses. The highest growth rate is evident among Protestant churches. In fact, Protestant membership tripled between 1978 and 1986, and in the final years of the twentieth century, Protestant membership in Costa Rican churches (like the Methodist and Assemblies of God, for instance) is estimated to include nearly 20 percent of the population. The *evangélicos'* faith has undoubtedly made its mark on Costa Rican society, with its emphasis on conversion and the adoption of a lifestyle meant to set its members apart from the surrounding culture.

PROTESTANT MISSIONARY ACTIVITY

The Mennonite church provides a useful illustration of Protestant missionary activity in Costa Rica. Rosedale Mennonite Missions (RMM)—part of the Conservative Mennonite Conference, a relatively small U.S. denomination—established a foreign mission in Costa Rica in 1961. Dominated by a conservative and literalist theology, as well as a commitment to the social well-being of individuals, RMM's activities abroad followed the tradition established among its North American congregations of merging evangelization with addressing physical needs.

Over the course of nearly 40 years, Rosedale Mennonite Missions has sent 100 individuals and five families to Costa Rica. Twenty-seven congregations have been established to date. From its inception, this church group has participated in an alliance of various Protestant denominations. But the contribution of the Mennonite church has been unique in its social pragmatism.

In urban areas, the Mennonite church has established new congregations, founded and taught in Bible institutes, and created day care centers for working mothers. Participants in RMM's Volunteer Service program have participated in an adult literacy program for many years, both in the capital and in the province of Guanacaste. All these activities have taken place within a strongly evangelical context, as churches were established alongside these social-service programs.

In rural areas, as well, these Mennonite volunteers have conducted Bible study while providing farming assistance, introducing pesticides, and improving the strain of grains that were used. Community development projects have included technical instruction in growing gardens to diversify the local diet, digging wells, and introducing better varieties of chicken to existing food-supply industries. Before rural health care reform was enacted in the 1970s, medical care was provided at various under-serviced outposts by Mennonite registered nurses. Also, RMM provided opportunities for enterprising individuals through small-business loans.

The height of RMM's mission activity took place throughout the 1970s; today the legacy of the Mennonite church is evident in its widespread national leadership and active congregations. The pacifist stance of this particular denomination struck a chord among the citizens of a country with no standing army. The Mennonite church's commitment to advancing social justice has also found common ground in a nation that tried to anticipate society's needs with the creation of extensive social welfare programs 50 years ago.

As is the case among numerous other Protestant groups, Mennonites have sent their missionaries to the Instituto de Lengua Española (Spanish-Language Institute) in San José for language training. Established in 1953, this school offers homestay placement along with a highly regarded program of language teaching. The institute estimates that over 3,000 North American Protestant missionaries have passed through its program.

Costa Rican Mennonite churches exhibit a trend shared by many Costa Rican congregations that have been established by U.S. mission personnel in that they follow a charismatic doctrine. Therefore their worship services may differ considerably from their U.S. counterparts. The adoption of local musical styles and other cultural expressions have served this church well in taking root in Costa Rican soil.

It is useful here to consider the historical context of Protestant mission activity in Costa Rica, from Bible distribution in the 1800s through the rise of Pentecostalism to today's evangelization via electronic media. The distribution of Bibles became "the most persistently carried out means by which

Protestant ideas were spread in Latin America" (Greenway 178). Within the liberal, reform-minded climate of the early nineteenth century, Protestant Bibles and schools were welcomed as signs of progress and modernization.

As independence and burgeoning nationhood spread throughout Latin America, its doors were opened to the rest of the world, and some missionaries viewed the "unchurched" Indian populations as fertile ground. North American Protestant missions provided translations of the Bible to native indigenous groups, as well as medical and educational services. In Central America, Moravian missionaries had reached the Miskito coast (within today's Nicaragua and Honduran territory) by the mid-1800s. Some theologians point to the revitalizing effect the translation of the Bible has had on threatened cultures. In Costa Rica, Mennonite missionaries were the first to work among the Bribrí Indians in the Talamanca region. Indeed, their translation work among the Bribrí anticipated a greater consciousness of the indigenous peoples' living conditions; and these missionaries have joined other groups, such as scholars and university students, to promote an appreciation for and protection of the historically neglected Indian communities.

In the early years of independence, the new Latin American governments encouraged the immigration of Europeans and North Americans, more as a means of exposing their citizens to liberal ideas than as a way to promote a Protestant doctrine. A heavy influx of missionaries soon followed; the emphasis of these missionary efforts was on schools, in many instances supplementing the lack of local government-sponsored initiatives in education that were endemic to this period of burgeoning nationhood.

Many of the schools that were founded by these liberal church groups were eventually secularized. However, some schools remain explicitly evangelical. The Colegios Monterrey and Metodista are a case in point; they are credited with initiating private bilingual (English-Spanish) education in the 1960s, and have since graduated several thousand students. The schools continue to be at the forefront of private education nationwide.

Today, the Protestant presence in Costa Rica is readily perceived—it is unmistakable, in fact. Hundreds of Protestant and Catholic churches coexist with churches in rural and urban areas; U.S. televangelists are recognized due to the wide transmission of their programs (in Spanish); the influence of North American church structure and liturgy is evident in the Sunday services; and it is estimated that in 2010, over 30 percent of the population will identify itself as evangelical.

A word should be said about the distinct influence of Pentecostalism on the Costa Rican religious scene. After World War II, Pentecostalism—a branch of Christian fundamentalism that advocates the expression of phenomena such as speaking in tongues and miraculous healing as evidence of spiritual blessing—caught fire and set the pace for rapid and unprecedented church growth. As perhaps can be argued about Latin America generally, many Costa Ricans demonstrate an openness to the manifestations of the supernatural. The cult of the Virgin and the rows of charms in the basement of the Basílica de los Angeles attest to this fact. The openness toward the supernatural is evident also in the energetic growth of the charismatic movements in both Catholic and Protestant circles.[2]

While the cultural openness and level of receptiveness to the supernatural account for part of the explosion in the growth of evangelical Protestant churches, it is also an important factor in the charismatic renewal movement within the Catholic church. The decade of the 1970s, particularly, witnessed an increased level of connectedness and association among Catholic and Protestant groups, which were united by their common charismatic identification. This commonality was demonstrated in the large, city-wide campaigns of evangelists such as the Reverends Luis Palau, Omar Cabrera, Billy Graham, and Jimmy Swaggart, as well as Father Francis McNutt.

The appeal of the evangelical Protestant message has only increased through the use of electronic media. Widespread exposure to this message has reduced social stigma, which in turn has helped make it socially acceptable to change from Roman Catholic to *evangélico*. In fact, the Costa Rican Protestant churches share significant affinities with their Catholic counterpart. The primarily conservative evangelical message echoes the official religion's investment in the status quo, and with the influx of American missionaries and other religious leaders, this status quo is increasingly reflecting U.S. religious values.

On the other hand, concern for the attrition rate among Protestants runs high in some of the more established missionary circles. In the aftermath of sustained economic crises in Costa Rica in the past two decades, religious institutions face significant challenges in making their spiritual message relevant, as they address growing social concerns and maladies brought about by a host of factors: increased poverty, immigration from neighboring countries; continuing pressure to compete in the global economy; the struggle to remain autonomous and peaceful amid a conflicted international community in the immediate vicinity; higher crime rates; and the threats of development and deforestation.

Catholic and Protestant Costa Rican institutional churches have not been particularly vocal in the political arena; at the same time, Costa Ricans have long enjoyed the rewards of a large and stable middle class, coupled with a pacifist commitment to democracy. At the end of the twentieth century, however, as the country grapples with intense economic pressures, questions are raised as to the ongoing role of religion. Perhaps in the coming century, these institutions will emerge in different roles.

NOTES

1. In Latin America, the term *evangélico* applies to a member of a church that is likely fundamentalist in biblical interpretation. Prosletyzing is central to the *evangélico* doctrine; church members may be urged not to participate in certain activities (drinking alcohol, or socializing with others who don't share their beliefs) in an effort to set themselves apart from those around them as a witness to their faith.

2. The fundamental impact of Pentecostalism is undeniable, with its patterns of church life that are relevant to the practice of religion in Costa Rica. Theologians account for the appeal of this doctrine in several ways. The worship style is culturally contextualized, that is, it is essentially compatible with the level of comfort with expressing emotion in Costa Rican society. In addition, Pentecostal leaders are nearly all Costa Rican, thus facilitating congregational identification with the church; the charismatic doctrine offers tangible evidence of consequences of following this path; and increased migration and urbanization creates a void and need for community and direction that the church aggressively seeks to provide (Greenway 190).

REFERENCES

Cardenal, Rodolfo. "The Church in Central America." In *The Church in Latin America (1492–1992)*, edited by Enrique Dussel. Wellwood, Eng.: Burns and Oates, 1992.

Cervantes Gamboa, Laura. "Origen y destino de las almas después de la muerte en la religión Bribrí." *Káñina* 17, no. 2 (1993): 213–23.

Dekker, James. "North American Protestant Theology: Impact on Central America." *Mennonite Quarterly Review* 58, supp. (August 1984): 378–93.

Drogus, Carol Ann. "The Rise and Decline of Liberation Theology: Churches, Faith, and Political Change in Latin America." *Comparative Politics* (July 1995): 465–77.

Greenway, Roger S. "Protestant Missionary Activity in Latin America." In *Coming of Age: Protestantism in Contemporary Latin America*, edited by Daniel R. Miller. Lanham, Md.: University Press of America, 1994.

Hallum, Anne Motley. *Beyond Missionaries: Toward an Understanding of the Protestant Movement in Central America*. Lanham, Md.: Rowman & Littlefield, 1996.

Martin, David. *Tongues of Fire: The Explosion of Protestantism in Latin America*. Oxford: Basil Blackwell, 1990.

Míguez Bonino, José. *Faces of Latin American Protestantism*. Translated by Eugene L. Stockwell. Grand Rapids, Mich.: Eerdmans, 1997.

Miller, Daniel R., ed. *Coming of Age; Protestantism in Contemporary Latin America*. Lanham, Md.: University Press of America, 1994.

Millet, Richard L. "Protestant-Catholic Relations in Costa Rica." *Journal of Church and State* 12 (Winter 1970): 41–57.

Molina, Iván, and Steven Palmer. *Historia de Costa Rica: Breve, actualizada, y con ilustraciones*. San José, Costa Rica: Editorial de la Universidad de Costa Rica, 1997.

Peck, Jane C. "Reflections from Costa Rica on Protestantism's Dependence and Nonlibertive Social Function." *Journal of Ecumenical Studies* 21 (Spring 1984): 181–98.

Troutman, Charles H. "Evangelicals and the Middle Classes in Latin America." Parts I and II. *Evangelical Missions Quarterly* 7, no. 2 (1971): 79–91; 7, no. 3 (1971): 154–63.

4

Social Customs

VISITORS TO COSTA RICA unfailingly remark on the warm hospitality of its citizens. Always evident is their genuine interest in others, the high value they place on social interaction, their festive celebration of ritual, the fact that they prize humor, their generously accommodating demeanor, and their extraordinary friendliness. Costa Ricans themselves have a deep appreciation for their country and culture: when a plane lands on Costa Rican soil, those on board often break into spontaneous cheering, clapping, and whistling. Their enthusiasm for their nation is endearing and contagious; yet their pride is tempered by the ingrained notion of being modest, of not calling attention to oneself, and of being *discreto* (discreet) in all things.

Certainly, Costa Ricans have much of which to be proud. Theirs is a stable democracy in a volatile region. Costa Rica is committed to peace within its borders and without: it abolished the army in 1948, and in 1987 its president was awarded the Nobel Peace Prize for his leadership in Central American peace initiatives. Costa Ricans have historically enjoyed the benefits of a large middle class and of a high level of prosperity, particularly when compared to that of the rest of Latin America.

Given that Costa Rica is part of the Central American region, such comparisons are unavoidable, and are the source both of an elitism of sorts among Costa Ricans and of some resentment from its neighbors. The vision set forth by a mid-century government coalition—one that led to Costa Rica's unusually extensive network of social services—continues to this day: its citizens have had long-term access to education, and health and social services, and at 97 percent, Costa Rica's literacy rate is among the highest in the Western

Women converse outside the entrance to a neighborhood *pulpería*. Photograph courtesy of Christy Halbert.

Hemisphere. In Costa Rica, hospitalization during childbirth is recognized as a universal right. In the 1990s, hospitals witnessed an influx of expectant mothers from neighboring countries; and these people were provided medical services free of charge. Such facts, which set this country apart from others, do result in feelings of superiority among many Costa Ricans, although they are loathe to admit to such an attitude.

Costa Ricans also take pride in the extraordinary biodiversity of their country, and indeed, this natural beauty is breathtaking. Costa Rica has protected a larger percentage of its territory than any other country on the planet. The conservation movement draws immense popular and official governmental support; however, many of these natural areas are constantly under threat due to the interference of investors—national and foreign—in economic-development projects, such as hotels on beaches near preserves. Corruption plays a role, too, as the bribing of local officials is all too common; the high legal standards frequently go unmet due to the high cost of enforcing them. This fundamental contradiction in the country's attitude toward its rich natural resources is puzzling, and according to social analysts, reflects a growing cultural crisis.

While the strength of Costa Rican culture lies partly in its adherence to tradition, in the careful preservation of what is uniquely its own, it must also counter this impulse to resist change when its survival is at stake. The apparent contradiction in its approach to the conservation of its natural resources is a case in point.

Perhaps this paradox may be explained somewhat by examining the implications of Costa Rica's role in providing a model of peace and stability for the rest of the world, a responsibility that is strongly impressed upon its citizens. At the same time, its culture fosters the assimilation of models of economic success and the latest technology from other countries and cultures (cell phone and Internet use are widespread, for example). This accounts in part for the great appeal of the United States for Costa Ricans; it also justifies their emphasis on image and on their portrayal of self to others.

For Costa Ricans, the presentation of self to others is of utmost importance, a cultural trait that is evident in the pride they take in their personal appearance. No matter their socioeconomic level, people are careful to always look their best, with pants pressed and shoes shined, fully made up, or wearing jewelry. It is not uncommon to see women in high heels even at the grocery store, a public environment where the image they project takes on great significance. In general, Costa Ricans dress up much more than their U.S. counterparts; and even when adults dress informally, tennis shoes are rarely worn. Personal grooming gives evidence of a meticulous eye for cleanliness and attention to detail. (Incidentally, it is common in many restaurants—particularly along highways—to spot a sink in the corner, separate from the restrooms, to facilitate washing one's hands before eating.) Projecting one's best image is always a clear goal, as a highly developed sense of formality underscores Costa Rican culture.

SOCIAL ENVIRONMENT

The level of formality in dress reflects the cultural importance of an individual's poise. Costa Ricans are very affectionate, for instance, yet they follow fairly rigid guidelines for social interaction: greetings are a case in point. When friends and family meet, the women greet each other with a kiss on one cheek (or in the air close to it) with a hand on the arm or shoulder, while speaking a phrase such as "*¿Cómo le va?*" (How are you doing?). Women and men may also greet each other similarly; meeting each other for the first time, men and women are likely to exchange only a handshake. Men may greet each other with a handshake or with an embrace and loud back-slapping.

During any social event, it is very important upon arriving to individually

A group of friends enjoys a morning *cafecito* (coffee break) at the Soda Tapia, a favorite landmark near the center of San José. Photograph courtesy of Christy Halbert.

acknowledge everyone in the room, and it is equally important to do so upon leaving. Not speaking to everyone present risks offending someone. This expectation of adherence to such a ritual underscores the traditional view of relations; and this formal behavior is consistent in dating patterns, as well.

DATING, THE FAMILY, AND GENDER ROLES

Formality in dating remains fairly widespread today, in spite of changes in other traditions. Until they are paired with one individual, Costa Ricans tend to go out in groups. However, *jalar* (dating one person exclusively) begins with a definite moment when one person, generally the male, *se le declara* (professes his intentions to another). Once the couple is officially dating, it is the male's responsibility to perform such chivalric duties as going to the woman's house to escort her to an event, walking on the side closest to the street, paying for all the evening's activities, and taking her home. Traditionally, the man is also permitted to visit the woman's home, provided her family members are present. The word used for this activity reveals the dynamics of the relationship: *marcar* means literally "to mark or keep track of." The supervised nature of these visits is expected, and the practice is deeply ingrained in Costa Rican dating patterns.

While the family is certainly central to the structure of Costa Rican society, family patterns are slowly changing. One in five families is headed by one parent, usually a woman; and 20 percent of all heads of family (defined as the person primarily responsible for meeting the family's physical needs) are over 60 years old. In recent years, there has been a steady increase in the number of older adults who live alone. This represents a significant, if not alarming, trend in a culture where the extended family has always provided the bulk of care for the elderly. In terms of gender, there is no statistical difference in the access women and men have to education. Yet, while women on average have a higher level of education and professional experience than men, they are paid less than their male counterparts for the same tasks, and the incidence of unemployment is higher among women. In this traditionally conservative culture, men have been granted a much greater degree of freedom in career choices, travel, living arrangements, and general life choices.

The recent development of the so-called *apartamento de soltera* (single woman's apartment) attests to the changes that are taking place in traditional interaction between the sexes. Whereas Costa Rican women are generally expected to remain with their parents until they marry (this expectation has not been so strongly applied to men), recently there has been a growing contingent of both single and divorced women living on their own or in the company of other women. The fact that more and more women are successfully implementing changes in the way they live is creating possibilities for other groups in society.

Costa Rican gays and lesbians are quick to point out that their lives are probably better in Costa Rica than they would be in other Central American countries. Contributing to this climate of relative openness are the absence of a repressive military and the recent creation of anti-discriminatory laws. Certainly, Costa Rica supports more gay businesses than other Central American nations, and in this respect, homosexual individuals are granted greater visibility. Within this traditionally conservative society, however, cultural and social prejudices still define the experience for many gays and lesbians. Individuals' families show support and acceptance in varying degrees; however, since gender roles are also fairly stereotypical, any deviation from the norm of heterosexuality may indeed result in negative sanctions.

Lesbian-owned and catering to a gay and lesbian clientele, the La avispa (The Wasp) dance club is one of a handful of public gathering places available to non-heterosexual individuals. Perhaps it is not surprising that, in a society that places great value on appearances and the projection of a narrowly defined image of what is and is not appropriate, gay Costa Ricans encounter great pressure to blend in quietly, to recess into the background and not draw attention to themselves. While some may perceive this as discretion and reward this behavior with tolerance, the fact remains that gays and lesbians have carved out only a minimal space in public life. Clubs like La avispa are therefore unusual in that they advertise that their clientele is gay; judging from the atmosphere within, it provides a joyful respite from an otherwise guarded existence.

Gay Costa Ricans have invented certain strategies to face the social pressures they feel. At La avispa, for instance, a New Year's party in July was established to provide a place for an early celebration of this holiday. During most holidays in Costa Rica, time with one's family takes precedence over all other relationships, and gay friends of a homosexual family member may not be welcomed at the family gathering. So on July 31, part of the country is already celebrating the start of a new year.

OTHER NATIONAL TRAITS

Generally, however, Costa Ricans are accommodating to a fault. Eager to please, striving to maintain the social order, and always interested in putting their best self forward, *para no quedar mal* ("so as not to make a bad impression," more or less) applies. They will routinely go to great lengths to make life easier, to soften a blow, to make things seem less harsh than they really are. For example, when asking a Costa Rican how long it takes to get somewhere, one may reasonably expect to add on an additional third to the estimate of time given: the person has simply tried to make the estimate more amenable—easier to accept—to the person asking. Some may consider this attitude evidence of admirable optimism; others might view it as a refusal to look reality in the face. Some visitors or new residents to the country are unaccustomed, for instance, to what they view as a maddeningly variable attitude toward punctuality.

Hora tica (Tico time) is a good-natured national joke for Costa Ricans. Simply put, the constraints of a schedule are subordinate to time spent in the company of others. One would be rude to put an end to a conversation with a friend or colleague only in order to adhere to some merely arbitrary appointment. Agreed-upon meeting times might be more accurately referred to as suggestions, rather than imperatives; chances are, in fact, that the other party is running late as well. In the business world, however, stated times are honored very conscientiously, and store hours, for instance, are strictly observed. There is even a phrase for what time schedule is to be adhered to: *hora americana* means punctuality.

In any event Costa Ricans, and those who have spent any time in this

A farmer's market on a typical Saturday in Escazú, a town on the outskirts of San José. Photograph courtesy of Christy Halbert.

country, know what to expect, so this looser view of time ceases to be a continual source of annoyance. This is not to say that Costa Ricans are either irresponsible, unable to keep to a schedule, or that they show complete disregard for others' valuable time. On the contrary, the impulse again to *quedar bien* (make a good impression) would make any Costa Rican extremely conscious of offending another's sensibilities and for this reason the person would want to respect others' needs absolutely, and in every situation.

LANGUAGE

Whenever the need arises to find some perspective in a given situation, Costa Ricans have come to rely on their extraordinary wealth of popular sayings. *Pura vida* (literally, pure life) has become the trademark response to the question, *¿Quihubo?* (What's up?), and reflects a very Costa Rican perspective: "all is well, life is good, I am content (or at least I will do all within my power to give that impression)."

Coming from the cherished traditions of the *campo* (rural area), Costa Rican sayings and proverbs are recycled continuously. Costa Rican speech sparkles with imagery: for example, to tease somebody who seems to be taking things too seriously, one might hear the comment that he or she is *más serio que un burro en lancha* (more serious than a donkey in a rowboat). Or the description of on-the-surface housecleaning may prompt the phrase, *por donde pasa la suegra* ("where the mother-in-law might pass by"). As these popular sayings reflect, humor is an essential factor in understanding Costa Rican culture. Every Costa Rican loves a good joke, and a good-natured ribbing is standard practice among friends. At the time of political elections, for instance, the candidates' popularity may be measured by the number and nature of jokes circulating about them.

Costa Rican speech patterns include several distinguishing characteristics that set them off from other Latin Americans. Trilled *r*'s are softened and slurred (what linguists term assibilation), so that a Costa Rican will pronounce the name of the country with a nearly whistled sound (the initial *r* in *Rica* is pronounced similarly to the *s* in *decision*). As mentioned before, Costa Ricans constantly use the diminutive ending, *-tico*, so that *chiquito* (very little)—already from chico (small)—becomes *chiquitico* (little bitty). However, the pervasive use of the *voseo* (a variation of the *vosotros*, roughly equivalent to "you all," conjugation) provides linguistic connections to other countries, namely of the Southern Cone (Chile and Argentina) as well as parts of Central America. Within Costa Rica, there is a difference in pronunciation in rural and urban speech; certainly, the English-speaking sectors of the southern Atlantic coast add another dimension to the national language. Known as *Mecatelio*, this language is a fusion of Spanish, standard English, and Jamaican English, and is spoken by descendants of Black Jamaicans who initially came to Limón to build the railroad in the late nineteenth century. And among a reduced group of people, Bribrí is the one remaining indigenous language still spoken in Costa Rica.

SPORTS AND LEISURE ACTIVITIES

Costa Ricans enjoy spectacular weather year-round and thus have ample opportunities for outdoor activities. Theirs is an enthusiastic appreciation for nature; the vegetation is lush, the rainfall is reliable, and flowers bloom in potted plants and along the roadside. In the Central Plateau especially, the mild weather eliminates the need for heating or air conditioning, so windows are often left open. Houses typically have a *patio de luz* (light patio), a small inner courtyard that is open to the sky, usually planted with grass and flowers or shrubs, and through it light streams into the rest of the house. It is as if the Costa Ricans are trying to find ways to capitalize on the extraordinary beauty of the outdoors.

This appreciation for their natural surroundings goes hand in hand with the value placed on physical activity and sports. While not all Costa Ricans may be sports fans, their way of life routinely incorporates exercise, mostly through walking. Even in metropolitan areas, where residents have come to rely on the excellent public transportation system, shoppers and commuters walk to get around the city. Walking is considered an essential activity, not a form of exercise, but the health benefits it provides are evident.

A large segment of the population is active in organized sports. The most popular activities are swimming, soccer, and cycling, although volleyball, tennis, running, and equestrian events have established a strong tradition as well. The cattle-raising province of Guanacaste is prized for its traditions in the training of horses, and dancing horses are a fixture of all major parades in San José.

In the early 1970s, the former international airport at La Sabana was converted into an enormous public park and recreation area. It is equipped with an Olympic-sized pool, an astounding number of soccer fields, and several basketball, volleyball, and tennis courts. The park also has a lake, a stadium (the site of presidential inaugurations), and an art museum. Located near downtown San José, the park is free and readily accessible, and on weekends it is packed with outdoor enthusiasts of all ages. Interestingly, El castillo (The Castle), a privately owned country club, has the only ice skating rink in Latin America.

Costa Rican national teams have represented the country in many international events. In the 1996 Olympics, Claudia Poll set a world record and won a gold metal for the 200-meter freestyle swim. Soccer teams regularly compete in world-class events, including the World Cup tournament. The mountainous terrain of Costa Rica provides challenging courses for cyclists; the annual national tour begins in Puntarenas and lasts five days. The country hosts an annual tennis tournament, La Copa del Café (The Coffee Cup), with participants from 40 nations; many enthusiasts play tennis in public parks and private clubs around the country.

Soccer, however, remains the undisputed favorite sport of Costa Ricans. Each of the seven provinces has its own professional team, and these players can make a good living. Soccer leagues in every conceivable organizational category abound: city and small-town teams, county-wide teams, even local women's teams have been established. Friendly rivalries based on soccer-team loyalties are common, and attendance at Sunday games is spirited: every weekend, crowds of 30,000 are in attendance at the national stadium. It is significant that the Costa Rican Cabinet includes the Department of Culture, Youth, and Sports. Such an organizational fusion provides clear evidence of the importance attributed nationally to sports and physical activity.

Another popular pastime is travel, both domestic and abroad. Reflective

Fans enjoy a Sunday match between the San Ramón and Grecia city teams. Women's teams, like the ones shown here, are gaining in popularity. Photograph courtesy of Christy Halbert.

of a certain socioeconomic level that Costa Ricans have long enjoyed, their love of travel also indicates their cosmopolitanism. Europe is quite popular as a destination. For example, to celebrate the *quinceañera*, a young girl's important 15th birthday, she is usually accompanied by one parent on her travels abroad; this event is akin to parents in the United States giving their daughter a car for high school graduation.

The United States is without question the most popular destination for Costa Ricans who travel abroad. Many go simply to shop, to visit relatives (particularly in Miami and Los Angeles), or to vacation. In fact, it is not uncommon for individuals to plan significantly far in advance for a month-long visit to the United States, and purchase a ticket to several different cities.

Domestic travel is also a popular pastime in this geographically diverse country. In the 1970s, the government launched a campaign called *Conozca su país* (Get to know your country). Its purpose was to promote Costa Ricans' travel within the country; at the time Costa Rica was experiencing a boom in the tourist industry that is only now leveling off. The government urged its citizens to discover what others from around the globe were flocking to

Sunday morning at a city park in downtown San José. Photograph courtesy of Christy Halbert.

see, encouraging them to explore the national parks system as their right and privilege.

Although Costa Ricans have long been avid lovers of the unique geography of each province, this travel campaign helped raise awareness of areas that had not previously been explored. A common destination for in-country travel is the fantastic variety of beaches that line the country on both coasts. From white sand to brown sand to shores turned black by ash from volcanic activity, Costa Rican beaches are some of the most beautiful in the world. During Holy Week, particularly, families and friends head to the coasts en masse and spend the days luxuriating at beachside resorts, camping on the beach, or staying in modest *cabinas*. Many beaches are bordered by national parks, adding other opportunities for appreciation of natural flora and fauna.

Costa Ricans also love to *salir a la calle* (literally, get out on the streets, or go out), whether it is out to shop, dance, eat, watch the latest films, go to the theater, take short trips to different parts of the country, or spend time with family and friends at each others' homes. Until recently, shopping was done in the style passed on from Old World settlers, at boutiques that lined the streets in downtown areas. The 1970s brought with them the development of *centros comerciales*, or a city block hollowed out with a parking lot like a courtyard, surrounded on three sides by rows of chain stores and specialty shops, much like the former downtown boutiques.

Today, Costa Ricans pride themselves on having the ease and luxury of U.S.-style shopping malls dotting the Central Plateau's cityscape. Some of these malls are elegant, showcasing the most recent trends in technology and fashion. Complete with food courts that include both U.S. and Costa Rican fast-food chains and restaurants, and with the latest video games, these malls have become hugely popular gathering places. Many are equipped with U.S. cinema franchises, catering to another favorite pastime in this country.

Following the more traditional pattern for grocery shopping, *pulperías*, or small, family-run convenience stores, usually appear every two or three blocks. These stores facilitated the daily purchase of food when refrigeration was not widespread; today the tradition of going to the store frequently persists, even though large superstore grocery chains are readily available. Another long-standing tradition is to buy the week's supply of fruits and vegetables at the local farmer's market. The overwhelming variety of produce tempts the eye, and for many families, it is a tradition to do the shopping together at these weekly markets.

Costa Ricans are avid fans of nightlife. Generally the nights are clear, the weather mild, and opportunities for entertainment abound. Theater and music performances provide a wealth of possibilities in venues as varied as the National Theater, the University of Costa Rica, or the Little Theatre Group of the Instituto Cultural Costarricense-Norteamericano. Costa Ricans are enthusiastic supporters of local talent, and participate in community theater, music concerts, festivals, and carnivals.

Dance is a favorite pastime in Costa Rica, from the traditional Latin forms of *cumbia, salsa,* and *merengue,* to the latest U.S. music. Clubs are usually packed after ten o'clock, with the dance floors crowded with well-dressed people. Protocol on the dance floor is fairly conservative: couples dancing dominates, and it is rare to find people dancing alone or even in small groups.

A wealth of clubs enrich the variety of the dance scene. Cocoloco, located within a mall in San José and catering to a younger crowd, plays exclusively pop or rock, either in English or Spanish. The popularity of Latin rhythms brings enthusiastic crowds to performances by local bands like Marfil, veteran performers of *salsa, cumbia,* and *merengue.* The Poas, named after one of Costa Rica's magnificent active volcanoes, is a hangout decorated with gourds and moss, dimly lit with green bulbs and notorious for its popularity with couples who, for one reason or another, find it necessary to be discreet about their liaison. Couples dance to *cumbias* in practiced, contoured rhythms. As mentioned, clubs like La avispa offer yet another option for a night of dancing.

HOLIDAYS

One common trait that unites all Costa Ricans is their love of celebration. Holidays are celebrated in the company of immediate family, extended family, and friends, old and new. It is not uncommon to extend spontaneous invitations to whomever one encounters in the course of planning such an event—these events tend to burgeon into quite large and lively celebrations. On Independence Day, San José Day, or New Year's Day, bombetas (firecrackers) are likely to be heard, as popping sounds come from all over. Most businesses are closed, and people gather in homes for celebrations, or take short day trips to the beach, a water park, or a place that serves *comida típica* (food typical of a particular region or from a Costa Rican tradition).

One popular spot is the Fiesta de Maíz (Corn Fair), a humble name for a beloved destination on holidays or Sunday afternoons. Nestled among the farmlands of Alajuela, the restaurant is popular also because the climate tends to be spectacular—warm, breezy, and sunny. On the menu at the Fiesta del Maiz is every conceivable derivative of corn: *atoles* (puddings), both sweet and salty; *tortillas de maíz*, a type of corn fritter, served with sour cream or melted butter; corn *tamales*; and various beverages made from corn. The restaurant is always packed with customers, who crowd around small tables in a very festive atmosphere.

The Christmas holiday season provides a good example of the way Costa Ricans enjoy celebrations. Strings of lights decorate windows and entrances in virtually every neighborhood. It is common for business to contribute to the holiday spirit by incorporating imitation snow in windowfront displays, in a country that has never seen a white Christmas. Most Costa Rican homes display a creche during this holiday, set on top of a bed of brownish tropical moss. A festive environment is underscored by unusually cool night breezes as people take to the streets, attending special concerts and other performances and *fiestas*, like the ones in Zapote, for example. This is, in effect, a carnival complete with rides, food stands, and a bullfight that is literally open to the public. Anyone can join the bull in the arena and try his or her hand at playing matador. Needless to say, there are always injuries, and sometimes fatalities. Grapes and apples, traditional holiday fare, are accompanied by *tamales*, an exotic and delicious combination of a cornmeal-based dough and chicken or pork, rice, olives, raisins, and special seasonings, wrapped in banana leaves, then boiled. Every household has its unique method of preparation; *tamales* are served every day for several weeks, accompanied by the traditional *agua dulce* (sweet water), a beverage made by dissolving shavings

A family buys banana leaves for *tamales*, in preparation for the holidays. Photograph courtesy of Christy Halbert.

from the *tapa*—a block of dark, raw sugar—in hot water. Of course, *rompope* (rum-laced eggnog) is on hand as well.

The importance of family in holiday celebrations simply cannot be overstated. Family members are much more likely to be automatically involved in birthdays, holidays, ceremonies, even vacations, than they would in the United States, for example. Extended family members as well as friends make up the community network, and a high priority is placed on seeing each other frequently, whether for coffee or an outing.

CUISINE

A Saturday may involve piling into a car and going in search of a food typical of a particular region. It would not be unusual to find the parents and children accompanied by a grandmother, a cousin, and a family friend. As Costa Ricans take great pride in their country and its regional distinctions, they seek out contact with, and the experience of, what they perceive as their "authentic culture." They go in search of *cajeta* in San Ramón, for instance; *cajeta* is a sugary confection made from creamy milk that is stirred patiently over low heat. The Costa Rican astronaut, Franklin Chang-Rodriguez, made *cajeta* famous when he took it on several space missions, and a coconut-and-orange variety was named *cajeta espacial*, or space *cajeta*, in his honor. Family groups seek out corn dishes like *chorreadas* in Guanacaste, seafood and ceviche (white fish marinated in lime juice to which finely chopped onion, tomato, and *culantro* has been added) in Puntarenas, or coconut milk– and oil-flavored dishes in Limón.[1]

Costa Ricans enjoy a tradition of fine eating, capitalizing on their rather astonishing wealth of fruits, tubers, and vegetables. The staples of their diet are rice, beans (mostly black but also small red ones), and corn tortillas, usually accompanied by creative and delicious combinations of lightly condimented vegetables in a salad. The traditional flavoring of food is not spicy; rather, cooks rely on more subtle flavors of herbs and natural seasonings. The mainstays of a Costa Rican kitchen are onion, *culantro* (a variety of cilantro, which is found increasingly in U.S. supermarkets), and *chile dulce* (fresh sweet red pepper).

Salads usually come in either a lighter version—shredded cabbage mixed with *culantro* and seasoned with lime juice or vinegar and salt—or the heavier version, such as *ensalada rusa* (Russian salad), prepared by boiling beets and potatoes, then mixing them with a mayonnaise dressing and finely chopped tomatoes, *culantro*, onion, and hard-boiled eggs.

The classic breakfast is *gallo pinto* (speckled rooster), a mix of leftover black beans and rice, tossed with lightly sauteed onion, *culantro*, and *chile dulce* and served with fried eggs, sour cream, and fresh tortillas. The traditional lunchtime dish is called *casado*, or married man, a humorous allusion to the kind of repetitive meals that a man purportedly expects once he marries. The dish is in fact quite varied: a large plate is spread with any combination of rice, beans, fried ripe plantains, salad, and spaghetti, and is accompanied by a piece of meat, chicken, or fish. As the midday meal is generally the heaviest, evening meals often consist of a simple soup.

Costa Rican cooks can do wonders with stews: *olla de carne* (meat stew) is a national dish, prepared slightly differently within each household but adhering to the indispensable ingredients of squash, field corn, tubers such as *yuca* or *ñampí*, potatoes, green plantains, and beef. Other typical dishes include *picadillos*, finely chopped vegetables (green beans, *chayote* squash, or potatoes) and beef; served with corn tortillas.

Snacks are known as *bocas* (literally, mouths) and accompany *cafecitos* (coffee breaks), alcoholic beverages, or are served as appetizers. They consist of either small sandwiches, miniature-sized filled pastries (sweet or salty), and tiny versions of *tamales* or *gallos* (roosters). *Gallos* usually consist of a small soft corn tortilla filled with a *picadillo*, a salad mix of tomato, cabbage, and hard-boiled egg. Desserts—if any are served—can include *arroz con leche*, or rice pudding; *tres leches* (three milks), a cake soaked with evaporated milk, condensed milk, and topped with whipped cream; *budín*, or bread pudding; and various coconut confections.

Meals are usually accompanied by fresh-fruit drinks—*frescos*—available year-round. They come in two varieties, *frescos en agua* (prepared with water) or *en leche* (with milk), prepared with bananas, papaya, or berries, for example. There are hundreds of varieties of fruit in Costa Rica, and most of them have been made into a *fresco*. Among the most distinctive is *cas*, an acidic fruit related to the *guayaba* (or guava) that is a natural thirst quencher. *Frescos* tend to be sweetened generously.

COFFEE

A description of Costa Rican cuisine would not be complete without addressing the importance of coffee. The traditional manner of preparation is to place heaping tablespoons of finely ground coffee in a cotton bag placed above a waiting carafe, and then to pour hot water over it slowly. Coffee is served rich and black or as *café con leche* (coffee with hot milk and liberal amounts of sugar) as an essential part of the morning routine and of the *cafecito de la tarde* (afternoon coffee break).

Today, Costa Rican coffee is recognized as being among the very best in the world, and its production has generated many export varieties. Coffee production has long dominated the Costa Rican economy, and it has accounted for the development of a coffee-rich oligarchy. Restored mansions exhibit the long-gone elegance and tradition of early nineteenth-century prosperity. Coffee provides an opportunity for conversation; it is a social equalizer of rich and poor; it beautifies the landscape with its eye-catching shrubs— its leaves are a vibrant green and, at harvest, the beans are a bright red. The November-to-February school holiday schedule developed in Costa Rica much as the May-to-August summer schedule did in the United States: school was planned around the demands of an agriculturally based economy that required all available hands to aid in the harvest. Coffee consumption and production created a powerful national icon. For instance, the five-*colón* bill, arguably one of the most beautiful paper currencies in existence, depicts

At a weekly fruit market, a vendor selling oranges out of the back of his truck takes the time to peel an orange for his customer. Photograph courtesy of Christy Halbert.

various stages of *la cosecha del café* (the coffee harvest). This same image was painted on the curved ceiling of the National Theater, and is a long-standing symbol of Costa Rican folklore.

NOTE

1. For more information on Costa Rican cooking, see Zaira Jiménez Córdoba's *Delicias típicas en su mesa* (Alajuela, Costa Rica: Litografía e Imprenta Alfonso, 1996). For regional dishes from the Caribbean coast, see Marjorie Ross de Cerdas' *La magia de la cocina limonense: Rice and beans y calalú* (San José, Costa Rica: Editorial de la Universidad de Costa Rica, 1991).

REFERENCES

Ansorena Montero, Aixa. "Negotiating Women's Legal Equality: Four Versions of a Law." In *The Costa Rican Women's Movement: A Reader,* edited by Ilse Abshagen Leitinger. Pittsburgh, Pa.: University of Pittsburgh Press, 1997.
Biesanz, Mavis Hiltunen, Richard Biesanz, and Karen Zubris Biesanz. *The Ticos:*

Culture and Social Change in Costa Rica. Boulder, Colo.: Lynne Rienner Publishers, 1999.

Córdoba, Zaira Jiménez. *Delicias típicas en su mesa*. Alajuela, Costa Rica: Litografía e Imprenta Alfonso, 1996.

Gagini, Carlos. *Diccionario de costarriqueñismos*. 4th ed. San José, Costa Rica: Editorial Costa Rica, 1989.

Gutiérrez Saxe, Miguel, ed. *Estado de la Nación en Desarrollo Humano Sostenible: Resumen del cuarto informe, 1997*. San José, Costa Rica: Proyecto Estado de la Nación, 1998.

Haber, Harvey, Dona Haber, and Lucinda Hilbrink. "National Parks, Reserves and Refuges." In *Insight Guides: Costa Rica*, edited by Harvey Haber. Boston: Houghton Mifflin, 1995.

Naranjo, Carmen. *Cinco temas en busca de un pensador*. 2d ed. San José: Editorial Costa Rica, 1989.

Ross de Cerdas, Marjorie. *La magia de la cocina limonense: Rice and beans y calalú*. San José: Editorial de la Universidad de Costa Rica, 1991.

5

Broadcasting and Print Media

IN SAN JOSÉ, Costa Ricans have access to a wide and well-funded array of media services and publications. The three major national newspapers are sold on practically every street corner, and many commuters can be spotted reading a paper on the bus. Glossy magazines and special-interest periodicals are readily found in supermarkets and bookstores throughout the city. However, their availability outside of the San José metropolitan area may be restricted, since Costa Rica—like other Latin American countries—still finds many of its resources overwhelmingly concentrated in the capital.

The pervasiveness of other media is exemplified by the ever-present transistor radio. Invariably, there is a radio playing in taxis and on public buses, and when walking along the street, sounds of Caribbean rhythms and songs from the U.S. Top Ten fill the air. In 1995, one or more televisions could be found in over 90 percent of Costa Rican households, and watching TV is a popular pastime. In a country where U.S. cultural icons are highly valued and sought after, Costa Rica's citizens enjoy access to cable television. Cable access is so widespread that at any given time, a viewer in Costa Rica can watch programs that are also being broadcast in any major U.S. city.

NEWSPAPERS

Costa Rica has long enjoyed freedom of the press. This fundamental democratic freedom was established in the early nineteenth century with the development of a local news press. This freedom was formally reiterated as a right by the Figueres government in 1948. The nation's largest and oldest daily newspaper, aptly named *La nación*, with a circulation of 75,000 in 1995, has set the tone for reporting that is followed by the other daily papers.

This paper's ideological perspective reflects the interests of its shareholders: financed by influential members of the business community, *La nación* has historically registered a conservative voice. Indeed, the paper went on record as being anti-Figueres during his presidency's far-reaching social reforms. In the decades following this reform era, the two other major daily newspapers came into existence, hoping to provide an alternative to the rightist coverage of the nation's leading newspaper. *La república* (circulation in 1995 of 55,000), founded in the 1950s, was sympathetic to Figueres, and for years represented a true counterpart to the ideological stance of *La nación*. In the 1960s, an afternoon paper, *La prensa libre* (The Free Press, circulation of 45,000 in 1995), started as a left-of-center publication. Today, however, newspaper reporting in the three major daily newspapers has converged into a monolithic, rightist perspective.

In fact, *La nación* is not simply a newspaper but a media conglomerate. In addition to a generous number of daily supplements, it publishes a half-dozen magazines, holds interests in other newspapers, and owns two of the largest radio stations in the country. Daily coverage is similar to that of most major newspapers around the world: domestic and international news, opinion editorials, business and the economy, arts, sports, entertainment and recreation, and letters to the editor. *Ancora* (Anchor), Sunday's cultural supplement, is a valuable medium for creating public awareness of and interest in Costa Rican arts and music, as well as in the writers, artisans, and musicians producing those works. Featuring interviews with leading intellectual figures, critical commentaries, and excerpts from literary works, *Ancora* has also contributed to the development of a collective appreciation of the arts, both regional and international.

Other weekly supplements include Sunday's *Revista dominical* (Sunday Review), an events showcase enhanced by interviews with local personalities. On Wednesdays, the educational supplement *Zurquí* (named after the *Zurquí* hills) targets a younger audience, and on Thursdays two other supplements appear: *En forma* (In Shape) reports on health and wellness issues; and *Tiempo libre* (Free Time) lists the calendar of social events in the Central Valley, naturally concentrating on those taking place in San José. Since 1995, *La nación* has been online. Its attractive Web site is updated daily, and provides a welcome link, especially to those readers living outside of Costa Rica.

Other print media that voice a different perspective from the mainstream press are available, including *Semanario Universidad*, the official University of Costa Rica weekly. Known for its coverage of international politics and arts, this publication is recognized for its leftist, anti-imperialist stance.

The urban landscape includes a message from the First Lady, "Peace begins at home." Photograph courtesy of Christy Halbert.

The Tico Times is an important feature of the news media in Costa Rica. Billing itself as "Central America's Leading English-Language Newspaper," it has been awarded international journalism prizes and is a mainstay of the sizable English-speaking expatriate population in Costa Rica. Founded in 1956, it also has a significant international circulation, and has been online since 1997. The staff of *The Tico Times* consists mostly of Americans who are long-term residents of Costa Rica. Along with reporting the local news, the cultural commentary from the perspective of non-native residents makes for interesting reading. A quick scan of the advertisements featured in *The Tico Times* reveals an emphasis on real estate and other services geared toward the individual wanting to relocate to Costa Rica.

As purveyors of information and perspective, journalists are courted by different interest groups in an informal but earnest lobbying effort. Government groups, banks, investors, and local businesses throw extravagant parties to which journalists are routinely invited. The status of journalists in Costa Rica is high; those with regular columns can become local celebrities. Certainly, they function as important opinion-makers.

MAGAZINES AND PERIODICALS

Costa Rica's relative prosperity in Latin America makes possible the publication of a fair number of magazines and periodicals. These range from glossy monthlies that target tourists, to evangelical Christian publications, to issues dedicated to conservation efforts. Publications that advocate environmental awareness and proactive measures to protect the environment and natural resources have acquired a growing number of international subscribers, as a result of ecotourism. *Gente 10* (People 10), a lesbian and gay-interest magazine, was founded in 1995, and its very existence is a testament to the growing visibility of the homosexual population. In a departure from previous times, advertisers pay to show themselves to be gay-friendly.

A number of scholarly journals are published in Costa Rica. *Káñina* (the past tense of "to dawn" in the Bribrí language) is a good example. Published by the University of Costa Rica, the journal showcases scholarship in fine arts, the humanities, and the social sciences. As an example of its diverse coverage, recent issues have featured a study of Bribrí funerary rites, a comparative analysis of Carlos Luis Fallas' *Marcos Ramírez* and Mark Twain's *Tom Sawyer*, a linguistic study of family names in the province of Heredia, an article on piano teaching methodology, and samples of original art, both visual and literary.

Foreign-funded periodicals have left their imprint on Costa Rican media as well. Primarily sponsored by aid organizations, such publications have made an important contribution to the dissemination of information. An international council began funding a far-reaching demographic analysis of Costa Rican society in 1994. The resulting publication—very useful in its concise reporting of a wide range of social and economic trends—appears annually as *Estado de la nación* (State of the Nation), and is posted on the Web as well. This merging of local and foreign media is representative of many such joint ventures that historically have characterized Costa Rican social development.

RADIO

The popularity and impact of the radio are unmistakable in Costa Rica. It has always provided an important link between the capital and far-flung locales, and today 130 radio stations fill the airwaves. Daily radio programming includes talk shows and soap operas, political and social commentary mixed with humor, educational and religious programs, and sports coverage.

It is not uncommon to listen to blaring romantic ballads while cleaning house. Many visitors to Costa Rica comment on the surprising pervasiveness on the radio of songs in English that are also popular in the United States; these are generally combined with music in the Caribbean traditions of *salsa, cumbia*, and *merengue*. Costa Ricans love music and it is played at any social gathering.

Another popular pastime is listening to sports commentators, who deliver a seemingly impossible, rapid-fire commentary in an excessively deep voice. During Sunday soccer matches, the trademark *gol* (goal), drawn out interminably, can be heard on radios the country over.

Costa Ricans' love of humor comes through in the many popular variety-style shows. *La Patada* (A Kick in the Pants), a program broadcast by Radio Sonora, features *concho*-style characters (a national archetype, of sorts) who provide raucous commentary on recent events, highlight blunders made by politicians, and generally provide a light-hearted perspective on the news. For serious commentary, listeners can tune in to the noon editorial, *La opinión*, practically an institution on Radio Reloj (Clock Radio), the radio station that announces itself with an exaggerated rolling of the *r*'s in its name.

In addition to these popular shows, evangelical Christian stations have blossomed since the 1980s. American missionaries were the first, for instance, to broadcast the Protestant message by radio and television. The radio station, Faro del Caribe (Lighthouse of the Caribbean), has transmitted broadcasts produced in Costa Rica and other areas of Latin America since the late 1940s. It includes programs targeted for the instruction and entertainment of children, mothers, and young people through Bible study, radio theater, advice, and music.

Radio programming has fulfilled other goals, like distance learning. In 1993, the government established the Costa Rican Institute of Radio Education in an effort to provide access to education to residents in rural areas. Programs such as "The Teacher in Your House" are broadcast from 12 noncommercial stations; these complement correspondence courses at both the elementary and secondary school levels. Lessons in English are immensely popular, and recently, programs have been broadcast in Bribrí as well.

TELEVISION

Costa Rican television transmission began in the 1950s; today there are a dozen commercial stations and one that is government-run. Channel 7's evening news program, *Telenoticias* (TV News), has been a fixture for many years, and generally follows the conservative tone set by the newspapers. Local television programming also includes soccer games and other sporting events (primarily bicycle races and swim meets), comedy shows, cooking and other how-to shows, programs giving religious and medical advice, and game shows and variety programs. Popularized during the 1970s, *El Show de Patiño* is remembered fondly by many as Costa Rica's first game show.

Costa Rican television also airs programs from the rest of Latin America, mostly soap operas from Mexico and Venezuela. Programs produced in the United States and dubbed in Spanish have proven to be hugely popular over the years, from *The Six Million Dollar Man, The Love Boat,* and *Dallas* to *Beverly Hills, 90210.* MTV programming, U.S. cartoons, and NBA games have also been part of this wave of imported U.S. culture.

The 1980s marked the advent of U.S. cable, bringing American sports and music coverage into even more Costa Rican homes. Now, satellite dishes abound as well. Greater access to such programming results in the English language being much more noticeable in daily life; its presence is almost routine. The sounds of Latin American Spanish, with its various regional dialects, are also shaping popular culture. Some worry about the changes in Costa Rican speech that have already become evident, using the more standard *tú* ("you") address for instance, rather than the regional *vos.* Others celebrate the cosmopolitan nature of such exposure, and welcome the pervasiveness of the English language, and of all things North American.

ELECTRONIC MEDIA

At the end of the twentieth century, the long reach of electronic media is in a sense making each country less insular, including Costa Rica. In addition, the effects of the Internet are becoming visible and unmistakable. Most importantly, the relatively low cost of Internet access has suddenly made available a much broader range of information, and provides almost instantaneous delivery.

Electronic media holds great potential for shaping and utilizing knowledge and information, allowing Costa Ricans to actively participate in the global economy. Though not all citizens have access to the Web or to information technology generally, this element of broadcast media is becoming increasingly a presence, and will surely define the future of broadcast media in this nation, as it has in others.

REFERENCES

Biesanz, Mavis Hiltunen, Richard Biesanz, and Karen Zubris Biesanz. *The Ticos: Culture and Social Change in Costa Rica.* Boulder, Colo.: Lynne Rienner Publishers, 1999.

Gutiérrez Saxe, Miguel, ed. *Estado de la Nación en Desarrollo Humano Sostenible: Resumen del cuarto informe, 1997.* San José, Costa Rica: Proyecto Estado de la Nación, 1998.

Haber, Harvey, ed. *Insight Guides: Costa Rica.* Boston: Houghton Mifflin, 1995.

Lara, Silvia, Tom Barry, and Peter Simonson. *Inside Costa Rica.* Albuquerque, N.M.: Resource Center Press, 1995.

6

Literature

IN SPITE OF the fact that its readership is rather limited beyond the borders of Central America, Costa Rica's literary tradition gives ample evidence of its quality, and merits increasing recognition. Beginning with Magón's vignettes portraying typical life at the turn of the century, and culminating with the experimental texts of the prolific Carmen Naranjo—nominated in 1998 for the Nobel Prize—Costa Rican writers have made a richly textured contribution to world literature. The backbone of the Costa Rican literary tradition is arguably the work of women writers; they have participated in— and often led the way to—every literary movement throughout this century. Since the 1970s especially, the voices of Black writers such as Quince Duncan have enriched the Costa Rican literary chorus.

The best known Costa Rican writers produced their works during the twentieth century; literary production was minimal before the last decade of the nineteenth century and came primarily in the form of serial installments published in newspapers. Joaquín García Monge's *El moto* (1900) is widely considered the first Costa Rican novel, making the transition between *cuadros de costumbre*—vignettes describing typical Costa Rican life, written in the tradition of social realism—and the extended prose of a full-fledged novel. It was only with the development of urban centers in the mid-1800s that theater flourished, and it was not until 1890 that the first collection of poetry was published. The relative brevity of this trajectory is misleading, however, as many significant works stand as proof of the talent of Costa Rican writers.

The wealth of literary production has taken place despite the difficulty of getting published. Publishing companies are underfunded and markets are small, so that making one's living exclusively as a writer is impossible. Writing as a vocation is, however, held in high esteem by Costa Ricans. Weekly newspapers include literary supplements and interviews with writers. The government, too, has supported publishing in several ways: the state-subsidized Editorial Costa Rica was established in 1961 and, along with private organizations, regularly recognizes writers with literature prizes. Another important publishing venue is the Editorial Universitaria Centro-americana, or EDUCA (Central American Universities Press): it is headquartered in San José (Carmen Naranjo served as its editor for many years), and has operated without outside funding since 1984. In spite of these difficulties, writers do get published, and the literature produced in Costa Rica today gives evidence of a sophisticated exchange of ideas among writers and the interplay of movements from around the globe.

It can be argued that prose is the nation's strong suit, although many published poets would disagree. Recent decades have witnessed renewed vigor in the production of plays that are generally used as a vehicle for social commentary. In the 1980s, the influx of exiled Chilean playwrights sparked a renewal of theater on the national scene. What is remarkable, however, is the exponential growth in the number of women writers in recent decades. Their participation is due in no small part to the efforts of Carmen Naranjo, one of the first women to be published and read widely abroad as well as in Costa Rica, who blazed a trail for other female writers to follow.

EARLY NARRATIVE

Costumbrismo was the first literary movement to be cultivated on Costa Rican soil, and it was instrumental in developing a sense of nationhood. Its style is given to drawing a realistic portrayal of daily life, enhanced by local speech and customs, as well as specific geographic locators. While Costa Rica has been spared much of the political strife that has informed many outstanding works of fiction elsewhere in Latin America, Costa Rican writers have portrayed their cultural context through the lens of both traditional and experimental narrative. For a country that is unique in Latin America, early Costa Rican literature provided engaging characterizations of the Tico sense of self.

In 1895 and 1896, Magón (Manuel González Zeledón) captured scenes from daily life, in weekly *cuadros* published in the Sunday edition of several newspapers. He and Aquileo Echeverría are credited with mythologizing the Costa Rican identity. Echeverría's *Concherías* (1905) still stands as the classic characterization of a Costa Rican prototype; his portrayal of the *concho* may be compared to that of the *jíbaro* in Puerto Rico, or the *gaucho* in Argentina, an archetype or "national self" of sorts in which Costa Ricans recognize exaggerated aspects of themselves. Written in verse—a *romance*, or eight-syllable lines with assonant rhyme—the *Concherías* created a dialogue between the *concho* and the narrator. The *concho* was portrayed as a simple, rural individual whose speech incorporated a wealth of folkloric references and quirky expressions. The narrator provided the reader a critical distance from this literary figure, while the dramatized dialogue lent itself to visualization.

The controversial essayist, Omar Dengo (1888–1928), subsequently challenged many of the stereotypes that had evolved at the time. In widely read essays published in newspapers and magazines, Dengo refuted commonly held concepts of the *concho*, for example, calling for an authentic appreciation of the rural Costa Rican individual. Dengo also admonished against the portrayal of a national character that had defined itself solely in relation to the other—whether it was a foreigner or someone of a non-white race—in a didactic effort, still praised today, to bring a critical consciousness to Costa Rican culture.

Carmen Lyra (1888–1949)

Writing under the pseudonym of Carmen Lyra, María Luisa Carvajal was the first woman writer to be widely published in the country, and she inaugurated the pivotal participation of women writers in Costa Rica's literary tradition. A look back shows evidence of her revolutionary subject matter: characters who were drawn from marginalized groups such as children, women, and banana workers. Lyra was a founding member of the Costa Rican Communist party in 1931, and her writing is always undergirded by social criticism. Her style, perspective, and subject matter make her an appropriate transitional figure whose literary trajectory mirrored social, political, and artistic changes of the early decades of the twentieth century.

A contemporary of Gabriela Mistral (the first Latin American awarded the Nobel Prize for Literature, in 1945), Lyra is best known for her collection of stories entitled *Los cuentos de mi Tía Panchita* (My Aunt Panchita's Stories, 1920). Lyra gathered stories, legends, and archetypes from around the world and recreated them within a local context. The geographical setting, historical references, and linguistic style are recognizably Costa Rican. Lyra also incorporated indigenous traditions in the stories of *Tatica Dios* (the Indian term, *tatica*, is a familiar form of address to one's father), *Tío Conejo* (Uncle Rabbit), and *Tío Coyote* (Uncle Coyote). Like Echeverría, Lyra has become a permanent fixture in the literature of Costa Rican folklore.

Carlos Luis Fallas (1909–66)

The publication of *Mamita Yunai* (1940) politicized Costa Rican literature, and it was the first novel in Central America to take on the abuses carried out by the banana companies, although Carmen Lyra had anticipated this theme in 1931 with her collection of short stories entitled *Bananos y hombres* (Bananas and Men). Carlos Luis Fallas (also known as Calufa) was a journalist and a member of the Communist party. Calufa based his narrative on observations made during his assignment as electoral official in Talamanca during the 1940 presidential elections. *Mamita Yunai* first appeared as weekly installments printed in a local newspaper later that year.

The novel's title is a play on the Spanish pronunciation of "united"; *Mamita* points to the dependent condition of its workers, one that was encouraged by the banana company. The first-person narrative recounts the experiences of Sibaja, who is on assignment for his political party in the Atlantic coastal region. Sibaja documents the exploitative nature of the United Fruit Company's domination as he describes the poor treatment of its employees— the Black and indigenous laborers—particularly the inadequate working conditions, and the company's destruction of the environment. La United Fruit is seen as a murderous presence, bringing only evil to the province. Although the characters are drawn somewhat stereotypically, they effectively give voice to the plight of the banana workers.

Mamita Yunai brought national and international attention to the deplorable working conditions within the transnational banana companies. This novel spurred similar denunciations by other Central American writers. Subsequently, seven novels were published in the next two decades in Panama, Honduras, and Guatemala on the theme of exploitation at the hands of foreign banana companies. Sympathizers embraced the cause for workers' rights; Carlos Luis Fallas himself was a leader in a major strike against the United Fruit Company in 1934.

Joaquín Gutiérrez (b. 1918)

The contributions of Joaquín Gutiérrez to Costa Rica's literary tradition rest in part on his portrayal of women, Blacks, and children. His 1950 novel, *Puerto Limón*, complements Calufa's work in its description of the 1934

banana workers' strike. The strike marked an important step in the quest for
equality for minorities in Costa Rica, as most of these workers were Black.
Gutiérrez successfully created in this work less stereotypical Black characters:
telling the story through Silvano's eyes, we witness a young Black man's
political coming of age. However, it would take another 30 years for readers
to hear Black Costa Ricans write about themselves.

Gutiérrez then cast his glance at another rural area of Costa Rica in *Mang-
lar* (The Mangrove Swamp, 1947). The narrative paralleled the sexual and
political maturation of its protagonist, Cecilia. The symbolism of the swamp
is evident in its fusion of the diverse natural elements, of water and land.
The lines of demarcation are blurred as Cecilia encounters the ambiguities
of adulthood. The novel broke ground when it portrayed the female psyche
and female eroticism, themes that would shortly be elaborated upon by Costa
Rican women writers themselves.

Joaquín Gutiérrez is best known, however, for a short novel entitled *Cocorí*
(1947). Set in Puerto Limón, this poignant story of a young Black child
stands as an indispensable part of Costa Rican literature and it has been
translated into several languages. *Cocorí* is credited with permanently im-
printing images of Black Costa Ricans onto the national consciousness.

TRANSITIONAL LITERARY FIGURES

Yolanda Oreamuno (1916–56)

La ruta de su evasión (The Path of Her Evasion, 1949) placed Oreamuno
at the vanguard of experimental narrative in Costa Rica. Her use of interior
monologue, nonlinear time and space, the centrality of language, and surrealist ruptures of thought aligns her with experimental novelists like William
Faulkner and Alain Robbe-Grillet. Oreamuno set Costa Rican narrative on
a course toward the innovations of postmodernism, and many writers have
followed in her wake.

Oreamuno's selection of themes, which are still in vogue years after her
death, also put her ahead of her time. For instance, she denounced domestic
violence and challenged the demarcation between the public and the private
sphere. Her novel provided an intimate portrait of the inner lives of a group
of women; Oreamuno set forth the family unit as a microcosm of the country
wherein the dysfunction of the small group would be evident in the larger.
Although she died young and destitute, she left behind an impressive literary
legacy.

Julieta Pinto (b. 1922)

A prolific writer since the publication of her first collection of short stories in 1963, Julieta Pinto's critically acclaimed text, *La vieja casona* (The Old House, 1967), has been translated and widely anthologized in the United States. Here, as in other texts, the realist portrayal is achieved successfully through the use of experimental literary technique: stream of consciousness dictates the narrative structure; linear chronology is disrupted; and causality is undermined.

Carmen Naranjo (b. 1931)

Carmen Naranjo's cultural influence cannot be underestimated. A writer and visual artist, she was the first woman to be appointed to the Cabinet as Minister of Culture, Youth, and Sports (in 1974). She is the founder of numerous organizations including the symphony orchestra and the National Theater Company, and has been editor of EDUCA for many years. In addition, Naranjo has held several international posts and is former ambassador to Israel. She has also led countless writer's workshops and is a mentor to at least one generation of writers. To date, Naranjo has published seven volumes of poetry (beginning in 1961), four plays, six collections of short stories (the most recent in 1998), and six volumes of essays, as well as six novels. Indeed, while this prolific writer has never made a living solely from publishing her works, her contribution to Costa Rican letters is incalculable.

The excellence of Naranjo's work has been recognized at home and abroad: her work has been frequently translated and widely anthologized, and she is the focus of growing scholarly attention in the United States. Her novel, *Diario de una multitud* (Diary of a Crowd, 1974), stands out as a smart and sensitive portrayal of middle-class life in Costa Rica. Naranjo is known for her knack of holding up to the light the foibles of the middle class. This novel is bitingly critical in places, and calls for a departure from apathy and growing alienation for the smug, self-contented class that is tempted to turn a blind eye to the ills of the larger society. The novel has been labeled an "antinovel," in its break from conventional characterization, nontraditional narrative stance, collage structure, and the significant demands it places on the reader. It is on par with postmodern works by Carlos Fuentes and other writers of the Latin American Boom.

The tales in *Ondina* (1983) earn her a definitive place in the short story genre alongside such impressive Latin American figures as Horacio Quiroga, Julio Cortázar, and Clarice Lispector. Set largely within the context of familial or romantic relationships, these stories display a mastery of the form as they treat the themes of sex-typing and gender roles, interpersonal conflict, the grotesque, perceptions of reality and fantasy, and eroticism. The 14 stories, many taking surprising turns after the style of O. Henry, mark a high point in Costa Rican literature.

Mujer y cultura (Woman and Culture) appeared in 1989 and symbolizes the vocational merging of Carmen Naranjo as both writer and activist. This readable collection of essays could be termed a companion text to the grass-roots movement for gender equality spearheaded by Naranjo during the 1980s. The Provecto de Igualdad Real (Bill for Women's True Equality) had as its primary objective the achievement of legal and actual or "real" equality for women: it sought to alter Costa Rican law where necessary to make explicit women's full equality with men, and also to call public attention to the regularly inconsistent application of the law when it came to women. The essays provided a literary and historical context for the social and legal changes taking place before the readers' eyes; essays ranged from a feminist revision of cultural myths (classical and modern) to a dissection of stereotypes of women's roles. Serving as a primer for historical and contemporary gender issues, *Mujer y cultura* had a powerful effect on Costa Rican consciousness, similar to the effect of Susan Faludi's *Backlash* (1991) on U.S. readers.

CONTEMPORARY WRITERS

Rima Rothe de Vallbona (b. 1931)

Although she has lived much of her adult life in the United States, Rothe de Vallbona publishes her work in Costa Rica and has made a significant contribution to Costa Rican letters. A literary scholar as well as a writer, she is best known for her short stories; the collection published in 1982, *Mujeres y agonías*, has received critical acclaim in Costa Rica and in the United States. In this, as in other works, her narrators resort to a variety of narrative techniques to portray daily human experience; indeed her *ouvre* could be said to showcase some of the major literary styles of the late twentieth century. Her work takes on the issues of contemporary society, including those in the political sphere and conceptualizations of gender roles.

Quince Duncan (b. 1940)

A descendant of English-speaking West Indian Blacks of the southern Atlantic coast, Quince Duncan writes of the experience of being Black in Costa Rica. Writing from within the Black community, he gives voice to the previously unexpressed; he has stated that his purpose is to fight against

Carmen Naranjo (center) and friends. Photograph courtesy of Christy Halbert.

continued disregard for the contributions made to society by Black Costa Ricans. The issue of stereotypes had been explored eloquently by the essayist Omar Dengo, whose essay *Bienvenidos los negros* (Welcome to the Black People, 1927) was the first work published in Costa Rica to warn against the dangers of racism.

Duncan's own contribution comes in his portrayal of Black coastal life and his depiction of race relations, all the while validating the Black Costa Rican experience. In two of his best-known novels, *Los cuatro espejos* (The Four Mirrors, 1973) and *La paz del pueblo* (The People's Peace, 1978), he reveals what is unmistakably the marginalization of the Black population, and shows both the latent and explicit racism of many cultural mores. He addresses a diverse readership, and clearly advocates a mutual effort at integration.

Duncan compiles a series of Black folk characters in his novels through the use of names—both English and African in origin—and by incorporating the dialects of the Atlantic coastal communities. He illustrates the convergence of the religious beliefs of Black Anglicans, Baptists, and Methodists that at the same time reveals significant preservations of African religious traditions. The widespread use of herbal treatments in this region, one historically underserved by conventional medicine, also shows the strength of traditions passed down through generations. Duncan is careful to showcase the variety of ideology and perspective within the Black community, even as he calls for unity of the generalized Costa Rican community.

Eulalia Bernard (b. 1935)

As a poet, academic, and political-office appointee, Eulalia Bernard has also significantly broadened her readers' knowledge about Afro-Caribbean life in Costa Rica. At the University of Costa Rica, she taught the first course in Afro-American studies offered in Latin America, and served for a time as cultural attaché to Jamaica.

Bernard's poetry challenges the "whitening" of Costa Rican history, and she rejects its tendency to turn a blind eye on its multiracial past. While Bernard's poetry can be read as a celebration of Black culture generally, her use of irony serves to confront stereotypes of Black men and women. Her poetry urges the reader to consider the integral participation of the Black community in the formulation of Costa Rican culture. In her bilingual collection, *My Black King* (1991), Bernard incorporates *Mecatelio*, or Limón Creole, which is a fusion of Spanish, standard English, and Jamaican English. This creole language becomes an important feature of her poems.

Tatiana Lobo (b. 1939)

Tatiana Lobo's novel, *Asalto al paraíso* (Assault on Paradise, 1992), provides another example of contemporary efforts to escape the whitewashing of history, and to recapture an authentic sense of Costa Rica's past. As a fictionalized account of the experiences of both a white Spanish settler escaping the Inquisition and a leader of the Boruca indigenous tribe, the novel offers a means of approaching a different dimension of Costa Rican identity. Set in Cartago and Talamanca between 1700 and 1710 and based on actual historical figures and events, Lobo's narrative showcases the contrast in worldview of the two characters. She explores the possibilities inherent in an encounter between cultures, and thereby simultaneously educates and entertains her readers.

Anacristina Rossi (b. 1952)

An important development in Costa Rican fiction in recent years has been the depiction of some of the ecological concerns arising in the wake of extensive development by the tourist industry. Rossi is a journalist whose investigation of the partial destruction of a nature preserve on the south Atlantic coast prompted her to write a short novel, only thinly veiled in its references to particular people and places. Her intent was both to expose the corruption of local officials dealing with foreign investors, and to make citizens aware of the environmental repercussions of the destruction of these areas. She was in fact documenting a representative case that followed an alarming trend. *La loca de Gandoca* (The Crazy Lady from Gandoca, 1992) quickly became a huge success, and galvanized popular support in an outcry to preserve Costa Rica's protected areas.

Dorelia Barahona (b. 1959)

Dorelia Barahona is part of a young generation of women writers, now in their forties, whose narratives document the coming of age during the 1970s, an era of intense social change in Costa Rica as in other parts of the globe. As adolescents, they witnessed a general surge of interest throughout Latin America in the promise of socialism in Chile and Cuba; they protested dictatorships entrenched in the region; they joined their voice to those of *la nueva canción* ("the new song," a folk tradition by songwriters who utilized more traditional and regional musical forms to address social and political matters), who were calling for a greater unity among the countries of the continent.

Barahona, like other members of this loosely knit group—among them Alicia Miranda Hena (*La huella de abril*, April's Trail, 1989) and Rosibel Morera Aguero (*Historias de un testigo interior*, Stories from an Inside Witness, 1990)—is from the upper middle class. Both her personal biography and the theme of her novel show evidence of another change, that of the increased visibility and flexibility of women's roles. Her 1990 novel, *De qué manera te olvido* (How Will I Ever Forget You), pays tribute to her friend Leda, who was killed after leaving Costa Rica to join the revolutionary forces in El Salvador. Barahona succeeds in conveying the horrors of war, made immediate by its proximity to Costa Rica's borders. She and other members of her generation, both male and female, write scenarios that bring to the forefront the violent consequences of El Salvador's alienated society. Her work has been recognized abroad, and her novel received the Juan Rulfo Primera Novela prize from the Mexican National Institute of Fine Arts.

PLAYS

The popularity of the theater has led many Costa Ricans to write original scripts that are regularly performed. In the 1980s, the immigrant community from the Southern Cone region of South America, fleeing dictatorships in Chile and Argentina, left their creative stamp on the Costa Rican theater. Drawing from the strength of the prolific theater tradition in their own countries, these playwrights, directors, and knowledgeable theatergoers impacted the dramatic literary scene in Costa Rica.

Alberto Cañas (b. 1920)

Both as a prolific writer of different genres and as a cultural ambassador, Alberto Cañas has made an enormous contribution to the arts of his country. In 1970, Cañas was appointed the first secretary of President Figueres' newly formed Department of Culture, Youth, and Sports, and has been intensely involved in promoting citizen participation in the arts. He began his career in theater in the mid-1950s, fusing existential concerns and technical experimentation. In his play, *En agosto hizo dos años* (Two Years Ago Last August, 1966), the stage becomes a screen, as the playwright borrows from cinematographic techniques to evoke the simultaneity of time. The notion of doubling characters serves also to comment on societal roles and expectations.

Samuel Rovinski (b. 1932)

One of the best-known Costa Rican playwrights—as well as a published novelist—is Samuel Rovinski, who furthers many of the themes initiated by Cañas. In *Un modelo para Rosaura* (A Model for Rosaura, 1964), the dialogue from the first scene begins to repeat itself in the last, conveying a circular notion of time. The insertion of the actor and director as actual characters serves to underscore the self-reflexive style of this play.

Rovinski's work treats a wide variety of subjects, from social critique of the influence of technology on contemporary society, to the Jewish experience in Costa Rica. In 1983, Rovinski focused on the recent events in El Salvador in a historical play entitled *El martirio del pastor* (The Pastor's Martyrdom). Characters are unnamed, and represent political or social sectors ("The nun" or "Oligarch 1," for example). Rovinski's technical infusion of lights, projection of newspaper and biblical texts on slides, and scenes from documentary films adds intensity to this sociopolitical critique. The work of another well-known Costa Rican playwright, Daniel Gallegos (b. 1930), develops the theme of violence in his critically acclaimed play, *En el séptimo círculo* (In the Seventh Circle), performed in 1982.

POETRY

The literary production of the surrealist poet Eunice Odio (1922–74) marked the beginning of a veritable deluge of women writers in the second half of the twentieth century. Her elaboration of vanguard poetry resulted in an excellent display of imagery, both in *Los elementos terrestres* (Earth Elements, 1948) and *Zona en territorio del alba* (A Zone in Dawn's Country, 1953). In the former, she makes use of images of natural elements, deconstructing and reconstructing organic materials in new ways; and in the latter, Odio explores the poetic voice and self-reflexion as she reclaims female expressions of sexuality and violence, among other themes.

In the development of poetry in general, Carmen Naranjo has been credited with linguistic renovation, beginning with her first critically acclaimed collection, *Canción de la ternura* (Song of Tenderness) in 1964. Indeed, the seven volumes of poetry she has published to date stand as an impressive record of the transitions of style and vision within poetry during the past four decades.

Another important poet is Julieta Dobles (b. 1943). Especially notable is her construction of the female subject and female eroticism. *Amar en Jerusalén* (To Love in Jerusalem, 1992) can be read as a feminist revalorization of those elements and activities that had been devalued precisely because they were feminine. A woman's world—her body, her sexuality, and her daily tasks—are recovered as valuable and important.

Ana Istarú (b. 1960) takes up the female subject as well in her collection, *La estación de fiebre* (Fever Season, 1983). Istarú reworks established love themes, with her erotic imagery adding another dimension. Her female subjects display an affirmation of their sexuality and actively seek its fulfillment.

Certainly, there are male writers who have contributed to the development of poetry in Costa Rica; and one poet who is particularly notable is Alfonso Chase (b. 1945). His poetry is overtly self-reflexive as he explores both existential and literary themes. For example, in his collection published in 1990, *Entre el ojo y la noche* (Between the Eye and the Night, 1990), he explores intertextuality, or the reference within a text to other literary texts, and he employs this device to critique cultural norms and traditions. In these poems, he makes reference to classical, biblical, and European literature as he illustrates the concept of a poem as literary re-creation of other texts.

The poetry of Carlos Cortés (b. 1962) adopts an ironic viewpoint as it explores the theme of poetry itself. In *Los pasos cantados* (The Sung Steps, 1987), Cortés follows centuries of tradition and once again the poem appears as a woman, but this woman is ultimately conscious of herself as a poem, and from this awareness comes a series of musings on the different literary concepts set forth in classical Spanish and Latin poetry. This poet thereby adopts a very contemporary stance on the poetic process.

REFERENCES

Berrón, Linda, ed. *Relatos de mujeres: Antología de narradoras de Costa Rica*. 3d ed. San José, Costa Rica: Editorial Mujeres, 1993.

Davis, Lisa E. "The World of the West Indian Black in Central America: The Recent Works of Quince Duncan." In *Voices from Under: Black Narrative in Latin America and the Caribbean*, edited by William Luis. Westport, Conn.: Greenwood Press, 1984. 149–62.

Leví, Enrique Jaramillo, ed. *When New Flowers Bloomed: Short Stories by Women Writers from Costa Rica and Panama*. Pittsburgh: Latin American Literary Review Press, 1991.

Lobo, Tatiana. *Assault on Paradise*. Translated by Asa Zatz. Willimantic, Conn.: Curbstone Press, 1998.

Martínex, Luz Ivette. *Carmen Naranjo y la narrativa femenina en Costa Rica*. San José, Costa Rica: EDUCA, 1987.

McKinney, Kitzie. "Costa Rica's Black Body: The Politics and Poetics of Difference in Eulalia Bernard's Poetry." *Afro-Hispanic Review* (Fall 1996): 11–20.

Baranjo, Carmen. *Mujer y cultura*. San José. Costa Rica: EDUCA, 1989.

———. *Ondina*. San José, Costa Rica: EDUCA, 1983.

———. "Problemas editoriales de Centroamérica." *Káñina* 12 (1988): 165–167.

———. *There Never Was a Once Upon a Time*. Translated by Linda Brilt. Pittsburgh Pa.: Latin American Literary Review Press, 1989.

Ortiz, María Salvadora. "Mamita Yunai: Novela de la plantación bananera." *Káñina* 16 (1992): 9–17.

Ramsay, Paulette. "The African Religious Heritage in Selected Works of Quince Duncan: An Expression of Cultural and Literary Marronage." *Afro-Hispanic Review* (Fall 1994): 32–39.

Ras, Barbara, ed. *Costa Rica: A Traveler's Literary Companion*. San Francisco: Whereabouts Press, 1994.

Rojas, Margarita, and Flora Ovares. *100 años de literatura costarricense*. San José, Costa Rica: Ediciones Farben, 1995.

7

Performing Arts

PERHAPS COSTA RICANS are natural performers. They are born into a culture rich with myriad popular sayings and endowed with a lavish tradition of storytelling. The popular sayings sparkle with the sly wit that characterizes Tico humor and are celebrated often, imbedded in stories that fuel a love of anecdote and gossip. By virtue of their cultural upbringing, Costa Ricans place a high value on humor and on an individual's ability to tell a joke or story. They seem inherently keyed into the reactions of others, automatically adjusting their tales to the taste of a particular audience. No social gathering takes place without at least one performance of this nature.

The performing arts in general permeate the Costa Rican cultural consciousness and social scene. In fact, public performance is considered integral to personal development: reciting romantic poetry, for instance, is an admired skill that is encouraged even at the elementary school level. Throughout the stages of a child's life, opportunities for participation in musical and theatrical performance abound. *Festivales de la canción* (music festivals) are popular with high-school students, and original compositions are received with great praise. Religious processions and civic parades, held on numerous occasions throughout the year, provide many venues for dramatic representation, prop construction, and costume making. Once a year, the national symphony orchestra, chorus, and dance company collaborate to produce an opera.

Costa Ricans also seem to have taken the art of impersonation to new heights. During political campaigns and the Christmas holidays, especially, improvised skits depict actual politicians or stock characters on television and radio, artfully combining entertainment with social commentary. For many,

Grupo de Cámara Surá performs in the Plaza de
la Cultura; the National Theater is to the right.
Photograph courtesy of Christy Halbert.

community theater provides an outlet for creativity with plays, choreographed
programs, and concerts. During end-of-the-year festivities, a *rondalla* (minstrel
group) is likely to be formed: composed of several singing guitarists, these community musicians will perform at parties, churches, or special events.

Another opportunity for performance that is ingrained in Costa Rican
culture is the tradition of *serenatas* (serenades). Almost any occasion can call
for a *serenata*: birthdays, Mother's Day, Father's Day, an upcoming trip, a
welcome back from a trip, a wedding engagement, or a noteworthy achievement. Typically, a serenade will take place once the singers are sure that the
intended is asleep. They will have gathered outside that person's front door.
After the performance, the singers and players will often be invited in for a
late snack. Another venue for musical expression can be observed regularly

in several malls in San José, where shoppers are treated to hours of live music peformed by string quartets.

While Costa Ricans may be natural performers, their ability is matched by a deeply ingrained cultural attitude of humility, wherein an individual must not boast of his or her achievements. Even so, at any social gathering a talented guitarist, singer, dancer, or storyteller will undoubtedly be present and will eventually be encouraged to perform. The pervasive impact of performing arts—and of so many individuals participating in them—has been supported in no small part by two institutions: the government and the media.

Newspapers carry extensive coverage of the performing arts; it is not uncommon to find over a dozen plays advertised on any given weekend. Interviews with local and international performers are regular features of weekend editions of *La nación*, and the arts in general are given a high status in Costa Rican society.

BACKGROUND

The socioeconomic reforms that were enacted in the 1940s were extended to the arts, with the intent of fostering cultural and artistic awareness in all regions of the country and among all social classes. It is the presidency of José Figueres, affectionately known as Don Pepe, that is credited with initiating a modern cultural renovation. The Figueres government founded the Castella Conservatory, an arts school that since 1953 has trained thousands of children and youth as musicians and dancers. And the state-subsidized Editorial Costa Rica (a publishing house), established in 1959, promotes the publication of original Costa Rican literary works.

In an anecdote that is recounted often, Don Pepe once said, "It is necessary to consider the quality of life as well as the standard of living. Why should we have tractors if we lack violins?" During his second presidential term, Don Pepe instituted the Ministry of Culture (which later became the Ministry of Culture, Youth, and Sports), with the playwright Alberto Cañas at the helm. Cañas' office oversaw the nation's cultural activities, coordinating workshops, classes, and performances and disseminating information regarding opportunities for involvement. The writer Carmen Naranjo eventually became head of the ministry, and in a short time the results of Don Pepe's inspiration were evident: today, the ministry sponsors weekly performances and contests in cities and towns all over the country, and it hosts an annual two-week International Arts Festival in San José. The Ministry of Culture, Youth, and Sports is now a respected institution, embodying the best of civic, educational, and government cooperation.

Don Pepe's vision touched the musical world particularly, and perhaps his most impressive cultural legacy is the creation of the Youth Symphony Orchestra during his second term. In the early 1970s, the diminished National Symphony Orchestra was in serious need of revitalization. The government tradition of aggressive problem-solving strategies paid off as the orchestra was strengthened, and a second symphony orchestra was born: foreign musicians were hired, with the stipulation that they teach an instrument to young people. What resulted is the only state-subsidized youth orchestra in the Western world. The Youth Symphony Orchestra has afforded invaluable instruction and opportunity for many Costa Rican youth. Today it performs internationally, and the Youth Symphony Orchestra has become a symbol of the power of government to do good. It also stands as a testament to enthusiastic popular support of the arts in Costa Rica.

THEATER

The city of San José boasts several impressive theaters. The first popular theater was the Teatro Variedades (Variety Theater). Built in 1891, it has the distinction of being the site of the first movie viewing in the country. The Teatro Melico Salazar has recently been restored, and its calender stays busy throughout the year. Both theaters bear the ornate markings of the Baroque style.

The most treasured theater is undoubtedly the National Theater. It was built in 1897, funded by members of the coffee-growing oligarchy. The story goes that in the late 1800s, a world-renowned opera singer named Adelina Patti was touring Central America but did not perform in Costa Rica because there was no suitable venue anywhere in the country. The coffee barons offered to pay a tax on every exported bag of coffee in order to build a theater. Construction began in 1890 and the theater was modeled after the Paris Opera House.

Built in the Renaissance style, the façade shows figures representing Music, Fame, and Dance; the likenesses of Ludwig van Beethoven and Pedro Calderón de la Barca, the great Spanish playwright, are visible on either side of the entrance. The building's four levels showcase a variety of luxurious appointments: marble floors and columns in the lobby; an elegant café and gallery; Italian marble sculptures and lush murals depicting Costa Rica's main exports; plush seating areas; and gilded, sculptured walls.

The acoustics are excellent in the horseshoe-shaped auditorium of the National Theater. These dimensions afford an attractive and comfortable proximity of performers to audience, creating a perfect environment for an evening of entertainment. The calendar of events at the National Theater is

As a crowd looks on, a street performer dives through a circle of knives. Photograph courtesy of Christy Halbert.

filled 320 days a year, with performances by an exciting blend of local and international actors, musicians, vocalists, and dancers. Even so, ticket prices are very affordable. This and other venues facilitate the eager participation in, and appreciative admiration for, the performing arts in Costa Rica.

Among other venues for theater performance is the Teatro El Angel (Angel Theater). Like other theaters, El Angel puts on new works written by Costa Rican writers as well as more classical works, such as those by Sophocles and Bertolt Brecht. The daily fare of plays in San José is quite varied, although most are comedies and social satires, which are often full of sexual innuendo. What distinguishes El Angel from other theaters is its origins: it was established in the 1970s by Chilean dissidents who fled the Pinochet dictatorship. The exceptional theatrical tradition in Chile and Argentina strengthened and revitalized Costa Rican theater, and today the opportunities for both performing and theater going abound.

The state universities are also active in theater production, and on the community-theater level, hundreds of plays and dramatic productions are in rehearsal at any given time all around the country. Not only does the high rate of participation in these shows guarantee an audience—as family members and friends support the performers—but the level of audience enthusiasm speaks volumes to the popularity of dramatic arts in Costa Rica.

A typical community-theater production will gather the talents (of varying abilities) of local singers, musicians, dancers, and actors to re-enact a history of Costa Rica. Following in the tradition of the *zarzuela*—the popular Spanish light opera—performers will sing original compositions, accompanied by several guitars, a percussionist, a pianist, and a bass player. Traditional regional dances are performed. Often, dancers and actors wear a different costume for each act, showing the considerable investment in a production of this kind.

DANCE

Although the National Dance Company has been around for quite some time, the popularity of modern dance has lagged behind other art forms until recently. In fact, a steady increase in touring dance companies from around the world, and a consistent stream of performances by students from the well-regarded university dance programs, has produced a slowly developing familiarity, appreciation, and appetite for more performances of this kind. Modern dance choreography is now a constant on the cultural scene.

Some observers have noted the curious contrast between the Costa Ricans' latecoming acceptance of modern dance, and their long-standing obsession with dancing: even young children will dance the *cumbia* with experienced ease, and nearly every party will involve dancing. It is important to note here the historical dimensions of dance as part of the cultural traditions of Costa Rica.

Bailes típicos

The province of Guanacaste is the birthplace of the vast majority of Costa Rican traditional dances. During national holidays, such as July 25, the date that commemorates the annexation of Guanacaste in 1824, celebrations often include a spirited display of these *bailes típicos* (typical dances).

An example is the *Caballito nicoyano* (Little Horse from Nicoya), harking from the mid-coastal zone of the province of Guanacaste. The premise of the dance, which is accompanied by a song by the same name, involves a courtship rite between a male cattle rancher and the woman he is wooing. The barefoot dancers are dressed in *campesino* style: the man wears white work pants, a long-sleeved white shirt, a *campesino* hat, a red cummerbund, and a red bandanna. (Male children who perform this dance usually appear on stage with a moustache penciled in on their upper lips.) The woman wears a white, off-the-shoulder blouse accented with lace, and a flowing, tiered skirt of bright colors. Her hair is pulled back and adorned with a fresh flower. The music begins with the clip-clop sound of hooves, and the dancers stay momentarily in place, embodying a young colt and a rancher. The man waves his bandanna over his head, simulating the motion of a lasso. Soon, the woman responds, mimicking a horse's movements, and the pursuit begins as they follow each other in a circle. Eventually, the rancher lassoes the colt. During the next stage of the dance, the dancers face each other as the woman tries to get away; the dance ends with an intensifying chase as she twirls toward him, and is finally caught.

Many of the *bailes típicos* draw on imagery from rural life in this cattle-growing region. In *El torito* (The Little Bull), dancers embody a bull (the male dancer) and a bullfighter (the female dancer), as they interact in the ranch's pen: he is portrayed as a sort of spirited rogue, attempting to kiss her; while she showcases a graceful femininity oblivious to the danger the bull presents, and eventually dominates him with her cape, represented by a bandanna.

However, many consider the *Punto guanacasteco* (Guanacaste dance step) the national typical dance. Its three phases include different stages of a courtship. From time to time, all the dancers pause in mid-dance and a male dancer will shout out a witty and sometimes racy *bomba*, a rhymed verse that comments on some aspect of the interaction depicted in the dance scene.

MUSIC

Native and Indigenous Musical Traditions

Anthropologist Laura Cervantes, from the University of Costa Rica, is one of the first scholars to research early indigenous instruments. Although few studies exist, she and others have found evidence of percussive instruments among the Bribrí and Cabécar groups in the Pacific coastal region: armadillo shells, maracas, wood drums, and flutes made out of bone (apparently, early cultures in the area did not have any stringed instruments).

Jorge Luis Acevedo, also on the faculty at the University of Costa Rica, has studied the indigenous groups in the Guanacaste region extensively. Basing his information in part on descriptions written by sixteenth-century chroniclers, and also on recovered artifacts (including many drums made of clay and shaped like animals), Acevedo surmises that music played a fundamental role in early cultures: Indians in the Nicoya region incorporated songs of all types and dances into special rituals and everyday life. He and others have identified one particular instrument, the *quijongo*, which is made of a thin, flexible wooden pole that is bowed by a string made of hemp fiber and attached to a hollowed-out *jícara* (gourd) to provide resonance. A percussion instrument, the *quijongo* is still played today, although a wooden box is substituted for the *jícara*.

Acevedo's studies also examine the development and construction of what became Costa Rica's national instrument, the marimba. This instrument is also part of the musical history of the Chiapas region of Mexico and Guatemala; scholars agree that it is African in origin. In Costa Rica, early marimbas were made from hollowed-out, elongated *calabaza* (a variety of squash) gourds set within a wooden frame whose top was lined with a panel of wooden keys, representing an octave.

Today, marimba keyboards range from three to seven octaves and can be played by one to four musicians; often, two marimbas are played by five musicians. The painstaking construction of a marimba has evolved into a revered art: made entirely by hand, wood is cut and dried under highly specific conditions, and building a single instrument may take several months. The preferred woods that are used for keyboards are *bálsamo* and *yámbaro*, while the wooden frame of the instrument is always made from *cedro amargo* (bitter cedar). One marimba musician who makes a living making the instruments boasted that the only non-native material used in the construction of his marimbas was German glue.

The historic background of music in the Guanacaste region plays well into the modern reverence for the form. Music is a constant in Costa Rican life, and is appreciated in all its dimensions, whether regional, classical, romantic *serenata*-style, reggae, calypso, pop, or Latin.

The Guanacaste Province

Guanacaste is considered the cradle of Costa Rican culture with good reason. Much of the country's folklore came from this area, and the province has contributed innumerable popular sayings, many dances, and a vast repertoire of love songs. Many of Costa Rica's best-known composers hail from this region, as well. However, there are other musical traditions that should be considered.

Traditional Costa Rican music is characterized by romantic ballads. Some typical pieces depict a scene in the life of a *campesino*, and others play homage to a hometown or province of origin. *Luna liberiana* (Liberian Moon), for example, sings to the beauty of the moon over Liberia, the capital of the province of Guanacaste. *Caña dulce pa'moler* (Sugar Cane to Grind), written by J. Daniel Zúñiga, is a song of longing, in which the singer wishes for those simple things that will make him happy: a field to grow sugar cane, his lover in his house, a pair of oxen. The instruments that are generally played with this music are one or two guitars, a pair of maracas (hollowed gourds filled with seeds), and a marimba.

Trío los ticos (The Ticos Trio) was founded by the prolific songwriter, Mario Chacón. This musical group reached its height of popularity during the 1950s and 1960s, and traveled abroad with the intent of creating awareness of Costa Rica's rich musical traditions. The trio accompanied itself with guitars, maracas, and marimba, and popularized countless ballads. Their versions of traditional songs from Guanacaste are still considered the standard by which to measure performance and interpretation of typical Costa Rican music.

The national anthem was written by José María Zeledón and Manuel María González in 1821. It seemed to anticipate the nation's pacifism, crafting a message of strength based on peace and hard work. But the writer of the unofficial national anthem of Costa Rica, the one that is preferred for its reverent tones, is anonymous and it is referred to only as the *Patriótica costarricense* (patriotic Costa Rican song). The first line begins, *Costa Rica es mi patria querida* (Costa Rica is my dear homeland), and as the song moves through a tribute to the wonders to be found within its borders, it pledges allegiance with fervor. Much like the contrast between the national anthem of the United States and "America the Beautiful," in Costa Rica the unofficial song is favored. For example, during a teachers' strike in 1995, educators from all over the country marched in the streets of San José, protesting the threat of a loss of retirement benefits. The protest was peaceful, and as the teachers stood momentarily outside a radio station, they broke out singing this unofficial anthem. The gathered crowds were hushed, as the song's quiet tones seemed to soothe differences and call for the respectful resolution of the issue at hand.

The Limón Province

The contributions of the province of Limón to Costa Rican musical performance should not be overlooked. While most citizens identify the Black coastal communities with reggae, and with the excesses of the annual Carnavales de Limón (Limón Carnival) that take place in October, there is much more to their traditions. Calypso music arrived in Costa Rica in the late 1800s through Limón, and brought with it the calypso dance form popularized by the carnival revelers.

However, many of the original compositions of Limón have been lost: due to their improvisational nature, most were not written down.[1] Calypso musicians did, however, inspire a large and very loyal following: the Riverside Orchestra was founded in 1937 by Johnny Steele, and soon became one of the most famous bands in the country. Steele played the saxophone, and together with five other musicians, brought calypso to the rest of Costa Rica. The memories of this time are still fresh for many long-time residents of Limón.

Musical Performance

The musical performance scene in San José is particularly vibrant. The national chorus offers many concerts a year, and travels continuously to various regions of the country. Brass bands play on Sundays in municipal parks, and recently the Grupo de Cámara Surá was established. A privately funded, elite group of singers, led by Angela María Cordero Morales, a professor of music at the National University, the Grupo de Cámara Surá has in five years made accessible a wide range of musical styles to the Costa Rican public. At Christmas, the group holds public concerts in the Plaza de la cultura (Culture Plaza) in downtown San José. Its repertoire covers many periods, styles, and regions, and has popularized South American musical styles as well.

Many other groups, representing all styles of music, perform at dance clubs throughout the country; the measure of their success generally is their ability to perform as dance accompanists. Two groups that have made a name for themselves on this scene are Marfil (Ivory) and the Taboga Band. Both can be considered Latin music performers, although they differ significantly from each other. Marfil is practically an institution: the group has been together for over 20 years. Playing a blend of Caribbean rhythms—*salsa, cumbia, merengue*—the band attracts huge crowds and still regularly performs at local nightclubs where dancing predominates. Marfil's performance includes dancing in sync, coordinating difficult moves and turns side by side on stage. The band includes percussion and brass instruments as well as synthesizers.

The Taboga Band is a younger band that recorded its first compact disc, *Ahora* (Now), in 1996. Their style reflects a trend on the contemporary music scene: blending traditional Latin rhythms with U.S. pop forms. The result is not always successful, but some of the Taboga Band's original compositions showcase local references and perspectives, which makes for interesting music.

Also new to the scene are groups like Amanecer (Dawn), an all-women band of singers, songwriters, and acoustic musicians. The themes of their songs center on environmental concerns, matters of gender equality, and Costa Rica's indigenous past. Their music adds an important voice to the contemporary music scene. The duo Edictus became immensely popular in the early 1990s, as their unique blend of violin and classical guitar reinterpreted songs from a variety of world traditions.

Music Reproduction

In recent years, the opportunities for music recording have increased substantially in Costa Rica. This represents a fairly significant change from the time when recording costs were prohibitive, and individual labels practically nonexistent. For many years, however, Sony music has had its Central American headquarters in San José; and perhaps this presence has facilitated the development of a small but growing local recording industry.

NOTE

1. For a thorough study of Black history and culture in Costa Rica, see *El negro en Costa Rica*, 5th ed., edited by Carlos Meléndez and Quince Duncan (San José: Editorial Costa Rica, 1978).

REFERENCES

Acevedo Vargas, Jorge Luis. *La música en Guanacaste*. San José, Costa Rica: Editorial de la Universidad de Costa Rica, 1980.

———. "La música de tradición oral de las reservas indígenas de Costa Rica y Guanacaste antes y después de la colonia." *Káñina* 11, no. 2 (1987): 229–49.

Cervantes Gamboa, Laura. "Información básica acerca de la música tradicional indígena de Costa Rica." *Káñina* 19, no. 1 (1995): 155–73.

Meléndez, Carlos and Quince Duncan. *El negro en Costa Rica*. 5th ed. San José, Costa Rica: Editorial Costa Rica, 1978.

Prado Quesada, Alcides. *Costa Rica: Su música típica y sus autores*. San José, Costa Rica: Lehman, 1961.

Searby, Ellen. *The Costa Rica Traveler*. 3d ed. Occidental, Calif.: Wyndham Bay Press, 1991.

8

Art

A CLOSE LOOK at the contemporary art scene in Costa Rica reveals an informal yet extensive network of painters, sculptors, woodworkers, and artisans. These artists contribute to a vibrant art community that benefits from visible government support. Since 1951, for example, the government-funded Casa del artista (House of the Artist) has offered free instruction in painting and sculpture. The Ministry of Culture, Youth, and Sports coordinates exhibitions and competitions, and government-commissioned sculptures frequently grace public spaces. Every year, the government also awards numerous art prizes. The Costa Rican public eagerly embraces the arts and yet, as happens in most of the world, it is difficult to make one's living as an artist.

For decades, the private sector has matched or exceeded the government's financial support of the arts: attesting to this fact are exhibitions in numerous galleries, schools, cultural centers, banks, and hotels, and in businesses as varied as hospital lobbies and car rental agencies. Many private institutions such as the Rotary Club award art prizes. Community-education courses in painting and sculpture are common and popular with students of all ages. Extensive media coverage of gallery showings and exhibitions, government-sponsored contests, and weekly features of individual artists help promote public interest as well.

Strong government support of the arts does not appear to impact freedom of artistic expression, and experimental art forms are encouraged. In 1994, for instance, the University of Costa Rica sponsored a graffiti contest on its campus. Another important development in the Costa Rican artistic scene in recent years is a byproduct of the purchasing power of tourists and their

Hazel de Vega, a local artist, at work in her home studio. Photograph courtesy of Christy Halbert.

interest in art: the potential for a greater number of individuals to earn a living as artists. However, by far most artists do not make their living exclusively from income generated from their art.

The multiple venues for exhibiting artwork, the high visibility of art and artists in the media, government sponsorship, and the growing income potential for Costa Rican artists have brought the average citizen familiarity with a wide variety of art forms; this in turn has cultivated an appetite for and appreciation of novel art forms. While some observers dismiss Costa Rica's artistic trajectory as one largely characterized by the imitation of European models, and as a small-scale affair generally, a fair assessment of Costa Rican art's tradition must recognize the power of popular interest and exposure to art in this country.

As a testimony to the value of art, the abundance of museums must also be acknowledged. Museums in Costa Rica are of two types. Visitors to the city of San José can choose from among numerous museums located in equally interesting buildings: for instance, the former National Liquor Factory, the old airport terminal, and an old prison. The Jade Museum sits atop the National Social Security office building, and it attracts visitors from around the world. The funding of museums of this category is inconsistent, however, and depends entirely on the sponsor, but these museums are generally well known and open to the public.

The other type of museum is often a small, unadvertised site—generally encountered in outlying areas from the capital—that displays the work of local artists, as well as recently popular indigenous artifacts. Other collections may simply be colonial antiques; in any case, these unofficial museums represent the appreciation of objects of art by the general populace. These museums can often double as gift shops: in fact, the market produced by tourism has caused rapid growth in entrepreneurial art, providing artisans and craftspeople with the means to live by their craft.

PAINTING

An overwhelming European influence can be readily perceived in Costa Rican art until the 1920s, when visual artists began producing works parallel to those of their literary counterparts. *Costumbrismo*—regional depictions of local color and customs—portrayed typical scenarios of daily life. As in literature, *costumbrismo* in painting represented an effort to capture those elements that defined "authentic" Costa Rican culture.

Teodórico Quirós and Fausto Pacheco were two of the first Costa Rican painters to work in the *costumbrista* style. They set the standard for a local tradition that continues to this day, with their portrayal of a *campesino* (an individual from a rural area, generally a farmer) habitat: adobe houses, set in a bucolic rural setting complete with bougainvilleas and trees. Two-toned in color and roofed with the traditional *tejas* (tiles), the *casa campesina* (rural dwelling) has become a visual cultural motif, along with the oxcart and coffee-picking basket. As symbols of Costa Rican culture, these icons have made their way into the permanent consciousness as well as into a profitable venue in the souvenir market. In the art scene today, watercolors are an especially popular medium for this traditional style.

Following the development and popularization of these regional and national images, the abstract period of the 1950s permanently changed the Costa Rican art world, as it expanded the possibilities for representation.

Painters showed influences of expressionism and other European movements, as they continued to produce original works. Max Jiménez began his career as a sculptor, and although his work was not recognized initially (his sculptures were shown in Costa Rica only after his death), today he is listed among the most influential sculptors in his country, and his work in stone, bronze, and wood is widely admired. After 1939, however, he abandoned sculpting and painted with oils exclusively. Jiménez' legacy might best be appreciated in his paintings, for he is considered the precursor of the "new art" of the 1930s. His paintings went deeper than the idealized view of Costa Rican culture to show its roots: images of Blacks and indigenous people were treated extensively in his work. Jiménez studied in London and lived much of his life abroad, but he maintained close ties to other Latin American artists and writers.

Another artist to paint in oils is Rafa Fernández. He uses muted blues and grays to depict female figures shrouded in mist; his work has been awarded national and international prizes. Other noted Costa Rican painters include Guillermo Jiménez, Fernando Castro, and Luis Fernando Quirós.

OTHER TWO-DIMENSIONAL MEDIA

Costa Rican artists have branched out from the tradition of oil painting into a variety of different mediums. Carlos Monge, art professor at the University of Costa Rica, stated, "If Costa Rica is not necessarily a country of great painters, it certainly is a country of great graphic artists" (256). Indeed, while several artists like Max Jiménez and Luisa Gonazález de Saenz have made significant contributions to painting in oils, experimentation with other forms and mediums has proliferated continuously in Costa Rican art. Herein lies its strength and uniqueness.

Joaquín Rodríguez del Paso is known for his drawings of human figures in Chinese ink: the ink is applied with a sharp bamboo pencil onto a wet paper canvas. Watercolor artists have a long tradition in Costa Rica, producing myriad images in all styles; Margarita Bertheau, a student of Luis Fernando Quirós, is the first well-known female watercolor artist. Noted contemporary watercolor artists include Magda Santonastasio, Hugo Sánchez, Luis Dael, and Virginia Vargas.

The muralists César Valverde and Francisco Amighetti have helped erase the traditional boundaries between the elitism of high art and the ordinary spaces of public life. Their murals can be appreciated in such diverse places as the ceiling of the National Theater, the private Lincoln School, and the National Bank in Alajuela.

WOODCUTS AND ENGRAVINGS

Costa Rica boasts an inspired tradition of woodcuts. This popular form has many enthusiasts, and a popular program in wood engraving is offered at the University of Costa Rica. The form's strong, simple lines lend themselves to a realistic portrayal of everyday life. Engravings tend to depict quotidian, or everyday, scenes: a woman in a kitchen; a crowd shooting fireworks; a pair of boots. Xylographers like Crisanto Badilla have achieved national recognition, and Magda Santonastasio has won numerous international and national awards for her engravings. Without a doubt, however, Francisco Amighetti is Costa Rica's best-known engraver, although he is also a muralist, watercolor artist, and poet. His color engravings especially have garnered him admiration around the world, and his work has been shown in museums of modern art in New York, Brazil, and Japan.

SCULPTURE

This art form has long been a popular one in Costa Rica, and today there are hundreds of sculptors, some of whom are able to make their living solely from their work. As with nineteenth-century painting in Costa Rica, sculpture followed the European classical models. Cemeteries in San José provide access to examples of early trends in sculpture: angels perched on ornate mausoleums reflect a primarily Italian influence. However, wood is by far the most popular sculptural medium, and like woodcuts, its long-standing tradition continues to provide an accessible art form. Along with the rest of Latin America, Costa Rica shares a love of public art, and commissioned works are highly visible in most public spaces.

Perhaps the best-known Costa Rican sculptor is Francisco Zúñiga, whose *Monumento al agricultor* (Monument to the Farmer) showcases his trademark themes and preference for public art. His work in bronze has for decades dominated the so-called nationalist movement celebrating the life and work of ordinary women and men. Although he has resided in Mexico for many years, his pieces are abundantly displayed in public spaces in Costa Rica, and he is considered an institution in his homeland.

WOODWORKING

At one time, Costa Rica's thick forests promised an unending supply of fine hardwoods. Indeed, for many years it was less expensive to build homes out of wood than other materials, and the wood furniture industry flourished as well. Beautiful woods were readily available: *caoba* (mahogony), the purple *nazareno* (known in English as purple heart, although the term in Spanish means literally *Nazarene*, an allusion to the purple robes of Christ), and the rich, dark tones of *cocobolo*, for example. A tradition of fine woodcrafts developed, tied to the long tradition of woodcutting and carving. Today, turned bowls and detailed boxes have become trademark Costa Rican crafts and a favorite of tourists.

Unfortunately, the high rate of deforestation that has plagued the country for decades has also had an impact on the wood industry. Recent conservation efforts to educate the populace are gradually bringing the desired results. Certain woods have been listed as endangered, and controls on exports have become much tighter. In recent years, the teak industry—designed in part to replace the shrinking resources in other woods like mahogony—has grown steadily. However, Costa Ricans continue to be very proud of their woods and their craftsmanship, and the prolific tradition of woodworking is very much intact today.

INDIGENOUS ARTISTIC TRADITIONS

A recent trend in Costa Rican art arises out of the current public interest in its indigenous past. Archaeologists, historians, sociologists, geographers, and literary scholars are beginning to apply their disciplinary insight to identifying and preserving indigenous artifacts.

One such program is carried out by the Art Department at the University of Costa Rica. Golfito, on the southwestern coast, has been chosen as a research site because of the evidence of early indigenous settlements. Their descendants have remained in the area, although they have been fairly isolated until now.

The motivation behind this program has been to teach awareness of the Indian past; the desired result is to cultivate a sense of appreciation for these early cultures, and in so doing, promote an acceptance of diversity. Another goal of this university-sponsored program is to create artisan cooperatives, so that Indians have a means of earning a living that affirms their heritage and simultaneously provides them with access to economic empowerment in contemporary Costa Rica. As a result, several artisan cooperatives are now producing art that is sold in tourist venues.

The influence of native indigenous traditions on Costa Rican art should not be underestimated. Recovered objects provide inspiration and integration of different physical forms, specific art-making techniques, and suggestions of the unique worldview held by the inhabitants of ancient Costa Rica. Contemporary artists in turn are identifying with those elements that come from native Indian traditions and incorporating them in their own works.

REFERENCES

Biesanz, Mavis Hiltunen, Richard Biesanz, and Karen Zubris Biesanz. *The Ticos: Culture and Social Change in Costa Rica.* Boulder, Colo.: Lynne Rienner Publishers, 1999.

Echeverría, Carlos Francisco. *Historia crítica del arte costarricense.* San José: EUNED, 1986.

Ferrero, Luis. *Escultores costarricenses (1973–1990).* San José, Costa Rica: Editorial Costa Rica, 1991.

"Magda Santonastasio: Grabadora, Premio Nacional Aquileo J. Echeverría, 1986." *Káñina* II, no. 1 (1987): 179–88.

Monge Carlos G. "Francisco Amighetti: 80 años." *Káñina* II, no. 2 (1987): 255–59.

Rodríguez, Rebeca M., and Blanca Ruiz R. "Max Jiménez: Sus grabados en el jaúl." *Káñina* 21, no. 2 (1997): 127–35.

Ulloa Barrenechea, Ricardo. *Pintores de Costa Rica.* 5th ed. San José, Costa Rica: Editorial Costa Rica, 1982.

Appendix A: Internet Resources

www.centralamerica.com/cr/info
Green Arrow's site devoted to Costa Rica, contains helpful historical references

www.infoweb.co.cr/galeria
Photogallery of Costa Rican physical spaces and architecture

www.lanacion.co.cr/
Online edition of Costa Rica's largest newspaper (also in English)

www.larepublica.co.cr/
Online edition of the country's second largest newspaper (only in Spanish)

www.supersite.incostarica.net
Full of varied information

www.ticotimes.co.cr/
Online version of Central America's leading English-language newspaper

www.tuanis.com
One of the best sites available, with interesting cultural commentary

Appendix B: Presidential Elections 1953–Present

Year	President-Elect	Voter Turnout
1953	José Figueres Ferrer	67.2%
1958	Mario Echandi Jiménez	64.67%
1962	Francisco J. Orlich Bolmarcich	80.9%
1966	José Joaquín Trejos Fernández	81.4%
1970	José Figueres Ferrer	83.3%
1974	Daniel Oduber Quirós	79.9%
1978	Rodrigo Carazo Odio	81.3%
1982	Luis Alberto Monge Alvarez	78.6%
1986	Oscar Arias Sánchez	81.8%
1990	Rafael Angel Calderón Fournier	81.8%
1994	José María Figueres Olsen	81.1%
1998	Miguel Angel Rodríguez Echeverría	69.9%

Appendix C: Costa Rica at a Glance

Capital: San José, founded in 1736

Language: Spanish, although Bribrí and Melicatelio are spoken as well

Currency: *Colón*, named for Christopher Columbus. The exchange rate in 1999 was 290 *colones* p/$1 U.S.

Territory: Divided into seven provinces: San José, Alajuela, Heredia, Cartago, Guanacaste, Puntarenas, and Limón

Size: Roughly the size of West Virginia, with a maximum length of 290 miles, a minimum width of 74 miles, and a maximum width of 162 miles

Highest Peak: Chirripó, at 12,535 feet above sea level

National Flower: *Guaria morada*, or purple orchid

National Tree: Guanacaste

Climate: Tropical, with dry (December to April) and rainy seasons; in the Central Plateau the climate hovers at 70° Fahrenheit year-round

Population: 3.5 million (49.46 percent female, 50.54 percent male)

Literacy: 97 percent

Life expectancy: 76 years

Glossary

alajuelense. Refers to a person originating from the city or province of Alajuela.

audiencia. Tribunal, or in this case a political and geographical boundary established in the Spanish colonial era.

bailes típicos. Traditional dances, most of them originating in the province of Guanacaste.

bomba. A rhymed verse, witty and sometimes risque, that is interjected during a traditional dance. The *bomba* is considered part of the accompanying music as well.

café. Coffee

cafecito. Coffee break, literally, "a little coffee."

calderonista. An individual who is a member of, or supports, Calderón's political party.

campesino/a. A person from a rural area, generally a farmer.

campo. Rural area

caoba. Mahogany, one of the hardwoods that are plentiful in Costa Rica.

cartaginés. Refers to a person originating from the city or province of Cartago.

casado. Literally, "married man," the *casado* is a rice-and-bean–based dish traditionally served at lunch, accompanied by any combination of rice, beans, fried ripe plantains, salad, spaghetti, and a piece of meat, chicken, or fish. The name is a humorous allusion to the kind of repetitive meals that a man purportedly can expect once he marries.

colegio. High school

colón. The national currency, named after Christopher Columbus, or Cristóbal Colón in Spanish. In 1999, the rate of exchange was nearly 200 *colones* to one U.S. dollar.

concho. An archetype or "national self" of sorts in which Costa Ricans recognize exaggerated aspects of themselves. It can mean rude or ignorant, as in *no seás concho* (Don't be a *concho*).

dichos ticos. Costa Rican sayings, typified by witty though tongue-in-cheek expressions, often utilizing slang or humor; for example, *Más feliz que una lombriz* (Happier than a worm, which rhymes in Spanish!) is the Costa Rican equivalent of the phrase, "Happy as a clam"; or, *Con toda la pata* (literally, With my whole leg) is typically used in response to the question, "How are you?" and means "just great"; or, *Se quedó viendo para el ciprés* ("She kept staring at the cypress") is the equivalent to the phrase in English, "She spaced out."

discreto. Discreet. Discretion is a highly valued quality in Costa Rican culture, and some say it is at the core of the national psyche.

encomienda. During Spanish colonial times, the indigenous population throughout Latin America was practically enslaved through this feudal system of indentured servanthood, in which individuals were tied indefinitely to the landowner whose land they worked.

escuela. School

evangélico. In Latin America, this term refers to a member of a Protestant church that is likely fundamentalist in biblical interpretation. Prosletyzing is central to the *evangélico* doctrine, and church members may abstain from drinking alcohol, for instance, in order to set themselves apart from those around them as a witness to their faith. The *evangélicos* represent the fastest-growing Christian contingent in Latin America.

filibustero. Mercenary soldier, most commonly refers to soldiers in William Walker's army, who participated in his ill-fated imperialistic attempt to annex the Central American territory to the United States in 1856.

gallo pinto. Meaning "speckled rooster," this is the classic Costa Rican breakfast consisting of leftover black or red beans and rice, tossed with sauteed onion, *culantro*, and red pepper, and served with fried eggs, sour cream, and fresh tortillas.

guanacaseco/a. Refers to a person originating from the province of Guanacaste.

herediana/a. Refers to a person originating from the city or province of Heredia.

hora tica. "Tico time" refers to the relaxed view of time in a country where appointments can run a standard 20 or 30 minutes late. This is not a sign of irresponsibility but of differing priorities, where personal contact is far more important than an artificial imposition of schedules. Costa Ricans generally clarify whether a stated appointment time is *hora tica* or *hora americana*, meaning "on time."

¿idiay? A typical Costa Rican phrase, literally "Well?" It is the rough equivalent of "What's up with that?"

jícara. Gourd

josefino. Refers to a person originating from the city or province of San José.

La negrita. "The Dark-Skinned One," also known as Our Lady of the Angels, is the patron saint of Costa Rica. She reportedly appeared in the form of a dark-skinned statue in 1653; today in Cartago, a basilica marks the spot.

limonense. Refers to a person originating from the city or province of Limón.

Mecatelio Spoken primarily in the Limón province, this language is a fusion of Spanish, standard English, and Jamaican English, and is spoken by descendants of Black Jamaicans who initially came to Limón to build the railroad in the late nineteenth century. For instance, *Falta trii yiez im get ten* (In three years he will be ten), as Trevor Purcell illustrates in *Banana Fallout* (120).

Meseta Central. Central Plateau: an area 15 by 40 miles at an altitude of 4,000 feet, and the site of the capital. Located in the mid-section of Costa Rica, over half of the population lives in San José and surrounding areas.

nazareno. Nazarene. A beautiful native hardwood, its name refers to the purple tones of the wood, like those of Jesus of Nazareth's robe.

pulpería. A small, usually family-run, store that sells a variety of goods; traditionally, people go several times a week to the neighborhood *pulperías*.

puntarenense. Refers to a person originating from the city or province of Puntarenas.

pura vida. "Pure life," the quintessential Costa Rican expression, conveys an attitude of optimism; it is often used in response to the greeting, "How are you?"

quedar bien. "To leave a good impression." It is often considered a national characteristic, and refers to Costa Ricans' extreme concern both for putting one's best self forward and for not risking offending anyone.

quijongo. A traditional percussion instrument made of a thin, flexible wooden pole that is bowed by a string made of hemp fiber, and attached to a hollowed-out gourd to provide resonance.

quinceañera. A 15-year-old girl, whose birthday is traditionally marked by an elaborate celebration.

tamal. Typically served at Christmas, *tamales* are a delicious combination of a cornmeal-based dough and chicken or pork, rice, olives, raisins, and special seasonings, wrapped in banana leaves, then boiled. Each household has its own traditional method of preparation.

teja. Tile for roofing, also slang for the amount of 100 *colones*.

Tica, Tico. An affectionate term used to refer to Costa Ricans; the word comes from their ubiquitous habit of using the diminutive suffix, "-tico," so that *chiquito* (very little)—already from chico (small)—becomes *chiquitico* (little bitty). This word can also be used as an adjective or a noun, as in *hora tica* (Costa Rican time).

Selected Bibliography

Acevedo, Jorge Luis. *La música en Guanacaste*. San José, Costa Rica: Editorial de la Universidad de Costa Rica, 1980.

Biesanz, Mavis Hiltunen, Richard Biesanz, and Karen Zubris Biesanz. *The Ticos: Culture and Social Change in Costa Rica*. Boulder, Colo.: Lynne Rienner Publishers, 1999.

Booth, John A. *Costa Rica: Quest for Democracy*. Boulder, Colo.: Westview Press, 1998.

Cardenal, Rodolfo. "The Church in Central America." In *The Church in Latin America, 1492–1992*, edited by Enrique Dussel. Wellwood, Eng.: Burns and Oates, 1992.

Córdoba, Zaira Jiménez. *Delicias típicas en su mesa*. Alajuela, Costa Rica: Litografía e Imprenta Alfonso, 1996.

Edelman, Marc, and Joanne Kenen, eds. *The Costa Rica Reader*. New York: Grove Weidenfeld, 1989.

Greenway, Roger S. "Protestant Missionary Activity in Latin America." In *Coming of Age: Protestantism in Latin America*, edited by Daniel R. Miller. Lanham, Md.: University Press of America, 1994.

Haber, Harvey, ed. *Insight Guides: Costa Rica*. Boston: Houghton Mifflin, 1995.

Lara, Silvia, Tom Barry, and Peter Simonson. *Inside Costa Rica*. Albuquerque, N.M.: Resource Center Press, 1995.

Leitinger, Ilse Abshagen, ed. and trans. *The Costa Rican Women's Movement: A Reader*. Pittsburgh: University of Pittsburgh Press, 1997.

Leví, Enrique Jaramillo, ed. *When New Flowers Bloomed: Short Stories by Women Writers from Costa Rica and Panama*. Pittsburgh: Latin American Literary Review Press, 1991.

Lobo, Tatiana. *Assault on Paradise*. Translated by Asa Tatz. Willimantic, Conn.: Curbstone Press, 1998.

Meléndez, Carlos, and Quince Duncan. *El negro en Costa Rica*. 5th ed. San José, Costa Rica: Editorial Costa Rica, 1978.

Molina, Iván, and Steven Palmer. *Historia de Costa Rica: Breve actualizada, y con ilustraciones*. San José, Costa Rica: Editorial de la Universidad de Costa Rica, 1997.

Naranjo, Carmen. *Mujer y cultura*. San José, Costa Rica: EDUCA, 1989.

———. *There Never Was a Once Upon a Time*. Translated by Linda Britt. Pittsburgh: Latin American Literary Review Press, 1989.

Palmer, Paula. *"What Happen": A Folk-History of Costa Rica's Talamanca Coast*. San José, Costa Rica: Ecodesarrollos, 1977.

Purcell, Trevor W. *Banana Fallout: Class, Color, and Culture among West Indians in Costa Rica*. Los Angeles: Center for Afro-American Studies Publications, 1993.

Ras, Barbara, ed. *Costa Rica Traveler's Literary Companion*. San Francisco: Whereabouts Press, 1994.

Rojas, Margarita, and Flora Ovares. *100 años de literatura costarricense*. San José, Costa Rica: Ediciones Farben, 1995.

Rolbein, Seth. *Nobel Costa Rica: A Timely Report on One Peaceful Pro-Yankee, Central American Neighbor*. New York: St. Martin's Press, 1989.

Ross de Cerdas, Marjorie. *La magia de la cocina limonense Rice and Beans y catalú*. San José: Editorial de la Universidad de Costa Rica. 1991.

Sikora, Jacobo Shifter, Lowell Gudmundson, and Mario Solera Castro. *El judío en Costa Rica*. San José, Costa Rica: EUNED, 1979.

Yashar, Deborah J. *Demanding Democracy: Reform and Reaction in Costa Rica and Guatemala, 1870's–1950's*. Stanford: Stanford University Press, 1997.

Index

Acuña, Angela, 39
Alajuela, 4, 71
Amanecer, 108
Amighetti, Francisco, 115
Arias, Oscar, 36–37
army, abolition of, 24
arts, government sponsorship of, 101–
2, 111–13

bailes típicos, 104–5
banana industry, 4, 15–17; workers'
strike, 16–17, 21, 88, 89
Barahona, Dorelia, 94
Basilica of our Lady of the Angels, 50
Bernard, Eulalia, 19, 93
biodiversity, xvii, 1
biological preserves: La Amistad Biosphere Reserve, 2; La selva, 1. *See
also* conservationism
Black culture, 4, 17–20; in literature,
89, 91–93. *See also* Limón
Bribrí, 4, 44, 105

caoba, 115–16
Cahuita. *See* Limón

Calderón, Rafael Angel, 20–21
Cañas, Alberto, 95
Carnavales de Limón, 4, 19, 107
Carrasco, Pancha, 11
Cartago, 3, 7, 8, 50
Carvajal, María Luisa, 87
Catholicism, 43, 45–53
Central America, 9–10, 15, 36–37, 45,
59, 63
Central American Federation, 48
Chase, Alfonso, 96
civil war, 21–22
Clarke, Maureen, 18
coffee, 74–75; industry, 11–14
Colegio Lincoln, 32, 114
Colegio Metodista, 55
Colegio Monterrey, 55
colonial period, 6–9. *See also encomien-
das*
communist party, 20, 87, 88
computers, 36. *See also* Internet ac-
cess
concho, 81, 87
conservationism, 1–3, 60–61
Cortés, Carlos, 96

costumbrismo: in literature, 86; in painting, 113
Country Day School, 32
currency, xvii, 74

dance, 70, 104–5
Dengo, Omar, 87, 92
dichos ticos, 65–66
Dobles, Julieta, 96
Duncan, Quince, 19, 91–93

ecotourism, xvii, 2–3
EDUCA (Central American Universities Press), 86, 90
education, 14, 29–36; private, 31, 32–34; public, 31–32
elections 14, 21–22, 35
encomiendas, 8, 12, 46

Fallas, Carlos Luis, 88
Fernández de Córdoba, 6
Figueres, José María, 18
Figueres, José (Pepe), 18, 23–25, 101–2
food, 71–74

García Monge, Joaquín, 85
Generation of 1888, 13
González, Gil, 7
González Víquez, Cleto, 14
González Zeledón, Manuel, 86
Guanacaste, 4, 67; music, 106–7; regional dance, 104
Guardia, General Tomás, 12–13, 15
Gutiérrez, Joaquín, 88

Heredia, 4
holidays, 71–72; religious, 50, 52; state, 52
Holy Week, 52, 69
homosexuality, 63–64, 80

independence, 8
indigenous populations, xvi, 4–7; artistic traditions, 116–17; musical traditions, 105–6; religion, 5, 44–45. *See also* Bribrí
Instituto Psicopedagogía Integral (IPI), 33
instruments, 105–6
Internet access 24, 82
Istarú, Ana, 96

Jiménez, Max, 114
Judaism, 44. *See also* Rovinski, Samuel

Káñina, 80
Keith, Minor Cooper, 15–16. *See also* banana industry

La lucha farm, 23
La nación, 78
La negrita, 50
La prensa libre, 78
La república, 78
La Romería, 50
La Sabana, 67
language, 65–66
Limón, 4, 44; music of, 107–8
Lobo, Tatiana, 93
Lyra, Carmen. *See* Carvajal, María Luisa

Marfil, 108
Mecatelio, 66, 93
Meiggs, Keith, 15. *See also* banana industry
Mennonites, 53–55
Ministry of Culture, Youth, and Sports, 90, 95, 101, 111
missions: Catholic, 45, 47–48; Protestant, 53–55
Monteverde Cloud Forest Preserve, 37–38

Mora Valverde, Manuel, 20–21. *See also* communist party
muralists, 114
museums, 113
music, 101–9

Naranjo, Carmen, 39, 90–91, 96, 101
National Dance Company, 104
national parks, 2, 69
National Theater, 102–3
National Youth Orchestra, 102
newspapers, 77. *See also La nación; La prensa libre; La república; The Tico Times*
Nobel Peace Prize, 36

Odio, Eunice, 96
oligarchy, coffee-growing, 11, 12, 14, 102
Olympics, 67
Oreamuno, Yolanda, 89

Pacheco, Fausto, 113
painting, 113–14
Panama Canal, 10
Partido Liberación Nacional (PLN), 29
Pentecostals, 55–56
Picado, Teodoro, 21–22
Pinto, Julieta, 90
playwrights, 94–95, 103
poetry, 96–97
press, freedom of, 77
Protestants, 43, 53, 54–57
provinces, 3–4. *See also names of specific provinces*
publishing, 85–86
Puntarenas, 4

Quirós, Teodórico, 113

radio, 81–82
railroad, construction of, 15–16, 18. *See also* banana industry
religious orders, 47
religious processions, 50, 52
Rich Coast, 6
Rossi, Anacristina, 93
Rothe de Vallbona, Rima, 91
Rovinski, Samuel, 95

San José, 1, 3, 10, 31, 77
Sanabria, Archbishop, 21
Santamaría Juan, 11
school calendar, 30. *See also* education
sculpture, 115
serenata, 100
social reforms, 14–15, 20–22
sports, 66
Surá, Grupo de Cámara, 100, 108

Taboga Band, 108
Talamanca 4, 7, 8, 93
Teatro El Angel, 103
television, 77, 82
theater, 102–4
Thiel, Bishop Bernardo Augusto, 49
The Tico Times, 79
time, notions of, 64
Tinoco, Federico, 14
travel, 68–69

United Fruit Company, 16–17, 21, 88. *See also* banana industry
Universidad Autónoma de Centroamérica (UACA), 34. *See also* education
University of Costa Rica, 31–32; Afro-American studies, 93; community service requirement, 31; recovery of indigenous artifacts, 4, 116

Vásquez de Coronado, Juan, 7
volcano, xx, xxiii, 1

Walker, William, 10–11
women: changing gender roles, 62–63; legal rights, 39–40; political involvement, 14, 22; in public office, 39; writers, 85, 87, 89–91, 96. *See also* Naranjo, Carmen
Women's True Equality Bill, 39–40, 91

woodcuts, 115
woodworking, 115–16

Youth Symphony Orchestra, 102

Zúñiga, Francisco, 115

About the Author

CHALENE HELMUTH is an assistant professor of Spanish at Centre College, Danville, Kentucky.

100140

SHAKESPEARE'S
ROMAN WORLDS

VIVIAN THOMAS

ROUTLEDGE
London and New York

First published 1989
by Routledge
11 New Fetter Lane, London EC4P 4EE
29 West 35th Street, New York, NY 10001

Phototypeset in 10/12 Times
by Input Typesetting Ltd, London
Printed in Great Britain
by Biddles Ltd, Guildford and Kings Lynn

British Library Cataloguing in Publication Data
Thomas, Vivian
Shakespeare's Roman worlds.   I. Title
822.3′3

Library of Congress Cataloging in Publication Data
Thomas, Vivian.
Shakespeare's Roman worlds/Vivian Thomas.
p.   cm.
Includes index.
ISBN 0 415 00756 9
1. Shakespeare, William, 1564–1616–Knowledge–Rome.
2. Shakespeare, William, 1564–1616. Julius Caesar.   3. Shakespeare,
William, 1564–1616. Antony and Cleopatra.   4. Shakespeare, William,
1564–1616. Coriolanus.   5. Rome in literature.   I. Title.
PR3069.R6T47   1989
822.3′3–dc19

ISBN 0 415 00756 9

For my wife, Audrey

CONTENTS

Acknowledgements   vii

Preface   ix

1   SHAKESPEARE'S ROMAN WORLDS   1

2   IMAGES AND SELF-IMAGES IN *JULIUS CAESAR*   40

3   REALITIES AND IMAGININGS IN *ANTONY AND CLEOPATRA*   93

4   SOUNDS, WORDS, GESTURES AND DEEDS IN *CORIOLANUS*   154

5   CONCLUSION   220

Notes   224

Bibliography   233

Index   242

ACKNOWLEDGEMENTS

I should like to express my gratitude to Professor Norman Sanders of the University of Tennessee and Dr Tom Matheson, Deputy Director of the Shakespeare Institute, University of Birmingham. They both sacrificed valuable time to read the manuscript, drew my attention to several mistakes, and made me rethink a number of points of substance. I owe a special debt of gratitude to Dr John Wilders, Professor at Middlebury College, Vermont, and Emeritus Fellow of Worcester College, Oxford, whose lectures first ignited my interest in the Roman plays. Thanks, too, are due to my students, whose persistent questions and acute comments have done so much to shape my perceptions of the plays. My greatest debt is to my wife, who typed and corrected the manuscript throughout its various stages and tirelessly sought to improve the clarity of expression. I am wholly responsible for the remaining errors or blemishes.

PREFACE

The 'infinite variety' of Shakespeare's Roman plays is reflected in the diversity of critical commentary to which they have given rise. As early as 1910, M.W. MacCallum's study, *Shakespeare's Roman Plays and their Background*, began an exploration of the relationship between Sir Thomas North's translation of Plutarch's *Lives of the Noble Grecians and Romans* and three of Shakespeare's Roman plays. Fascination with this aspect of the plays has continued – a succinct and convenient account is provided by Kenneth Muir in *The Sources of Shakespeare's Plays* (1977). The wider question of 'sources' and 'influences' has been subject to much discussion and has been analysed recently by Robert S. Miola in 'Shakespeare and his sources: observations on the critical history of *Julius Caesar*' (*Shakespeare Survey*, vol. 40 (1987), pp. 69–76).

A number of important studies have given consideration to Shakespeare's creation of a social universe in the Roman plays, and the influences exerted on the dramatist's perceptions of the classical world. The most abbreviated list would have to include: J.E. Phillips, *The State in Shakespeare's Greek and Roman Plays* (1940); T.W. Baldwin, *William Shakespeare's Small Latine and Lesse Greeke* (1944); J.A.K. Thompson, *Shakespeare and the Classics* (1952); Virgil K. Whitaker, *Shakespeare's Use of Learning* (1953); Terence Spencer, 'Shakespeare and the Elizabethan Romans' in *Shakespeare Survey*, vol. 10 (1957); Wilbur Sanders, *The Dramatist and the Received Idea* (1968); Reuben A. Brower, *Hero and Saint: Shakespeare and the Graeco-Roman Heroic Tradition* (1971); J.L. Simmons, *Shakespeare's Pagan World: The Roman Tragedies* (1973); Paul A. Cantor, *Shakespeare's Rome: Republic and Empire* (1976); Robert S. Miola, *Shakespeare's Rome* (1983); Charles Martindale (ed.) *Ovid Renewed* (1988); and John W. Velz's recent article 'Cracking strong curbs asunder: Roman destiny and the Roman hero in *Coriolanus*' (*English Literary Renaissance* 13 (1983), pp. 58–69) in which he suggests that 'new dimensions emerge in Shakespeare's Roman world if one stands on the *Aeneid* to observe it'.

Consideration of broad critical studies of the plays or specialist aspects such as imagery gives rise to an enormous list of significant essays and monographs, including such varied contributions as: G. Wilson Knight, *The Imperial Theme* (1930); John Palmer, *Political Characters of Shakespeare* (1945); Maurice Charney, *Shakespeare's Roman Plays: The Function of Imagery in the Drama* (1961); John Holloway, *The Story of the*

Night (1961); Ernest Schanzer, *The Problem Plays of Shakespeare* (1963); Jan Kott, *Shakespeare our Contemporary* (1965); Derek Traversi, *Shakespeare: The Roman Plays* (1963); Emrys Jones, *Scenic Form in Shakespeare* (1971); Janet Adelman, *The Common Liar: An Essay on 'Antony and Cleopatra'* (1973); Michael Long, *The Unnatural Scene: A Study in Shakespearean Tragedy* (1976); Walter C. Foreman Jr, *The Music of the Close: The Final Scenes of Shakespeare's Tragedies* (1978); Philip J. Highfill Jr, (ed.), *Shakespeare's Craft* (1982); and J. Leeds Barroll, *Shakespearian Tragedy, Genre, Tradition and Change in 'Antony and Cleopatra'* (1984). Two recent books which indicate a growing tendency to emphasize the political and historical dimensions of the plays are: John Wilders, *The Lost Garden: A View of Shakespeare's English and Roman Histories* (1978) and Alexander Leggatt, *Shakespeare's Political Drama: The History Plays and the Roman Plays* (1988). The new historicist school of criticism has also given rise to interesting commentaries on these plays. Three books which contain a few essays devoted to some of the Roman plays and which give a broad guide to the vigour of this approach are: Jonathan Dollimore, *Radical Tragedy: Religion, Ideology and Power in the Drama of Shakespeare and his Contemporaries* (1984); Patricia Parker and Geoffrey Hartman (eds), *Shakespeare and the Question of Theory* (1985); Jean E. Howard and Marion F. O'Connor (eds), *Shakespeare Reproduced: The Text in History and Ideology* (1987).

The above list of works dealing with various aspects of the Roman plays is merely representative and does not even touch on the hundreds of specialist articles which in recent years have enhanced critical appreciation of the plays. Fortunately, there are some useful surveys of critical work on the plays: J.C. Maxwell's article 'Shakespeare's Roman Plays: 1900–1956' in *Shakespeare Survey* vol. 10 (a volume devoted to the Roman plays); John W. Velz, *Shakespeare and the Classical Tradition: A Critical Guide to Commentary, 1660–1960* (1968); Stanley Wells (ed.), *Shakespeare: Select Bibliographical Guides* (first printed in 1973: revised 1990 to take account of books and articles published in the intervening fifteen years).

There are points of tangency and occasional overlap between this and previous studies, but there is no attempt to replicate anything that has been well done – for example, providing detailed exploration of Shakespeare's engagement with the classical world through such writers as Ovid and Virgil. The distinguishing feature of this study is that it endeavours to convey a clear idea of the relationship between the characters and events in Shakespeare's plays and the main narrative sources on which the four Roman plays are based, while simultaneously undertaking a critical analysis of the plays through the perspective of Shakespeare's Roman worlds, particularly the creation and operation of the value system. Hence these plays are perceived as political plays, histories and tragedies. Critical works devoted to the Roman plays frequently omit consideration of *Titus Andronicus*. Here, critical analysis of *Titus* is undertaken in the opening chapter, which commences with an exploration of the nature of Shakespeare's Roman worlds. *Julius Caesar*, *Antony and Cleopatra*, and *Coriolanus* each have a separate chapter devoted to them because, in each case, critical analysis of the plays involves a thorough examination of Shakespeare's response to the characters and events found in Plutarch and subsidiary sources. The assumed narrative source material for *Titus* does not afford such rich opportunity for analysis as that provided by Plutarch's great work. Indeed, G.K. Hunter has recently argued (*Notes and Queries*, 30 (1983)) that the chap-book version generally held as the chief narrative source of the play derives from the ballad which in turn is based on the play. The ubiquitous influence of Ovid's *Metamorphoses* on *Titus* is widely recognized and is not, therefore, explored here.

The texts used for this study are the New Arden Edition of the respective plays: *Titus Andronicus*, edited by J.C. Maxwell (1953), *Julius Caesar*, edited by T.S. Dorsch (1955), *Antony and Cleopatra*, edited by M.R. Ridley (1965) and *Coriolanus* edited by Philip Brockbank (1976). All quotations from Sir Thomas North's translation of Plutarch are taken from vol. V of Geoffrey Bullough's *Narrative and Dramatic Sources of Shakespeare* (1966). My continuing references to 'Plutarch' rather than 'North' are not, of course, intended to diminish recognition of the influence of North's language on Shakespeare.

This book is designed to appeal to a wide audience, from the general reader to the specialist student of Shakespeare. Although no attempt has been made to employ the apparatus or terminology of the historicist approach, much of the critical analysis is congruent with this new school of thought because the focus of attention is the relationship between characters, values and the dynamics of social change, including exploration of the relationship between history and myth.

This study contains an extensive bibliography, but one that is confined to books in order to keep it within reasonable bounds. Limitation of space and the necessity of keeping critical assessment taut have precluded discussion of many interesting studies which are highlighted by inclusion in the select bibliography.

1

SHAKESPEARE'S ROMAN WORLDS

Thou art a Roman; be not barbarous
(*Titus Andronicus*, I.i.378)

The aim of this book is to show how a clear understanding of Shakespeare's exploration and articulation of Roman values provides an invaluable means of gaining fresh critical insights into the Roman plays. The most striking feature of these plays is that, more than any other group of plays or any individual play, they create an intense sense of a social universe – not just a sense of place but an awareness of the values, attitudes, aspirations, and idiosyncrasies of the different Romes which are portrayed in *Titus Andronicus*, *Julius Caesar*, *Antony and Cleopatra* and *Coriolanus*. Shakespeare gives a palpable sense of the Roman world in diverse ways: the physical landmarks of Rome, such as the Tiber and the Capitol, are mentioned with great frequency; there are numerous references to Roman manners and customs – the Feast of Lupercal in the opening scenes of *Julius Caesar* for example; political and religious institutions and officials are ever present, such as tribunes, aediles, patricians, augurers, flamens (priests) or lictors (ushers); the mythology of the pantheon and references to the gods pervade the plays; and Roman history, including most vitally its Trojan origins, is focused in the minds of the major participants. Yet, when all this is recognized, the most important reason for feeling such an intense awareness of the peculiar quality of these societies is the articulation of Roman values. These values are not platitudinous precepts but deeply held convictions about the relative worth of different kinds of human actions. Consequently, it is possible to identify those qualities which are most esteemed in these Roman worlds. The central values are: service to the state, constancy, fortitude, valour, friendship, love of family and respect for the gods. It is not surprising that the relative importance attaching to these central values varies from play to play because Shakespeare portrays a changing Rome. The catalyst of conflict is the collision of values or the divergence between personal aspirations and obligations to the society. But if the relative importance accorded each of these values changes through time they all continue to

1

shape perceptions and are persistently invoked to commend or condemn human behaviour.

Shakespeare's interest in Rome encompassed the whole of his dramatic career. *Titus Andronicus*, written around 1590, is his first tragedy and may have been his first play. Although the events encapsulated in the play ostensibly relate to a late period of Roman history (possibly around the fourth century AD), Shakespeare conveys the feeling of an embryonic Rome. He returns to the vision of a primitive Rome in *Coriolanus*, the last of his tragedies (written around 1607–8). *Julius Caesar*, the dramatist's first play to draw on Plutarch, was composed in 1599, virtually the mid-point in his career. *Antony and Cleopatra* (c. 1606–7) was written when he was at the height of his powers.

In the primitive Rome of *Coriolanus* it is valour which is the chief virtue, because this is a period when the very existence of Rome is dependent on the courage of its warriors and citizens to do battle with its immediate neighbours. Moving from the world of 494–491 BC to the period of *Julius Caesar*, 45–42 BC, is to move from a primitive to a mature and sophisticated Rome; a society with a rich heritage, proud of its democratic institutions. Valour is no longer the most important value, though it has its place. The foremost means of serving the state is through a commitment to its political life. Yet pursuit of this objective involves conflict with the popular leadership of an outstanding individual who embodies Roman 'greatness' or destiny. Co-mingling with these revered values are political ambition, friendship and favouritism. Here is Rome at the crossroads. The Rome of *Antony and Cleopatra* (40–30 BC) is not merely different from the Rome of *Julius Caesar*, it is juxtaposed with a society whose values are totally antithetical to those of Rome: the Rome of Octavius Caesar may appear opportunist or even decadent when viewed from the perspective of the past, but compared with Egypt it is austere. Ironically, the great Roman general who turns his back on Roman values and becomes Egyptianized is extolled, retrospectively, by the abstemious and puritanical Octavius, as the embodiment of the greatest Roman virtues. For Octavius Caesar, Antony is the fallen angel. His description of the Antony of old is the outstanding exposition of Roman virtue in these plays (I.iv.55–71). A further irony is that in the age of Empire, rather than a great warrior, general, political thinker or orator, what Rome needs and acquires is the supreme civil servant.

The purpose of this study is to analyse the values in the plays and their role in generating conflict, and to make a close examination of Shakespeare's handling of his source material. Special emphasis is given to Sir Thomas North's translation of Plutarch's *Parallel Lives of the Noble Grecians and Romans*. Geoffrey Bullough has, in *Narrative and Dramatic Sources of Shakespeare*, provided an excellent collection of those sources which Shakespeare may have consulted in addition to North's Plutarch.

(Volume V of Bullough's huge editorial work contains the relevant 'lives' from Plutarch and excerpts from narrative and dramatic sources which Shakespeare may have used.) Where the evidence of particular use of other sources is strong it is worth scrutinizing Shakespeare's response to them. However, as Plutarch is without doubt Shakespeare's main source, it is his response to the events and characters portrayed by the famous Greek which is of primary significance. The source material for *Titus Andronicus* is of a very different kind from that of Plutarch's *Lives*, which is why a separate chapter is not devoted to that play.

Plutarch's work is a fascinating historical narrative in its own right, but it holds a special place in Shakespearian scholarship because, along with the works of Hall and Holinshed, it is one of the three most important source books known to have been used by the dramatist. It is evident that Shakespeare composed three of his Roman plays with this volume at his elbow. He follows the narrative very closely, occasionally lifting whole passages, and frequently taking words and phrases directly from North's translation.

Plutarch, who lived from approximately AD 46 to 120, was a native of Chaeronea, where he spent most of his life. He went on numerous embassies to Rome and delivered lectures there. His *Moral Essays* achieved great popularity during the Renaissance. His *Parallel Lives of the Noble Grecians and Romans* was conceived as a study comparing famous pairs of men from the two great cultures who were alike in personality, shared similar circumstances or lived at approximately the same time. His stated objective was a pursuit of character within a social and historical context rather than a work of historical narrative or analysis. Part of the fascination of the book lies in Plutarch's desire to go behind the scenes, to scrutinize the small and mundane actions of these men as well as their famous deeds. As Plutarch expresses the point in his *Life of Alexander*: 'The noblest deedes doe not always shew men's vertues and vices, but often times a light occasion, a word, or some sporte, makes men's natural dispositions and manners appear more plaine, then the famous battells wonne.'[1] Plutarch's *Lives* made its way into English via the French translation of Professor Jacques Amyot of Melun (1513–93). This French translation appeared first in 1559 and had achieved considerable popularity when Sir Thomas North became acquainted with it during his embassy to France on behalf of Elizabeth I. His English translation was published in 1579. Its impact was such that there were three reprints during Shakespeare's lifetime: 1593, 1603, and 1612.

A brief but valuable commentary on Shakespeare's use of Plutarch is provided by Kenneth Muir in *The Sources of Shakespeare's Plays*.[2] At the other extreme, an extensive examination of the relationship between Shakespeare and Plutarch was undertaken by MacCallum (*Shakespeare's Roman Plays and their Background*) in 1910.[3] The Arden editions of the plays are also useful in this respect. However, the intention in this volume is to provide a close analysis of Shakespeare's use of his source material and to integrate this inquiry with a critique of the plays. Essentially, Shakespeare departs from the sources in five ways. Some of these techniques are used simply to achieve economy; others have a more direct bearing on his shaping of characters and events. First, he conflates events, such as the Feast of Lupercal and Caesar's triumph over Pompey's sons in the opening scene of *Julius Caesar*. Second, he omits actions which figure prominently in Plutarch, for example, Mark Antony's disastrous Parthian campaign and his savage treatment of Cicero (he orders the murder, dismemberment and public display of the head and hands of his political antagonist). Third, he changes important points of detail: Menenius (in Livy) is a man of plebeian origins; in Shakespeare's play he is a thoroughgoing patrician; the dispute between Cassius and Brutus over who should lead the right flank at Philippi is transferred to Octavius and Antony. Fourth, Shakespeare develops characters or details which he finds in his source material. Enobarbus, for example, is little more than a name in Plutarch, but from one incident (the man, suffering from an ague, deserts Antony before the battle of Actium and dies almost immediately) Shakespeare creates a major character. Similarly, Aufidius and Menenius receive only a small mention in Plutarch but they emerge as prominent character studies in *Coriolanus*. Finally, he invents such features as Caesar's deafness and his rescue from the Tiber by Cassius.

Part of the difficulty of getting these plays into proper focus is the tendency to consider them 'essentially' as tragedies with a significant (or sometimes insignificant) political or historical dimension. The substance and vision inherent in the Roman plays is such that the perspective of tragedy is inadequate to provide a thoroughgoing critical appreciation of them. In addition to illuminating many points of detail, both large and small, it is the aim of this study to provide coherent answers to several broad questions. First, what kind of characterisation does Shakespeare find in Plutarch and in his subsidiary sources? Second, how numerous and significant are the changes Shakespeare makes to his source material? Third, how does his understanding and articulation of Rome and Roman values influence the structuring of his plays and the dramatic conflicts – and how does the relative importance of values change from one play to another? Fourth, how does the 'weight' of politics and history influence the texture of the plays: to what extent are they 'histories' or 'tragedies' and how important is this question in gaining a deeper insight into the critical dilemmas posed by the plays?

Clearly, *Titus Andronicus* stands apart from the three plays traditionally categorized as Roman. This early play lacks the rich historical source material which Shakespeare was able to draw on for his mature Roman plays, but it merits more than passing consideration because it reflects so clearly Shakespeare's early awareness of the potency of Roman values in shaping society. Too often dismissed as journeyman work or as an attempt to emulate Kyd's highly successful revenge tragedy, this play provides valuable insights into Shakespeare's exploration of the relationship between the conflicting values of warfare and civilised living.

The most perceptive comments on the relationship between Shakespeare's Roman worlds and the sixteenth-century context are made by T.J.B. Spencer in his essay 'Shakespeare and the Elizabethan Romans'. He opens his discussion by citing the praise Shakespeare has received for his ability to create a genuine sense of Rome and Romanness in his plays. Nahum Tate and Dryden are quoted, but most telling is Pope's acknowledgement that Shakespeare was 'very knowing in the customs, rites and manners of Antiquity', adding even more significantly, 'In *Coriolanus* and *Julius Caesar*, not only the Spirit, but Manners, of the *Romans* are exactly drawn; and still a nicer distinction is shewn, between the manners of the *Romans* in the time of the former and of the latter.'[4] This comment is particularly perceptive, revealing his awareness that Shakespeare creates not a Roman world but Roman worlds. Spencer is not so much struck by these expressions of admiration for Shakespeare as by the time when they were made: 'The odd thing is that this veracity or authenticity was approved at a time when Shakespeare's educational background was suspect; when the word "learning" practically meant a knowledge of Greek and Roman writers'.[5] Despite such keen appreciation of the authentic feel of Shakespeare's Rome by writers who had doubts about his learning, others, such as Thomas Rymer and Dennis, sneered at what they saw as gross deficiencies in Shakespeare's attempt to recreate Rome on the stage, especially the virtual absence of a sense of the dignity of Rome.[6] Whereas these critics were exceptional in their views, the eighteenth century produced many complaints about Shakespeare's use of anachronisms, which range from clocks, billiards, and caps to a reference to the sound of a battery. It was implicit recognition of the solidity and authenticity of Shakespeare's Roman worlds that caused irritation with his anachronisms.

Spencer points out that

Ancient, and in particular Roman, history was explored as the material of political lessons, because it was one of the few bodies of consistent and continuous historical material available . . . In writing his Roman plays Shakespeare was touching upon the gravest and most exciting as well as the most pedantic of Renaissance studies, of European scholarship.[7]

Yet despite the significance and popularity of Roman history, Spencer argues, England was not endowed with good historical writing on Greece or Rome. Perhaps the figures of Livy and Tacitus cast too strong a shadow over would-be chroniclers of Roman history. The two exceptions to this general reticence are significant. The works of William Fulbecke[8] and Richard Reynolds[9] convey a clear impression of their association of order and dignity with Empire as opposed to Republic. A translation of Appian in 1578 under the title *An Auncient Historie and Exqisite Chronicle of the Romanes Warres, both Civile and Foren* cites as the main headings the turmoil, greed, and destruction which characterized Roman history, all of which led to 'an evident demonstration, That peoples rule must give place and Princes power prevayle'.[10] On the basis of what seems to be sound evidence Spencer concludes:

> in spite of literary admiration for Cicero, the Romans in the imagination of the sixteenth century were Suetonian and Tacitan rather than Plutarchan . . . it required a considerable intellectual feat to substitute the Plutarchan vision of Rome (mostly republican) for the customary line of the Imperial Caesars. Montaigne and Shakespeare were capable of that feat. Not many others were.[11]

Rather than taking up a position that was powerfully present in his own society, therefore, Shakespeare adopted a strongly independent and iconoclastic standpoint in the creation of his Roman plays. He was fascinated by the characters and stories of Brutus, Antony, and Cleopatra that were so well known in his society; but he was determined to ground their actions in a clearly conceived and articulated vision of Rome – one profoundly influenced by his reading of Plutarch. However, it must be remembered that Shakespeare entered the world of Rome dramatically before writing *Julius Caesar* in 1599. *Titus Andronicus* may have been inspired by the success of Kyd's *The Spanish Tragedy*, but even so Shakespeare had, for the first time, to meet the challenge of creating a sense of a highly specific social universe. Indeed, the play was entered in the Stationers' Register in 1594 as 'a Noble Roman Historye' and published later that year as a 'Most Lamentable Romaine Tragedie' – a claim which Spencer feels is justified by the standards of the sixteenth century. Arguing for the play's portrayal of a sense of Rome which would appear impressively authentic to the sixteenth-century audience, Spencer makes some significant observations:

> The play does not assume a political situation known to Roman history; it is, rather, a summary of Roman politics. It is not so much that any particular set of political institutions is assumed in *Titus*, but rather that it includes *all* the political institutions that Rome ever had. The author seems anxious, not to get it all right, but to get it all in . . . It seems to be a quintessence of impressions derived from an eager reading of Roman history rather than a real effort at verisimilitude. Still, I think

that *Titus* would easily be recognised as typical Roman history by a sixteenth-century audience.[12]

Putting aside for a moment the inconsistencies with regard to political institutions (which are not surprising since the events in question do not belong to a known period of Roman history), Shakespeare very powerfully evokes the sense of a Roman world which is palpable, and reveals that even before his encounter with Plutarch he set himself the highest standards in creating a social and political universe. It was Plutarch who gave Shakespeare the foothold for transcending the achievement of *Titus*. As Spencer suggests, 'It was probably the most serious experience that Shakespeare had of the bookish kind'.[13]

There can be little doubt that the reading of Plutarch's *Lives* constituted a watershed in Shakespeare's dramatic career. Plutarch's work clearly conveyed to the dramatist an intense sense of a social universe – a world in which values were clearly articulated, and permeated every aspect of life. It was this feeling, greatly accentuated by Shakespeare, which constituted the cornerstone for his subsequent writing of three Roman plays. Shakespeare saw his characters primarily as *social* beings: autonomous, individual, idiosyncratic, but powerfully influenced by the values of their culture. Spencer, referring to Brutus and Caesar, insists that

> the reassessment and reconsideration of such famous historical figures was a common literary activity in the Renaissance, not merely in poetry and drama (where licence is acceptable), but in plain prose, the writing of history. It seems hardly legitimate to talk about 'tradition', to refer to 'traditional' opinions about Caesar and Brutus, when in fact the characters of each of them had been the subject of constant discussion.[14]

Although in literature and history the deeds of these characters had been assessed in terms of morality and political effectiveness, nobody prior to Shakespeare had integrated actions, motives and personalities into the social and political universe. The very word 'Rome' rings through Shakespeare's plays with a powerful vibration. It is this profound awareness of the social ethos permeating the thought and actions of these plays which gives a sense of the reality and the solidity of ancient Rome.

Many critics have acknowledged the importance of the social ethos in the plays. They have not, however, explored the ways in which perception of these values animates actions and conflicts at every level. It is not simply a matter of a cultural contrast between Rome and Egypt, for example, but the significance of a cultural contour map which is different for each Rome depicted in the plays. One critic to demonstrate the significance of the role of values in the Roman plays is Paul A. Cantor in *Shakespeare's Rome: Republic and Empire*. But rather than perceiving Shakespeare's interest as the interaction between values and character, he sees Shakespeare's central concern as one of portraying the different kinds of Rome. Cantor expresses the matter succinctly:

> I want to emphasize that I do believe that the three Roman plays form a kind of historical trilogy, dramatizing the rise and fall of the Roman Republic, in a sense the tragedy of Rome itself, in which the Republic is corrupted and eventually destroyed by its very success in conquering the world.[15]

This view represents an admirable counterbalance to critics who have paid little attention to the role of values in influencing conflicts and actions in the plays, but it carries this awareness to the opposite extreme by elevating the society above the characters as Shakespeare's centre of interest. Cantor quite rightly states that 'In studying the Roman plays we gradually become aware that Shakespeare could hardly have understood Romans without understanding Rome'. Nor can there be any objection made to Cantor's claim that 'since *Coriolanus* begins with the creation of the tribunate, and goes on to dramatise its precarious survival through a grave constitutional crisis, the play provides a portrait of the origins of republicanism in Rome'.[16] But Shakespeare's artistry in creating a palpable feeling of primitive Rome has not been undertaken for its own sake – as historian or sociologist. Rather, he has animated and vitalized this society in order to provide a firm grounding for his drama. What is admirable about Cantor is that he has recognized the extent to which Shakespeare was fascinated by the social ethos. The dramatist is clearly captivated by the tension generated between deeply ingrained habits of thought and the pragmatic and opportunist responses of virtually everyone in coming to terms with fundamental social change. Shakespeare lived in a society where such tensions were being experienced and was, no doubt, intrigued by the presentation of the moment of breaking point in Plutarch. He saw this situation as providing much more than background for the setting of *Coriolanus* – it was an integral feature of the tragedy. But it is the human tragedy which is the centre of Shakespeare's interest.

It is because of the significance of the political and historical dimensions of these plays that they have presented so many difficulties for critics who have wanted to analyse them in terms that apply to *Hamlet* or *King Lear*, where the political and historical aspects are relatively minor. The Roman plays are history plays and political plays as well as being tragedies. Their multifaceted nature should, therefore, be recognized and enjoyed. They can be called tragedies but they constitute a special kind of tragedy – a unique blend of history, politics and tragic fall. Unless this mixture is appreciated, and savoured, critics and theatregoers will be unduly perplexed and disappointed – a feeling clearly articulated by Janet Adelman in *The Common Liar: An Essay on 'Antony and Cleopatra'*:

In the history plays, diversity of perspective and opacity of character are tolerable because the protagonist of the plays is England itself: all the major characters are to some degree minor characters in that pageant; no character need make exclusive claim to our interest. But Rome is not in any sense the protagonist of *Antony and Cleopatra*; though its matter is historical, the total world created by the play is not. And principles tolerable in the history plays set up intolerable tensions in *Antony and Cleopatra* because they so frequently undercut the pretensions of the characters in whom we are most interested. We and the lovers are forced to live, for the moment, in an uncomfortably historical world, a world in which no motive or emotion is sure, no judgement absolute.[17]

This comment raises the whole question of genre. What useful distinction can be made between a history play and a tragedy? One thing that these plays have in common is that they are based on what Shakespeare believed was historical fact – though he doubtless had a sense of the differences in quality of the historical materials with which he dealt. John Wilders, in *The Lost Garden: A View of Shakespeare's English and Roman History Plays*, suggests that at one level the distinction between the histories and tragedies is at the very least blurred:

The only immediately obvious feature which the histories have in common is that they all deal with the history of England. A case could be made for describing some of Heminge's and Condell's 'histories' as 'tragedies', particularly *Richard II* and *Richard III*, both of which have dominant heroes and are distinguished from the other histories in the table of contents by the description '*THE LIFE AND DEATH*'. Again, some of the Folio tragedies could well be considered histories: *Julius Caesar* has no central, commanding hero of the magnitude of Hamlet or Macbeth and this play, too, is described as '*THE LIFE AND DEATH*' of Julius Caesar. The superficial evidence suggests, then, that the distinction between Shakespeare's histories and his tragedies is not as clear-cut as the Folio division implies.[18]

However, having cast doubt on the validity of treating these groups of plays as separate entities, Wilders goes on to suggest that there is one very important sense in which the histories and tragedies are different:

The difference seems to lie in the role of the tragic hero. Whereas a history play portrays the fortunes of many characters as they play their roles in a nation's continuing life, a tragedy is devoted chiefly to the struggles of one character, and his death, depicted as the outcome of the conflicts which occupy the play, gives to the ending of a tragedy a sense of absolute finality. A Shakespearean tragedy has what Peter Ure calls 'the order and unity of biography', a unity implied by the old title

'*THE LIFE AND DEATH*'. But whereas the death of a tragic hero conveys a sense of an ending, the impression created by a history play is that the life of a nation has neither beginning nor ending.[19]

This is a very useful distinction and enables us to draw a fairly clear line between such plays as *Hamlet* and *King Lear* on the one hand and any of the plays in the history cycles or even *King John* and *Henry VIII*. However, when this criterion is applied to a consideration of the Roman plays, it soon becomes apparent that their historical dimension too is much greater than in the other tragedies. Certainly at the end of *Julius Caesar* and *Antony and Cleopatra* we have our eyes on the future of Rome as well as focusing on the personal tragedies of the central characters. This is less true of *Coriolanus*, but the political dimension of this play is so strong that it has a distinctly different feel from a play like *Macbeth*. So although the Roman plays may legitimately be referred to as tragedies they have a special quality that makes thém distinctive. It is not merely a sense of historical continuity which they share with the English histories but a distinct feeling of political identity, institutions and conflicts. If the identity of England as a place and a symbol is clearly articulated in Shakespeare's ten history plays, the sense of Rome as place and symbol is even more powerfully articulated in all four Roman plays.

How does Shakespeare achieve this and what are the implications? The sense of Rome as an historical entity redolent with suggestion has received careful consideration by Robert Miola who maintains that Rome

> is sometimes metaphor, sometimes myth, sometimes both, sometimes neither. Despite its metamorphoses, Rome maintains a distinct identity. Constructed of forums, walls, and Capitol, opposed to outlying battle-fields, wild, primitive landscapes, and enemy cities, Rome is a palpable though ever-changing presence. The city serves not only as a setting for action, but also as central protagonist. Embodying the heroic traditions of the past, Rome shapes its inhabitants, who often live or die according to its dictates for the approval of its future generations.[20]

Miola has a keen sense of the shaping power of Rome, of its multifarious associations and of the influence exerted by its values and its entrenched sense of destiny. For him the central Roman ideals explored in Shakespeare's plays are 'constancy, honour and *pietas* (the loving respect owed to family, country, and gods)'.[21]

Cantor, in attempting to draw together the main threads in the interwoven fabric of the Roman ethos, comments:

> It is difficult to find one English word to cover this complex of austerity, pride, heroic virtue, and public service that constitutes Romanness in Shakespeare, in the way that the one word *eros* describes the force in

Antony and Cleopatra that manifests itself in such diverse forms as hunger, thirst, sexual desire and 'immortal longings'. Perhaps the best word to describe the side of human nature developed in a character like Coriolanus is *spiritedness*, a term which has the advantage over alternatives like *heart* or *courage* of immediately calling to mind public spiritedness. The distinguishing characteristic of the Republican Romans in *Coriolanus*, and *Julius Caesar* as well, is that their spiritedness is ordinarily directed toward the service of the public.[22]

Regardless of the adequacy or otherwise of the term 'spiritedness' for encapsulating Roman values, Cantor, like Miola, has a firm grasp of the way in which these values are powerfully projected so as to inform our sense of a distinctive Roman world in each of the plays. However, he is at pains to contrast the living, breathing Roman values in *Coriolanus* and *Julius Caesar* with their absence in *Antony and Cleopatra*. As he puts it:

> Though many critics talk about Rome as a value in *Antony and Cleopatra*, the characters in the play are conspicuously silent on the subject. Not a word is spoken about the good of Rome in the course of the play: all one ever hears is the characters' concern for their relative positions in the pure power struggle in the Empire.[23]

This statement is by no means true, because Octavius' denunciation of Antony in terms which portray him as the quintessential Roman, *before* he met Cleopatra, is arguably the best example in all four plays of what it means to be a Roman (I.iv.55–71). Nevertheless, Cantor is making an important and valid distinction between the potency of Roman values in *Julius Caesar* and *Coriolanus* compared with *Antony and Cleopatra*. In *Antony and Cleopatra* there has been a distinct dilution of Roman values: political advantage is more important than public service. It is easy, therefore, to see the Roman world of *Antony and Cleopatra* as set free from Roman values, but such a view fails to comprehend the ways in which these values still percolate the society. Not only is Mark Antony the heroic *past* incarnate, but the opportunist Octavius Caesar finds the Roman ideal of austerity congenial to his puritanism: he clearly feels that the Roman value of abstemiousness validates his actions against Antony, who has turned his back on his society. This is not cynicism but reflects the subtle interweaving of personal ambition with a cultural heritage. The division between Rome of the past and present, and Egypt, finds expression in Antony. As he suddenly leaves Cleopatra, to deal energetically with matters of state, she says 'He was dispos'd to mirth; but on the sudden/A Roman thought hath struck him.' (I.ii.79–80). The contrast between the cultures is accentuated by Shakespeare's drawing of Octavius' character, which is distinctly puritanical. The division between the Roman Republic and the Rome of the Emperors on which Cantor insists, therefore, has a

11

great deal of validity, but it in no way negates the contrast which has frequently been made between Rome and Egypt. It is refinement of this contrast which is called for rather than its rejection.

Cantor makes a number of perceptive and illuminating comments in comparing the world of *Antony and Cleopatra* with that of *Coriolanus*. Referring to the latter he points out that 'the simple acts of eating and drinking never once occur on the stage during the entire play'. In criticising the Rome/Egypt dichotomy which has characterized some valuable criticism of *Antony and Cleopatra*, he argues that 'In most formulations, Egypt is associated with images of eating and drinking, while Rome is associated with images of temperance and abstinence', yet 'Our impression of how widespread indulgence has become in the world of *Antony and Cleopatra* can only be confirmed when we see even the usually abstinent Octavius caught up in the general round of drunkenness in Rome.'[24] This last comment misrepresents the nature of the scene on Pompey's barge (including its essentially masculine nature which contrasts sharply with the deeply feminine associations of Egypt). Nevertheless, though Cantor carries his argument much further than the evidence will bear, he does provide a wonderfully vigorous and telling commentary on the contrast between the Rome of *Coriolanus* and the Rome of *Antony and Cleopatra*:

> In conclusion, the fundamental opposition between *Coriolanus* and *Antony and Cleopatra* is implied in the opening scenes of the plays. *Coriolanus* begins in the everyday world of the city, *Antony and Cleopatra* in a lavish imperial court remote from the cares of daily life . . . Whereas *Coriolanus* begins in an atmosphere of necessity and urgency, with Rome plagued by famine and open revolt, *Antony and Cleopatra* begins in an atmosphere of luxury and languor, with the hero dismissing news from Rome and idly wondering: 'What sport to-night?' . . . *Coriolanus* reveals Rome in its pristine and uncorrupted state, with both the virtues and defects of its lack of sophistication. The Rome of *Antony and Cleopatra*, by contrast, is sophisticated to the point of decadence, a world in which the possibilities for living like a traditional Roman have been virtually played out, leaving a man like Antony to search out new pleasures to 'sharpen' his jaded 'appetite'.[25]

What Shakespeare does, in each of the Roman plays, is to give us a vision of a society which is so impregnated by its value system that characters do not merely interact with each other but with the history, goals and aspirations of Rome. Cicero's injunction was, for the most part, actively assented to: 'This, then, ought to be the chief end of all men, to make the interest of each individual and of the whole body politic identical'.[26] But how precise can we be in specifying the values which animate Shakespeare's Rome? How does the relative weight attaching to these values vary from one play to another? What values are constant throughout the

Roman plays? The more accurately these questions can be answered the closer we are able to move in the direction of acquiring a clear critical understanding of the plays.

The fundamental values which permeate the Roman plays are: service to the state, fortitude, constancy, valour, friendship, love of family and respect for the gods. The relative importance of these values varies according to the condition of Rome and its stage of development. Most of these values reinforce each other, but occasionally there is an intense conflict of values. Normally the great Roman attributes of fortitude, constancy and valour are cultivated to ensure that a man fulfils the goal of serving the state; likewise, due respect for the gods is an essential duty in ensuring that they look favourably on Rome. The demands of friendship can, of course, place a man in conflict with his desire to serve his country: such is the fate of Brutus in having to choose between his personal attachment to Julius Caesar and his loyalty to the Republic of Rome. For Brutus, service to his society means the preservation of a particular kind of Rome – a free, democratic Rome. The case of Coriolanus is more complicated. He devotes himself, body and soul, to his society and to his family. His initial problem arises when he is asked by his mother to stand for political office. He has served Rome in a superhuman way on the battlefield but knows full well that his nature cannot endure the compromises required in the political arena. He tells his mother:

> Know, good mother,
> I had rather be their servant in my way
> Than sway with them in theirs.
> (II.i.200–2)

Above all, he cannot pretend to sympathize with the plebeians: his patrician contempt must have free reign. Ultimately, love of his mother overcomes his resistance. As a consequence he is placed in a position where he jeopardizes the political equilibrium of the state. He perceives his banishment as a betrayal by the patricians (he has not fought for the plebeians so their behaviour causes him little anguish) and determines to revenge himself on 'ingrateful Rome' (that is, the intellectual, emotional, and physical crucible in which his spirit was forged). He is deterred from the final assault by appeals to his love of family and his loyalty to Rome. Ranged against these powerful forces is a burning desire for revenge created by an intense sense of betrayal – betrayal by all he has known and loved. The deeply inculcated values of devotion to family and service to Rome triumph over the passionate thirst for revenge.

Mark Antony is the total antithesis of Coriolanus. He implicitly rejects all that Rome stands for in allowing himself to be seduced by Cleopatra. Along with Cleopatra goes a whole set of beliefs which are antithetical to Roman values. As he embraces a new culture Antony relinquishes his martial qualities. The price paid by the Egyptianized Antony is the total loss of the Roman qualities of vigour and efficiency. Symbolically this is represented by means of the loss of his sword ('O, thy vile lady!/She has robb'd me of my sword' (IV.xiv.22–3)) and his final inability to despatch himself efficiently. Ironically, Mark Antony is described by Octavius as having been the embodiment of Roman virtue. As he berates Lepidus about Antony's frivolous escapades in the East he suddenly recreates a picture of the Antony of former times:

> Antony,
> Leave thy lascivious wassails. When thou once
> Was beaten from Modena, where thou slew'st
> Hirtius and Pansa, consuls, at thy heel
> Did famine follow, whom thou fought'st against,
> Though daintily brought up, with patience more
> Than savages could suffer. Thou didst drink
> The stale of horses, and the gilded puddle
> Which beasts would cough at: thy palate then did deign
> The roughest berry, on the rudest hedge;
> Yea, like the stag, when snow the pasture sheets,
> The barks of trees thou browsed. On the Alps
> It is reported thou didst eat strange flesh,
> Which some did die to look on: and all this –
> It wounds thine honour that I speak it now –
> Was borne so like a soldier, that thy cheek
> So much as lank'd not.

(I.iv.55–71)

This wonderful speech, which is based on Plutarch's account of Antony's suffering and resilience, accumulates enormous power and resonance by reason of being placed in the mouth of Octavius. The very character who despises Antony for his betrayal of Roman ideals and values renders the most vivid description of the greatness that was Antony. This is not the kind of picture that Mark Antony creates of Julius Caesar on the day he overcame the Nervii, rather it is the portrayal of a true Roman in defeat. Endurance, fortitude, constancy: these are the values which are extolled. The changes Shakespeare makes from Plutarch all have the effect of accentuating these qualities: Plutarch's 'puddle water' becomes 'the stale of horses'; where the historian states that Antony's 'chiefest want . . . was famine' but that 'he was of such a strong nature, that by pacience he would overcome any adversitie, and the heavier fortune lay upon him, the more constant shewed he himself', the dramatist gives famine the vitality and persistence of a wild beast ('at thy heel/Did famine follow'). Where Plutarch comments that Antony was 'brought up in all finenes and superfluitie' Shakespeare has 'Though daintily brought up', and he drinks that 'Which beasts would cough at'; he eats 'strange flesh/Which some did die to look on', and all this suffering 'Was borne so like a soldier, that thy cheek/So much as lank'd not'.

A major value which appears throughout the Roman plays (except in *Titus Andronicus*) is contempt for the plebeians. Coriolanus is the only character who denigrates the plebeians to their faces, but the feeling is universal. Two criticisms of the people are continually articulated by patricians. The first is that the common men are unstable, subject to the conflicting views and pressures which are directed towards them. Second, they are denounced for being dirty. Most readers or auditors would notice this feature but few would recognize the ubiquity of this attitude. This is partly because every expression of contempt is tightly interwoven into the dramatic structure. Casca, for instance, reveals his attitude while simultaneously giving full rein to his assumed persona as detached cynic. Having described Caesar's rejection of the crown, he goes on to provide a colourful description of the plebeians or the 'rabblement' as he calls them (a wonderful piece of verbal inventiveness):

> the rabblement hooted, and clapp'd their chopt hands, and threw up their sweaty night-caps, and uttered such a deal of stinking breath because Caesar refus'd the crown, that it had, almost, choked Caesar; for he swounded, and fell down at it. And for mine own part, I durst not laugh, for fear of opening my lips and receiving the bad air.
>
> (I.ii.240–7)

He illustrates Caesar's control of the crowd by means of a comparison with the actors' manipulation of the audience: 'If the tag-rag people did not clap him and hiss him, according as he pleas'd and displeas'd them, as they use to do the players in the theatre, I am no true man' (I.ii.255–8). Casca gives full scope to his own theatrical performance by imitating the response of a group of girls to Caesar's fit before concluding with a devastating indictment of their gullibility – or his cynicism: 'Three or four wenches, where I stood, cried, "Alas, good soul", and forgave him with all their hearts; but there's no heed to be taken of them; if Caesar had stabb'd their mothers, they would have done no less' (I.ii.268–72).

Significantly, the term 'plebeian' is seldom used in the plays. Rather, such epithets as 'tag-rag people' are employed to reveal the speaker's disdain and to suggest that they consist of a gallimaufry, a mixture, lacking clear shape or direction. Moreover, the parallel between the relationship of actor to audience and patrician to plebeian occurs on a number of occasions in *Julius Caesar* and *Coriolanus*. Casca describes Caesar's manipulation of the crowd, and the latter's astute response to the signals which he receives from them. Simultaneously, we see Casca's own attempt to play a role in which he will appear worldly wise and cynically detached. He saves a powerful if ambiguous piece of news as a parting shot: 'Marullus

and Flavius, for pulling scarfs off Caesar's images, are put to silence'
(I.ii.282–3). At the other end of the spectrum from Casca's 'performance'
is Octavius Caesar's dismissal of the news that Pompey is attracting a great
deal of popular support:

> This common body,
> Like to a vagabond flag upon the stream,
> Goes to, and back, lackeying the varying tide,
> To rot itself with motion.
>
> (I.iv.44–7)

Octavius uses two words which effectively embody and convey a sense of
the worthlessness and cowardly subservience of the commonality: 'vagabond' and 'lackeying'. Finally, his contempt for the plebeians and his
insistence on their ineffectuality is encapsulated in the word 'rot'. Octavius
does not analyse the reasons for the movement of the plebeians away
from himself towards Pompey; rather he dismisses this turnabout as
characteristic.

Antony, who proves to be the greatest manipulator of the people in the
Roman plays, dismisses them without the scorn of Octavius or the biting
sarcasm of Casca, merely contenting himself to reflect on a sad
commonplace:

> Our slippery people,
> Whose love is never link'd to the deserver
> Till his deserts are past, begin to throw
> Pompey the Great, and all his dignities
> Upon his son . . .
>
> (I.ii.183–7)

The sense of the plebeians as dirty and foul-smelling is forcefully asserted
by Cleopatra:

> mechanic slaves
> With greasy aprons, rules, and hammers shall
> Uplift us to the view. In their thick breaths,
> Rank of gross diet, shall we be enclouded,
> And forc'd to drink their vapour.
>
> (V.ii.208–12)

The characteristics of uncleanliness and inconstancy are brought out effectively, with a distinct comic element, in the dialogue between Menenius
and the plebeians. The old patrician refers to the advancing citizens as
'clusters' before chastising them for causing the exile of Coriolanus and
precipitating the crisis:

> You are they
> That made the air unwholesome when you cast

> Your stinking greasy caps in hooting at
> Coriolanus' exile.
>
> (IV.vi.130–3)

Their irresponsibility, inconstancy and comic inadequacy is revealed by their defensive comments, but they do not appear as contemptible in the eyes of the audience as they do in the eyes of their social superiors. Of course, no character in the Roman plays can match Coriolanus for vituperation. His expressions of contempt have a unique quality.

Another vital feature of Shakespeare's Roman world is that it is essentially masculine. The cardinal Roman virtues relate primarily to the male. Indeed, when Octavius denounces Antony he insists that his great adversary has relinquished his manhood. Antony, he claims, is

> not more manlike
> Than Cleopatra; nor the Queen of Ptolemy
> More womanly than he . . .
>
> (I.iv.5–7)

Women, for Octavius, are associated with weakness and inconstancy. As he expresses the point,

> women are not
> In their best fortunes strong; but want will perjure
> The ne'er-touched vestal . . .
>
> (III.xii.29–31)

Octavius' description of the Antony who is in thrall to the Egyptian queen is the total antithesis of the Antony of old who epitomized the Roman virtues of courage, constancy and durability (I.iv.55–71). A little reflection reveals just how powerfully women embody masculine qualities in the plays. Volumnia is the supreme example of the Roman matron, in contrast to the gentle femininity that characterizes Coriolanus' wife. Their contemplation of Coriolanus' dangers and actions in battle is revealing:

> VOLUMNIA Methinks I hear hither your husband's drum;
> See him pluck Aufidius down by th'hair,
> As children from a bear, the Volsces shunning him.
> Methinks I see him stamp thus, and call thus:
> 'Come on you cowards, you were got in fear
> Though you were born in Rome.' His bloody brow
> With his mail'd hand then wiping, forth he goes
> Like to a harvest man that's task'd to mow
> Or all, or lose his hire.
> VIRGILIA His bloody brow? O Jupiter, no blood!
> VOLUMNIA Away you fool! it more becomes a man
> Than gilt his trophy. The breasts of Hecuba

17

When she did suckle Hector, look'd not lovelier
Than Hector's forehead when it spit forth blood
At Grecian sword contemning . . .

VIRGILIA Heavens bless my lord from fell Aufidius!
VOLUMNIA He'll beat Aufidius' head below his knee,
And tread upon his neck.

(I.iii.29–47)

Even Portia makes her plea to Brutus in terms that assert her masculine qualities, though the scene as a whole reveals her gentleness, warmth and attractive femininity:

I grant I am a woman; but withal
A woman that Lord Brutus took to wife;
I grant I am a woman; but withal
A woman well reputed, Cato's daughter.
Think you I am no stronger than my sex,
Being so father'd, and so husbanded?
Tell me your counsels, I will not disclose 'em.
I have made strong proof of my constancy,
Giving myself a voluntary wound
Here, in the thigh: can I bear that with patience,
And not my husband's secrets?

(II.i.292–302)

More remarkably, Cleopatra, who represents the chief threat and challenge to Roman values, finally succumbs to them, promising to die 'after the high Roman fashion' (IV.xv.87). Just before killing herself she asserts:

My resolution's plac'd, and I have nothing
Of woman in me: now from head to foot
I am marble-constant: now the fleeting moon
No planet is of mine.

(V.ii.237–40)

Here is the supreme renunciation of the qualities of variety, luxury, indulgence and extravagance associated with the most vital woman of all. She strips herself of the very elements which made her enchanting. Now is the moment for capriciousness to give way to constancy.

Although it is possible to enumerate the values which pervade all the Roman plays, it is evident that the relative emphasis attaching to these values varies from one play to another. In *Coriolanus* Shakespeare portrays a primitive Rome. Rome has acquired a sense of identity, of superiority even, but it is also aware of its precariousness. In such a situation the most effective way of serving the state is through physical courage. As Cominius makes the point,

> It is held
> That valour is the chiefest virtue and
> Most dignifies the haver . . .
>> (II.ii.83–5)

Again, in asserting his right to speak out in defence of Coriolanus, Cominius reveals the depth of the individual's obligation to the state:

> I have been consul, and can show for Rome
> Her enemies' marks upon me. I do love
> My country's good with a respect more tender,
> More holy and profound, than mine own life,
> My dear wife's estimate, her womb's increase
> And treasure of my loins . . .
>> (III.iii.110–15)

This commitment to service is total and authenticated by battle scars: there is no question of calculation – here is a fundamental statement of principles which form the essential substance of living, rather than a presentation of abstract precepts.

When we move to the Rome of *Julius Caesar* the sense of service is again powerfully articulated by Brutus:

> If it be aught toward the general good,
> Set honour in one eye, and death i'th'other,
> And I will look on both indifferently;
> For let the gods so speed me as I love
> The name of honour more than I fear death.
>> (I.ii.84–8)

Once more, service to the society is the paramount value transcending the importance of life itself; but here there is no automatic suggestion of physical courage on the battlefield. Although Brutus and Cassius have to take to the battlefield, the whole feel of the play is that public service is manifested primarily in the councils of state. Indeed, the central issue of the play revolves around the threat to the opportunity for political service through the usurpation of power by Caesar. This is a politically mature Rome with a sophisticated culture and a proud history. The powerful orator and statesman Cicero makes a brief appearance; Cato's greatness is invoked; Lucius Junius Brutus' legendary feat of freeing Rome from the last of its kings constitutes a critical element in the emotional pressure of events; and Cassius, in describing his rescue of Caesar from the Tiber, displays an awareness of the unbroken history of Rome from its very foundation:

> I, as Aeneas, our great ancestor,
> Did from the flames of Troy upon his shoulder

The old Anchises bear, so from the waves of Tiber
Did I the tired Caesar.

(I.ii.111–14)

Here, then, is a self-conscious Rome: a society aware of its past as a living organism, as an essential part of existing reality, which is a source of strength and duty; achievements and ideals impose ethical demands. But there is a sense of idealism being threatened. The play opens with a celebration of Caesar's latest victory, but he has triumphed over Romans, not foreigners. Flavius and Marullus immediately introduce us to a world of political conflict. Their dialogue reveals that Caesar is hated and feared, but the common people are unreflecting: those who formerly cheered Pompey now celebrate Caesar's triumph over Pompey's sons. Whereas *Coriolanus* opens with a starving mob desperately attempting to assert itself, and going on to achieve a constitutional foothold in society, the crowd in *Julius Caesar* appears content and footloose, constituting a potential force available to those most able to manipulate them. The plebeians, then, are outsiders, observers of the political process who become insiders only during political crises. They have been absorbed into the body politic while being simultaneously neutralized. The feeling at the outset is that they have their bread and circuses but have no more power and influence than they possess in *Coriolanus* once they have secured their tribunes. The cobbler can bait his social superior with impunity, suggesting a degree of social control which is free and subtle rather than tight and brutal (surely the point Shakespeare wishes to convey through the cobbler's banter). In this mature Rome political conflict is not between patrician and plebeian but takes place within the patrician class. With this political maturity there is a subtle undermining of Roman values. Brutus is the exceptional man. Antony seems to speak the truth when he says,

All the conspirators save only he
Did that they did in envy of great Caesar;

(V.v.69–70)

Significantly, the pleas to Brutus to free Rome from the tyranny of Caesar are manufactured by Cassius (as opposed to representing a genuine appeal by diverse people as they are in Plutarch). Cassius admits in his soliloquy that if he held Brutus' place in Caesar's affection he could never be persuaded to join the conspiracy. This is a world where Roman values still exert a powerful influence, but personal antagonisms and political ambitions are breaking through the fabric. Brutus is drawn into the conspiracy because his reputation as a man of integrity will serve to provide political credibility to the conspirators. This reveals that values still count but that they are also subject to manipulation by ambitious men. The proscription scene is stunning in its display of political cynicism: a death list of political adversaries is drawn up in a cold and brutal way with relatives sacrificed to buy the deaths of personal rivals; Caesar's will is distorted to raise funds; and Lepidus is drawn in as a make-weight to deflect opprobrium from Antony and Octavius – who clearly intend to remove him when the time is ripe.

By the time we reach *Antony and Cleopatra* Rome has moved far beyond the stage of tension between democracy and potential dictatorship. The nominally threefold world is effectively a two/fold world in which two powerful men compete for absolute control. But Roman values and ideals have not been jettisoned. Octavius believes in the Roman world and Roman destiny; he is conscious of past achievements and the need for an ordered Empire. The vision of Rome has moved physically from city to Empire, but the qualities that made Rome are magnificently invoked by Octavius in his picture of the old Antony. Nevertheless, Rome has reached the point where the supreme leader is not a magnificent warrior like Coriolanus, an admired idealist like Brutus, or a commander of political genius like Julius Caesar. Rather he is the quintessential civil servant and political manipulator. He is no orator, no fighter, no great general – nor is he a charismatic leader: he is simply aware of the nature of the world in which he lives, and possesses the will and dedication to overcome obstacles to his sole domination. Perhaps the finest example of dramatic irony in the whole of Shakespeare occurs when Antony pleads with Octavius Caesar to 'Be a child o'the time' (II.vii.98). This man is precisely that and is determined to become, in the words of Thidias, 'The universal landlord' (III.xiii.72) or, as he is described by Cleopatra, 'Sole sir o'the world' (V.ii.119).

It would be a mistake, however, to see the Rome of *Antony and Cleopatra* as being devoid of its old ideals. Those ideals are viewed with greater detachment and are used by individuals for their own ends rather than constituting essential principles by which life is lived. But Caesar's personal temperament is sympathetic to the Roman ideal of austerity. He is puritanical in outlook and suffers no tension between his political and private lives (with one possible exception, but even the sacrifice of his beloved sister to political expediency seems to cause him no heartache). Octavius Caesar is the quintessential political man: for him politics is life. He does not devote himself to public service; instead he gathers to himself control of the Roman Empire in order to fulfil his personal aspirations. There can be no danger of Octavius Caesar falling foul of his great uncle's desire to appear the public servant ('What touches us ourself shall be last serv'd' (III.i.8)).

The marked shift in the values that animate the political life of Rome in this play is most effectively revealed by Pompey's response to Menas' offer to cut the throats of Antony, Octavius and Lepidus:

> Ah, this thou shouldst have done,
> And not have spoke on't! In me 'tis villainy,
> In thee, 't had been good service. Thou must know,
> 'Tis not my profit that does lead mine honour;
> Mine honour, it. Repent that e'er thy tongue
> Hath so betray'd thine act. Being done unknown,
> I should have found it afterwards well done,
> But must condemn it now. Desist, and drink.
>
> (II.vii.72–9)

Pompey is not appalled by the suggestion, but is unwilling to have his reputation damaged by sanctioning the act. This is a world in which the leading politicians are willing to contemplate the basest acts but realize that there still exists a constraint in the form of values to which their countrymen, even politicians, subscribe. But Pompey goes further and attempts to put a gloss of moral purpose on his whole enterprise:

> 'Tis not my profit that does lead mine honour;
> Mine honour, it.
>
> (II.vii.75–6)

Here is an expression of the desire to have a moral purpose. Ironically, Octavius, who is the fortunate beneficiary of this squeamishness, has no moral qualms when it comes to disposing of the political opponents with whom he sits down to eat. He kills them all in turn but always in a way which lends the colour of justification to his actions. Even when he finally defeats Antony he invites the bystanders to consult their correspondence in order to see for themselves how he was blameless in the conflict (V.i.73–7). Octavius has it both ways: total control but with a public presentation of 'facts' that exonerate him from any suggestion of being the guilty party.

Cantor suggests that Shakespeare perceived the decline in the moral values of Rome, and with a feeling of sorrow portrayed the process in these three plays. The argument being pursued here is that Shakespeare became powerfully aware of the enormous role of values in shaping Roman society and in influencing the lives of famous historical characters such as Coriolanus and Brutus, but that rather than being concerned with the rise and decline of Rome he was fascinated by the changing texture of Roman society and by the nature of the interaction between these characters and their society. Shakespeare's Roman worlds are so powerfully recreated that they are fascinating in themselves, but the greatest fascination of all is in observing the interplay between proclivities, idiosyncrasies, ambitions, strengths and weaknesses of characters, and the arena of social and political values in which they act out their roles.

The Most Lamentable Romaine Tragedie of Titus Andronicus, to use the title which was printed on the three Quarto editions, is usually excluded from discussions of Shakespeare's Roman plays on the grounds that first, it does not share the source material which is the foundation upon which Shakespeare constructs *Julius Caesar*, *Antony and Cleopatra* and *Coriolanus*; and second, that it is a straightforward 'revenge tragedy'. A third reason, more often implied than made explicit, is that this is early Shakespeare (possibly the dramatist's first play) or not wholly Shakespeare, and consequently is inferior to the truly Roman plays. There is no doubt that the source material available to Shakespeare for *Titus* is of an entirely different nature from Plutarch's *Lives*, but that the play is 'merely' a revenge tragedy (possibly intended to cash in on the popularity of Kyd's *The Spanish Tragedy*) is open to serious challenge, as is the question of its dramatic power, which has been demonstrated by two great productions: Peter Brook's of 1955 with Sir Laurence Olivier as Titus, and most recently by the Royal Shakespeare Company's towering production staged at the Swan Theatre in 1987/8 (directed by Deborah Warner with Brian Cox in the title role).

When considering the Rome portrayed in *Titus* Terence Spencer implied that the dramatist was cavalier in his treatment of Roman institutions, being more concerned 'not to get it all right, but to get it all in'.[27] Given that Shakespeare was not, however, dealing with the historically familiar and well-documented histories found in Plutarch, he exercised a great deal of freedom in shaping the characters, events and society portrayed in *Titus*. What is immediately striking is that he worked assiduously to create an intense sense of Rome, and a very specific Rome, even if the institutional forms embodied in the play are drawn from diverse periods. As Spencer points out, 'One could say almost without paradox that, in many respects, *Titus Andronicus* is a more typical Roman play, a more characteristic piece of Roman history, than the three great plays of Shakespeare which are generally grouped under that name'.[28]

Shakespeare's commitment to the creation of a Roman world is recognized by a number of scholars, though it is true, as Miola claims, 'Probably the most striking feature of modern critical reaction to *Titus Andronicus* is the persistent refusal to consider it one of Shakespeare's Roman plays'.[29] Miola himself is ardent in his espousal of *Titus* as a Roman play, and in an impressive chapter enumerates many of its Roman features (he makes the interesting observation that the word Rome appears more frequently in this play than in *Julius Caesar* and *Antony and Cleopatra* together); he is thorough in tracing all the classical allusions, paying special attention to those relating to Troy. He concludes that 'despite the crudity of content and technique, *Titus Andronicus* is an important engagement with Rome and Romans'.[30] Likewise, Nicholas Brooke in *Shakespeare's Early Tragedies* points out that

23

Rome has always for Shakespeare the emotive suggestion of political greatness, and also of political curiosity: his interest in a society different from Tudor England is manifest here in the presentation of a fusion of democracy with Imperial power that pre-figures the political interest of *Julius Caesar* or *Coriolanus*.[31]

Bullough also makes the point that 'The designer of the plot seems to have been interested both in the political ideal of order and unity in the State and in the ancient traditions of Rome from which the later Empire departed'.[32] Although the prose story is set in the late fourth century AD 'in the Time of Theodosius',[33] the only Andronicus of Roman history bearing any resemblance to the protagonist of the story is Andronicus Comnenus who was Emperor of Byzantium (1183–5). Shakespeare realized that the story had little to do with Rome or history, and so was completely free to create the kind of social universe he desired. What is significant is that he does not opt for Rome as a vague background but endeavours to create the feeling of a distinct Roman world. In his other Roman plays Shakespeare was tied very closely to sharply delineated historical events, personalities and institutions. Here he is free, yet chooses to create a palpable sense of Rome and Roman qualities, quite unlike his approach in *King Lear* and *Macbeth*, where background matters and informs the action in subtle ways but does not become a conscious entity as does Rome in *Titus Andronicus*.

One of the most intriguing features of *Titus* is its seminal quality: it spawns two divergent lines of development. One, a concern with human values and their fusion into a social ethos, leads to an exploration of the relationship between the personal and political in the Roman plays. The other development is concerned much more directly with good and evil, the bestial and the spiritual, with the political being pushed to the periphery, a development which reaches its apogee in *King Lear*. The Rome of *Titus Andronicus* aspires to human greatness and achievement, but it is characterized by a confusion of values and lacks an effective mechanism for choosing a leader. This problem is articulated in the opening scene where Marcus, on behalf of the people, offers the position of Emperor to Titus because he is the most deserving man in Rome – that is, because his service to the state has been greatest. But this service has been on the battlefield and so does not signify that he would constitute an ideal choice of political leader – as experience soon demonstrates. Although Titus declines the honour, he nevertheless makes a decisive entry into the political arena by choosing between the two contenders for power. It would take very little political judgment to realize that Saturninus is too unstable to be trusted with political authority, but Titus is either totally blind to his deficiencies or feels that there is some vestige of tradition in favouring the elder brother. Rather than being confused about the

24

institutional forms prevailing in this unhistorical Rome, Shakespeare is exploring the dangers of a system which lacks coherence: a system of primogeniture may place a political incompetent, or worse, in power; a vaguer system of inheritance is likely to produce factionalism and conflict; while the choice of a military hero is almost a formula for disaster. The most attractive feature of the political framework in this Rome is the vulnerability of the Emperor to overthrow by the people – a constraint which is not adequate in the face of a subtle and devious ruler (qualities Saturninus lacks but which Tamora brings to the leadership).

Quite unlike the later Roman plays, the individual voices of plebeians are unheard. They are appealed to directly, and there is a sense of their goodwill and honesty. They are not vacillating; nor are they subject to the contempt of their social superiors (as they are in the later Roman plays). Their choice of Marcus, an eminently good man, as tribune, speaks strongly for their sound judgment. Even so there is a sense of an inadequately articulated political framework. Once the initial political misjudgment occurs, the territory encompassed by the play becomes more elemental, exploring the depths of human depravity and savagery. No thought is given to the *institutional* barbarism of human sacrifice by the victims of *individual* savagery. Instead there is a gradual realization of the fragility of civilized society. The society which creates poetry and reveres learning is also 'a wilderness of tigers'. It is because of this fact that the interrogation of human values and their articulation through social and political systems is crucial. Once the bestiality of Tamora, her family and her lover is defeated through Titus' monstrous revenge, Rome achieves another chance of establishing a just and coherent institutional framework. Marcus and Lucilius show promise of providing good leadership – in an alliance with their ancient enemies, the Goths. Even so, the future is uncertain. The audience is made aware of the nature of the political difficulties. In *King Lear* concern with the fate of Lear and Cordelia is overwhelming. The audience is aware of the need for moral leadership but is not able to focus on the future. At the end of *Titus* there is a profound sense of the need to establish a humane and durable *political system*. Both plays suggest that human society is always vulnerable to a bestiality that may be kept in check but can never be eradicated. The political awareness, however, is much greater at the end of *Titus* – one indicator that this play merits inclusion in any discussion of the Roman plays.

The doubts about Shakespeare's authorship of *Titus* commenced with the wholly unsubstantiated comments of Edward Ravenscroft in 1687, but, as Stanley Wells points out in a recent introduction to the play,

both his criticism and his doubts have been loudly echoed until well into the twentieth century. They have gone hand in hand because the fundamental reason why people have doubted that Shakespeare wrote the play has been that they found it so distasteful.[34]

G.R. Hibbard rightly comments that

> normally the evidence for Shakespeare's sole authorship – the fact that it was attributed to him by Francis Meres in his *Palladis Tamia* (1598), and its inclusion in the First Folio – would be accepted as decisive.[35]

The techniques employed to cast doubt on Shakespeare's authorship were subject to withering criticism by E.K. Chambers in 1924,[36] but it was not until 1943 with the publication of *The Authorship of 'Titus Andronicus'* by Hereward T. Price that there was an emphatic assertion of Shakespeare's sole authorship. Price made many perceptive comments on several facets of the play and drew attention to its anticipation of key elements in *Othello* and *King Lear*.[37] Dover Wilson, the editor of the New Cambridge edition of the play, remained unconvinced by Price and credited the overall design of the play, along with most of Act I, to George Peele.[38] Significantly, he expressed a low opinion of the play. Although Bullough asks the rhetorical question, 'could any other dramatist but Shakespeare have written this *tour de force*?', and goes on to claim that 'the rhetorical skill and flexibility, the sustained power of dramatic movement shown throughout . . . suggest that Shakespeare planned the play' he loses the courage of his convictions by adding the proviso that Shakespeare 'probably wrote most of it', leaving room for the possible collaboration of Peele.[39] The editor of the Arden edition, J.C. Maxwell, weighed the evidence carefully and was led towards the conclusion that Shakespeare was the sole author but suffered a loss of nerve and allowed for the influence of Peele in the first act.[40] Sylvan Barnet, editor of the Signet edition (1953), finds no reason to ascribe part of the work to other hands,[41] a view shared more recently by E.M. Waith, the editor of the Oxford edition of the play.[42] Wells appears to have an open mind on the subject.[43] The view offered here is that *Titus Andronicus* is wholly Shakespeare's and is a masterly and powerful play judged not only by the standard of Shakespeare's contemporaries but by the standards of Shakespeare himself.

The stage history of *Titus* is meagre. As Stanley Wells points out, 'it was the first Stratford-upon-Avon production of *Titus Andronicus*, by Peter Brook in 1955, that really brought the play back into the repertory and established Titus himself as a great tragic role'. However, despite the impact of Laurence Olivier's 'overwhelming performances as Titus',[44] Brook cut over 650 lines. John Barton's productions at the Old Vic (1957) and in Stratford-upon-Avon (1981) were both performed as parts of a double bill so that cutting was even more severe (850 lines). The 1987–8 production at the RSC's Swan Theatre, therefore, constituted a watershed in several respects: it was uncut; it was performed in an Elizabethan-type theatre; and it accepted all the challenges presented by the text: the grotesque humour, the presentation of all the horrors, including the multiple deaths at the final banquet, and the powerfully structured rhetoric. There was a total absence of embarrassed laughter. The laughter evoked by the text was given full rein by the actors but they never lost control: the momentary release accomplished, the fierce tension was quickly re-established. Much of the power of difficult moments (that is, moments that appear difficult from reading the text) arose from the actions and responses of those characters surrounding the speaker. For instance, when Titus burst into laughter before replying to Marcus' puzzled question, 'I have not another tear to shed', the latter's expression changed from bewilderment to pity. During the fly-killing scene (III.ii) the audience was confronted by the face of Lavinia tortured with anguish as Titus frantically pursued the logic of his fractured mind. Embarrassed laughter was impossible. Likewise, when Titus killed Lavinia (she was sitting on his lap) by means of a sudden movement that broke her neck there was a gasp of horror from the audience. The scene, just prior to that, in which Titus cuts the throats of Demetrius and Chiron, was one of terrifying realism: the sheer deliberation of the scene with the broken Lavinia advancing with the bowl between her stumps generated a feeling of terror and pity such as the present writer has previously never experienced in the theatre. In the final scene the exchange of looks between Titus and Tamora drained any possibility of embarrassed laughter as the Queen gradually gained a realization that her sons really *were* in the pie. Her attempt to remove the bits from her mouth aroused enormous empathy even for this tigress. The subsequent surge of killings provided a climax of horror rather than detachment through absurdity. Similarly, the moment of near farce when Titus, Marcus and Lucilius debate over who shall give his hand to ransom Titus' sons, took place with Lavinia writhing on stage, presenting a picture which eliminated any suggestion of burlesque. As Titus' hand was amputated he was cradled by a seemingly compassionate Aaron in a scene which revealed the emotional value of physical propinquity. The tearing of this vision by Aaron's later exclamation '[I] almost broke my heart with extreme laughter' (V.i.113) made his comments all the more horrific.

As the editor of the Arden edition points out,

No source for *Titus* survives in a form which we know to have been available to Shakespeare. But a single copy (in the Folger Library) of a mid-eighteenth-century chap-book giving a version not based on Shakespeare may be in essentials pre-Shakespearian . . . Its title-page claims that it is 'Newly Translated from the Italian Copy printed at Rome', and it may indeed be of Italian origin. The ballad, 'The Lamentable and Tragicall History of Titus Andronicus', which is printed with the prose story, and is also included in Percy's *Reliques* as 'Titus Andronicus's Complaint', is entirely dependent on the prose story, though some of the stanzas have been rearranged to bring the order of events into closer conformity with the play. All the differences between the prose story and the play are compatible with the hypothesis that the former is substantially identical with the source of the latter.[45]

Eugene M. Waith, in commenting on this source, adds,

We can be sure, however, that behind it lie the stories of the rape of Lucretia, of Appius and Virginia, probably of Thyestes, and most certainly of the rape of Philomela. Shakespeare of course knew these stories as well as the Titus-story which they influenced. How much he may have been affected by Seneca is debatable.[46]

Emrys Jones, in *The Origins of Shakespeare*, advances a persuasive argument for the influence of a Latin translation of Euripides' *Hecuba*.[47] It is not necessary to trace the connections between these diverse sources and Shakespeare's play, but it is instructive to note the changes which the dramatist makes from the prose story (assuming, as seems highly probable, that the story contained in the chap-book is identical or very close to the version used by Shakespeare).

The differences between the prose story and the play can be summarized as follows: Shakespeare invents the dispute about the succession along with Titus' election and his disastrous choice of Saturninus. Likewise, the dramatist invents the sacrifice of Alarbus. In the prose story Lavinia is betrothed to the Emperor's *son*. Her rape and mutilation are quite separate from the murder of her betrothed. Shakespeare conflates the incidents of the murder of Bassianus (the Emperor's brother and rival) and the rape of Lavinia, and locates her as a central element in the family conflict which erupts as a result of Saturninus choosing her for his wife. Whereas all three of Titus' surviving sons are executed in the prose story, Shakespeare preserves Lucilius so that he can return with an army of Goths and attempt to establish a new order in Rome at the end of the play. Thus the play ends as the story does not with a strong Emperor at the helm. Two character changes are also significant. The Emperor is a gullible weakling in the story, whereas in the play, although he is governed by Tamora, he displays a vicious streak and is dangerously unstable. The character of Aaron undergoes an even more remarkable transformation. In contrast to the story, where he is primarily the Queen's instrument, he becomes his own master in the play, exhibiting a dynamism, energy, guile and viciousness which makes him a frightening adversary and the embodiment of evil. Aaron is not in thrall to his vices as Tamora is, nor is he merely an inhuman monster like Demetrius and Chiron: he is, rather, a self-conscious villain who revels in causing pain and suffering. He is, indeed, dedicated to iniquity and ultimately proclaims his creed openly. Those who have found a humanity in his care of his child completely misunderstand the nature of his egotism: his is not the natural tenderness of parent for child, it is the projection of self into the future. The final difference between story and play is that the Roman–Goth conflict of the former is diminished, as the central dramatic clash occurs between the family of Tamora and her entourage on the one hand and the Andronici on the other. This reshaping by Shakespeare is highly significant because there is no simple duality between Rome and the barbarians: Rome becomes increasingly barbaric under the influence of Tamora, but the Goths in their support of Lucilius become the instruments for transforming Rome from the wilderness of tigers to an ordered community.

Although the setting of *Titus* is nominally the fourth century AD and does, therefore, relate to a historically later period than the other Roman plays, it *feels* earlier. Indeed, Shakespeare has gone to great lengths to convey a sense of a primitive Rome. Paradoxically, Shakespeare's first attempt at writing a Roman play, though dealing with the latest historical period encompassed by them, conveys an impression of a very early Rome – the embryo of the state which is embodied in the later plays. One crucial difference between this play and the others is that it contains no political substance. There are political factions but the basis of the factionalism appears to be purely personal. Conflicting political values are never articulated. What is enormously powerful is a sense of Rome: Rome as a physical setting, as a family possessing a proud ancestry traceable to Troy. The invocation of images of Troy begins in this play and continues throughout the Roman plays. Moreover, there is a tension between the self-perception of a pious, proud, close-knit community imbued with a sense of civilization, and the practice of barbaric religious rites. Whereas all the other Roman plays exhibit antagonism between patricians and plebeians, in this play no such strain is perceived. At no point are the people spoken of contemptuously by the patricians. The felt sense of pressure is between the aspiration for a truly civilized society with respect for learning, and the immediate exhibition of a barbarous ritual which sets the tragedy in motion.

Indeed it is only through an immediate awareness of the Roman quality of the play that Titus' killing of his son becomes anything other than the wilful act of a vicious character who is thereafter unable to command the sympathy of the audience. Shakespeare is careful to create an intense, pulsating feeling of Rome from the opening moments of the play. Even before the entrance of the triumphant Titus, the brothers and competitors for the throne of Rome, Saturninus and Bassianus, address the people directly. Saturninus opens the play with his plea:

Noble patricians, patrons of my right,
Defend the justice of my cause with arms;
And, countrymen, my loving followers,
Plead my successive title with your swords . . .
                            (I.i.1–4)

While Bassianus commences his appeal for support with the line: 'Romans,
friends, followers, favourers of my right' (I.i.9), Marcus in rejecting both
claims announces that Titus is the people's choice as due reward for his
'many good and great deserts to Rome' (I.i.24). These include courage
and sacrifice:

                    five times he hath return'd
Bleeding to Rome, bearing his valiant sons
In coffins from the field,
                            (I.i.33–5)

As the captain makes a path for Titus' entrance he too speaks in ringing
terms of 'Rome's best champion' (I.i.65). The first words spoken by Titus
are 'Hail, Rome' before paying tribute to his sons in a manner which
emphasizes the family of the Andronici and the family of Rome with its
ancestry in Troy:

Romans, of five and twenty valiant sons,
Half of the number that King Priam had,
Behold the poor remains, alive and dead.
These that survive, let Rome reward with love;
These that I bring unto their latest home,
With burial amongst their ancestors.
                            (I.i.79–84)

As the history, traditions and suffering of Rome are encapsulated in Titus'
speech, so the values of Rome are soon subject to severe scrutiny. Titus'
eldest son Lucius calls for a sacrifice in the name of Roman religion:

Give us the proudest prisoner of the Goths,
That we may hew his limbs, and on a pile
Ad manes fratrum sacrifice his flesh
Before this earthy prison of their bones,
That so the shadows be not unappeas'd,
Nor we disturb'd with prodigies on earth.
                            (I.i.96–101)

Despite Tamora's desperate but logical plea that her sons no less than
those of Titus have merely served their country, Titus accedes to Lucius'
request, giving him Alarbus, Tamora's eldest son. The triumphant exclamation of Lucius is significant:

Away with him, and make a fire straight,
And with our swords, upon a pile of wood,
Let's hew his limbs till they be clean consum'd.
(I.i.127–9)

Two of the most important images in the play relate to plants and limbs
and one of the masterly features of the language is the way in which
images are paralleled, echoed and juxtaposed to contrast what is beautiful
and natural with what is ugly and unnatural. It is ironic that Lucius is the
auditor when Aaron describes the rape and mutilation of Lavinia:

They cut thy sister's tongue and ravish'd her,
And cut her hands and trimm'd her as thou sawest.
(V.i.92–3)

Lucius is naturally horrified by the expression and cries 'O detestable
villain! Call'st thou that trimming?' (V.i.94).

The sacrifice is an action of institutionalized barbarity, whereas the
rape and mutilation is one of inhuman savagery. Shakespeare is evidently
concerned with probing the depths of human viciousness, and this play
can be seen very clearly as a precursor of *King Lear* (including the powerful animal imagery, with society being viewed as a 'wilderness of tigers')
while Iago is in a direct line of descent from Aaron. Lucius reports,

See, lord and father, how we have perform'd
Our Roman rites: Alarbus' limbs are lopp'd,
And entrails feed the sacrificing fire,
Whose smoke like incense doth perfume the sky.
(I.i.142–5)

Shakespeare is provoking questions about the nature of Roman rituals
not only by presenting an account of the events but by means of the
incongruity of the language employed by Lucius, with limbs 'lopp'd' like
branches and 'entrails' feeding a fire which then 'perfumes' the sky. The
numerous references to books, and Titus' beautifully expressed offer to
Lavinia:

Come, and take choice of all my library,
And so beguile thy sorrow,
(IV.i.34–5)

emphasize the gap between Roman belief in their civilized values and
the barbarous action of the sacrifice. Even the ravenous tigress Tamora
denounces the action as 'cruel, irreligious piety!' (I.i.130). If Roman
religion is subject to critical scrutiny, so too is Roman pride. Titus kills
his son Mutius for barring his way in Rome. The whole quarrel arises
from Titus' passionate desire to serve Saturninus. He declines the offer

31

of being made Emperor; chooses the elder of the Emperor's sons to succeed; and immediately accepts Saturninus' offer of marrying Lavinia without consulting her or even being aware that she is about to become the wife of Bassianus. An alert, politically self-interested Titus could have glory and status but he doesn't even think in such selfish terms. So deeply moved is he by the opposition of his sons that he is reluctant to allow the burial of Mutius in the family tomb. Titus commits a terrible wrong out of a zealous desire to serve Rome in a totally unselfish way. Significantly, Tamora warns Saturninus against the immediate casting off of Titus on the grounds that the people may supplant him and elect Titus because the Romans consider ingratitude 'a heinous sin' (I.i.448). A concomitant of service and loyalty in Rome, therefore, is gratitude – a value which remains strong in all the Roman plays as two vivid lines from *Julius Caesar* and *Coriolanus* testify. Antony comments on Caesar's recognition of Brutus as one of the assassins:

> Ingratitude, more strong than traitors' arms,
> Quite vanquish'd him: then burst his mighty heart;
>   (III.ii.187–8)

While Aufidius anticipates Coriolanus as 'pouring war/Into the bowels of ungrateful Rome' (IV.v.130–1).

Thus, throughout the play, Shakespeare invokes a powerful sense of Rome. The Roman people are appealed to directly at the beginning and end of the play (and their voice is decisive); there is an awareness of officials and social classes such as tribunes and patricians; the physical solidity of Rome, with the Capitol as its symbolic centre, is strongly contrasted with the wilderness beyond the walls; its history including the trials and tribulations of wars and its origins in Troy (there are eight references to Troy including some which are extensive) impregnates the play; references to the gods are frequent and Titus appeals directly to them; and finally there is an awareness of a Roman ethos of service, the highest achievement being sacrifice in war – a point emphasized by Titus (III.i.4), Marcus (III.i.167–70) and the Captain (I.i.65).

If all these elements link *Titus* closely with the later Roman plays it differs from them in a number of significant ways. There are fewer *real* political issues than there are in *Coriolanus* and *Julius Caesar*. Likewise, the exploration of the quest for power and the contrasts between *political* personalities and styles are much less potent than in *Antony and Cleopatra*. At the dramatic centre of *Titus* is a moral clash. The brothers Bassianus and Saturninus, who are seeking power at the outset of the action, can be distinguished in terms of good and bad (though Saturninus is more foolish and unstable than vicious). Titus' initial judgments, including sanctioning the sacrifice of Alarbus, leave him politically vulnerable and exposed to Tamora's thirst for revenge. But ironically, the natural savagery and iniquity of Aaron, Tamora and her sons Demetrius and Chiron, are such that they do not need a motive for their subsequent actions. Titus, on the other hand, does resort to inhuman actions as a consequence of being driven partially mad through the horrors that he is made to endure. Despite claims to the contrary, the imagery is interwoven with great imaginative force and subtlety. There are a series of powerful contrasts. In terms of the animal imagery Tamora is described as a 'ravenous tiger' (V.iii.5), her sons as 'hell-hounds' (V.ii.144) and 'bear-whelps' (IV.i.96). Aaron is a 'hellish dog' (IV.ii.77) while Lavinia is the doe or hart. The bird, animal and plant images frequently relate to inherited characteristics: as a Goth says of Aaron, 'But where the bull and cow are both milk-white,/They never do beget a coal-black calf' (V.i.31–2); or, as he asserts himself, 'For all the water in the ocean/Can never turn the swan's black legs to white' (IV.ii.101–2); and, as Lavinia says of Chiron, ''Tis true the raven doth not hatch a lark' (II.iii.149).

The sense of the plant kingdom in its contrasting guises is evoked with great power and persistence: young Marcius is a 'tender sapling' (III.ii.50); Lucius is a 'Brave slip' (V.i.9); Titus and Marcus 'are but shrubs, no cedars we' (IV.iii.45); Aaron's son is 'base fruit' and 'fruit of bastardy' (V.i.43 and 48); Saturninus hangs his head 'As flowers with frost, or grass beat down with storms' (IV.iv.71); Lavinia's tears are like 'honey-dew/Upon a gather'd lily almost withered' (III.i.112–13) while the cheeks of Titus and Marcus 'are stain'd, like meadows yet not dry,/With miry slime left on them by a flood' (III.i.125–6); Lavinia is a 'spring' 'stain'd with mud' a 'goodly summer' whom Chiron and Demetrius have with their 'winter mix'd' (V.ii.170–1).

References to water are diverse and ubiquitous culminating in its most delicate representation as tears which contrast with the violent waters of 'a wilderness of sea', 'envious surge' and 'brinish bowels' (III.i.94–7). Body parts are significant throughout, frequently relating to the physical mutilations which occur, but being developed in other ways too, with the eye receiving that special attention which it is accorded in *Troilus and Cressida* and *King Lear*. Music is frequently invoked and is closely related to these images. A good example of imagery forming an integral part of the verbal and dramatic structure occurs during the woodland scenes which culminate in the murder of Bassianus and the rape and mutilation of Lavinia. Titus leads his band forth to awaken the newly weds for the hunt with the words:

The hunt is up, the morn is bright and grey,
The fields are fragrant and the woods are green.
Uncouple here and let us make a bay,
And wake the emperor and his lovely bride,

And rouse the prince, and ring a hunter's peal,
That all the court may echo with the noise.

                                        (II.ii.1–6)

This fresh and inviting description is soon followed by Tamora's perspective of the wood as a demi-paradise:

My lovely Aaron, wherefore look'st thou sad
When everything doth make a gleeful boast?
The birds chant melody on every bush,
The snake lies rolled in the cheerful sun,
The green leaves quiver with the cooling wind,
And make a chequer'd shadow on the ground;
Under their sweet shade, Aaron, let us sit,
And, whilst the babbling echo mocks the hounds,
Replying shrilly to the well-tun'd horns,
As if a double hunt were heard at once,
Let us sit down and mark their yellowing noise;
And after conflict, such as was suppos'd
The wand'ring prince and Dido once enjoyed,
When with a happy storm they were surpris'd,
And curtain'd with a counsel-keeping cave,
We may, each wreathed in the other's arms,
Our pastimes done, possess a golden slumber,
Whiles hounds and horns and sweet melodious birds
Be unto us as is a nurse's song
Of lullaby to bring her babe asleep.

                                        (II.iii.10–29)

The delicate beauty and sheer tenderness of this description contrasts with Aaron's demand for action:

This is the day of doom for Bassianus;
His Philomel must lose her tongue to-day,
Thy sons make pillage of her chastity,
And wash their hands in Bassianus' blood.

                                        (II.iii.42–5)

But even more striking is Tamora's description of the very same place in entirely different language when Bassianus and Lavinia arrive in the grove followed by Demetrius and Chiron. In mock fear and apprehension she describes the threatening character of the natural world:

Have I not reason, think you, to look pale?
These two have tic'd me hither to this place:
A barren detested vale you see it is;
The trees, though summer, yet forlorn and lean,

34

Overcome with moss and baleful mistletoe:
Here never shines the sun: here nothing breeds,
Unless the nightly owl or fatal raven:
And when they show'd me this abhorred pit,
They told me, here, at dead time of the night,
A thousand fiends, a thousand hissing snakes,
Ten thousand swelling toads, as many urchins,
Would make such fearful and confused cries,
As any mortal body hearing it
Should straight fall mad, or else die suddenly.
                                    (II.iii.91–104)

In the fine Stratford production of 1987/8, Tamora's two sons immitated
the creatures cited by her and seemed to be playing a game. Bassianus
joined in and both the audience and the character received a violent shock
as he was suddenly stabbed. The beautiful woodland glade of Tamora's
earlier description immediately acquired all the baleful qualities of the
second. As Demetrius informed Tamora that Lavinia was to be raped
before being mutilated he used a metaphor that gathered into itself a
peculiar horror: 'First thrash the corn, then after burn the straw'
(II.iii.123). This line is paralleled by Marcus in the closing phase of the
play where he uses a closely allied image to describe the renewal of Rome:

O, let me teach you how to knit again
This scattered corn into one mutual sheaf,
                          (V.iii.70–1)

This pattern of contrasts is repeated in the scene where the mutilated
Lavinia is discarded by Tamora's sons – a scene rendered profoundly
shocking in the Stratford production as the sons emerged imitating the
crawl of Lavinia, before sitting astride her and spitting in her face, finally
releasing her with taunts:

DEMETRIUS So, now go tell, and if thy tongue can speak,
      Who 'twas that cut thy tongue and ravish'd thee.
CHIRON Write down thy mind, bewray thy meaning so,
      And if thy stumps will let thee play the scribe.
DEMETRIUS See how with signs and tokens she can scrowl.
CHIRON Go home, call for sweet water, wash thy hands.
DEMETRIUS She hath no tongue to call, nor hands to wash;
      And so let's leave her to her silent walks.
CHIRON And 'twere my cause, I should go hang myself.
DEMETRIUS If thou hadst hands to help thee knit the cord.
                                    (II.iv.1–10)

In contrast to this brutal contempt for the human body, Marcus on discovering his niece creates a vision of the loveliness and delicacy of the human form and of man's capacity to feel and describe it:

> Speak, gentle niece, what stern ungentle hands
> Hath lopp'd and hew'd and made thy body bare
> Of her two branches, those sweet ornaments,
> Whose circling shadows kings have sought to sleep in,
> And might not gain so great a happiness
> As half thy love? Why dost not speak to me?
> Alas, a crimson river of warm blood,
> Like to a bubbling fountain stirr'd with wind,
> Doth rise and fall between thy rosed lips,
> Coming and going with thy honey breath.
> But, sure, some Tereus hath deflow'red thee . . .
> A craftier Tereus, cousin, hast thou met,
> And he hath cut those pretty fingers off,
> That could have better sew'd than Philomel.
> O, had the monster seen those lily hands
> Tremble like aspen-leaves upon a lute,
> And make the silken strings delight to kiss them,
> He would not then have touch'd them for his life.
> Or had he heard the heavenly harmony
> Which that sweet tongue hath made,
> He would have dropp'd his knife, and fell asleep,
> As Cerberus at the Thracian poet's feet.

$$(II.iv.16-51)$$

Marcus' description simultaneously projects the horror of the particular violation and the appalling sense of recognition that in all times and places there are human beings who possess a capacity for savagery that is truly terrifying.

Close examination of the text together with an awareness of the impact of two great stage productions by the Royal Shakespeare Company, reveals the misplaced nature of the criticism to which the play has been subject. As thoughtful a commentator as Bullough has suggested that 'Often the impression given is of detachment rather than of complete immersion in the story' which 'again recalls Ovid's urbane presentation of strange happenings'.[48] Much more surprising is M.C. Bradbrook's statement that 'the horrors are all classical and quite unfelt, so that the violent tragedy is contrasted by the decorous imagery. The tone is cool and cultured in its effect'.[49] Waith has expressed a similar view and Bullough makes a specific reference which is wholly at variance with theatrical experience, when he writes of the dramatist's 'bad taste, as in Marcus's prettifying of Lavinia's mutilation'.[50] What in fact Marcus' speech does is to give expression to a refined sensibility confronted with the consequence of inhumanity which is incomprehensible – and this speech contrasts with the language and action of Chiron and Demetrius, two creatures devoid of human compassion. Here is the clash of good and evil represented in *King Lear*. Marcus' speech embodies numerous references to the delicacy of nature, to music, to the parts of the body and to tears. This juxtaposition of the natural world and tears is continued in the next scene as Titus is left pleading in the streets on behalf of his sons, after the judges and senators have passed him by, and is continued when he sets eyes on Lavinia:

> What fool hath added water to the sea,
> Or brought a faggot to bright-burning Troy?
> My grief was at the height before thou cam'st,
> And now like Nilus it disdaineth bounds.
>
> (III.i.68–71)

A little later there is a juxtaposition of the violence of unbridled nature with extreme delicacy as Titus expresses his own anguish and the pain of Lavinia's suffering:

> For now I stand as one upon a rock
> Environ'd with a wilderness of sea,
> Who marks the waxing tide grow wave by wave,
> Expecting ever when some envious surge
> Will in his brinish bowels swallow him. . . .
> Gentle Lavinia, let me kiss thy lips,
> Or make some sign how I may do thee ease.
> Shall thy good uncle, and thy brother Lucius,
> And thou, and I, sit round about some fountain,
> Looking all downwards to behold our cheeks
> How they are stain'd, like meadows yet not dry,
> With miry slime left on them by a flood?
> And in the fountain shall we gaze so long
> Till the fresh taste be taken from that clearness,
> And made a brine-pit with our bitter tears?
>
> (III.i.93–129)

The kissing is characteristic of the play: bodies are mutilated but the tenderness of feeling that joins father–daughter, father–son, child–grandfather and brothers is continually expressed in kissing and culminates in young Lucius kissing his dead grandfather. Love, tenderness and the delicate touching of bodies exists in a world of terrifying violence and physical mutilation so that the object of contemplation is humanity itself rather than the body politic. The inadequacy of the response of those critics who have seen this play as a failure (or at best mere journeyman work) was revealed in the Stratford production which held audiences stiff with horror and released them occasionally into laughter, but a laughter that was sealed or confined, and which was never embarrassing or gave any credence to the view that the play contains large elements of burlesque. (Robert B. Heilman, for example, suggested that in *Titus* 'the reciprocal acts of revenge become parodistic, the frantic exacerbation of melodramatic appeal a caricature'.[51]) Likewise, although the significance of the influence of Kyd's *The Spanish Tragedy* cannot be denied, the Stratford production gave a tremendous sense of Shakespeare having a clear perception of his own design, which was remarkable more for its independence of Kyd than its similarity. The sense of the parallels were also beautifully pointed up in the Stratford production. For instance, the 'game' played by Demetrius and Chiron prior to the murder of Bassianus was taken up by Titus when, having persuaded Tamora to leave her sons, he grasped them around the shoulders in jocular manner before wrenching their necks together with frightening power. Brian Cox, who played Titus, displayed the ability to provoke a laugh and kill it instantly – a quality Shakespeare felt was attainable but which most modern critics have not believed possible. For instance, as he emerged at the banquet in his chef's attire he welcomed individuals and groups before looking down at the pie which he held, crying, 'And welcome, all' (V.iii.28). The power of 'horrid laughter' (to use Nicholas Brooke's term), its function as a necessary release and the effectiveness of the grotesque were all manifest in a production that revealed Shakespeare's astonishing control of the audience. Rather than feeling any embarrassment as Lavinia left the stage with Titus' hand between her teeth the audience was stilled and transfixed with horror. Likewise the preparations for the banquet were completed to the tune, whistled by the cooks, 'Off to work we go'. While the preparations proceeded, Marcus stood horrified and was momentarily embraced by Lucius. Marcus (Donald Sumpter) was played as an enormously sympathetic character with his own inner strength and overwhelming compassion. He it is who gently cradles the child of Tamora and Aaron as he attempts to knit Rome together under the guidance of the surviving remnant of the Andronici family (Lucius, the last of Titus' twenty-five sons).

Miola is confident that Rome has a new Aeneas in Lucius, who keeps his oath to spare Aaron's child:

> The restraint of emotion here, the tacit recognition of higher obligations than personal satisfaction, the steady refusal to pursue a violent course of vengeance that will shed innocent blood – all suggest that Lucius has changed from an impetuous bloodthirsty youth to a man capable of wise leadership.[52]

What he omits to mention is that Lucius is bound by his oath. There is, however, clear recognition of the need to establish new moral boundaries.

Perhaps the child's survival, and Marcus' gentle care of it, attests to the emergence of a more civilized Rome. Even so the closing scene poses a number of questions. After the numerous references to inherited characteristics – ''Tis true the raven doth not hatch a lark' (II.iii.149) – the question that inevitably arises is, what kind of man will Aaron's child grow into? And will any society be freed from cycles of tranquillity and terror? Finally, how well do men learn and what capacity do they display for incorporating those lessons into social institutions which are both humane and durable?

These questions reveal both the affinities which this play shares with the later Roman plays and the contrasts. The mind is focused on present horrors and the capacity of human beings to behave with extreme savagery, as in *King Lear*, but there is also contemplation of the future and the relationship between the body politic and human values. It is this latter dimension which links the four plays – especially the feeling of the self-consciousness of the Roman worlds.

2

IMAGES AND SELF-IMAGES IN *JULIUS CAESAR*

But I am constant as the northern star,
Of whose true-fix'd and resting quality
There is no fellow in the firmament.

(III.i.60–2)

I shall have glory by this losing day
More than Octavius and Mark Antony
By this vile conquest shall attain unto.

(V.v.36–8)

Why, man, he doth bestride the narrow world
Like a Colossus, and we petty men
Walk under his huge legs, and peep about
To find ourselves dishonourable graves.

(I.ii.133–6)

O, he sits high in all the people's hearts:
And that which would appear offence in us,
His countenance, like richest alchemy,
Will change to virtue and to worthiness.

(I.iii.157–60)

The most notable feature of Shakespeare's use of his source material in *Julius Caesar* is the way in which he conflates events. This process begins in the opening scene where the dramatist combines Caesar's triumph over Pompey's sons (October, 45 BC) with the Feast of Lupercal (15 February, 44 BC). Among other things this conjunction points up the incongruity between a celebration of the founding of Rome and the triumph of one great Roman general over the sons of an equally revered Roman. In the midst of these celebrations comes the warning from a soothsayer – an event which, according to Plutarch, occurred much earlier. Again there is a passage of a month between Cassius' initial suggestion to Brutus that he join the conspiracy and the evening preceding the assassination. In the play there is a feeling of headlong pace. Even more significant is the way in which the dramatist conflates the events following the assassination. In

Plutarch's account, Brutus first makes a speech in the Capitol 'to win the favour of the people and to justify that they had done'.[1] On the following day he made a second speech in the market place which was less than wholly successful. Two days after the assassination the matter was discussed in the Capitol, with Antony supporting Cicero's suggestion that the conspirators be rewarded with honours but that Caesar's edicts stand and that he receive the appropriate praises. Brutus supported Antony's request to take charge of the funeral arrangements, thereby enabling him to stir up the crowd against the conspirators. Shakespeare concentrates these events into the meeting between Antony and the assassins immediately after Caesar's death and the forum scene.

The dramatist totally omits the historical breach between Antony and Octavius which began with antagonistic manoeuvring and culminated in battle which Antony lost (referred to by Shakespeare in *Antony and Cleopatra* where Octavius describes Antony's retreat over the Alps – I.iv.55–71). When Antony gained the support of Lepidus, Octavius found it expedient to join forces with them in order to gain political ascendancy. Historically, the proscription scene occurred several months after the assassination. This brief but chilling scene encapsulates a negotiation which lasted three days and took place on the Isle of Pharos. Finally, the three weeks which separated the battles at Philippi are conflated into a single day. Hence Plutarch's description of events which are spread over a period of three years between October, 45 BC and 42 BC are powerfully concentrated by Shakespeare into a brief but indefinite time-scheme. The feeling is one of a continuous and rapid unfolding of events taking place in a matter of days, except for a time lapse between the fleeing of Brutus and Cassius from Rome and their meeting at Philippi.

Shakespeare's invention of Calpurnia's sterility and Caesar's deafness are significant. When Caesar reminds Antony to touch Calpurnia in the chase it is the first glimpse of his new-found superstition later emphasized by Cassius (II.i.195). The deafness in one ear brings a rich vein of irony to the moment when a physically declining Caesar is asserting his superhuman invulnerability. Here Shakespeare points up a disjunction between the reality and Caesar's acceptance of his cultivated public persona. Cassius' wonderfully malicious description of Caesar's physical vulnerability and his own role in rescuing him from the Tiber is also Shakespeare's invention – an invention which is striking given Plutarch's description of Caesar saving himself from the Egyptians in Alexandria by means of his excellent swimming (even supporting precious books on his head!). There is no historical basis for the meeting of the adversaries before the battle of Philippi. This scene enables Shakespeare to develop personality contrasts and conflicts in which the audience are reminded by Cassius that had his will prevailed over Brutus, Mark Antony would not be standing there. Even more significant is the transference of Plutarch's description of the

41

dispute between Brutus and Cassius over who should lead the more prestigious right flank to Octavius and Antony in the play. This brief conflict brings out the rough directness of the young Octavius in refusing to be overborne by the experienced Antony and provides in embryo the rivalry which will blossom into a quest for domination of the Empire in *Antony and Cleopatra*.

Some of the minor but significant changes made by Shakespeare are closely tied up with characterization. Plutarch portrays Caesar as a man who is affable, courteous, generous, magnanimous, calculating and ambitious. He ranks him as second only to Cicero as an orator and goes on to describe how this talent, along with other attributes, were put to the service of his political aspirations. Two little incidents which are indicative of Caesar's ambition are recorded by the historian. On encountering a poor village in the Alps, Caesar responded to his friends' jests about the pursuit of political office by earnestly proclaiming, 'for my parte, I had rather be the chiefest man here, then the second person in Rome'.[2] When in Spain he fell to weeping and responded to the bewilderment of his associates by saying 'Doe ye not thinke . . . that I have good cause to be heavie when king Alexander being no older than myselfe is now, had in old time wonne so many nations and countries: and that I hitherunto have done nothing worthy of my selfe?'[3] His triumphs in Spain and the arrangement of the subsequent peace brought him the admiration of his soldiers and great wealth.

Caesar's enemies took secret delight in his huge financial outlays, designed to gain friends and win popular support, believing that he would exhaust his financial resources. And indeed, it seems that he acquired a debt of 1300 talents before he obtained any public office. As overseer of a road-building project he even contributed some of his own money to ensure its successful completion – confident that such an 'investment' would eventually yield a substantial return. At one stage the impatience of Caesar's creditors was such that he was obliged to resort to Crassus, the richest man in Rome. However, Crassus was very willing to oblige him, for by that time Caesar's influence was such that he was able to provide support for his wealthy friend against Pompey. In due course Caesar reconciled these powerful adversaries and managed to forge an alliance with them. This reconciliation of Crassus and Pompey brought Caesar immediate political gain as they supported his election to consulship. Once elected he adopted populist policies, such as redistribution of land and the provision of free corn to the people, which brought him into conflict with the majority of senators. Rather than submit to political pressure he invoked the support of Crassus and Pompey. It soon became apparent that Caesar was not content merely to be one major political force among many. He cemented his relationship with Pompey by giving him his daughter Julia in marriage, even though she had been promised to

Servilius Caepio. Not wanting to disappoint the latter unduly, he promptly arranged for him to marry Pompey's (now discarded) wife. She too had been promised elsewhere but Caesar accepted that it was not possible to satisfy everyone.

On marrying Calpurnia, Caesar arranged for his father-in-law to succeed him as Consul and then created antagonism by appointing as tribune a notorious character, P. Colordius, because of his hostility to Cicero. Despite these character defects Caesar's star was soon in the ascendant as a consequence of his victories in Gaul. These triumphs greatly enhanced his stature as a general and as a man possessed of immense physical courage. He also gained a reputation in the wars for liberality and magnanimity. Caesar's willingness to place himself in great physical danger was recognized as part of his quest for honour, but his determination to overcome all physical disabilities, including epilepsy, was so remarkable that it won him unqualified admiration:

> For, concerning the constitucion of his bodie, he was leane, white, and soft skinned, and often subject to headache, and otherwile to the falling sickenes: (the which tooke him the first time, as it is reported, in Corduba, a citie of Spayne) but yet therefore yeelded not to the disease of his bodie, to make it a cloke to cherishe him withall, but contrarilie, tooke the paines of warre, as a medicine to cure his sicke bodie fighting alwayes with his disease, travelling continually, living soberly, and commonly lying abroade in the field.[4]

As for his soldiers, Plutarch comments, 'he was so entirely beloved of his souldiers, that to doe him service . . . if Caesars honor were touched, they were invincible'.[5]

Plutarch states that Caesar had long anticipated a battle for primacy with Pompey and manoeuvred accordingly. The death of his daughter Julia in childbirth removed the bond that tied them. The critical moment arrived when Caesar was ordered to dismiss his army and return to Rome. Instead, after some hesitation, he crossed the Rubicon and marched on Rome to confront Pompey's army. The latter, mistakenly overestimating the strength of Caesar's force, fled, thereby relinquishing an important legal as well as military advantage. In order to finance his war preparations Caesar did not hesitate to take by force the treasure from the temple of Saturn. Pompey finally made a stand at Pharsalia where he was easily outmanoeuvred by Caesar who instructed his soldiers to ensure that Brutus come to no harm. He not only pardoned Brutus, but all those, including Cassius, for whom he pleaded. Caesar wrote to his friends in Rome that his greatest pleasure had been to save the lives of those who had taken up arms against him.

Caesar's final battle, which was fought in Spain, was against the sons of Pompey. Plutarch records, with considerable emotion, the hostility which

Caesar aroused by celebrating this particular victory in Rome (an emotion which is conveyed powerfully in Shakespeare's opening scene of the play):

> the triumphe he made into Rome . . . did as much offend the Romanes, and more, then any thing that ever he had done before: bicause he had not overcome Captaines that were straungers, nor barbarous kinges, but had destroyed the sonnes of the noblest man in Rome, whom fortune had overthrowen. And bicause he had plucked up his race by the rootes, men did not thinke it meete for him to triumphe so.[6]

Despite the offence caused by this triumph, Plutarch continues, the Romans appointed him perpetual Dictator which 'was a plaine tyranny: for to this absolute power of Dictator, they added this, never to be affraied to be deposed'.[7] Although Plutarch expresses distaste for the title bestowed on Caesar and the other honours that were heaped on him (supported even by those who hated him out of the desire to gain office) he declares that Caesar conducted himself with admirable restraint – pardoning former enemies and elevating some (such as Cassius and Brutus) to high office. He ordered the setting-up of Pompey's statues once more and granted free distribution of corn and the provision of feasts and festivities for the people. What Plutarch leaves open to interpretation is the extent to which such actions were the consequence of political calculation rather than generosity of spirit. For instance, he cites Cicero's comments on Caesar's re-establishment of Pompey's statues: by this means 'he made his owne to stand the surer'.[8]

Within the compass of a few pages Plutarch gives Shakespeare a great deal of valuable material for the first two scenes of the play. First, Plutarch points to the main reason for the antagonism which Caesar attracted: 'the chiefest cause that made him mortally hated, was the covetous desire he had to be called king: which first gave the people just cause, and next his secret enemies, honest colour to beare him ill will'.[9] Plutarch goes on to narrate events that suggest Caesar was desirous of the title of king but determined to test public reaction before revealing his ambition. Caesar, on his return to Rome, rebuked those who called him king as soon as he discerned that the vast majority were offended by the title. Again, at the Feast of Lupercal Antony presented Caesar with a 'Diadeame wreathed about with laurell' which brought forth a cry of approval and rejoicing but 'not very great' and 'done onely by a few, appointed for the purpose'. When Caesar rejected the crown (twice as opposed to Shakespeare's thrice), 'then all the people together made an outcrie of joy'.[10] The historian makes it clear, therefore, that this is no whim of Antony's but a rehearsed scheme to make another test of popular feeling. Shakespeare conveys this in a much more interesting way. In a few strokes he heightens the whole scene, providing a vivid portrait of Casca, who dramatizes the incident while playing the part of the cynically detached observer.

These few pages also record Caesar's arrogance in refusing to stand to greet the senators who came to present him new honours. When he became aware of the hostility caused by his action he tore open his collar and invited his friends to cut his throat – a histrionic action for which he later felt ashamed. Shakespeare dramatizes the incident, again using Casca, thereby gathering up and accentuating the elements of farce and embarrassment.

There is a fairly flat account of how the tribunes Marullus and Flavius imprisoned those who 'first saluted Caesar as king'[11] and later removed the 'Diadeames' from Caesar's images. For these actions they are deprived of their tribuneships. Shakespeare's handling of this incident is instructive. In the opening scene he uses Marullus and Flavius to demonstrate political opposition to Caesar and to reveal the naivety and susceptibility of the common people. In the following scene Casca, by way of a footnote to his description of Caesar's rejection of the crown, adds 'Marullus and Flavius, for pulling scarfs off Caesar's images, are put to silence' (I.ii.282–3). This terse and ambiguous comment strikes an ominous note: political opponents are quickly removed – and killed? What does 'put to silence' mean? A modern audience would probably interpret this comment as meaning put to death. Shakespeare either intended this interpretation or, what is more likely, deliberately used an ambiguous expression to keep the audience wondering about the precise nature of Caesar's power and aspirations. There is certainly no ambiguity in his source: these men are simply deprived of their office (though this in itself reveals Caesar's impatience with opponents and his capacity to effect his will).

Shakespeare uses numerous details of the 'straunge and wonderfull signes that were sayd to be seene before Caesars death',[12] including the flames which sprang forth from the slave's hand, the noise on the night and Calpurnia's dream, who 'untill that time, was never geven to any feare or supersticion',[13] and the many ominous signs discovered by the soothsayers, including Caesar's sacrifice of a beast that had no heart. The Soothsayer, who had previously warned Caesar about the Ides of March, cautions, 'but yet they are not past'.[14] A point not taken up by Shakespeare is Plutarch's account of a discussion which took place the day before the assassination. Caesar declared that his preference was 'Death unlooked for'.[15]

The arguments put forward by Decius Brutus, including the reinterpretation of Calpurnia's dream, are all taken up by Shakespeare. Caesar had such confidence in this man, Plutarch comments, that 'in his last will and testament he had appointed him to be his next heire'.[16] Artemidorus had gained knowledge of the conspiracy and attempted to impart it to Caesar. He handed Caesar the warning with the words 'reade this memoriall to your selfe, and that quickely, for they be matters of great waight and touche you neerely'. Shakespeare comes close to this very expression, but whereas Plutarch adds, 'Caesar tooke it of him, but coulde never reade it, though he many times attempted it, for the number of people that did salute him',[17] Shakespeare's Caesar takes advantage of the occasion to display his commitment to the primacy of public duty over private interest: 'What touches us ourself shall be last serv'd' (III.i.8).

At this point Plutarch makes an interesting interpolation. Whereas he normally stands apart from the events, attempting to provide a clear statement of the relevant details and circumstances (citing alternative accounts where conflicting descriptions have been advanced), here he writes as a fatalist. Artemidorus tries hard to give the memorial to Caesar but is prevented by the surge of the crowd, even though he continues to follow the procession. Taking this and subsequent events together Plutarch concludes:

> For these things, they may seeme to come by chaunce: but the place where the murther was prepared, and where the Senate were assembled, and where also there stoode up an image of Pompey dedicated by him selfe amongest other ornaments which he gave unto the Theater: all these were manifest proofes that it was the ordinaunce of some god, that made this treason to be executed, specially in that verie place. It is also reported, that Cassius (though otherwise he did favour the doctrine of Epicurus) beholding the image of Pompey, before they entred into the action of their traiterous enterprise: he did softly call upon it, to aide him.[18]

Plutarch also makes an obscure observation about Cassius suddenly breaking into 'a furious passion, and made him like a man halfe besides him selfe'.[19] Shakespeare makes sense of this incident by making Cassius believe that Caesar is being warned of the plot.

Shakespeare uses Plutarch's brief description of the contrived pleas on behalf of Publius Cimber, but creates for Caesar a speech which suggests he has fallen victim to the image of the great man. Then the dramatist gives Caesar a telling little comment of which there is no hint in the narrative. Insisting on the futility of pleading he says, 'Doth not Brutus bootless kneel?' (III.i.75). If Shakespeare accords Brutus a special position at this point, Plutarch provides justification for this view a little later. Caesar fiercely resists the assassins until he realizes that Brutus is one of them. The picture of the assassination created by Plutarch is vivid, revealing Caesar's courage, the ensuing chaos, and the way in which the assassins unintentionally wounded one another:

> Metellus at length, taking his gowne with both his handes, pulled it over his necke, which was the signe geven the confederates to sette apon him. Then Casca behinde him strake him in the necke with his sword, howbeit the wounde was not great nor mortall, bicause it seemed, the

feare of such a develishe attempt did amaze him, and take his strength from him, that he killed him not at the first blowe. But Caesar turning straight unto him, caught hold of his sword, and held it hard: and they both cried out, Caesar in Latin: O vile traitor Casca, what doest thou? and Casca in Greeke to his brother, Brother, helpe me. At the beginning of this sturre, they that were present, not knowing of the conspiracie were so amazed with the horrible sight they sawe: that they had no power to flie, neither to helpe him, not so much, as once to make any outcrie. They on thother side that had conspired his death, compassed him in on everie side with their swordes drawen in their handes, that Caesar turned him no where, but he was striken at by some, and still had naked swords in his face, and was hacked and mangeled amonge them, as a wilde beaste taken of hunters. For it was agreed among them, that every man should geve him a wound, bicause all their partes should be in this murther: and then Brutus him selfe gave him one wounde about his privities. Men reporte also, that Caesar did still defende him selfe against the rest, running everie waye with his bodie: but when he sawe Brutus with his sworde drawen in his hande, then he pulled his gowne over his heade, and made no more resistaunce, and was driven either casually, or purposedly, by the counsell of the conspirators, against the base whereupon Pompeys image stoode, which ranne all of a goare bloude, till he was slaine. Thus it seemed, that the image tooke juste revenge of Pompeys enemie, being throwen downe on the ground at his feete, and yelding up his ghost there, . . . For it is reported, that he had three and twenty wounds apon his body: and divers of the conspirators did hurt them selves, striking one body with so many blowes. When Caesar was slaine, the Senate (though Brutus stood in the middest amongest them as though he would have sayd somewhat touching this fact) presently ran out of the house, and flying, filled all the city with marvelous feare and tumult.[20]

Caesar's death was marked by the appearance of a comet which remained visible for seven nights. The darkening of the sun also damaged the fruit. But the most clear indication that the gods were offended by the murder, Plutarch states, was the appearance of an apparition before Brutus.

Plutarch's *Life of Brutus* opens by noting that Marcus Brutus was a descendant of Junius Brutus, whose statue was set up in Rome because of the courage he displayed in driving out the Tarquins, the last kings of Rome. However, the historian promptly draws a contrast between the two personalities: Junius was so severe that he ordered the execution of his own sons; Marcus Brutus, on the other hand, 'framed his manners of life by the rules of vertue and studie of Philosophie, and having imployed his wit, which was gentle and constant, in attempting of great things: me thinkes he was rightly made and framed unto vertue'.[21] Brutus' mentor was his uncle Marcus Cato, whose daughter Portia he married. Plutarch describes Brutus' mastery of Latin and his qualities as an orator, going on to illustrate his favoured style of Greek oratory – a style which Shakespeare unmistakably adopts for Brutus' forum speech:

> But for the Graeke tongue, they do note in some of his Epistells, that he counterfeated that briefe compendious maner of speach of the Lacedaemonians. As when the warre was begonne, he wrote unto the Pargamenians in this sorte: I understand you have geven Dolobella money: if you have done it willingly, you confesse you have offended me: if against your wills, shewe it then by geving me willinglie.[22]

Very early in his account of Brutus' character and life, Plutarch mentions an event which must have startled and impressed Shakespeare. He states that when Caesar and Pompey took up arms against each other, it was assumed Brutus would side with Caesar because Pompey had executed Brutus' father. And indeed, prior to this conflict Brutus would not deign to speak to Pompey. However, 'Brutus preferring the respect of his countrie and common wealth, before private affection, and perswading himselfe that Pompey had juster cause to enter into armes then Caesar: he then tooke parte with Pompey'.[23] Here we have in essence the character of the man who could conspire the assassination of his benefactor for the good of his country and who, in Shakespeare's play, tells Antony that even if he were Caesar's son he would be satisfied that the assassination was justified. The source of this breathtaking naivety is surely to be found in Plutarch's description of the man who joins forces with his own father's murderer for the good of his country.

During the battle of Pharsalia, Caesar instructed his men to take Brutus alive or to let him go if he would not surrender. Plutarch gives the following explanation for this act of extreme magnanimity:

> Some saye he did this for Serviliaes sake, Brutus mother. For when he was a young man, he had bene acquainted with Servilia, who was extreamelie in love with him. And bicause Brutus was borne in that time when their love was hottest, he perswaded him selfe that he begat him.[24]

Brutus did escape from the battle and wrote to Caesar who 'did not onelie pardon him, but also kept him always about him, and did as muche honor and esteeme him, as any man he had in his companie'.[25] Plutarch provides further hints as to why Caesar had a special regard for Brutus. At Brutus' intercession Caesar pardoned Cassius and the King of Libya, whose plight seemed hopeless, and commented, 'I knowe not, sayd he, what this young man woulde, but what he woulde, he willeth it vehementlie'.[26] This quality of vehemence, of passion, of giving himself completely to a cause, provides a vital component of Shakespeare's characterization. Plutarch adds that when confronted by suitors Brutus would never yield to flattery or false persuasion but 'being moved with reason and discretion, did alwayes encline to that which was good and honest'.[27]

The historian then embarks on a fascinating discussion of the triangular relationships between Caesar, Brutus and Cassius. The latter two were linked through marriage as Brutus' sister Junia was the wife of Cassius. However, they fell out over the pursuit of the Praetorship (chief judge) of the city. Caesar felt that Cassius was the more deserving on the basis of his military exploits but he nevertheless appointed Brutus to the post:

> Cassius cause is the juster, sayd he, but Brutus must be first preferred. Thus Brutus had the first Praetorshippe, and Cassius the second: who thanked not Caesar so much for Praetorshippe he had, as he was angrie with him for that he had lost.[28]

Plutarch explores all the possibilities for Caesar's preference, including such cynical interpretations as the desire to promote conflict between Cassius and Brutus or because he feared Brutus' 'great minde, authority, and frends'.[29] Cassius, in cautioning Brutus against Caesar, used neither of these suggestions but 'sayd Caesar gave him, not to honor his vertue, but to weaken his constant minde, framing it to the bent of his bowe'.[30]

Caesar, Plutarch suggests, was wary of Brutus so that he 'did not trust him overmuch', but, 'he trusted his good nature, and fayer condicions'.[31] When cautioned by friends against Antony and Dolabella, Caesar 'aunswered, that these fat long heared men made him not affrayed, but the leane and whitely faced fellowes, meaning that, by Brutus and Cassius'.[32] It would appear from Plutarch's account that Caesar realized that he could not depend on Brutus' unqualified support, but he thought him incapable of duplicity. Caesar also felt that the long-term political interests of Brutus would deter him from serious opposition. As Plutarch puts it,

> I am perswaded that Brutus might in dede have come to have bene the chiefest man of Rome, if he could have contented him selfe for a time and have bene next unto Caesar, and to have suffred his glorie and authoritie, which he had gotten by his great victories, to consume with time.[33]

Indeed, continues Plutarch, Brutus would have been prepared to do this, 'But Cassius being a chollericke man, and hating Caesar privatlie, more then he did the tyrannie openlie: he incensed Brutus against him'.[34] The historian enumerates various personal reasons for Cassius' antagonism towards Caesar but also gives him credit for strong political conviction: 'For Cassius even from his cradell could not abide any maner of tyrans'.[35] Shakespeare attached little importance to this comment: the Cassius of the play is a passionate man for whom personal considerations are of overriding importance.

Plutarch gives a clear indication of widespread dissatisfaction with Caesar's behaviour and the perception of the threat he represented to political freedoms and traditions. There is a genuine appeal to Brutus to redress these wrongs:

But for Brutus, his frendes and contrie men, both by divers procurementes, and sundrie rumors of the citie, and by many bills also, did openlie call and procure him to doe that he did. For, under the image of his auncester Junius Brutus, that drave the kinges out of Rome, they wrote: O, that it pleased the goddes thou wert now alive, Brutus: and againe that thou wert here amonge us nowe. His tribunall (or chaire) where he gave audience during the time he was Praetor, was full of suche billes: Brutus, thou art a sleepe, and art not Brutus in deede.[36]

In Shakespeare's play these appeals are forged by Cassius and his associates in order to convince Brutus of the groundswell of opposition to Caesar and, more importantly, to persuade him that he is the man all Romans perceive as the supreme defender of freedom.

Both the historian and the dramatist emphasize the strategic role of Brutus in the conspiracy: his reputation as a man of integrity was essential in affording the conspirators political credibility. The only deviation Shakespeare makes at this point is that his Cassius is fully aware of the need for Brutus from the outset. Plutarch states that,

Nowe when Cassius felt his frendes, and did stirre them up against Caesar: they all agreed and promised to take parte with him, so Brutus were the chiefe of their conspiracie. For they told him, that so high an enterprise and attempt as that, did not so muche require men of manhoode, and courage to drawe their swordes: as it stoode them uppon to have a man of suche estimacion as Brutus, to make everie man boldlie thinke, that by his onelie presence the fact were holie, and just. If he tooke not this course, then that they shoulde goe to it with fainter hartes, and when they had done it, they shoulde be more fearefull: bicause everie man woulde thinke that Brutus woulde not have refused to have made one with them, if the cause had bene good and honest.[37]

The historian provides some deft touches in his account of the development of the conspiracy. During the debate over whether they should invite Cicero to join the conspiracy, Plutarch states that

they durst not acquaint Cicero with their conspiracie, although he was a man whome they loved dearelie, and trusted best: for they were affrayed that he being a coward by nature, and age also having increased his feare, he woulde quite turne and alter all their purpose, and quenche the heate of their enterprise, the which speciallie required hotte and earnest execucion, seeking by perswasion to bring all thinges to suche safetie, as there should be no perill.[38]

Despite the approval of his fellow-conspirators, Shakespeare's Brutus disagrees because he feels Cicero would insist on becoming the leader. Ironically, Brutus immediately assumes leadership and makes a number of vital decisions – all of which are wrong. Plutarch writes admiringly of their remarkable confidence in each other, disdaining to undertake an oath of secrecy. Such an oath-taking is proposed in Shakespeare's play but Brutus rather self-righteously dismisses the idea. The historian draws a sharp contrast between Brutus' ability to appear perfectly natural and unperturbed in public while being racked with anxiety at home. This perturbation does not arise from doubts about the justice of the act, but relates to 'the daungers that might happen'.[39] Shakespeare's Brutus is concerned exclusively with the morality of the action. Indeed, these conspirators barely look beyond the assassination, and when they do (by proposing that Antony be killed along with Caesar) Brutus exercises a veto.

The substance of the scene in which Portia pleads with Brutus to open his heart to her is provided by Plutarch. Having described the wound and the ensuing fever he continues,

Then perceiving her husbande was marvelouslie out of quiet, and that he coulde take no rest: even in her greatest payne of all, she spake in this sorte unto him: 'I being, O Brutus, (sayed she) the daughter of Cato, was married unto thee, not to be thy beddefellowe and companion in bedde and at borde onelie, like a harlot: but to be partaker also with thee, of thy good and evill fortune. Nowe for thy selfe, I can finde no cause of faulte in thee touchinge our matche: but for my parte, howe may I showe my duetie towardes thee, and howe muche I woulde doe for thy sake, if I can not constantlie beare a secret mischaunce or griefe with thee, which requireth secrecy and fidelity? I confesse, that a womans wit commonly is too weake to keepe a secret safely: but yet, Brutus, good educacion, and the companie of vertuous men, have some power to reforme the defect of nature. And for my selfe, I have this benefit moreover: that I am the daughter of Cato, and wife of Brutus. This notwithstanding, I did not trust to any of these things before: untill that now I have found by experience, that no paine nor griefe whatsoever can overcome me.' With those wordes she shewed him her wounde on her thigh, and tolde him what she had done to prove her selfe. Brutus was amazed to heare what she sayd unto him, and lifting up his handes to heaven, he besought the goddes to geve him the grace he might bring his enterprise to so good passe, that he might be founde a husband, worthie of so noble a wife as Porcia: so he then did comfort her the best he coulde.[40]

Shakespeare heightens this account not only by introducing a wider vocabulary and more effective diction, but by injecting a greater sense of urgency into Portia's appeal. In particular Shakespeare uses a series of rhetorical questions with a play on the words 'sick', 'by', 'you', 'yours' and 'vows':

> Is Brutus sick, and is it physical
> To walk unbraced and suck up the humours
> Of the dank morning? What, is Brutus sick?
> And will he steal out of his wholesome bed
> To dare the vile contagion of the night,
> And tempt the rheumy and unpurged air
> To add unto his sickness? No, my Brutus;
> You have some sick offence within your mind,
> Which, by the right and virtue of my place,
> I ought to know of; and, upon my knees,
> I charm you, by my once commended beauty,
> By all your vows of love, and that great vow
> Which did incorporate and make us one,
> That you unfold to me, your self, your half,
> Why you are heavy . . .
>
> (II.i.261–75)

As the emotional temperature rises Portia kneels before Brutus and continues her plea with great force and dignity:

> BRUTUS   Kneel not, gentle Portia.
> PORTIA I should not need, if you were gentle Brutus.
>   Within the bond of marriage, tell me, Brutus,
>   Is it excepted I should know no secrets
>   That appertain to you? Am I your self
>   But, as it were, in sort or limitation,
>   To keep with you at meals, comfort your bed,
>   And talk to you sometimes? Dwell I but in the suburbs
>   Of your good pleasure? If it be no more,
>   Portia is Brutus' harlot, not his wife.
> BRUTUS You are my true and honourable wife,
>   As dear to me as are the ruddy drops
>   That visit my sad heart.
>
> (II.i.278–90)

Once more questions are used as the key structural element. Shakespeare adopts the word 'harlot' from his source but he intensifies its power by prefacing it with the wonderfully effective phrase 'Dwell I but in the suburbs/Of your good pleasure?' There is not so much as a hint in the source material to give Shakespeare even the embryo of Brutus' moving reply – a response that elevates him in the mind of the audience.

On the day of the assassination Portia, despite her resolution, was so overcome by anxiety that she collapsed and was taken to bed. When Brutus received the news, 'it grieved him, as it is to be presupposed: yet he left not of the care of his contrie and common wealth, neither went home to his house for any news he heard'.[41] Indeed, Brutus retained the presence of mind to calm his associates with a look when they were on the brink of panic, believing momentarily that the conspiracy was being exposed.

The importance of Brutus to the conspiracy is reiterated by Plutarch – who, incidently, referring to them as 'conspirators', says parenthetically, 'if so they shoulde be called'.[42] He describes Caesar's desperate fight to escape his assailants until he sees Brutus 'with a sworde drawen in his hande readie to strike at him: then he let Cascaes hande goe, and casting his gowne over his face, suffered everie man to strike at him that woulde'.[43] This sentence, along with the account of Caesar's concern for Brutus' safety at Pharsalia, his pardon and subsequent generosity, constitute the only evidence of a special relationship between the two men. Plutarch never writes of them embracing or working closely together. This strange lacuna is taken up by Shakespeare in his play. We hear Caesar chastise those soliciting for the repeal of Cimber's banishment with the words 'Doth not Brutus bootless kneel?' (III.i.75); Brutus' sorrowful aside as he is invited, as a friend, to drink wine with Caesar prior to the assassination (II.ii.126–9); and finally Caesar's dying words as he is confronted by Brutus in the role of assassin: '*Et tu, Brute?* – Then fall Caesar!' (III.i.77). But we never *experience* an expression of deep friendship between them. Antony's assertion that Brutus was 'Caesar's angel' (III.ii.183) is unreliable because at that moment he is infiltrating into the minds of the people a sense of Brutus' betrayal of his friend. There is, then, something strangely enigmatic about the Caesar–Brutus relationship both in Plutarch's narrative and in the play.

Plutarch is unequivocal in stating that only Brutus opposed the killing of Antony. The reasons advanced by the conspirators were: first, Antony was 'a wicked man'[44] who favoured tyrany; secondly, he held great sway with the soldiers; thirdly, he was daring and had considerable influence by virtue of holding the office of Consul. These reasons certainly made Antony a potentially dangerous adversary. Brutus, however, argued that it was 'not honest' and that there was hope of reform in Antony, who, on the death of Caesar, 'would willingly helpe his contry to recover her libertie'.[45] Initially, Antony did indeed play the role of peacemaker. The day after the conspiracy, the Senate granted pardons and established order. Antony sent his son to the Capitol as pledge and encouraged the conspirators to come down and engage in mutual acts of goodwill and even invited Cassius home to supper. The following day the Senate commended Antony for his behaviour and granted offices to Brutus and his associates. Just when everything seemed to have been resolved Antony moved that Caesar's will be 'red openly' and that he be buried honourably. 'Cassius stowtly spake against it. But Brutus went with the motion, and agreed unto it',[46] and this, Plutarch states, was Brutus' 'second fault' (the first being his opposition to the killing of Antony). When the people learned that they were the recipients of 75 drachmas each and had been bequeathed gardens and arbours they 'loved him, and were marvelous sory for him'.[47] Having set the stage, Antony walks on to it:

> Afterwards when Caesars body was brought into the market place, Antonius making his funerall oration in praise of the dead, according to the aunchient custom of Rome, and perceiving that his wordes moved the common people to compassion: he framed his eloquence to make their harts yerne the more, and taking Caesars gowne all bloudy in his hand, he layed it open to the sight of them all, shewing what a number of cuts and holes it had upon it. Therewithall the people fell presently into such a rage and mutinie, that there was no more order kept amongest the common people.[48]

From this brief but suggestive comment, Shakespeare draws inspiration for Antony's powerful oration. Whereas Plutarch does not indicate whether Antony had been playing a waiting game or merely acting in response to propitious circumstances, Shakespeare leaves no doubt about Antony's calculation. Plutarch makes it plain that when their houses were attacked 'the conspirators forseeing the daunger before, had wisely provided for them selves, and fled'.[49] Brutus was alone in failing to foresee the outcome. These critical miscalculations by Brutus form a structural feature of the play.

The riot also resulted in the strange murder of Cinna, who was mistaken for his namesake, one of the assassins. This Cinna was a friend of Caesar's who left his sick-bed to attend the funeral after experiencing a dream in which Caesar led him to supper against his will. The incident evidently fired Shakespeare's imagination, because he created out of it a chilling scene consisting of an amalgam of tragedy and farce. It is this incident which persuaded Brutus and Cassius to flee from Rome 'within a fewe dayes after'.[50]

Brutus and Cassius fled to Antium and waited for the pendulum to swing their way again, being conscious, as Plutarch puts it, of the 'fickle and unconstant' nature of the 'multitude'.[51] Indeed, this change of attitude did occur because of Antony's arrogant and dictatorial behaviour, but Brutus, fearing the presence of Caesar's soldiers who might seek revenge, did not return to Rome. Thus into the vacuum stepped the young Octavius, 'the sonne of Julius Caesars nece, whome he had adopted for his sonne, and made his heire, by his last will and testament'.[52] Antony initially underestimated this young man and attempted to push him aside when he arrived in Rome, but Octavius soon began 'to curry favor with the common people'. He 'tooke upon him his adopted fathers name, and made distribution amonge them of the money which his father had bequeathed unto them'.[53] By a variety of strategems Octavius outmanoeuvred Antony and, with the backing of Cicero, gained the support of the Senate, driving Antony out of Italy. The rejoicing was shortlived, however, for Octavius maintained an army and stood for Consul although it was contrary to law. When the Senate turned to Brutus for salvation, Octavius made overtures to Antony. Although he was only twenty years old, Octavius was made Consul. He soon appointed judges to condemn and sentence Brutus and Cassius. Moving with speed and ruthless efficiency Octavius Caesar divided the Empire between Antony, Lepidus and himself. The triumvirate then 'set up billes of proscription and outlawry, condemning two hundred of the noblest men of Rome to suffer death, and among that number, Cicero was one'.[54]

In response to developments in Rome, Brutus and Cassius each gathered an army and joined forces in Smyrna. Plutarch describes with admiration their achievement:

> So they were marvelous joyfull, and no lesse coragious, when they saw the great armies together which they had both leavied: considering that they departing out of Italy, like naked and poore banished men, without armor and money, nor having any shippe ready, nor souldier about them, nor any one towne at their commaundement: yet notwithstanding, in a short time after they were now met together, having shippes, money and souldiers enowe, both footemen and horsemen, to fight for the Empire of Rome.[55]

Though the circumstances of their meeting were propitious they soon fell to quarrelling. Plutarch prefaces his account of the dispute with character portraits:

> And men reputed [Cassius] commonly to be very skilfull in warres, but otherwise marvelous chollerick and cruell, who sought to rule men by feare, rather then with lenitie: and on the other side he was too familiar with his friends, and would jest too brodely with them. But Brutus in contrary manner, for his vertue and valliantnes, was well-beloved of the people and his owne, esteemed of noble men, and hated of no man, not so much as of his enemies: bicause he was a marvelous lowly and gentle person, noble minded, and would never be in any rage, nor caried away with pleasure and covetousnes, but had ever an upright mind with him, and would never yeeld to any wronge or injustice, the which was the chiefest cause of his fame, of his rising, and of the good

will that every man bare him: for they were all perswaded that his intent
was good . . . as for Cassius, a hot, chollerick and cruell man, that
would oftentymes be caried away from justice for gayne: it was certainly
thought that he made warre, and put him selfe into sundry daungers,
more to have absolute power and authoritie, then to defend the libertie
of his contry . . . And in contrary manner, his enemies them selves did
never reprove Brutus, for any such chaunge or desire. For, it was sayd
that Antonius spake it openly divers tymes, that he thought, that of all
them that had slayne Caesar, there was none but Brutus only that was
moved to doe it, as thinking the acte commendable of it selfe: but that
all the other conspirators did conspire his death, for some private malice
or envy, that they otherwise did beare unto him.[56]

Shakespeare incorporates (in the quarrel scene) some of the characteristics
ascribed to Cassius. The crucial last section forms the basis of Antony's
panegyric over Brutus' body at the end of the play.

The two quarrels between Brutus and Cassius described in Plutarch are
conflated by Shakespeare to a single event. The historian records that
Cassius sent Brutus one-third of his funds despite the opposition of his
colleagues. In the play, Brutus denounces Cassius for not sending a share
of the funds when he himself is unable to raise the money by such 'vile'
means. The first quarrel, recounted by Plutarch, is inspired by the mutual
hostility of the captains and ends with the intervention of the Cynic poet;
the second arises out of Brutus' condemnation of Lucius Pella for taking
bribes. What Shakespeare does with this material is to shape a magnificent
scene in which Cassius reveals his yearning for Brutus' love. Cassius'
assertion that he is a 'better' soldier than Brutus (later amended to 'elder')
is Shakespeare's invention (perhaps inspired by the knowledge that Cassius
was the better soldier). His passionate desire to retain the new-found
amity is such that he is unwilling to oppose Brutus over the battle plans
even though he knows them to be wrong. We also gain a sense of Brutus
as a profoundly troubled man, grieving over the death of Portia and
possibly burdened with a feeling of guilt for the murder of Caesar (if only
at a subconscious level). The dramatist uses the Cynic poet to point up a
contrast between these major figures: Cassius is amused; Brutus outraged.

The omens turned against Brutus and Cassius the day before the battle
of Philippi. The eagles that had followed them so faithfully suddenly
departed. Not unduly alarmed by this, they were, nevertheless, scrupulous
in undertaking the religious rites that preceded battle. Despite the
thoroughness of their spiritual observances they encountered more bad
omens, disconcerting leaders and men alike. Even more demoralising for
Brutus was the appearance of a strange 'image' which said 'I am thy ill
angell, Brutus, and thou shalt see me by the citie of Philippes'. This did
not prevent Brutus winning the first battle, but shortly before the second

battle, 'this spirit appeared again unto him, but spake never a word'.[57] The historian describes the last conflict of views between Cassius and Brutus, as they contemplate the forthcoming battle:

> Cassius was of opinion not to trye this warre at one battell, but rather to delay tyme, and to drawe it out in length, considering that they were the stronger in money, and the weaker in men and armors. But Brutus in contrary manner, did alway before, and at that tyme also, desire nothing more, then to put all to the hazard of battell, as soone as might be possible: to the ende he might either quickely restore his contry to her former libertie, or rid him forthwith of this miserable world.[58]

Plutarch goes on to describe how Brutus engaged in lively conversation over supper while a forlorn Cassius turned to Messala, saying, 'I protest unto thee, and make thee my witnes, that I am compelled against my minde and will (as Pompey the great was) to jeopard the libertie of our contry, to the hazard of a battel.'[59] Shakespeare uses these lines almost word for word and records another significant piece of information imparted by Plutarch – that the following day was Cassius' birthday. The sense (though not the structure nor the beauty) of the leaders' parting speech, is taken from Plutarch,[60] as is Brutus' condemnation of Cato's suicide, allied with his own determination to kill himself rather than be taken captive.

Cassius' generosity of spirit again emerges when Brutus requests the right wing of the attack. Cassius concedes this privilege even though he is the older and more experienced soldier. In the event Brutus' orders were misunderstood. The result was that his attack was a hopelessly disorganized affair. Even so Messala's men stormed through Octavius' camp and would have killed him, but he was absent either through sickness or on the advice of a friend who had received a premonition on the previous evening. Despite the disordered nature of Brutus' attack his force triumphed whereas that of Cassius failed. Had there been a clear perception of the situation, victory would have fallen to Brutus and Cassius:

> For nothing undid them, but that Brutus went not to helpe Cassius, thinking he had overcome them, as him selfe had done: and Cassius on the other side taried not for Brutus, thinking he had bene overthrowen, as him selfe was.[61]

Plutarch goes on to recount how Cassius, having fled, stood on a hill attempting to discern Brutus' position: 'howebeit Cassius him selfe sawe nothing, for his sight was verie bad'[62] (a point of detail picked up by Shakespeare). Titinius rode out to evaluate the situation, and was greeted by Brutus' men. Unfortunately his colleagues mistakenly believed he had been taken captive; Cassius retired to his tent with the words 'I have lived to see one of my best frendes taken, for my sake, before my face'.[63] He was later found with his head severed; his slave Pindarus 'was never seene more'.[64] When Titinius returned to discover the error he blamed himself for delay and promptly killed himself. Brutus on his arrival at the camp was confronted by this grim sight. Praising Cassius he called him 'the last of all the Romanes, being unpossible that Rome should ever breede againe so noble and valiant a man as he'[65] – words closely echoed by Shakespeare.

Whereas Shakespeare compacts the deaths of Cassius and Brutus, Plutarch recounts how Brutus restored the morale and confidence of his men, provided them with two thousand drachmas each, and promised them that should they prevail over the re-organised armies of Antony and Caesar, 'he would geve them the sacke and spoyle of two cities, to wit, Thessalonica, and Lacedaemon'. Plutarch is saddened by having to recount this, and can find no mitigation except by comparison with the behaviour of men who have no claim to any moral stature:

> In all Brutus life there is but this only fault to be found, and that is not to be gainesaid: though Antonius and Octavius Caesar did reward their souldiers farre worse for their victory. For when they had driven all the naturall Italians out of Italie, they gave their souldiers their landes and townes, to the which they had no right: and moreover, the only marke they shot at in all this warre they made, was but to overcome, and raigne.[66]

Despite the difficulties confronting Brutus – such as the indiscipline of Cassius' soldiers once his stern hand had been removed – he had an enormous advantage over his enemies who were camped in low-lying marshland which was cold and damp. Moreover, Brutus' navy had secured an overwhelming victory on the same day that the land battle had been fought, with the result that he had the prospect of plentiful supplies whereas Antony and Octavius faced a dearth. All Brutus had to do was to stand and hold his ground. Unfortunately, the news of the sea victory was delayed for twenty days. The night before the second battle, one Cilodius, who had intelligence of the outcome of the sea battle in Octavius' camp, attempted to impart the news to Brutus but was disbelieved and prevented from seeing him. That night the 'monstrous spirit'[67] again appeared before Brutus in his tent. On the day of the battle there were several other strange events, all of which were unfavourable to Brutus.[68] As the battle was about to commence one of his bravest captains rode out before Brutus' very eyes and surrendered to the enemy. Despite all these setbacks Brutus fought well and lost only because of the cowardly behaviour of Cassius' soldiers. Brutus, Plutarch comments, 'in the middest of the conflict, did all that was possible for a skillful Captaine and valliant souldier: both for his wisedom, as also for his hardinesse, for the obtaining of victorie'.[69]

A number of small details of the battle recorded by Plutarch are taken up by Shakespeare: the courage of the son of Marcus Cato, who calls aloud his name and that of his father in the battle; Lucilius, Brutus' friend, surrenders to a group of soldiers heading for his leader and diverts them by pretending to be Brutus. Shakespeare follows Plutarch closely when Lucilius addresses Antony:

Antonius, I dare assure thee, that no enemie hath taken, nor shall take Marcus Brutus alive: and I beseech God keepe him from that fortune. For wheresoever he be found, alive or dead: he will be found like him selfe.

And Antony's response:

I doe assure you, you have taken a better bootie, then that you followed . . . For, I had rather have suche men my frendes, as this man here, then enemies. Then he embraced Lucilius, and at that time delivered him to one of his frendes in custodie, and Lucilius ever after served him faithfullie, even to his death.[70]

Again, Plutarch's description of Brutus seeking the aid of his friends to commit suicide is followed faithfully by Shakespeare:

Now, the night being farre spent, Brutus as he sate bowed towards Clitus one of his men, and told him somewhat in his eare, the other aunswered him not, but fell a weeping. Thereupon he proved Dardanus, and sayd somwhat also to him: at length he came to Volumnius him selfe, and speaking to him in Graeke, prayed him for the studies sake which brought them acquainted together, that he woulde helpe him to put his hande to his sword, to thrust it in him to kill him. Volumnius denied his request, and so did many others: and amongest the rest, one of them sayd, there was no tarying for them there, but that they must needes flie. Then Brutus rising up, We must flie in deede sayd he, but it must be with our hands, not with our feete.[71]

The substance of Brutus' dying words is also taken by Shakespeare from Plutarch:

Then taking every man by the hand, he sayd these words unto them with a cheerefull countenance: It rejoyceth my hart that not one of my frends hath failed me at my neede, and I do not complaine of my fortune, but only for my contries sake: for, as for me, I thinke my selfe happier than they that have overcome, considering that I leave a perpetuall fame of our corage and manhoode, the which our enemies the conquerors shall never attaine unto by force nor money, neither can let their posteritie to say, that they being naughtie and unjust men, have slaine good men, to usurpe tyrannical power not pertaining to them.[72]

The dramatist, however, effects subtle shifts which casts an ironical light on Brutus. For the words 'It rejoyceth my hart that not one of my frends hath failed me at my neede' Shakespeare has

> My heart doth joy that yet in all my life
> I found no man but he was true to me.
> (V.v.34–5)

The sentence in Plutarch does not provoke any thought of Brutus' own personal betrayal of Caesar; Shakespeare's lines heighten our consciousness of that betrayal – and Brutus' lack of awareness of it. Likewise, Shakespeare's lines give Brutus a more abrasive, over-confident quality not present in Plutarch:

> I shall have glory by this losing day
> More than Octavius and Mark Antony
> By this vile conquest shall attain unto.
> (V.v.36–8)

The difference in tone invites the audience to think about historical judgments. Brutus was by no means extolled in the way he imagined: even those most favourably disposed towards him were ambivalent, whereas many authorities reviled him. One thing to emerge clearly from the play is that Brutus precipitates the very defeat of democracy that he sought to preserve. It takes Mark Antony's generous and tender words to leave the audience with a feeling of the nobility of Brutus (V.v.68–75).

Plutarch comments that some said Strato held Brutus' sword for him, and that both he and Messala gave themselves up to Octavius, who accepted their offers of service. Shakespeare follows this closely, including Strato's words on being brought before Octavius: 'Caesar, beholde, here is he that did the last service to my Brutus'.[73] One significant difference is that the dramatist gives these events a political edge. The feeling is conveyed that Antony and Octavius do not act out of a sense of generosity or good fellowship but that they are shrewdly gathering capable and loyal men around them as a matter of self-interest.

One fascinating change by Shakespeare is that he omits Antony's magnanimous gesture of giving orders for Brutus' body to be 'wrapped up in one of the richest cote armors he had'.[74] Instead Antony speaks the beautiful panegyric delivered over the body of Brutus. Plutarch provides an ambiguous footnote on the death of Portia in which he cites the views of earlier writers who stated that she 'tooke hotte burning coles, and cast them into her mouth, and kept her mouth so close, that she choked her selfe'.[75]

In his evaluation of Julius Caesar's rule, Plutarch comes down heavily against the justice of his assassination, asserting:

Howbeit Caesars power and government when it came to be established, did in deede much hurt at his first entrie and beginning unto those that did resist him: but afterwardes, unto them that being overcome had received his government, it seemed he rather had the name and opinion onely of a tyranne, then otherwise that he was so in deede. For there never followed any tyrannicall nor cruell act, but contrarilie, it seemed that he was a mercifull Phisition, whom God had ordeyned of speciall grace to be Governor of the Empire of Rome, and to set all thinges againe at quiet stay, the which required the counsell and authoritie of an absolute Prince. And therefore the Romanes were marvelous sorie for Caesar after he was slaine and afterwardes would never pardon them that had slaine him.[76]

And he goes on to insist that Brutus could not escape censure for murdering his benefactor:

the greatest reproache they could object against Brutus, was: that Julius Caesar having saved his life, and pardoned all the prisoners also taken in battell, as many as he had made request for, taking him for his frende and honoring him above all his other frends. Brutus notwithstanding had imbrued his hands in his blood.[77]

Nevertheless, Plutarch defends Brutus on the basis that his motives were of the highest – even his enemies agreeing that he sought only 'to restore the Empire of Rome againe, to her former state and government'.[78] The historian also makes the point that despite the difficulties of planning the assassination it was successfully accomplished because Brutus chose 'honest men, or else that by his choyse of them, he made them good men'.[79] Finally, Plutarch claims the purity of Brutus' motives are demonstrated by the honourable burial afforded him by one of his enemies, Antony, while the other, Octavius, 'reserved his honors and memories of him'.[80]

In his account of Cicero's life, Plutarch reveals Octavius' use of him in order to obtain the Consulship and to drive Antony from Rome. When, however, it was to Octavius' advantage to join forces with Antony and Lepidus, not only did he 'divide the Empire of Rome with them, as if it had bene lands left in common between them' but he also agreed that Cicero's name be added to the proscription list. Plutarch describes the horse-trading with evident disgust:

Some say that Caesar stuck hard with Cicero the two first dayes, but at the third, that he yeelded and forsooke him. The exchaunge they agreed upon betwene them, was this. Caesar forsooke Cicero: Lepidus, his owne brother Paulus: and Antonius, Lucius Caesar, his uncle by the mothers side. Such wrath tooke place in them, as they regarded no kindred nor blood, and to speake more properly, they shewed that no brute or savage beast is so cruell as man if with his licentiousnes he have liberty to execute his will.[81]

He then describes the way in which Cicero was captured and murdered – the boy who betrayed his escape route being an enfranchised slave educated by Cicero, and one of the chief murderers a man acquitted of murder in a case where Cicero defended him. Even more disgusting than the details of the killing is what follows:

> So Cicero being three score and foure yeares of age, thrust his necke out of the litter, and had his hed cut of by Antonius commaundement, and his hands also, which wrote the Orations (called the Philippians) against him . . . When these poore dismembred members were brought to Rome, Antonius by chaunce was busily occupied at that time about the election of certaine officers: who when he heard of them and saw them, he cried out alowde that now all his outlawries and proscriptions were executed: and thereuppon commaunded his head and his hands should straight be set up over the pulpit for Orations, in the place called Rostra. This was a fearefull and horrible sight unto the Romanes, who thought they saw not Ciceroes face, but an image of Antonius life and disposicion . . .[82]

Of the numerous subsidiary sources available to Shakespeare for details of characters and events, two of the most interesting are Suetonius and Appian. Some of their observations are particularly worth noting as possible influences on the dramatist.

Suetonius' *The Historie of Twelve Caesars*, translated by Philemon Holland (printed in 1606), provides a fascinating character sketch of Julius Caesar, an account of his passion for honours, and a description of the assassination and events leading up to it. First, there is a fine physical description and an insight into the almost comic insecurities of the great man, such as his delight in being able to wear the laurel garland to conceal his baldness.

> Of stature he is reported to have bene tall; of complexion white and cleare; with limbs well trussed and in good plight; somewhat full faced; his eies black, lively, and quick; also very healthfull, saving that in his latter daies he was given to faint and swoune sodainly; yea, and as he dreamed, to start and be affrighted: twice also in the midst of his martiall affaires, he was surprized with the falling sicknes. About the trimming of his body, he was over-curious: so as he would not onely be notted and shaven very precisely, but also have his haire plucked, in so much as some cast it in his teeth, and twitted him therewith. Moreover, finding by experience, that the deformity of his bald head was oftentimes subject to the scoffes and scornes of back-biters and slaunderers, hee tooke the same exceedingly to the heart: and therefore he both had usually drawne

downe his haire that grew but thin, from the crowne toward his fore-head: and also of all honours decreed unto him from the Senate and People, he neither received nor used any more willingly, than the privi-ledge to weare continually the triumphant Lawrel guirland. Men say also, that in his apparel he was noted for singularity, as who used to goe in his Senatours purple studded robe, trimmed with a jagge or frindge at the sleeve hand: and the same so, as hee never was but girt over it, and that very slack and loose . . .[83]

Suetonius goes on to write that he was given to 'carnall pleasures' dishon-ouring 'many Dames' in the process, but that 'most especially hee fancied Cleopatra'.[84] If his appetite was excessive when it came to women, Sue-tonius acknowledges Caesar's indifference to food and drink. He recounts a fascinating incident in which Caesar's fellow guests declined to partake of 'olde ranke oile' set before them, while Caesar consumed it with relish, 'because he would not be thought to blame his Host either for negligence or rusticitie'.[85]

The historian emphasizes Caesar's susceptibility to flattery and his weak-ness for honours:

he not only tooke upon him excessive honours, to wit, continued Consul-ship, perpetuall Dictature, and Presidency of Manners; and more than so, the forename of Emperour, the Surname Father of his Countrie; his statue among the Kings, an eminent seate of Estate raised above the rest in the *orchestra*, among the Senatours: but hee suffered also more stately dignities than beseeming the condition of a mortall wight to bee decreed and ordained for him: namely, a golden Throne in the Curia, and before the Tribunal: a sacred Chariot and therein a frame carrying an Image, at the solemne pomp of his Games *Circenses*: Temples, Altars, his owne Images placed neere unto the Gods: a sacred Bedloft for such Images to be bestowed upon: a *flamen*, certaine *Luper-ci*: and the denomination of one moneth after his owne name. Besides, no honourable offices there were but he tooke and gave at his owne pleasure.[86]

Suetonius' description of the assassination brings out Caesar's physical courage and his sense of dignity. Moreover, it reveals two accounts of Caesar's last moments: one in which he says nothing; and the other in which he refers to Brutus as 'and thou my sonne'.

Then Caesar catching Cassius by the arme thrust it through with his stile or writing punches; and with that being about to leape forward he was met with another wound and stayed. Now when he perceived himselfe beset on everie side and assailed with drawne daggers he wrapped and covered his head with his gowne: but withall he let downe the large lap with his left hand to his legges beneath, hiding thereby the inferiour part also of his bodie, that he might fall more decently: and so, with 3 and 20 wounds he was stabbed: during which time he gave but one grone, without any worde uttered, and that was at the first thrust; although some have written, that as M. Brutus came running upon him he said 'And thou my sonne'.[87]

In assessing the antagonism provoked by Caesar, Suetonius claims that 'the greatest envie and inexpiable hatred he drew upon himselfe' occurred when 'al the Senatours in generall came unto him with many and those most honourable decrees, he received them sitting still before the Temple of Venus Genitrix'.[88] The man whose courtesy was such that he swallowed bad oil rather than embarrass his host, and whose discretion and judgment gained him political power and astonishing military triumphs, was capable of making a fatal error of decorum, merely to assert his own importance. This last element is powerfully present in Shakespeare's characterization.

Among the most significant of the probable sources reproduced by Bullough is Appian's *The Civil Wars*. The section dealing with Antony's speech at Caesar's funeral may have offered numerous suggestions for Shakespeare. First, Appian records how Antony opened his oration by referring to his role as 'Consul, of a Consul, friend, of a friend, and kinsman, of a kinsman (for Antony was partly his kinsman)'. Shakespeare's Antony insists 'He was my friend, faithful and just to me' (III.ii.87). And this element of friendship is the fulcrum on which the argument is balanced, as Antony insinuates a contrast between Caesar's loyalty as a friend and Brutus' disloyalty and betrayal of friendship. Second, Appian draws attention to the way in which Antony used Caesar's body as a focal point: 'Antonie directed his countenance and hands to Caesars body' and mixed 'pitie and indignation' – key features adopted by Shakespeare. Third, Antony invites the citizens to 'purge' themselves of 'this unkindnesse'. Shakespeare writes of the wound inflicted by Brutus, 'This was the most unkindest cut of all' (III.ii.185). Fourth, after Antony had stirred the crowd to a passion creating 'an uproare' and swearing that he was 'ready to revenge', he 'waxed colde, and recanted hys wordes'. Shakespeare's Antony, having created the same commotion, exerts exactly the same restraint:

Good friends, sweet friends, let me not stir you up
To such a sudden flood of mutiny.

(III.ii.212–13)

Fifth, Antony, having 'gyrded' his gown 'that he might better stirre his handes', sang a hymn to Caesar, then 'rehearsed the warres, the fights, the victories, the nations that he had subdued to his Countrey, and the great booties that he had sent, making every one to be a marvell'.[89]

Shakespeare's Antony does not provide this catalogue of victories but at one point makes the critical observation,

> He hath brought many captives home to Rome,
> Whose ransoms did the general coffers fill:
> Did this in Caesar seem ambitious?
>
> (III.ii.90–2)

Shakespeare's Antony reminds his audience of Caesar's triumphs but turns them into acts of public service rather than a quest for personal glory. Later in the speech he refers to one of Caesar's greatest victories but does so in a way that makes it appear an inadvertent reference, made only because it is associated with the gown worn by Caesar when he was struck down:

> If you have tears, prepare to shed them now.
> You all do know this mantle. I remember
> The first time ever Caesar put it on;
> 'Twas on a summer's evening in his tent,
> That day he overcame the Nervii.
>
> (III.ii.171–5)

The intense realization of this event – ''Twas on a summer's evening in his tent' and the subtlety of the reference to one specific triumph, exerts a much more powerful hold on the imagination of the crowd than the reiteration of a list of victories, but it is hard to believe that Shakespeare was not influenced in this respect by Appian's description. Next Appian recounts how Antony

> falling into moste vehement affections, uncovered *Caesars* body, holding up his vesture with a speare, cut with woundes, and redde with the bloude of the chiefe Ruler, by the which the people lyke a Quire, did sing lamentation unto him, and by this passion were againe repleate with ire.[90]

Shakespeare's Antony, of course, makes much greater use of the gown, specifying the perpetrators of each rent in the bloodstained garment. But even this detail may have been suggested by Appian who says of Antony:

> Then made he *Caesar* hymselfe to speake as it were in a lamentable sort, to howe many of his enemies he hadde done good by name, and of the killers themselves to say as in an admiration, *Did I save them that have killed me*? This the people could not abide, calling to remembraunce, that all the kyllers (only *Decimus* except) were of *Pompeys* faction, and subdued by hym, to whom, in stead of punishment, he had given promotion of offices, governments of provinces and armies, and thought *Decimus* worthy to be made his heyre and son by adoption, and yet conspired hys death.[91]

Clearly, the significance of this description is to emphasize the ingratitude and disloyalty of men to whom Caesar had been benefactor. Shakespeare imaginatively enters into the mind of the historical Antony, perceives his intent, but devises a more effective means for achieving the desired emotional pressure. Shakespeare's Antony follows Appian's Antony in the next move and goes beyond him. Appian tells how Antony brought

> the Image of *Caesar*, made of waxe, for hys body it selfe lying flat in the Litter, could not be seene. Hys picture was by a devise turned about, and .xxiii. wounds wer shewed over al his body, and his face horrible to behold. The people seeing this pittifull picture, coulde beare the dolour no longer, but thronged togyther, and beset the Senate house, wherein *Caesar* was kylled, and set it a fyre, and the kyllers that fledde for their lives.

Shakespeare's Antony reveals the body itself:

> Kind souls, what weep you when you but behold
> Our Caesar's vesture wounded? Look you here!
> Here is himself, marr'd, as you see, with traitors.
> (III.ii.197–9)

The response in both cases is explosive – but whereas in Appian's account the crowd storm off to take their destructive revenge, including the horrible killing of Cinna, whom they 'cruelly tore . . . to peeces, and lefte not one parte to be put in grave',[92] Shakespeare's crowd is restrained in order to hear the will – the will which establishes them as Caesar's heirs: a will which, in all the historical accounts, had been made known before the funeral.

A comparison of Appian's account with Shakespeare's powerful scene reveals the way in which Shakespeare absorbed the impact of detail and submerged himself imaginatively into the historical situation while simultaneously translating these events into a dramatic structure with all its possibilities and limitations. What emerges from an examination of the source material used by Shakespeare is the sense of a scrupulous mind ranging over the details and having its imagination kindled by excitement. The contrast between what enters the crucible of the imagination and what emerges from it generally leaves the reader awed, but it is perhaps possible to catch a glimpse of the process of metamorphosis.

William and Barbara Rosen, '*Julius Caesar*: the speciality of rule', make the telling point that,

> In striving for fullness and accuracy of assessment, Plutarch shifts from a favourable account of a character's traits and actions to an unfavourable point of view and back again with a startling abruptness, and usually refuses a final judgement.[93]

This enigmatic quality of the characters found in Plutarch could hardly have been more stimulating for the dramatist. However successful Shakespeare was in bringing these characters to life, he retained some of the mystery and opacity to be found in Plutarch's portraits. Critics still hold conflicting views about the central characters, and much of the critical work on the play has been devoted to analysing the thought processes and actions of Brutus and Julius Caesar. Brutus' orchard soliloquy alone has given rise to a great deal of fascinating discussion. The diversity of critical assessments of the main characters and the movements of audience sympathy has led to a recognition that the play is, in the words of Adrian Bonjour, a 'drama of divided sympathies'.[94] As Geoffrey Bullough suggests, Shakespeare 'seems to have wished to compose an objective and impartial picture of the interrelationship of Brutus and Cassius, Caesar, Antony and Octavius, while entering as little as possible into the complexities of the political situation'.[95] In the process of dramatising a momentous historical event, Shakespeare not only captivates his audience by provoking an active participation in evaluation of character, morality and political judgment, but simultaneously creates a landmark in the history of drama. As W. Warde Fowler observed in his *Roman Essays and Interpretations*, 'The idea that a good man could do incalculable harm from the best possible motives was, as far as I know, a new one in tragedy'.[96] Willard Farnham echoed this comment in *Shakespeare's Tragic Frontier*: 'Before Brutus there had been no tragic hero on the English stage whose character had combined noble grandeur with fatal imperfection'.[97] But Shakespeare's innovation did not stop there, as *Julius Caesar* has been seen as a play belonging to or embodying various genres: a tragedy in the mould of *Hamlet*, *Othello*, *King Lear* or *Macbeth*; a revenge tragedy belonging to the clearly identifiable strain emanating from Kyd's *Spanish Tragedy*; a Roman history; and a political play. Ernest Schanzer, for instance, points out in *Shakespeare's Problem Plays* that

> The two elements which Aristotle thought necessary for the profoundest tragedy, *peripeteia* and *anagnorisis*, an ironic turn of events which makes an action have the very opposite effect of that intended, and the realization of this by the agent, are thus seen to be fundamental to our play. They are found, in varying degrees of prominence, in all of Shakespeare's mature tragedies.[98]

Norman Rabkin argues persuasively in 'Structure, convention and meaning in *Julius Caesar*' that 'The action of the play makes clear sense in terms of revenge tragedy',[99] while Hugh M. Richmond claims that 'There is thus a supreme irony in the last scene of the play, which definitively eliminates the possibility of treating Brutus as a tragic hero, and requires instead that we see the action as a study of political forces'.[100] These viewpoints are open to debate but there can be no doubt that there is a strong political element in the play. Indeed, a great deal of the fascination of the play has arisen out of a recognition of the complex interplay between the public and private worlds. As L.C. Knights has expressed the matter, in 'Personality and politics in *Julius Caesar*':

> We notice, too, how often the word 'love' appears in this play. I haven't made a count, but it must be about two dozen times, which is perhaps rather surprising in a political play. Again and again the characters speak of their love – their 'dear love' or their 'kind love' – for each other, just as they seem to find a special satisfaction in referring to themselves as 'brothers'. Now the effect of all this is not only one of pathos or simply irony. The focus of our attention, I have said, is the public world: from the arena of *that* world, personal life – where truth between man and man resides – is glimpsed as across a gulf. The distance between these two worlds is the measure of the distortion and falsity that takes place in the attempt to make 'politics' self-enclosed.[101]

Just as the interplay between the political and private spheres has been recognized, so too is there an awareness of the peculiarly Roman quality of the play. In addition to the prominence given to topography, officers, customs and traditions, the very names of the chief participants carry a resonance. As R.A. Foakes has observed in 'Language and action in *Julius Caesar*',

> The names of Caesar (211 times), Brutus (130 times), and to a much lesser degree Cassius (69 times) and Antony (68 times) echo through the play, and are used frequently where a pronoun would occur in the other tragedies. Besides contributing to the formality and dignity of the play, the names of Caesar and Brutus in particular have their own special meanings. The word Caesar had long been in use to signify an all-conquering, absolute monarch, and is used in the play with this implication . . . The name of Brutus is equated with honour . . . The names of Caesar and Brutus thus have symbolic qualities, and represent a concept as well as an individual character. Two other names which have much importance are that of Rome and Roman (72 times in the play), and the name of liberty. The fact that he is a Roman should in itself indicate certain qualities in a man . . . it is significant that after the end of Act III the words 'Rome' and 'Roman' occur only in the mouths of the rebels until the final tribute of Antony to Brutus:
>
> > This was the noblest Roman of them all.
> >
> > (V.v.68)
>
> The conspirators, especially Brutus and Cassius, associate themselves with Rome as the home of truth, honor, liberty, and manliness . . .[102]

There is, however, something paradoxical associated with the intensity of the feeling of Rome and the urgency of political conflict. The nature of the political situation is never clear. As Alexander Leggatt suggests in *Shakespeare's Political Drama*,

> The play gives little sense of the republican constitution; Caesar seems to be not overturning an established order but moving into a political vacuum. Instead of a clear system we have an ideal of Romanness, something inherent in the blood, guaranteeing integrity of behaviour.[103]

The precise position prevailing in Rome at the beginning of the action has been clearly stated by R.A.G. Carson in 'The Ides of March':

> In modern political thought the term dictatorship means the exercise of unconstitutional supreme power; but in the Roman Republic the dictatorship was an office to which a man was constitutionally appointed at a crisis of the State's affairs. When the crisis was safely over, the dictator resigned his appointment, as Sulla had done. In Caesar's case, however, the appointment had been given him for life; and on some of his coins his portrait appears coupled with the title *Dictator Perpetuus*.
>
> In addition, at the end of 45, Caesar was given the consulship, in normal times the chief annual magistracy of the Roman state, for a period of ten years. The *Praefectura Morum*, a reviewing authority which controlled entry into the Senate, was also now bestowed on him permanently. More to the point, it was Caesar alone who had command of armed forces.
>
> As the year 44 opened, the great political question in men's minds, not least in that of Caesar himself, must have been how his supreme power was to be given a durable expression. Doubtless Caesar could have maintained his autocracy for his lifetime; but the experience of the Civil Wars had shown that Roman political organization was inadequate to control and perpetuate a widespread empire. It must have been Caesar's purpose, as a statesman, to establish a system that would continue beyond his lifetime. Contemporary sources, which Shakespeare followed in close detail, allege that Caesar's intended solution was the establishment of a monarchy.[104]

Shakespeare has deliberately left the audience with a feeling of uncertainty about the precise nature of the constitutional position in Rome, because that uncertainty is part of the excitement which is engendered from the opening lines of the play. The audience is immediately caught up in the flow of political passions and is made curious about political allegiances and conflicts. It is the personalities, their perceptions, values, affections and antagonisms, rather than constitutional niceties, that capture the imagination. The central political issue, whether Julius Caesar seeks to become a king and thereby suffocate Roman democracy, is clearly understood but never resolved. Moreover, the blurring of issues is part of the

living reality of the political world. The imagery conveys a sense that for
many of Caesar's opponents he has already grown too big. It is Brutus in
his orchard soliloquy who clears Caesar of abuse of power, but for the
other conspirators even the possession of that power is excessive and
intolerable. Brutus is both over-scrupulous – refusing to condemn Caesar
for his acquisition of power – and insufficiently scrupulous – condemning
him to death out of fear of his possible future actions as a king.

The essentially political nature of *Julius Caesar* is manifest in the opening scene of the play. The language of Flavius and Marullus is prosiac and
direct. Their questions carry a sense of urgency and frustration.

> FLAVIUS Hence! home, you idle creatures, get you home:
> Is this a holiday? What, know you not,
> Being mechanical, you ought not walk
> Upon a labouring day without the sign
> Of your profession? Speak, what trade art thou?
>
> (I.i.1–5)

But rather than gaining the respect of the crowd, they are teased and
baited by the cobbler (who is evidently not in awe of his social superiors).
This truculence and vitality followed by submission, suggests that the
plebeians constitute a significant but unstable element in the political life
of Rome. The tribunes' indictment of them creates a visual image of the
city and its inhabitants full of movement and vigour:

> MARULLUS Wherefore rejoice? What conquest brings he home?
> What tributaries follow him to Rome,
> To grace in captive bonds his chariot wheels?
> You blocks, you stones, you worse than senseless things!
> O you hard hearts, you cruel men of Rome,
> Knew you not Pompey? Many a time and oft
> Have you climb'd up to walls and battlements,
> To towers and windows, yea, to chimney-tops,
> Your infants in your arms, and there have sat
> The livelong day, with patient expectation,
> To see great Pompey pass the streets of Rome:
> And when you saw his chariot but appear,
> Have you not made an universal shout,
> That Tiber trembled underneath her banks
> To hear the replication of your sounds
> Made in her concave shores?
> And do you now put on your best attire?
> And do you now cull out a holiday?
> And do you now strew flowers in his way,
> That comes in triumph over Pompey's blood?

70

Be gone!
Run to your houses, fall upon your knees,
Pray to the gods to intermit the plague
That needs must light on this ingratitude.

(I.i.32–55)

This speech vibrates with a sense of Rome as a physical reality, and as the embodiment of a distinct ethos. The charge of inconstancy and ingratitude, the betrayal of Rome's heroic past, encapsulated in the name of Pompey, will be repeated by Mark Antony, but then the symbol of Roman achievement will be Julius Caesar. As the crowd disperse the diction and tone once more become prosaic – it then rises with the last four lines of the scene, presenting the image of a powerful Caesar, and a political antagonism which is intense:

These growing feathers pluck'd from Caesar's wing
Will make him fly an ordinary pitch,
Who else would soar above the view of men
And keep us all in servile fearfulness.

(I.i.72–5)

Already, then, in this brief opening scene there is a sense of a pulsating Rome; a Rome in which the ordinary people seem unthinking but vigorous; a Rome in which there is fervid political conflict and an acute awareness of the past, but with a history and destiny that is still being shaped as well as weighing on the present.

Without being fully conscious of the fact, the audience is caught up in the swirl of political tension; it is made aware of the peculiar atmosphere of Rome. The physical landmarks of the city resonate in the speech of Marullus, while Pompey's fame and his defeat by Caesar animate its history. His greatness cannot be forgotten, and those who oppose Caesar recall Pompey's name to cast a shadow over Rome's all-powerful leader. This image of Pompey as a factor, a virtual participant in the existing political struggle, constitutes one of the most fascinating aspects of a play which vibrates with a sense of history and the attempt to shape Rome's destiny.

In this play, as in no other, Shakespeare explores the significance of personal and political images and self-images. The audience is immediately presented with perceptions of images and self-images which are subjected to telling ironies. All the images used by Caesar's detractors are intended to disparage him by showing his power as disproportionate. Instead, they have the effect of reinforcing the image of the demi-god. Cassius' image as he attempts to draw Brutus into the conspiracy is a good example:

Why, man, he doth bestride the narrow world
Like a Colossus, and we petty men

71

Walk under his huge legs, and peep about
To find ourselves dishonourable graves.

(I.ii.133–6)

Conversely, when Cassius attempts to belittle Caesar by describing his
rescue of the great leader from the Tiber, his reference to Rome's origins
in Troy is vivid, but he succeeds neither in elevating himself nor in demean-
ing Caesar:

Caesar cried, 'Help me, Cassius, or I sink.'
I, as Aeneas, our great ancestor,
Did from the flames of Troy upon his shoulder
The old Anchises bear, so from the waves of Tiber
Did I the tired Caesar. And this man
Is now become a god, and Cassius is
A wretched creature, and must bend his body
If Caesar carelessly but nod on him.

(I.ii.110–17)

The *effect* of Cassius' story is to reveal his personal malice towards Caesar.
This awareness is reinforced when he describes Caesar's epilepsy:

He had a fever when he was in Spain,
And when the fit was on him, I did mark
How he did shake; 'tis true, this god did shake;
His coward lips did from their colour fly,
And that same eye whose bend doth awe the world
Did lose his lustre; I did hear him groan;
Ay, and that tongue of his, that bade the Romans
Mark him and write his speeches in their books,
Alas, it cried, 'Give me some drink, Titinius,'
As a sick girl. Ye gods, it doth amaze me
A man of such a feeble temper should
So get the start of the majestic world,
And bear the palm alone.

(I.ii.118–30)

Whereas Plutarch points to the admiration Caesar gained through his
ability to endure physical disabilities and hardships, Shakespeare's antagonistic Cassius attempts to use the disability as a means of belittling him.
All he achieves is the alienation of the audience and the embarrassed
detachment of Brutus. It is ironic that at the end of the dialogue Cassius
feels able to express satisfaction:

I am glad
That my weak words have struck but thus much show
Of fire from Brutus.

(I.ii.173–5)

It is not Cassius' comments that have exerted an influence on Brutus but the latter's cogitations and the noises off-stage, which he fears may be the culmination of Caesarism by the crowning of Caesar. Only Cassius' brief reference to Brutus' ancestor has touched the right vein. The calculating political man has failed in his act of persuasion because he has allowed his personal animus to show through his ostensible public concern for Roman democracy.

Cassius, though possessing keen political judgment, is a political failure because he gives way to personal feelings. He knows that the success of the conspiracy requires Antony's death, but submits to the inferior judgment of Brutus. Again, he accepts Brutus' disastrous decision to fight the final battle at Philippi in order to preserve their newly restored friendship. Cassius is a man for whom personal feelings override abstract political considerations. He muses to himself after drawing Brutus a few steps towards the conspiracy:

> Well, Brutus, thou art noble; yet I see
> Thy honourable mettle may be wrought
> From that it is dispos'd: therefore 'tis meet
> That noble minds keep ever with their likes;
> For who so firm that cannot be seduc'd?
> Caesar doth bear me hard; but he loves Brutus.
> If I were Brutus now, and he were Cassius,
> He should not humour me.
>   (I.ii.305–12)

Brutus represents the opposite case. But it is not merely his opposition to dictatorship and his commitment to democracy that causes him to join the conspiracy. It is, above all else, his self-image as the preserver of Roman democracy. Cassius could not have seduced Brutus in any way except by appealing to the public image of Brutus as the protector of Roman democracy. Brutus' susceptibility to his image as servant of Rome is apparent in his opening dialogue with Cassius:

> What is it that you would impart to me?
> If it be aught toward the general good,
> Set honour in one eye, and death i'th'other,
> And I will look on both indifferently;
> For let the gods so speed me as I love
> The name of honour more than I fear death.
>   (I.ii.83–8)

Cassius is quick to respond to this cue with the line, 'Well, honour is the subject of my story' (I.ii.91). Alas for Cassius, he is distracted from the most seductive approach by his passionate hatred of Caesar, but having given vent to his feelings (and perhaps recognizing his failure to elicit the desired response) he touches on the right nerve in Brutus by means of a crucial historical reference:

> Age, thou art sham'd!
> Rome, thou hast lost the breed of noble bloods!
> When went there by an age, since the great flood,
> But it was fam'd with more than with one man?
> When could they say, till now, that talk'd of Rome,
> That her wide walks encompass'd but one man?
> Now is it Rome indeed, and room enough,
> When there is in it but one only man.
> O, you and I have heard our fathers say,
> There was a Brutus once that would have brook'd
> Th'eternal devil to keep his state in Rome
> As easily as a king.

> (I.ii.148–59)

The response is immediate but qualified. Brutus is anxious about what might happen rather than with the present situation. Even in his orchard soliloquy Brutus does not indict Caesar on the basis of what he is. His action is predicated on what Caesar may become. If Cassius is less than wholly successful in his attempt to seduce Brutus, he at least discovers his friend's weak spot. The forged pleas, ostensibly from the citizens of Rome appealing to Brutus to save Roman democracy, are his next ploy. (The appeals are genuine in Plutarch.) The language Brutus uses in response to these letters is wholly revealing of his self-image:

> Shall Rome stand under one man's awe? What, Rome?
> My ancestors did from the streets of Rome
> The Tarquin drive, when he was call'd a king.
> 'Speak, strike, redress!' Am I entreated
> To speak, and strike? O Rome, I make thee promise,
> If the redress will follow, thou receivest
> Thy full petition at the hand of Brutus.

> (II.i.52–8)

Brutus' perception of himself as the selfless servant of Rome, the man of total integrity and honour, never wavers. This is revealed in its least attractive light in his conflict with Cassius (though he is under great strain and suffering intense personal anguish having just heard of Portia's death):

> There is no terror, Cassius, in your threats;
> For I am arm'd so strong in honesty
> That they pass by me as the idle wind,
> Which I respect not.

> (IV.iii.66–9)

Again, as he faces death Brutus expresses two highly specific consolations:

> Countrymen,
> My heart doth joy that yet in all my life
> I found no man but he was true to me.
> I shall have glory by this losing day
> More than Octavius and Mark Antony
> By this vile conquest shall attain unto.
> (V.v.33–8)

It never occurs to Brutus that he betrayed a friend and patron when he took part in the conspiracy. He is confident that he will be vindicated and honoured by history. The fact that Rome may be much worse placed under Antony and Octavius than it was under Caesar evades him, or he fails to accept responsibility for having helped (albeit unintentionally) to create that situation. Brutus' self-image, then, insulates him from self-criticism. That he can still be a highly sympathetic and appealing presence on the stage was demonstrated by Roger Allam's performance at Stratford-upon-Avon in 1987/88, but the sympathy is qualified by recognition of the limitations of his self-awareness and his failures of political judgment – strands which are tightly interwoven by Shakespeare.

Brutus' first political miscalculation stems from personal misjudgment. When Cassius advocates the assassination of Antony along with Caesar he advances sound reasons based on a firm understanding of human affection:

> I think it is not meet,
> Mark Antony, so well belov'd of Caesar,
> Should outlive Caesar: we shall find of him
> A shrewd contriver; and you know, his means,
> If he improve them, may well stretch so far
> As to annoy us all; which to prevent,
> Let Antony and Caesar fall together.
> (II.i.155–61)

Brutus' response is not devoid of substance but he totally underestimates the power of personal feeling in the political sphere. Not only that, but he dismisses the military potential of Antony by resort to a metaphor. In the process he is able to validate the murder of Caesar by transforming it to a blood sacrifice, a ritual for the purgation of Rome:

> Our course will seem too bloody, Caius Cassius,
> To cut the head off and then hack the limbs,
> Like wrath in death and envy afterwards;
> For Antony is but a limb of Caesar.
> Let's be sacrificers, but not butchers, Caius.

> We all stand up against the spirit of Caesar,
> And in the spirit of men there is no blood.
> O, that we then could come by Caesar's spirit,
> And not dismember Caesar! But, alas,
> Caesar must bleed for it. And, gentle friends,
> Let's kill him boldly, but not wrathfully;
> Let's carve him as a dish fit for the gods,
> Not hew him as a carcass fit for hounds.
> And let our hearts, as subtle masters do,
> Stir up their servants to an act of rage,
> And after seem to chide 'em. This shall make
> Our purpose necessary, and not envious;
> Which so appearing to the common eyes,
> We shall be call'd purgers, not murderers.
> And for Mark Antony, think not of him;
> For he can do no more than Caesar's arm
> When Caesar's head is off.
>
> (II.i.162–83)

Cassius panders to Brutus' vision of the ritualization of the murder as a convenient evasion, but quickly returns to the point of substance:

> Yet I fear him;
> For in the ingrafted love he bears to Caesar . . .
>
> (II.i.183–4)

Unlike Brutus, Cassius recognizes that most men carry their personal feelings into public life. Likewise, the astute politician thinks it foolish to take an unnecessary risk. This conflict, and the contrast between personalities, recurs as soon as the assassination has been effected. Brutus is naive enough to give Antony the assurance that:

> Our reasons are so full of good regard,
> That were you, Antony, the son of Caesar,
> You should be satisfied.
>
> (III.i.224–6)

This is a characteristic of the historical Brutus who took up arms on behalf of Pompey, the murderer of his own father, against Caesar because he believed that Pompey's cause was the better.

In contrast, Cassius observes Antony warily, first presenting him with the prospect of political advancement:

> Your voice shall be as strong as any man's
> In the disposing of new dignities.
>
> (III.i.177–8)

And later, attempting to corner him with a specific commitment:

I blame you not for praising Caesar so;
But what compact mean you to have with us?
Will you be prick'd in number of our friends,
Or shall we on, and not depend on you?
(III.i.214–17)

When Antony makes the audacious move of requesting to speak in Caesar's funeral, Cassius is astonished by Brutus' assent and quickly tries to
retrieve the situation. But Brutus persists in his second political blunder,
confident that so long as he speaks first Antony poses no threat. This
assumption, together with the acceptance of Antony's word that he will
not use the occasion to indict the conspirators, is enough to maintain
Brutus' confidence. (In the 1983/84 production at Stratford-upon-Avon,
Emrys James playing Cassius was the last of the conspirators to leave the
stage. Alone with Antony he moved in close to his adversary, finally
holding a sword at his throat. Cassius' dilemma was made explicit.) Both
Cassius and Antony are men who will break their word without a second
thought when it is a matter of political advantage. For Brutus his word is
his bond, and honour transcends political advantage or even survival. The
question arises, therefore, what hope does the idealist have in the political
arena?

Even during the blazing quarrel which takes place in the tent at Sardis,
Cassius never refers to these fatal miscalculations by Brutus – and Brutus
never recognizes them. Indeed, he is so oblivious of these errors that he
has no hesitation in overriding Cassius – the more experienced general –
with the decision to fight at Philippi. Cassius' only reference to their
differences of opinion over the fate of Antony occurs during the parley
when he is provoked by Antony into exclaiming:

Flatterers? Now, Brutus, thank yourself.
This tongue had not offended so to-day,
If Cassius might have rul'd.
(V.i.45–7)

Even when the incompetence of Octavius allows Brutus an initial advantage in the battle he almost manages to lose the initiative by giving the
word too early. (In the historical battle Brutus' soldiers fell to plunder
instead of racing to the aid of Cassius, who was hard pressed by the much
more formidable Antony.)

Any account of the character and actions of Brutus that omits references
to the moments of tenderness with Portia, or his young boy Lucius, will
inevitably make him appear aloof or even cold. These scenes are crucial
in conveying the current of warmth and gentleness which is part of Shakespeare's Brutus. The deficiency in Brutus is not one of coldness, or lack
of feeling, but his remarkable capacity to elevate the political over the

77

personal, and his self-image as the repository and guardian of Roman democracy. Brutus' tragedy stems from his inability to step outside this perception of himself. He shows a kind of acuteness when he cautions Cassius,

> Into what dangers would you lead me, Cassius,
> That you would have me seek into myself
> For that which is not in me?
>
> (I.ii.62–4)

He cannot be enticed by the suggestion of power, but he fails to recognize that his self-image as saviour of Rome involves a great deal of egotism and arrogance. The self-image is, moreover, corrupting. Brutus feels justified in killing Caesar because Rome *may* become subject to the tyranny of monarchic dictatorship. (Once the decision is made he talks to the conspirators as though they were all on Caesar's death list.) The ugliness of murder can be transformed into sacrifice. Finally, in justifying the assassination to the people he presents Caesar's tyranny as a fact:

> Had you rather Caesar were living, and die all slaves, than that Caesar were dead, to live all free men?
>
> (III.ii.23–5)

There is no evidence, merely assertion.

Although Brutus admits in his forum speech that Caesar loved him, and Cassius states as much in his soliloquy, Shakespeare never presents Brutus and Caesar together as friends. Caesar signifies Brutus' special status when he responds to the pleading of Decius Brutus with the comment 'Doth not Brutus bootless kneel?' (III.i.75), and Brutus expresses personal sympathy for Caesar in his orchard soliloquy:

> I know no personal cause to spurn at him,
> But for the general. He would be crown'd:
> How that might change his nature, there's the question.
>
> (II.i.11–13)

and again in his aside as Caesar invites the conspirators to take wine with him on the morning of the assassination:

> CAESAR Good friends, go in, and taste some wine with me;
> And we, like friends, will straightway go together.
> BRUTUS [*Aside*] That every like is not the same, O Caesar!
> The heart of Brutus earns to think upon.
>
> (II.ii.126–9)

Nevertheless, there is no suggestion that Brutus is, to use Antony's term, 'Caesar's angel'. The enigmatic nature of the relationship is maintained in Caesar's final words, '*Et tu Brute?* – then fall Caesar' (III.i.77). The central thrust of Antony's forum speech is the ingratitude of Brutus in betraying his friend and patron. That is, however, a finely calculated means of winning over the people. Shakespeare presents Julius Caesar and Brutus as friends without investing the relationship with any show of deep feeling that is accessible to the audience. This diminishes the sense of personal betrayal by Brutus without removing it. In doing this Shakespeare is not moving away from Plutarch's presentation. The historian insists on Brutus' debt to Caesar rather than indicating a close emotional bond. What Antony does is to invert Brutus' argument that political duty overrides personal affection or obligation; he realizes full well that the people standing in front of him possess a clearer sense of personal ties and loyalties than they do of abstract political principles. Indeed, he fully exploits the twin assumptions of Brutus' nobility and friendship to Caesar, exposing betrayal and ingratitude to undermine any belief in Brutus as an 'honourable man'.

Antony is prepared to blacken Brutus when it is politically expedient but honours him in passing judgment over his body. Thus Antony does one thing in the political arena and another at the moment when Brutus passes into history. This process of characters assessing themselves, being assessed by others, and speaking and acting in a way which exposes them to the judgment of history and the audience is part of the underlying structure of the play. This feature of characters seeing themselves as actors on the stage of history is highlighted most dramatically immediately after the assassination:

> CASSIUS Stoop then, and wash. How many ages hence
> Shall this our lofty scene be acted over,
> In states unborn, and accents yet unknown!
> BRUTUS How many times shall Caesar bleed in sport,
> That now on Pompey's basis lies along,
> No worthier than the dust!
> CASSIUS So oft as that shall be,
> So often shall the knot of us be call'd
> The men that gave their country liberty.
> (III.i.111–18)

The audience is jolted into recognition of themselves as being distant observers of the historical event while the characters see themselves as historical personages frozen momentarily, but soon to be absorbed and judged by the flow of history. In this way the dramatist provokes questions about the very nature of historical knowledge: were the events and characters really like this? The difficulty of 'knowing' is underlined by Shakespeare in the very process of character drawing and presentation.

The paradox inherent in this presentation of a self-consciously historical moment is that the key figures have yet to attain their goal. There has been little thought beyond the assassination. Once it is achieved there is a consciousness of the need to complete the process and to re-establish the political framework without Julius Caesar. At that very moment a servant arrives and imparts Antony's message. The firm rhetorical structure of the speech suggests a cool and calculating Antony – a character who has made a swift assessment of the situation and is ready to act with guile and daring:

> Thus, Brutus, did my master bid me kneel;
> Thus did Mark Antony bid me fall down;
> And, being prostrate, thus he bade me say:
> Brutus is noble, wise, valiant, and honest;
> Caesar was mighty, bold, royal, and loving:
> Say I love Brutus, and I honour him;
> Say I fear'd Caesar, honour'd him, and lov'd him.
> If Brutus will vouchsafe that Antony
> May safely come to him, and be resolv'd
> How Caesar hath deserv'd to lie in death,
> Mark Antony shall not love Caesar dead
> So well as Brutus living; but will follow
> The fortunes and affairs of noble Brutus
> Thorough the hazards of this untrod state,
> With all true faith. So says my master Antony.
>   (III.i.123–37)

As R.G. Moulton comments in *Shakespeare as a Dramatic Artist*,

> In the whole of Shakespearean Drama there is nowhere such a swift swinging round of a dramatic action as is here marked by this sudden up-springing of the suppressed individuality in Antony's character, hitherto so colourless that he has been spared by the conspirators as a mere limb of Caesar.[105]

Even when he arrives and is distracted by the bloody corpse Antony is able to end his speech by referring to the assassins as 'The choice and master spirits of this age' (III.i.163). His grasping of the bloody hand of each of the assassins is an act of supreme daring, as the most naive must recognize that there is the possibility that their names are being inscribed on Antony's death list. The discerning Cassius is obviously alarmed (Sean Baker as Cassius in the 1987/8 RSC production was quick to remove his hand from Antony's grasp). Having 'stopped' the action, then, Shakespeare quickly accelerates it, absorbing the audience and the characters into the excitement of the conflict. Antony, successful in outmanoeuvring Brutus despite Cassius' opposition, is left alone to give full vent to his feelings, and pledges himself to the destruction of the conspirators. His speech provides a harsh judgment on Brutus' 'sacrifice' and creates an image of destruction which ranges widely beyond Rome to encompass the whole of Italy. The speech reveals Antony's love of Caesar and his willingness to be the bloodthirsty revenger by inflicting massive suffering on the innocent. The passionate Antony is also ruthless, and so the pendulum of sympathy swings back towards the conspirators.

If Brutus falls victim to his self-image, so too does Julius Caesar. His first entrance is preceded by the critical comments of Marullus and Flavius, the tenor of which suggest a character who is arrogant and enjoys an impius triumph over noble sons of Rome. His first appearance is very brief but it creates an adverse impression: he speaks of himself in the third person, accepts the sycophancy of Antony and Casca without demur and adopts the posture of infallible seer in responding to the caution of the Soothsayer. Before he returns from the chase, sympathy has been moved marginally in his favour, or at least held in suspension, because Cassius' criticisms are so evidently based on personal envy. His second entrance is subdued, but Caesar's first comment is incisive even though it is expressed in the metaphorical language of political assessment:

> Let me have men about me that are fat,
> Sleek-headed men, and such as sleep a-nights.
> Yond Cassius has a lean and hungry look;
> He thinks too much: such men are dangerous.
>
> (I.ii.189–92)

When Antony seeks to reassure him, Caesar discerns a central feature of Cassius' inner world (a feature the audience experiences only through Caesar's eyes). He prefaces it, however, with a comment which projects his public persona. The image has become the man:

> ANTONY Fear him not, Caesar, he's not dangerous.
> He is a noble Roman, and well given.
> CAESAR Would he were fatter! But I fear him not:
> Yet if my name were liable to fear,
> I do not know the man I should avoid
> So soon as that spare Cassius. He reads much,
> He is a great observer, and he looks
> Quite through the deeds of men. He loves no plays,
> As thou dost, Antony; he hears no music.
> Seldom he smiles, and smiles in such a sort
> As if he mock'd himself, and scorn'd his spirit
> That could be mov'd to smile at any thing.
> Such men as he be never at heart's ease
> Whiles they behold a greater than themselves,
> And therefore are they very dangerous.
> I rather tell thee what is to be fear'd

Than what I fear; for always I am Caesar.
Come on my right hand, for this ear is deaf,
And tell me truly what thou think'st of him.

(I.ii.193–211)

Caesar returns to the image of the invulnerable man at the end of the speech, but is obliged to direct Antony to his good ear. The audience is made aware of Caesar's physical decline while the great man himself is unaware of any incongruity.

No sooner has Caesar made his exit than another indication of his physical infirmity is provided by Casca's description of events – a clearly biased account, but his sneering tells against Caesar. All the earlier comments on Caesar portray him as a kind of demi-god, but Casca's picture reveals a small, histrionic man whose limited success is achieved only through the naivety and stupidity of the people:

Marry, before he fell down, when he perceiv'd the common herd was glad he refus'd the crown, he pluck'd me ope his doublet, and offer'd them his throat to cut. And I had been a man of any occupation, if I would not have taken him at a word, I would I might go to hell among the rogues. And so he fell. When he came to himself again, he said, if he had done or said anything amiss, he desir'd their worships to think it was his infirmity. Three or four wenches, where I stood, cried, 'Alas, good soul', and forgave him with all their hearts; but there's no heed to be taken of them; if Caesar had stabb'd their mothers, they would have done no less.

(I.ii.260–72)

Before Caesar reappears his character is revealed through the eyes of others. Brutus, in weighing the possible justification for the assassination, admits:

and, to speak truth of Caesar,
I have not known when his affections sway'd
More than his reason.

(II.i.19–21)

Cassius, fearing that he will not go to the Capitol, portrays him as a man who has become superstitious:

But it is doubtful yet
Whether Caesar will come forth to-day or no;
For he is superstitious grown of late,
Quite from the main opinion he held once
Of fantasy, of dreams, and ceremonies.

(II.i.193–7)

Decius Brutus reveals a particularly unattractive feature of Caesar (not to mention himself) when he comments on his susceptibility to flattery:

> Never fear that: if he be so resolv'd,
> I can o'ersway him; for he loves to hear
> That unicorns may be betray'd with trees,
> And bears with glasses, elephants with holes,
> Lions with toils, and men with flatterers;
> But when I tell him he hates flatterers,
> He says he does, being then most flattered.
> Let me work . . .
>   (II.i.202–9)

When Caesar makes his next appearance, responding to Calpurnia's pleas to stay at home in response to the auguries, the strange events of the night and her dreams, he is more histrionic than ever, and despite his newly acquired superstition, determined to live up to his self-image:

>   Danger knows full well
> That Caesar is more dangerous than he.
> We are two lions litter'd in one day,
> And I the elder and more terrible,
> And Caesar shall go forth.
>   (II.ii.44–8)

Nevertheless, he momentarily yields to Calpurnia's persuasions,

> Mark Antony shall say I am not well,
> And for thy humour I will stay at home.
>   (II.ii.54–5)

Although he has agreed to tell a white lie, in the ensuing discussion with Decius Brutus, Caesar disdains such an evasion and puts on a display of arrogance and contempt towards the Senate:

> CAESAR And you are come in very happy time
>   To bear my greeting to the senators,
>   And tell them that I will not come to-day:
>   Cannot, is false; and that I dare not, falser;
>   I will not come to-day. Tell them so Decius.
> CALPURNIA Say he is sick.
> CAESAR   Shall Caesar send a lie?
>   Have I in conquest stretch'd mine arm so far,
>   To be afeared to tell greybeards the truth?
>   Decius, go tell them Caesar will not come.
> DECIUS Most mighty Caesar, let me know some cause,
>   Lest I be laugh'd at when I tell them so.

CAESAR The cause is in my will: I will not come;
    That is enough to satisfy the Senate.
                     (II.ii.60–72)

Having reinterpreted Calpurnia's dream, Decius Brutus then goes on to seduce Caesar:

               The Senate have concluded
To give this day a crown to mighty Caesar.
If you shall send them word you will not come,
Their minds may change. Besides, it were a mock
Apt to be render'd, for some one to say,
'Break up the Senate till another time,
When Caesar's wife shall meet with better dreams.'
If Caesar hide himself, shall they not whisper,
'Lo, Caesar is afraid'?
                     (II.ii.93–101)

Caesar immediately succumbs. In doing so he is diminished in the eyes of the audience: for all his arrogance he is clearly alarmed that his public image will be damaged, and that is sufficient to dull his critical awareness. This determination to play up to his public image is fatally manifest on his way to the Capitol. Artemidorus thrusts the crucial warning into his hand with the words,

    O Caesar, read mine first; for mine's a suit
    That touches Caesar nearer.
                     (III.i.6–7)

In Plutarch Caesar fails to read the warning because he is unable to do so in the throng. Shakespeare's Caesar seizes the opportunity to make a public display of his self-denying service to the commonwealth: 'What touches us ourself shall be last serv'd' (III.i.8). What appears to Caesar as an astute move proves fatal (though Ernest Schanzer is not alone in attributing this action to 'Caesar's scrupulous and unselfish administration of justice').[106]

It is in the Capitol that Caesar gives full vent to his assertiveness as the supreme Roman. After chastising Metellus Cimber with fawning he moves on to a vivid description of himself as being the unique embodiment of Roman constancy, employing a comparison that presents him as a demi-god:

    I could be well mov'd, if I were as you;
    If I could pray to move, prayers would move me;
    But I am constant as the northern star,
    Of whose true-fix'd and resting quality
    There is no fellow in the firmament.

The skies are painted with unnumber'd sparks,
They are all fire, and every one doth shine;
But there's but one in all doth hold his place.
So in the world: 'tis furnish'd well with men,
And men are flesh and blood, and apprehensive;
Yet in the number I do know but one
That unassailable holds on his rank,
Unshak'd of motion; and that I am he,
Let me a little show it, even in this,
That I was constant Cimber should be banish'd,
And constant do remain to keep him so.

(III.i.58–73)

Dowden has remarked perceptively that 'The real man Caesar disappears for himself under the greatness of the Caesar myth. He forgets himself as he actually is, and knows only the vast legendary power named Caesar'.[107] The dramatist, nevertheless, affords us glimpses of the real man. John Palmer, in *Political and Comic Characters of Shakespeare*, comments on Caesar welcoming his colleagues before departing for the Capitol, 'He has a word for everyone and it is the right word. This is the real Caesar, courteous and accessible, who has it in him to win hearts and command respect'.[108] More recently, Alexander Leggatt has said of Caesar's bequest of his private arbours and orchards to the people of Rome, 'This is Caesar at his most amiable'.[109] But it is the Caesar of the relaxed private world, endowed with fine human qualities, who points up even more sharply the surrender of the man to the image.

Both Brutus and Julius Caesar are portrayed as flawed characters. They show poor judgment at critical moments, but ultimately they are victims of misguided self-perception. Both are subject to the pressures of their society. Brutus' position in Rome is clearly articulated by Casca and Cassius:

CASCA O, he sits high in all the people's hearts:
    And that which would appear offence in us,
    His countenance, like richest alchemy,
    Will change to virtue and to worthiness.
CASSIUS Him and his worth and our great need of him
    You have right well conceited.

(I.iii.157–62)

Brutus not only recognizes his special standing but exaggerates it. This is his chosen role and in accepting it he is prepared to subordinate all personal claims to the wider requirements of his society. However, he is so intent on fulfilling the mission to save Rome from tyranny that he is insufficiently scrupulous in evaluating the real position of Caesar and the consequences of his removal. Brutus' great weakness is that he longs to acquire the title of liberator of his beloved Rome. This weakness is not simply the product of egotism but arises from a passion for his conception of Rome: its history and its mission. At the heart of this vision is a feeling about the way in which Rome should be governed by selfless men giving freely of their personal attributes. At the very least Julius Caesar is an obstruction to the free flow of service and political debate; the nominal governors of Rome are reduced and belittled. The fatal culmination of this process, for Brutus, is the creation of a king. This is the symbol of the destruction of the free, creative essence of Rome. This way of thinking is clearly alien to Caesar. Puffed-up with his military victories, fully conscious of his service to Rome and his value as the leader of his society, he has become detached from an awareness of a central feature of the political life of Rome. Praised, honoured and flattered, the military genius has fallen victim to the public image of the great man. As he assumes the public mantle more completely so his perspicacity is diminished. Caesar has the political wisdom and personal perception to see right through Cassius, but these qualities are blunted by his belief in the invulnerability of the great man, Caesar.

Shakespeare preserves a degree of sympathy for both men that is much greater than the most careful critical analyses can suggest, because of the subtle interweaving of representations of the characters by events and other characters. For instance, Casca's parting shot after his unattractive portrait of Caesar, 'Marullus and Flavius, for pulling scarfs off Caesar's images, are put to silence' (I.ii.282–3), comes as a shock, which is doubly frightening because of its context. Then the antagonism felt towards Caesar is partially offset by Cassius' soliloquy in which it is evident that he is manipulating Brutus, his motives being much more personal than political. It is difficult, therefore, to provide a critical account which does justice to or adequately reflects the subtle and swiftly changing feelings which occur in the theatre.

It is, of course, the sight of the bloody murder itself which wins most sympathy for Caesar. The action appears ignoble, unheroic and inhuman – regardless of any political justification. Ironically, Caesar's stature grows from that moment as all retrospective glances are to his greatness rather than to his all too apparent human deficiences. Equally, sympathy for Brutus grows out of disgust at the calculation and political cynicism of Antony and Octavius, his deep personal loss of the loving Portia, and the disintegration and defeat of his armies in the final phase. Cassius, too, appears warmly sympathetic as he struggles against his own failures (unwillingness to send financial support to Brutus and his personal intervention in support of a wrong-doer) and his desperate desire to retain the love and friendship of Brutus. Audience sympathy for Cassius is accentuated by the knowledge that had his political judgments prevailed the conspiracy might not have ended in ignominious defeat.

True to the political nature of this play, Shakespeare accentuates the feeling of pity for Brutus and Cassius by creating an awareness of the calculation of Antony and Octavius. They dispute over who shall lead the more prestigious right flank and are manoeuvring for precedence even before they have won the day. As they achieve victory their nominal magnanimity in absorbing the quality soldiers who have served Brutus and Cassius is seen as shrewdly self-interested. These two characters are devoid of illusions or public images. They are natural politicians who are neither moulded nor burdened by Roman history and values: they are professionals in using social reality and symbols in the quest for personal power.

The cold cynicism of the proscription scene is not equalled in the play. It is the more shocking for coming hard on the heels of the scene of mob violence in which Cinna the poet is murdered. When it seems that there can be nothing worse than this senseless cruelty, the audience is confronted by politicians calmly drawing up a death list of political opponents: bargaining the deaths of antagonists with the lives of relatives and associates. Mark Antony is at his least attractive when he pours scorn on the makeweight Lepidus. It is ironic that Octavius, the defender of Lepidus, is the man who will dispose of both when the time is ripe. This boorish and cynical Mark Antony does not, of course, rival the historical personage portrayed by Plutarch who had Cicero dismembered, and his head and hands put on public display. Shakespeare could not risk the exposure of the character who was to become the flawed hero of his next Roman play.

Even Cassius' worst fears are surpassed in the forum scene as Antony reveals a thorough understanding of the citizens and displays consummate control of their emotions. This speech provides the greatest example of the power of rhetoric in the whole of Shakespeare. Each step is carefully calculated, while the rhythm of speech is controlled by the refrain 'honourable men', which moves from seeming respect through irony and sarcasm to bitter contempt.

As Antony produces the will, he feels the waves of approval and excitement crashing against him. He employs the refrain for the seventh and final time, carrying irony and sarcasm to a crescendo of indignation:

Will you be patient? Will you stay awhile?
I have o'ershot myself to tell you of it.
I fear I wrong the honourable men
Whose daggers have stabb'd Caesar;
(III.ii.151–4)

Before reading the will, however, Antony is masterly in presenting a vivid picture of one of Caesar's famous triumphs. He fills his audience with horror by displaying Caesar's tattered and bloody robe after creating a vision of it in its pristine condition. As Brents Stirling points out in *Unity in Shakespearian Tragedy*, Antony recreates and inverts Brutus' ritualization of the murder so that 'Brutus' transformation of blood into the heady wine of sacrifice is reversed both in substance and in ceremony'.[110] He is then ready to create the final shock by displaying the mutilated corpse:

> If you have tears, prepare to shed them now.
> You all do know this mantle. I remember
> The first time ever Caesar put it on;
> 'Twas on a summer's evening in his tent,
> That day he overcame the Nervii.
> Look, in this place ran Cassius' dagger through:
> See what a rent the envious Casca made:
> Through this the well-beloved Brutus stabb'd;
> And as he pluck'd his cursed steel away,
> Mark how the blood of Caesar follow'd it,
> As rushing out of doors, to be resolv'd
> If Brutus so unkindly knock'd or no;
> For Brutus, as you know, was Caesar's angel.
> Judge, O you gods, how dearly Caesar lov'd him.
> This was the most unkindest cut of all;
> For when the noble Caesar saw him stab,
> Ingratitude, more strong than traitors' arms,
> Quite vanquish'd him:
>
> (III.ii.171–88)

'Valiant' Casca becomes 'envious' Casca, and Brutus, after being referred to as 'Caesar's angel', becomes a Judas. The mood of the crowd so increases in excitement that they have to be restrained and reminded that they have not yet heard the will. The details of the will, at the end of this speech, are sufficient to make each man feel a personal attachment to Caesar. The crowd has been transformed from supporters of Brutus to the instrument of Antony. What we *see* next, however, is not the destruction of one of the conspirators, but the horrible murder of an innocent man. Rather than the revival of democracy, which was the ostensible purpose of the assassination, we see anarchy.

Caesar, Brutus, Cassius and Antony are all drawn on a grand scale: Shakespeare conveys a vivid sense of personalities, and distinctive idiosyncrasies and weaknesses. Perceptions of these characters emanate not only from their words and actions, but from the comments and assessments of others. For instance, despite several attempts by individuals to show Caesar in a bad light, the images involved simply convey the enormity of his stature in Rome. Only Casca manages to deflate the image. Paradoxically, the hollowness of Caesar's 'greatness' is exposed by his own desperate attempt to live up to the image. There's a feeling that the Julius Caesar observed in the play is a lesser man than he was earlier in his career: the man has been absorbed by the image; now subject to flattery and superstition, Caesar shows only flashes of his former insight and courage. When Antony expresses shock at the sight of the corpse:

> O mighty Caesar! dost thou lie so low?
> Are all thy conquests, glories, triumphs, spoils,
> Shrunk to this little measure?
>
> (III.i.148–50)

his words could apply metaphorically to the living Caesar seen on the stage. Likewise, Antony's encomium on Brutus portrays a character who transcends the living Brutus seen on the stage. Shakespeare's audience has seen only the anguished Brutus who, drawn into the conspiracy, struggles to justify the assassination to himself by creating a mental formulation which will assuage his conscience. His admirable qualities as public man of unquestioned integrity stem from the same source as his vulnerability: his sense of the Roman world and his place in it as servant and protector of its ideals. This commitment enables him to kill his friend – and then to represent it as a sacrifice rather than a murder. But it also deprives him of the ruthlessness to undertake the politically expedient killing of Antony. Indeed, his scrupulousness presents Antony, albeit inadvertently, with a platform to defeat the conspirators. Ironically, the awareness of his own integrity and doubt about the moral rectitude of Cassius leads him to assume control of the conspiracy and to override the views of his brother-in-arms, who is politically and militarily more experienced and astute. Purity of intention is all that matters to Brutus, and his evident dismay in his encounters with the ghost of Caesar reveals that he has never been able to completely satisfy himself that the murder was justified. Added to this anguish is awareness of his sacrifice of Portia, whom he loves dearly, to his public responsibilities. Most critics assume that one of the two announcements of Portia's death is redundant, as the dramatist intended only the one to remain in the text. But the dual presentation enables the audience to experience the suffering and inner turmoil in his quarrel with Cassius, and later to allow him to present a stoic, public response when he receives the news for the second time. In the recent Stratford production Roger Allam effectively conveyed a sense of Brutus' anguish at the beginning of the scene by burning a letter and crumbling the ashes in his hand. Brutus, then, emerges as the 'noblest Roman', as a man suited to serve as a living model of Roman *gravitas*, an essential contributor to the political life of the state, but wholly unsuited to the role of conspirator and political leader.

In his assessment of Brutus' character and failure William Hazlitt argued:

Those who mean well themselves think well of others, and fall a prey to their security. The humanity and sincerity which dispose men to resist injustice and tyranny render them unfit to cope with the cunning and power of those who are opposed to them.[111]

Dowden, on the other hand, gave a different slant to the commitment of Brutus:

It is idealists who create a political terror; they are free from all desire for blood-shedding; but to them the lives of men and women are accidents; the lives of ideas are the true realities; and, armed with an abstract principle and a suspicion, they perform deeds which are at once beautiful and hideous . . .[112]

Perhaps the most remarkable feature of Shakespeare's presentation of Cassius is the way in which he moves from being an unattractive political manipulator at the beginning of the play to the sympathetic character at the end. (Indeed, in the 1983/84 production at Stratford-upon-Avon, Cassius, played by Emrys James, was overwhelmingly the most sympathetic character on the stage.) Yet, despite this astonishing transition, it seems impossible to square the character of Cassius with Brutus' words spoken over his dead friend:

Are yet two Romans living such as these?
The last of all the Romans, fare thee well!
It is impossible that ever Rome
Should breed thy fellow.

(V.iii.98–101)

Cassius has revealed a great capacity for love, a desperate desire to have Brutus' love, and has demonstrated the soundness of his political judgment. The parting between Brutus and Cassius is the most moving in the whole of Shakespeare. Moreover, the deep affection which he inspired in those around him should not be overlooked, as it is powerfully demonstrated in V.iii. As Alexander Leggatt comments:

He and Titinius literally die for each other. We have seen Cassius pleading for Brutus' love and never quite getting it. All we see of his relationship with Titinius, earlier in V.iii, is two men simply working together, making no parade of their friendship. The revelation of the depth of that friendship is a flash of the unexpected, a touch of unprogrammed humanity in a world of controlled display.[113]

Yet Brutus' expression 'the last of all the Romans' implies an idealism and detachment which seems wholly at odds with what has been seen of the living Cassius. Cassius is attractive because of his essentially human qualities – vices as well as virtues. What Caesar saw as malice emanating from the pressures of a coldly analytical mind and envious nature is misguided. He rightly assesses Cassius' potential for conspiracy but fails to fully comprehend his adversary's nature. Had Caesar shown to Cassius the affection he bestowed on Brutus he would have found a loyal friend rather than a deadly enemy – as Cassius' soliloquy clearly indicates:

> Caesar doth bear me hard; but he loves Brutus.
> If I were Brutus now, and he were Cassius,
> He should not humour me.

(I.ii.310–12)

Personal affection rather than commitment to Roman values is Cassius' chief quality. That does not, however, imply that Cassius is indifferent to the state of Rome. He is undoubtedly opposed to Caesarism. Unlike Brutus he could accept the distortion of Roman political life if he loved and was loved by the supreme leader. Nevertheless, Brutus' judgment should not be lightly dismissed as the excess of generosity engendered by compassion. Set Cassius alongside Mark Antony and Octavius Caesar and Brutus' claim no longer appears as wildly exaggerated.

Shakespeare's portrait of Antony suggests a warm emotional commitment to Caesar, and the sense of a man determined to avenge his murdered friend. What Antony does not convey, however, is any feeling of a commitment to Roman values. He is a political opportunist who displays astonishing calculation from the moment of Caesar's death. His forum speech reveals great insight into the minds of the common people and a masterly ability to manipulate language and feelings. It is the contrast between this public performance (and Shakespeare enables the audience to detect and savour every moment of the control of the crowd) and his display of cold, almost uncouth cynicism which makes the proscription scene so shocking. If Antony appears as the supreme politician, unfettered by values and ideals, he seems warmhearted when contrasted with Octavius Caesar. Although Shakespeare presents no more than a cameo of Octavius, it is sufficient for a good actor to reveal stubbornness and steely ambition operating under the control of an unemotional character. The time gap between the writing of *Julius Caesar* and *Antony and Cleopatra* is astonishingly wide, given the way in which Shakespeare has so carefully prepared for the future collision of Antony and Octavius at the end of the play.

This sense of the future coming to life is powerfully evoked at the end of the play and diminishes the personal tragedy associated with the deaths of Brutus and Cassius. During the course of the action the Roman world has changed. Even without the benefit of historical hindsight the impression is created that the 'dogs of war' have a lot more running to do. The new equilibrium which has been established is unstable. This is a brave new world in which there will be little room for philosophical considerations. In a play dominated by images of blood, hunting, metal and space or room,

91

there is a sudden contraction. The visual image which dominates the closing phase of the play, which sees the death of young Cato on the battlefield and several suicides, is the sword. The arena for civil conflict in *Julius Caesar* is Rome itself. Whereas the Rome of *Julius Caesar* could still accommodate the antagonistic watchfulness of Brutus and Cassius, but where Marullus and Flavius are perhaps put to death for pulling scarves off Caesar's images, the Rome of the triumvirate has already produced a bloodbath and is in the hands of vigorous politicians for whom even the Roman Empire will prove too small.

3

REALITIES AND IMAGININGS IN *ANTONY AND CLEOPATRA*

> Think you there was, or might be such a man
> As this I dreamt of?
>
> (V.ii.93–4)

Geoffrey Bullough suggests that Plutarch 'was one of the few Roman historians to treat the lovers with any sympathy'.[1] Nevertheless, anyone comparing Plutarch's portrayal with Shakespeare's central characters is immediately struck by the extent to which the dramatist omits several important references to their actions and attitudes in order to maintain sympathy for them. Shakespeare's Octavius Caesar, on the other hand, is a more calculating and manipulative character than his counterpart in Plutarch. Consequently, Shakespeare seems to be influenced by two considerations: first, how to make Antony and Cleopatra sufficiently attractive to win audience sympathy; secondly, to penetrate the narrative account to discover motives and character traits that lie below the surface.

According to the historian, Antony was physically impressive: 'he had a goodly thicke beard, a broad forehead, crooke nosed and there appeared such a manly looke in his countenaunce, as is commonly seene in Hercules pictures, stamped or graven in mettell'.[2] Antony, whose family traced its ancestry back to Hercules, attempted to accentuate this resemblance, even wearing his garments in a way reminiscent of the ancient hero: 'when he would openly shewe him selfe abroad before many people, he would alwayes weare his cassocke gyrt downe lowe upon his hippes, with a great sword hanging by his side, and upon that, some ill favored cloke'.[3] The attractive features of Antony's personality which emerge from Plutarch are his courage, conviviality and liberality. His vices were at least as strong as his virtues: he was corrupt, lecherous and cruel. Immensely popular with the soldiers, he had the rare ability to mingle and drink with them as their equal while retaining their respect. As Plutarch expresses it:

> things that seeme intollerable in other men, as to boast commonly, to jeast with one or other, to drinke like a good fellow with every body, to sit with the soldiers when they dine, and to eate and drinke with them souldier-like: it is incredible what wonderfull love it wanne him

93

amongest them . . . But besides all this, that which most procured his rising and advauncement, was his liberalitie, who gave all to the souldiers, and kept nothing for him selfe.[4]

The duality in Antony's nature is clearly shown by two incidents. The first, which won Antony great praise, was the bestowing of a magnificent coat to cover Brutus' body on the funeral pyre. The soldier entrusted with the task attempted to steal the coat and was promptly executed by Antony. The second is taken from Plutarch's extensive account of Antony's disastrous Parthian wars. In his eagerness to return to Cleopatra he started his campaign during the winter instead of resting his army in Armenia until the spring; he then rushed ahead with his main force, leaving behind his engines of battery, which were soon captured. This led to the loss of 10,000 men and doomed the campaign to failure. Eventually Antony's main force was surrounded and placed in severe jeopardy. In one battle alone he lost 3,000 men, with 5,000 badly wounded. After this display of mismanagement and incompetence Antony went to the tents of the sick and wounded to comfort them. Rather than reviling him for his poor leadership they pitied him:

> shewing him the best countenaunce they coulde, tooke him by the hand, and prayed him to go and be dressed, and not to trouble him selfe for them, most reverently calling him their Emperour and Captaine: and that for them selves, they were whole and safe, so that he had his health . . . the care he tooke at that time to help, visite, and lament those that were sicke and wounded, seeing every man to have that which was meete for him: that was of such force and effect, as it made them that were sicke and wounded to love him better, and were more desirous to do him service, then those that were whole and sound.[5]

On his retreat from Parthia Antony took a muster which revealed a death toll from sickness and battle of 24,000. Even so he made his men sleep in the fields in winter, and lost a further 8,000, in his anxiety to return to Cleopatra. Here we have the enigma of the man who could commit acts of great folly, weep and feel deeply for his wounded soldiers, return their love and respect, and then, out of his passion for Cleopatra, cast away thousands of lives.

The contrast between Antony's magnanimity and viciousness is clearly revealed by comparing his treatment of Enobarbus and Cicero. When deserted by the former, Antony expressed his sorrow and sent Enobarbus' treasure after him. Cicero, however, aroused Antony's bitter antagonism by denouncing him in his Philippics. When Antony formed the triumvirate with Lepidus and Octavius they spent three days haggling over the proscription list. Antony fought hard to have Cicero executed, and he did not stop there: he had the body dismembered and the head and hands put on display. Moreover, 'when the murtherers brought him Ciceroes head and hand cut of, he beheld them a long time with great joy, and laughed heartily, and that oftentimes for the great joy he felt'.[6] Plutarch comments on this event more than once with burning indignation:

> Antonius suffered his Uncle by his mother's side to be slaine, that he might have his will of Cicero to kill him: a thing so damnable, wicked, and cruell of it selfe, that he hardlie deserved to have bene pardoned, though he had killed Cicero, to have saved his Uncles life.[7]

At another point Plutarch describes Cicero's capture and murder:

> So Cicero being three score and foure yeares of age, thrust his necke out of the litter, and had his head cut of by Antonius commaundement, and his hands also, which wrote the Orations (called the Philippians) against him . . . When these poore dismembred members were brought to Rome, Antonius . . . commaunded his head and his hands should straight be set up over the pulpit for Orations, in the place called Rostra. This was a fearefull and horrible sight unto the Romanes, who thought they saw not Ciceroes face, but an image of Antonius life and disposicion . . .[8]

Whereas the Antony of the play is made more attractive than his historical counterpart, the opposite is true of Octavia – Shakespeare totally suppresses her outstanding qualities. Octavia's loyalty to Antony and his mistreatment of her were critical in turning popular opinion in Rome against him. Before being deserted by Antony, Octavia bore him two children and undertook two embassies to her brother in an attempt to reconcile them. Her first mission was successful in bringing about a new concorde but the second was doomed to failure. Plutarch records that Octavius allowed his sister to set out on her peace mission to Antony 'not for his respect at all (as most authors doe report) as for that he might have an honest culler to make warre with Antonius if he did misuse her, and not esteeme of her as she ought to be'.[9] The cynical behaviour of Octavius was rewarded by Antony's maladroitness. He requested Octavia to stay in Athens and send him the two thousand soldiers and generous supplies she had assembled. Meanwhile Antony was so effectively seduced by Cleopatra's wiles that he postponed his second proposed Parthian campaign, even though the Persians were engaged in civil war. When Octavia returned to Rome, Octavius instructed her to leave Antony's house. She refused. Moreover, she continued to look after Antony's children, including those borne by Fulvia, and to act as his ambassador. But, as Plutarch points out, her diligence in serving Antony's interests contributed significantly to the decline of his popularity:

> when Antonius sent any of his men to Rome, to sue for any office in

the common wealth: she received him very curteously, and so used her selfe unto her brother, that she obtained the thing she requested. Howbeit thereby, thinking no hurt, she did Antonius great hurt. For her honest love and regard to her husband, made every man hate him, when they sawe he did so unkindly use so noble a Lady.[10]

Antony intensified the antagonism of the Romans by holding a ceremony in the square of Alexandria in which Cleopatra and her children, magnificently and appropriately dressed (the Queen as Isis), were awarded kingdoms. Octavius was able to present a vivid picture of Antony disposing of Roman territory as if it were his personal property. Once the tension between Antony and Octavius gave way to preparation for war Antony continued to blunder. He gathered up his forces and spent several days feasting and celebrating on the Isle of Samos. Meanwhile Caesar was struggling, in the face of considerable hostility, to raise the funds to support his own army. Instead of launching an attack Antony 'gave Caesar leysure to make his preparacions, and also to appease the complaints of the people'.[11] In the midst of this inaction Antony's only positive decision was to order Octavia out of his house, thereby attracting contempt for his ignoble and ungrateful action and disdain for his poor judgment in handling the strategic and military situation. Antony's subservience to Cleopatra is revealed by the way in which his friends and advisers were threatened for disagreeing with her and were forced to flee for their own safety.

Commenting on Antony's greatest military triumph, Plutarch exposes his political motivation:

For the greatest and most famous exploye Antonius ever did in warres (to wit, the warre in the which he overthrew Cassius and Brutus) was begon to no other ende, but to deprive his contriemen of their libertie and freedom.[12]

He goes on to point out that many of the victories ascribed to Antony were in fact accomplished by his 'Lieutenauntes'[13] – a point taken up by Shakespeare (III.i.16–27) – while at a critical moment in the most important battle of his life (Actium) he betrayed his devoted followers 'so beastlie left them that loved him best, and were most faithfull to him'.[14] In his summing up of Antony's actions Plutarch denouces him for his breach of the 'lawes and ordinaunces'[15] of Rome by marrying Cleopatra while still being married to Octavia. He commends Antony's resolve to avoid capture but disparages the execution: 'Antonius . . . slue him selfe, (to confesse a troth) cowardly, and miserably, to his great paine and griefe: and yet was it before his bodie came into his enemies hands'.[16]

The portrait of Antony that emerges from these pages is nothing like as attractive as the character who appears in the play. Nevertheless, the word 'bountie' is quite firmly attached to Antony in Plutarch's account.

The dramatist provides a chilling proscription scene in *Julius Caesar*, but neither in that play nor in *Antony and Cleopatra* is there any reference to the mutilation of Cicero and Antony's joyful response to the news. Again, Shakespeare makes no reference to Antony's irresponsible and incompetent Parthian campaign. The warmhearted and generous Octavia of the narrative is a colourless creature in the play. Antony's betrayal, therefore, is not nearly as distasteful as it is in Plutarch's narrative. Perhaps the surprising thing is not that Shakespeare excises actions and events that show Antony in an intolerably bad light, from the standpoint of a dramatic hero, but that he encapsulates so much of Antony's folly and weakness while still making him an attractive, sympathetic character. Shakespeare's Lepidus makes the excuse for Antony that his vices merely serve to show up his virtues more brightly, and this is a view generally shared by the audience. The Antony who emerges from the pages of Plutarch is a dissolute and vicious individual whose attractive features are so few in comparison with his vices that rather than redeeming him they merely serve to mitigate the feeling that he was a thoroughly bad man.

Having enumerated Antony's finer qualities and weaknesses, Plutarch describes his meeting with Cleopatra. He prefaces this description with the observation that the Egyptian queen represented the final undoing of Antony:

> Antonius being thus inclined, the last and extreamest mischiefe of all other (to wit, the love of Cleopatra) lighted on him, who did waken and stirre up many vices yet hidden in him, and were never seene to any: and if any sparke of goodnesse or hope of rising were left him, Cleopatra quenched it straight, and made it worse then before.[17]

She was particularly dangerous to Antony because she was at her most formidable:

> For Caesar and Pompey knew her when she was but a young thing, and knew not then what a worlde ment: but nowe she went to Antonius at the age when a womans beawtie is at the prime, and she also of best judgement.[18]

But Cleopatra was not merely a mature voluptuary: she was highly intelligent, a gifted linguist and endowed with a voice and manner that made her captivating. Indeed, it was these attributes, along with her acute awareness of them, rather than physical beauty, which made her so enchanting. As Plutarch puts it:

> Now her beawtie (as it is reported) was not so passing, as unmatchable of other women, nor yet suche, as upon present viewe did enamor men with her: but so sweete was her companie and conversacion, that a man could not possiblie but be taken. And besides her beawtie, the good

grace she had to talke and discourse, her curteous nature that tempered her words and dedes, was a spurre that pricked to the quick. Furthermore, besides all these, her voyce and words were marvelous pleasant: for her tongue was an instrument of musicke to divers sports and pastimes, the which she easely turned to any language that pleased her. She spake unto few barbarous people by interpreter, but made them aunswere her selfe, or at the least the most parte of them: as the Aethiopians, the Arabians, the Troglodytes, the Hebrues, the Syrians, the Medes, and the Parthians, and to many others also, whose languages she had learned. Whereas divers of her progenitors, the kings of Aegypt, could scarce learne the Aegyptian tongue only, and many of them forgot to speake the Macedonian.[19]

Plutarch's description of Cleopatra is anything but static. He presents cameos of the lovers in all sorts of 'fond and childish' pastimes:

For she, were it in sport, or in matter of earnest, still devised sundrie new delights to have Antonius at commaundement, never leaving him night nor day, nor once letting him go out of her sight. For she would play at dyce with him, drinke with him, and hunt commonly with him, and also be with him when he went to any exercise or activity of body. And somtime also, when he would goe up and downe the citie disguised like a slave in the night, and would peere into poore mens windowes and their shops, and scold and brawle with them within the house: Cleopatra would be also in a chamber maides array, and amble up and downe the streets with him, so that oftentimes Antonius bare away both mockes and blowes. Now, though most men misliked this maner, yet the Alexandrians were commonly glad of this jolity, and liked it well, saying verie gallantly, and wisely: that Antonius shewed them a commicall face, to wit, a merie countenaunce: and the Romanes a tragicall face, to say, a grimme looke.[20]

Although Plutarch conveys a sense of Cleopatra's guileful manipulation of Antony there is too a feeling of fellowship, of mutual delight. There is a strong playful element in the lovers' relationship which is almost childishly irresponsible. It is as if Cleopatra liberated a side of Antony's personality that had formerly been repressed and which he found refreshing.

The overwhelming sense of luxury and magnificence of Cleopatra, almost as a goddess, is conveyed by the description of the first meeting of the lovers:

she disdained to set forward otherwise, but to take her barge in the river of Cydnus, the poope whereof was of gold, the sailes of purple, and the owers of silver, which kept stroke in rowing after the sounde of the musicke of flutes, howboyes, citherns, violls, and such other instruments as they played upon in the barge. And now for the person of her selfe: she was layed under a pavillion of cloth of gold of tissue, apparelled and attired like the goddesse Venus, commonly drawen in picture: and hard by her, on either hand of her, pretie faire boyes apparelled as painters doe set forth god Cupide, with little fannes in their hands, with the which they fanned wind upon her. Her Ladies and gentlewomen also, the fairest of them were apparelled like the nymphes Nereides (which are the mermaides of the waters) and like the Graces, some stearing the helme, others tending the tackle and ropes of the barge, out of the which there came a wonderfull passing sweete savor of perfumes, that perfumed the wharfes side, pestered with innumerable multitudes of people. Some of them followed the barge all alongest the rivers side: others also ranne out of the citie to see her comming in. So that in thend, there ranne such multitudes of people one after an other to see her, that Antonius was left post alone in the market place, in his Imperiall seate to geve audience: and there went a rumor in the peoples mouthes, that the goddesse Venus was come to play with the god Bacchus, for the generall good of all Asia. When Cleopatra landed, Antonius sent to invite her to supper to him. But she sent him word againe, he should doe better rather to come and suppe with her. Antonius therefore to shew him selfe curteous unto her at her arrivall, was contented to obey her, and went to supper to her: where he found such passing sumptuous fare, that no tongue can expresse it. But amongest all other thinges, he most wondered at the infinite number of lightes and torches hanged on the toppe of the house, geving light in everie place . . .[21]

Here is not merely an awareness of luxury, but a surrender to the world of feeling. The senses are appealed to through colour, sound, touch, ('cloth of gold of tissue') and scent. Beginning with the colloquial 'I will tell you', Shakespeare's Enobarbus recreates the supreme moment:

The barge she sat in, like a burnish'd throne
Burn'd on the water: the poop was beaten gold;
Purple the sails, and so perfumed that
The winds were love-sick with them; the oars were silver,
Which to the tune of flutes kept stroke, and made
The water which they beat to follow faster,
As amorous of their strokes. For her own person,
It beggar'd all description: she did lie
In her pavilion – cloth of gold, of tissue –
O'er-picturing that Venus where we see
The fancy outwork nature. On each side her,
Stood pretty dimpled boys, like smiling Cupids,
With divers-colour'd fans, whose wind did seem
To glow the delicate cheeks which they did cool,

99

And what they undid did . . .
Her gentlewomen, like the Nereides,
So many mermaids, tended her i'the eyes,
And made their bends adornings. At the helm
A seeming mermaid steers: the silken tackle
Swell with the touches of those flower-soft hands,
That yarely frame the office. From the barge
A strange invisible perfume hits the sense
Of the adjacent wharfs. The city cast
Her people out upon her; and Antony,
Enthron'd i'the market-place, did sit alone,
Whistling to the air; which, but for vacancy,
Had gone to gaze on Cleopatra too,
And made a gap in nature.

(II.ii.191–218)

Shakespeare incorporates all the elements in Plutarch's magnificent description but makes the vision more vivid: the barge 'burn'd on the water'; the diversity of instruments is reduced to the 'tune of flutes'. The sense of touch is more delicate and intense: the winds are 'love-sick' with the 'purple' sails; the water caresses the oars 'As amorous of their strokes'; 'the silken tackle/Swell with the touches of those flower-soft hands'. It is 'A strange invisible perfume hits the sense'. The people are no longer like buzzing insects who pester: 'The city cast/Her people out upon her'. Antony is not simply left 'post alone in the market-place'; even the air, 'but for vacancy,/Had gone to gaze on Cleopatra too,/And made a gap in nature'. What in Plutarch is exotic and magnificent becomes in Shakespeare both more intensely realized and fantastic. Fact and fancy co-mingle; the whole vision is both too wonderful to be true and too clearly delineated to be false. And the words come from the mouth of a 'souldier only' to impress Romans who have not witnessed the magic of the East. This vision is the ultimate expression of a culture which contrasts totally with that of Rome. Here is the sense of a world which is the antithesis of all that Rome stands for. When the dramatist absorbed and transformed this passage from Plutarch/North, he did not confine it to a magnificent set-piece but used it to epitomize a contrast that pervades the play. Significantly, Shakespeare's Enobarbus builds up to this description by responding to Maecenas' questions about the abundance and extravagance of Egypt:

MAECENAS Eight wild-boars roasted whole at a breakfast, and but twelve persons there; is this true?
ENOBARBUS This was but as a fly by an eagle: we had much more monstrous matter of feast, which worthily deserved noting.

(II.ii.179–83)

The material for this incident is drawn from an amusing story told to Plutarch by his grandfather, Lampryas, who knew a physician acquainted with one of Antony's cooks:

> he tooke him to Antonius house, (being a young man desirous to see things) to shew him the wonderfull sumptuous charge and preparation of one only supper. When he was in the kitchin, and saw a world of diversities of meates, and amongest others, eight wild boares rosted whole: he began to wonder at it, and sayd, Sure you have a great number of ghests to supper. The cooke fell a laughing, and answered him, No (quoth he) not many ghestes, nor above twelve in all: but yet all that is boyled or roasted must be served in whole, or else it would be marred straight. For Antonius peradventure will suppe presently, or it may be a pretie while hence, or likely enough he will deferre it longer, for that he hath dronke well to day, or else hath had some other great matters in hand: and therefore we doe not dresse one supper only, but many suppers, bicause we are uncerteine of the houre he will suppe in. Philotas the Phisition tolde my grandfather this tale.[22]

This intimate story conveys a wonderful sense of abundance and extravagance. What is remarkable is not that the dramatist uses it but that it is used with such economy and dramatic effect.

A complete contrast to the portrait of Cleopatra found in Plutarch is provided by Flavius Josephus. *The Antiquities of the Jews* was translated by Thomas Lodge in 1602, and it seems probable that Shakespeare was acquainted with this work. If so, he totally ignores the portrait of the ruthless and avaricious Egyptian which emerges from those pages:

> About the same time there grew certaine troubles and alterations in Syria: for that Cleopatra continually sollicited and importuned Antony, and whetted on his displeasure against all, perswading him to remoove all from their governments, and to bestow the same on her selfe. And for that Antony loved her extremely, she was in great estimation and credit with him: and being in her owne nature inclined to covetousnesse, shee abstained from no kinde of corrupt dealing and wickednesse. For knowing that the kingdome should descend unto her brother, she caused him to be poisoned, when he was but fifteene yeeres olde: as for her sister Arsinoe, she caused her to be slaine by Anthonies meanes at such time, as she made her prayers in the temple of Diana at Ephesus. Moreover in what place soever she understood that there was any hope to get money, whether it were in robbing of temples, or in breaking open sepulchers; she would be possessed thereof: neither was there any religious place so sacred, from whence she tooke not away the ornaments. Furthermore there was not any thing so prophane and interdicted, which she laid not hands on to satisfie her unbridled avarice.

Neither was the whole world sufficient enough to content this magnificent Ladie, who was made slave to her owne desires; and her disordinate appetite was such, that all the riches in the world were not able to saciate and fill the same. For this cause she incessantly importuned Antonius to take from others, to be liberall towards her.[23]

Entirely different in tone is an anonymous work dating from around the thirteenth century. This manuscript, entitled *The Deeds of Caesar*, gives a description of Cleopatra's physical attractiveness and an account of her death. The author states that Cleopatra was 'very beautiful, and she exerted herself greatly to deck herself out to please Caesar'.[24] One intriguing element in this account is the description of a conversation over dinner between Julius Caesar and Achoreus the high priest:

This Achoreus, who was an astrologer, spoke in answer to Caesar's questions and told him everything, the order of the planets, and how in Ethiopia there are black men; he told of the Nile and how it grows and how it diminishes through the virtue of the planet called Mercury.[25]

Did this comment provide the imaginative spark for a brief but vital moment in the play where Antony responds to Octavius Caesar's questions about the role of the Nile in the economic life of Egypt? (II.vii.17–23.) What this passage conveys is a sense of the intellectual curiosity of the Romans, their desire to understand the societies with which they came into contact – including, crucially, their economic foundations.

If Shakespeare paints Antony in colours far more attractive than Plutarch, he quite decidedly alters the picture of Octavius to his detriment. In *The Life of Octavius Caesar* which was added to the 1603 edition of Plutarch's *Lives*, and was almost certainly read by Shakespeare, the opening sentence reads: 'He was very modest and continent in all the parts of his life, saving that he was somewhat given to women'.[26] Shakespeare's character is evidently 'continent', abstemious and fastidious, but no womanizer. Quite the contrary. His harsh denunciations of Cleopatra as a whore and his obvious distaste for Antony's amorous adventures are articulated in a way which gives the impression of a man who finds sex distasteful. He obviously holds women in low esteem. The only woman for whom he expresses any feeling is his sister, Octavia, and his affection for her is clearly deep and genuine. His abstemiousness is indicated early on in Plutarch's account where it is stated that 'he drunke very little wine' and that 'In his ordinarie diet he banished superfluity of meates'. This accords perfectly with Shakespeare's character, but the comment that 'he delighted to be merry and pleasant among his friends, or to bring in pleasant players of commedies to passe the time away'[27] is totally at variance with the Octavius of the play. For Shakespeare's character political life is all-embracing, and his one genuinely emotional bond is with his sister – whom he is willing to use as a pawn on the political chessboard.

At no time in the play does Octavius make a joke or give the impression that he has any personal relationships (leaving aside his sister) – nor is there any sign of personal affection towards him. He is respected and admired for his political qualities and provides, therefore, a much sharper contrast with the Antony of the play, whose emotional life is very rich. The contrast between the two is highlighted during the scene on Pompey's barge where Antony immerses himself in the festivities, enjoying the physical contact, camaraderie and drinking, while Octavius is ill at ease, reluctantly drinking a second cup of wine before announcing his departure – like the closure of a board meeting, which for him, it is. Plutarch says of Octavius that he had 'so comely a face' that he disconcerted his antagonists as soon as they looked on him. Moreover, 'he had very cleare and lively eyes'. Though physically attractive he was later subject to many infirmities, and immediately after the civil war 'he left armes and horses' because 'he was never any great souldier'.[28] There is no hint of Octavius' attractive physical attributes or demeanour in Shakespeare's play, nor any sense of facial animation. The reference to lack of soldiership does, however, find expression in the play, as the impression gleaned is of a man who listens closely to his advisers – though such counselling takes place behind closed doors, with decisions being publicly announced by Octavius.

Shakespeare's character gives little sense of great intellect or humility but Plutarch says of Octavius that 'he was learned in the liberall sciences, very eloquent, and desirous to learne'.[29] The only manifestation of intellectual inquisitiveness in the play occurs in the scene of revelling on Pompey's barge where Antony is responding to Octavius' enquiry about the organization of agriculture in Egypt (whereas the drunken Lepidus confines his enquiries to the nature of crocodiles). But this moment rather gives a sense of Octavius' thoroughness in discovering the principles of land management because of its implications for Roman rule – a typical piece of Roman acquisition of knowledge which is essential for the preservation of the Empire. Again Shakespeare adduces no sign of Octavius' eloquence, though he does reveal him as the consummate political controller. This control is beautifully exhibited in the confrontation with Pompey (II.vi.1–59), though he never utters more than a few words.

Plutarch rounds off his description of Octavius by referring to his pleasing voice, his careful study in speech training and eloquence, and his attachment to good books. Perhaps surprisingly, the historian says that 'He was somewhat, and too much given to divinations: he was marvellously afraid of thunder and lightening: he had a great confidence in dreames, and in such like vanities'.[30] The enumeration of his achievements in public office commence with his attainment of consulship at the age of 20 years and conclude with the observation that,

It is a wonderfull thing that he could winde himselfe out of so many great affaires and warres, that he could within foure and twenty yeares of age, restore againe into so good estate the common wealth of Rome, turmoiled and troubled with so many proscriptions and civill warres as it was. And that afterwards so long as he commaunded alone, he did so firmely establish this Monarchie'.[31]

Yet, despite this attractive portrait, Plutarch does record events which expose facets of Octavius' character that Shakespeare seized upon to create an individual who was considerably at variance with this highly favourable account.

What, then, are the most significant departures of Shakespeare from his source material in his portrayal of the central characters? First, Antony is transformed into a much more attractive character. There is no hint of his life of lechery, drunkeness, debauchery and corruption in Rome while acting as Julius Caesar's right-hand man. All the references to the life of Antony before he met Cleopatra relate to his greatness as a general. Even more importantly, two major historical events are ignored: Antony's disastrous handling of his Parthian campaigns with the needless loss of thousands of men, and his responsibility for the murder and mutilation of Cicero. It is true that Antony cuts a very unattractive figure in the proscription scene in *Julius Caesar*, but in *Antony and Cleopatra* there is not the slightest allusion to the ugly brutality which Plutarch recounts with such evident disgust. Arguably, references to the activities of the young Antony in Rome are irrelevant to the actions and events of this play; similarly mistreatment of Cicero is not germane to any incident in the play. Nevertheless, Shakespeare does not develop the character traits implicit in these actions. Quite the contrary. It is impossible to imagine Shakespeare's Antony stooping to the vile acts that are related by Plutarch. Shakespeare's creation of an attractive Antony – albeit one who degrades himself at Actium and reveals a high degree of naivety and incompetence – is clearly a dramatic necessity. Plutarch's Antony could not gain the sympathy of the audience for ten minutes. Dramatically, Shakespeare could quite easily have dropped any reference to the Parthian campaigns. In fact he creates a scene which centres on Ventidius and Silius (III.i). This scene does not, however, allude in any way to the fiasco for which Antony was responsible. Rather, it highlights an interesting political point: namely, how generals are normally accredited with the successes achieved by their subordinates, who dare not risk success which deflects glory away from their superiors, and how this jealousy can diminish efficiency. Plutarch relates that Ventidius was a man of humble origins who owed his promotion to Antony's favour. This remarkable individual was the only Roman to secure victory over the Parthians – and Antony arranged his triumph in Rome as a reward. Either he stopped short of eclipsing

Antony, or the latter displayed a generosity of spirit rare among generals. The relevant passage is intriguing:

> Ventidius was the only man that ever triumphed of the Parthians untill this present day, a meane man borne, and of no noble house nor family: who only came to that he attained unto, through Antonius frendshippe, the which delivered him happie occasion to achieve to great matters. And yet to say truely, he did so well quit him selfe in all his enterprises, that he confirmed that which was spoken of Antonius and Caesar: to wit, that they were alway more fortunate when they made warre by their Lieutenauntes, then by them selves.[32]

The second major transformation of the source material relates to Antony and Octavia. The length of the time they lived together is greatly contracted, their two children go unmentioned, and most importantly of all, the role played by this remarkable woman, who served as Antony's envoy in Rome even after he had deserted her, is suppressed. Her two attempts to mediate between Octavius and Antony are contracted to one. Thus the woman of character, intelligence and generosity of spirit is reduced to a pale and colourless character in the play. Apart from her outstanding virtues, Plutarch states the general view that Cleopatra 'nether excelled Octavia in beawtie, nor yet in young yeares'.[33]

Third, Shakespeare's Octavius has none of the attractive features delineated by Plutarch. He has no charm or eloquence: he is a very effective political leader who devotes his energies entirely to political manoeuvring. His one intimate personal relationship is with his sister and even she can be used for political advantage. He is perceptive, ruthless and fully aware of the need to draw on the experience and understanding of his closest associates. Even so they remain totally subordinate, neither giving nor receiving any sign of affection. He is the antithesis of Antony. Shakespeare's Octavius is such a clearly drawn character – fastidious, abstemious, observant and devoid of personal warmth – that it is impossible to imagine him sharing Antony's susceptibility to women, a 'weakness' which Plutarch ascribes to him. Shakespeare's character attracts admiration rather than affection. Antony is loved and can cause his men to weep after he has failed miserably as a general and leader. This latter enigma is, of course, powerfully present in Plutarch, when Antony is comforted by the wounded soldiers whom he has failed so lamentably during the Parthian campaign.

Fourth, if Shakespeare suppresses Antony's most unattractive features and diminishes the more likeable elements of Octavius found in Plutarch, he accentuates Cleopatra's charm, vivacity and capriciousness. It is easy to understand Antony's dotage. Moreover, the role of her children is so reduced in the play that her whole emotional intensity is fixed on Antony. Whereas Plutarch emphasizes Cleopatra's anxiety about her children when contemplating suicide, there is only one brief reference to their vulnerability in the play – Octavius' thinly disguised threat (V.ii.130–1).

Fifth, the greatest character change from the source material is Enobarbus. He has no character at all in Plutarch. Mentioned only three times, the most significant reference is to his desertion of Antony *before* Actium (he deserts *after* the battle in the play) and his subsequent sudden death. From such unpromising material Shakespeare draws inspiration for the creation of a central character – one through whom a great deal of our perception of events is filtered.

Turning from character to events, one major historical change made by Shakespeare, which is masterly in terms of the shaping of the play, is Antony's initial departure from Egypt. Historically, Antony left for Parthia, received news of the turmoil created in Rome by Fulvia, and so re-set his course in order to re-establish political equilibrium in Rome. The threat of Pompey was a relatively minor affair. Shakespeare reshapes events so that Antony leaves for Rome in response to Octavius' request for aid against Pompey. The news of Fulvia's death, with its political repercussions, comes fast on the heels of Caesar's missive. Antony's tardy response to Octavius' request for help puts him in a position of some embarrassment, which Octavius exploits by pretending that Antony had a hand in the rebellion precipitated by Fulvia. Shakespeare thus creates a powerfully emotional atmosphere for the meeting of Antony and Octavius, and this is heightened by the great danger to Caesar of Pompey's approach. In these circumstances Antony has every reason to feel uncomfortable and defensive, but he has no reason for making any substantial concessions to Octavius – who badly needs his support. But it is in precisely these circumstances that Antony is manoeuvred into a position where he agrees to marry Octavia – even though he can have no serious intention of being loyal to her. Moreover, Octavius himself makes it plain that this is no marriage of convenience. If Antony fails Octavia he will create an irrevocable breach between them. Still, Antony, in order to smooth over a short-term difficulty, makes a decision, the long-term consequences of which are highly damaging if not catastrophic. Antony's first major decision in the play, therefore, is revealed as an act of great folly.

The next major decision made by Antony, apart from his desertion of Octavia, is his determination, despite all advice to the contrary, to allow Cleopatra to accompany him to Actium and to fight at sea. In Plutarch's account Antony's failure in his conflict with Octavius came earlier, as he had the opportunity of engaging Caesar while the latter was beset by the difficulties of raising money for the campaign. Shakespeare does not refer to this, but underlines Antony's slowness of response by crediting Octavius with superhuman speed. We are constantly struck by the shrewd calculation, adroitness, and sheer physical speed of Octavius. Ironically, both in historical fact and in the play, Antony is in the position of being able to win the battle of Actium despite having made the foolish decision of engaging in a naval battle. It is his astonishing flight after Cleopatra which brings about disaster. Historically, even after the sea battle was lost the army held firm for seven days awaiting Antony's return. Had he done so he might well have overcome Octavius. Instead he retired to the island of Pharos, building himself a house by the sea and living in isolation like Timon of Athens. Shakespeare ignores that period and instead concentrates Antony's feeling of shame and desolation in a single scene (III.xi).

Another key change by Shakespeare is that the news of Octavius' assault on Pompey and the 'turning-off' of Lepidus comes as a surprise to Antony. In Plutarch the account of Octavia's successful reconciliation of brother and husband concludes with an exchange of ships for land soldiers in which it is clear that Octavius is going to make his attack on Pompey with Antony's approval: 'After they had taken leave of eache other, Caesar went immediately to make warre with Sextus Pompeius, to gette Sicilia into his handes'.[34]

Shakespeare's response to Plutarch's account of the events immediately preceding the battle of Actium is fascinating. Plutarch describes how Octavius is able to build up hostility to Antony by describing the gift of large parts of the Eastern Empire to Cleopatra and her children – undertaking such action in ceremonials that are anathema to the Romans – while Antony's wife resides in Rome, conscientiously and lovingly fulfilling both domestic and political roles on his behalf. Thus Antony totally alienates his supporters in Rome. This is of crucial importance because Octavius himself generates great hostility through the imposition of taxes necessary for financing his campaign. The immediate reasons for the conflict advanced by Antony in the play, and Octavius' response to them, come directly from Plutarch. Octavius retained the ships loaned him by Antony; he refused to share with Antony lands and resources plundered from Lepidus and Pompey; finally, Octavius had divided Italy among his own soldiers, leaving nothing for Antony's men. Octavius justified his actions by claiming that he had not received a share of Antony's Eastern conquests.

As the preparations proceed Cleopatra seeks to join Antony in the battle. But whereas in the play Antony assents to this request in the face of strong opposition from all his friends and advisers, because he is in thrall to Cleopatra, Plutarch puts forward a slightly different account:

So Antonius, through the perswasions of Domitius [Enobarbus], commaunded Cleopatra to returne againe into Ægypt, and there to understand the successe of this warre. But Cleopatra, fearing least Antonius should againe be made friends with Octavius Caesar, by the meanes of his wife Octavia: she so plyed Canidius with money, and filled his purse, that he became her spokes man unto Antonius, and told him there was no reason to send her from this warre, who defraied so great a charge:

neither that it was for his profit, bicause that thereby the Ægyptians would then be utterly discoraged, which were the chiefest strength of the army by sea: considering that he could see no king of all the kings their confederats, that Cleopatra was inferior unto, either for wisedom or judgement, seeing that longe before she had wisely governed so great a realme as Ægypt, and besides that she had bene so long acquainted with him, by whom she had learned to manedge great affayres. These fayer perswasions wan him: for it was predestined that the government of all the world should fall into Octavius Caesars handes.[35]

Plutarch's last sentence is fascinating. First, it brings out the crucial importance of the decision to allow Cleopatra to go to the war (the implication being that Antony would have won the battle had he not deserted his post to follow Cleopatra at the vital moment). Secondly, it conveys a sense of destiny at work in human affairs – though not in a simple way. In order for Octavius to triumph at Actium, Antony has to desert his men.

Another significant 'cut' by Shakespeare is Plutarch's vivid description of the festivities which took place on the Isle of Samos:

Thus, all their forces being joyned together, they hoysed sayle towards the Ile of Samos, and there gave them selves to feasts and sollace. For as all the kings, Princes, and communalties, peoples and cities from Syria, unto the marishes Maeotides, and from the Armenians to the Illyrians, were sent unto, to send and bringe all munition and warlike preparation they could: even so all players, minstrells, tumblers, fooles, and jeasters, were commaunded to assemble in the Ile of Samos. So that, where in manner all the world in every place was full of lamentations, sighes and teares: onely in this Ile of Samos there was nothing for many dayes space, but singing and pyping, and all the Theater full of these common players, minstrells, and singing men. Besides all this, every citie sent an oxe thither to sacrifice, and kings did strive one with another who should make the noblest feasts, and give the richest gifts. So that every man sayd, What can they doe more for joy of victorie, if they winne the battell? when they make already such sumptuous feasts at the beginning of the warre?[36]

All this takes place while Caesar is scrambling money together to raise an army. Had Antony forgone the festivities and accelerated his preparations he would have caught Octavius unprepared:

Octavius Caesar understanding the sodain and wonderful great preparation of Antonius, he was not a litle astonied at it, (fearing he should be driven to fight that sommer) bicause he wanted many things, and the great and grievous exactions of money did sorely oppresse the people . . . Hereuppon, there rose a wonderfull exclamation and great uprore all Italy over: so that among the greatest faults that ever

Antonius committed, they blamed him most, for that he delayed to give Caesar battell. For he gave Caesar leysure to make his preparacions, and also to appease the complaints of the people. When such a great summe of money was demaunded of them, they grudged at it, and grewe to mutinie upon it: but when they had once paied it, they remembred it no more.[37]

In the play, the feeling is conveyed that Antony is never in a position to gain an advantage over Caesar; the latter is always several steps ahead in his preparations. Indeed, when Antony is told of Caesar's progress he can hardly credit the news and is rebuked by Cleopatra – in contrast to Plutarch's account where Cleopatra says: 'And what daunger, I pray you, said she, if Caesar keepe at Toryne?'[38]

Given Shakespeare's frequent references to fortune in the play, and his adoption of the omens in Plutarch for *Julius Caesar*, it is perhaps surprising that he makes so little use of the numerous omens recounted by Plutarch – all of which are adverse to Antony:

Before this warre, as it is reported, many signes and wonders fel out. First of all, the citie of Pisaurum which was made a colony to Rome, and replenished with people by Antonius, standing upon the shore side of the sea Adriatick, was by a terrible earthquake sonck into the ground. One of the images of stone which was set up in the honor of Antonius, in the citie of Alba, did sweate many dayes together: and though some wyped it away, yet it left not sweating still. In the citie of Patras, whilest Antonius was there, the temple of Hercules was burnt with lightning. And at the citie of Athens also, in a place where the warre of the gyants against the goddes is set out in imagerie: the statute of Bacchus with a terrible winde was throwen downe in the Theater. It was sayd that Antonius came of the race of Hercules, as you have heard before, and in the manner of his life he followed Bacchus: and therefore he was called the new Bacchus. Furthermore, the same blustering storme of wind, overthrew the great monstrous images at Athens, that were made in the honor of Eumenes and Attalus, the which men had named and intituled, the Antonians, and yet they did hurt none of the other images which were many besides. The Admirall galley of Cleopatra, was called Antoniade, in the which there chaunced a marvelous ill signe. Swallowes had bred under the poope of her shippe, and there came others after them that drave away the first and plucked downe their neasts.[39]

Only the last of these omens finds its way into the play, and that in an abbreviated form: 'Swallows have built/In Cleopatra's sails their nests' (IV.xii.3–4). Nevertheless, Shakespeare creates a feeling of the operation of fate, which is manifested most strongly in the form of the soothsayer.

In enumerating the rival forces Plutarch provides the list of kings who backed Antony. This roll-call of kings, which gives a powerful sense of the exotic, is seized upon by Shakespeare. Once the balance of forces has been specified, Plutarch is explicit in his criticism of Antony's decision to fight by sea – once more this is fully utilized by Shakespeare:

> Now Antonius was made so subject to a womans will, that though he was a great deale the stronger by land, yet for Cleopatraes sake, he would needes have this battell tryed by sea: though he sawe before his eyes, that for lacke of water men, his Captaines did presse by force all sortes of men out of Graece that they could take up in the field, as travellers, muletters, reapers, harvest men, and younge boyes, and yet could they not sufficiently furnishe his gallies: so that the most part of them were empty, and could scant rowe, bicause they lacked water men enowe. But on the contrary side, Caesars shippes were not built for pompe, highe, and great, onely for a sight and bravery, but they were light of yarage, armed and furnished with water men as many as they needed, and had them all in readines, in the havens of Tarentum, and Brundusium.[40]

While the two leaders are making proposals and counterproposals about the venue for the battle, Caesar moves with such swiftness that Antony's fleet is caught unprepared:

> Caesar had quickly passed the sea Ionium, and taken a place called Toryne, before Antonius understoode that he had taken shippe. Then began his men to be affraid, bicause his army by land was left behind.

Antony's response to this precarious situation is to undertake a desperate bluff – which is successful:

> So he armed all his water men, and set them in order of battell upon the forecastell of their shippes, and then lift up all his rancks of owers towards the element, as well of the one side, as the other, with the prooes against the enemies, at the entry and mouth of the gulfe, which beginneth at the point of Actium, and so kept them in order of battell, as if they had bene armed and furnished with water men and souldiers. Thus Octavius Caesar beeing finely deceyved by this stratageame, retyred presently.[41]

This incident is ignored by Shakespeare but great emphasis is given to Octavius' speed which is echoed throughout the remainder of the play. Indeed, Antony follows up this successful stratagem by cutting off Caesar from supplies of fresh water. Here is the shrewd Antony: Shakespeare never allows him this degree of astuteness; his very thought processes have become clogged and befuddled by Cleopatra.

At this point in the narration Plutarch gives a simple but moving account of Enobarbus' betrayal of Antony and the latter's response:

Furthermore, he delt very friendly and curteously with Domitius, and against Clepatraes mynde. For, he being sicke of an agewe when he went and tooke a litle boate to goe to Caesars campe, Antonius was very sory for it, but yet he sent after him all his caryage, trayne, and men: and the same Domitius, as though he gave him to understand that he repented his open treason, he died immediately after.[42]

Canidius, previously bribed by Cleopatra, suddenly does an about turn and attempts to persuade Antony to abandon the sea battle and take up a better position for fighting on land. However, 'notwithstanding all these good perswasions, Cleopatra forced him to put all to the hazard of battel by sea'.[43]

Shakespeare draws fully on the historian's description of Antony's refusal to behave rationally in the face of Cleopatra's persuasions, and adopts, in abbreviated form, the comment of a soldier in the midst of preparations, cited by Plutarch:

O noble Emperor, how commeth it to pass that you trust to these vile brittle shippes? what, doe you mistrust these woundes of myne, and this sword? let the Aegyptians and Phaenicians fight by sea, and set us on the maine land, where we used to conquer, or to be slayne on our feete.[44]

Despite relinquishing his main advantage and employing his weakest resources against Caesar, Antony achieves equality in the sea battle (he even has a slight advantage in Shakespeare) when Cleopatra panics.

Howbeit the battell was yet of even hand, and the victorie doubtfull, being indifferent to both: when sodainely they saw the three score shippes of Cleopatra busie about their yard masts, and hoysing saile to flie . . . There Antonius shewed plainely, that he had not onely lost the corage and hart of an Emperor, but also of a valliant man, and that he was not his owne man . . . he was so caried away with the vaine love of this woman, as if he had bene glued unto her, and that she could not have removed without moving of him also. For when he saw Cleopatraes shippe under saile, he forgot, forsooke, and betrayed them that fought for him.[45]

After Antony caught up with Cleopatra's ship and boarded it the enormity of his action struck him with full force. After a brief skirmish with one of his pursuers,

he returned againe to his place, and sate downe, speaking never a word as he did before: and so lived three dayes alone, without speaking to any man. But when he arrived at the head of Taenarus, there Cleopatraes women first brought Antonius and Cleopatra to speake together, and afterwards, to suppe and lye together.[46]

Even then Antony was able to retrieve the situation. However, he was too demoralized to seize the opportunity:

> Antonius sent unto Canidius, to returne with his army into Asia, by Macedon. Now for him self, he determined to crosse over into Africk, and toke one of his carects or hulks loden with gold and silver, and other rich cariage, and gave it unto his friends: commaunding them to depart, and to seeke to save them selves. They aunswered him weeping, that they would nether doe it, nor yet forsake him. Then Antonius very curteously and lovingly did comfort them, and prayed them to depart.[47]

Antony's capacity to attract such devotion after deserting his men, is astonishing. Even the navy held out until 'five howers within night'. Plutarch goes on to emphasize that Antony still had the resources to overcome Caesar:

> Many plainely sawe Antonius flie, and yet could hardly beleeve it, that he that had nyneteene legions whole by lande and twelve thowsand horsemen upon the sea side, would so have forsaken them, and have fled so cowardly: as if he had not oftentimes proved both the one and the other fortune, and that he had not bene throughly acquainted with the divers chaunges and fortunes of battells. And yet his souldiers still wished for him, and ever hoped that he would come by some meanes or other unto them. Furthermore, they shewed them selves so valliant and faithfull unto him, that after they certainly knewe he was fled, they kept them selves whole together seven daies.[48]

Having fled from Actium, Cleopatra attempted to convey a vast quantity of treasure by ship to Asia – even taking the ships overland across what is now the Suez canal. The hostility of the Arabians finally persuaded her to withdraw from this enterprise. As for Antony, he built a house by the sea on the Isle of Pharos, 'and dwelt there, as a man that banished him selfe from all mens companie: saying that he would lead Timons life'. When Canidius arrived to tell him that all the army was lost and several of his former supporters had joined with Caesar, he seemed indifferent, but finally left his retirement and joined Cleopatra in Alexandria. 'He was no sooner comen thither, but he straight set all the city of rioting and banketing againe, and him selfe to liberalitie and giftes'. Indeed, they celebrated a new order, Synapothanumenon ('signifying the order and agreement of those that will dye together') to replace their previous order of Amimetobion, meaning 'no life comparable'.[49]

In anticipation of her suicide Cleopatra tested a great many poisons on condemned prisoners:

> So when she had dayly made divers and sundrie proofes, she found none of all them she had proved so fit, as the biting of an Aspicke,

the which only causeth a heavines of the head, without swounding or complaining, and bringeth a great desire also to sleepe . . .[50]

Nevertheless, Antony and Cleopatra retained the hope of gaining a reprieve from Caesar. They were reduced to sending as their ambassador the schoolmaster of their children, 'Cleopatra requesting the realme of Ægypt for her children, and Antonius praying that he might be suffered to live at Athens like a private man, if Caesar would not let him remaine in Ægypt'.[51] This request, and Octavius' tart reply, are adopted by Shakespeare: 'Caesar would not graunt unto Antonius requests: but for Cleopatra, he made her aunswere, that he would deny her nothing reasonable, so that she would either put Antonius to death, or drive him out of her contrie'.[52]

Octavius chose as his messenger one Thyreus, 'a verie wise and discreete man' noted for his eloquence.[53] This is sufficient hint for Shakespeare to devise Octavius' cynical instructions to his messenger:

> From Antony win Cleopatra, promise,
> And in our name, what she requires; add more,
> From thine invention, offers: women are not
> In their best fortunes strong; but want will perjure
> The ne'er-touch'd vestal: try thy cunning, Thidias.
>   (III.xii.27–31)

Unfortunately for Thyreus, his reception by Cleopatra is so favourable that Antony becomes jealous and has him whipped. Shakespeare incorporates the action and part of the message ascribed to Antony by Plutarch: 'and bad him tell him that he made him angrie with him, bicause he shewed him selfe prowde and disdainfull towards him, and now especially when he was easie to be angered, by reason of his present miserie'.[54] Shakespeare makes an alteration that allows him to continue the contrast that runs right through the play, of the successful Antony of the past, with the failure of the present:

> Get thee back to Caesar,
> Tell him thy entertainment: look thou say
> He makes me angry with him. For he seems
> Proud and disdainful, harping on what I am
> Not what he knew I was.
>   (III.xiii.139–43)

The dramatist also picks up the point that it is Cleopatra's birthday. As part of the process of mollifying and reassuring Antony, she celebrates it 'with such solemnitie, that she exceeded all measure of sumptuousnes and magnificence'.[55] Whereas in Shakespeare these revels constitute a shortlived interlude before the attack by Caesar, in historical terms

Octavius was obliged to return to Rome to deal with domestic difficulties before gathering up his forces for the final thrust against Antony the following year. When he returned and captured the city of Pelusium the rumour spread that the city was surrended by Seleucus on Cleopatra's instructions. Consequently, Cleopatra was hard put to convince Antony that the story was false.

Caesar approached Alexandria with caution for fear that Cleopatra would destroy the magnificent treasures that she had built and amassed there. However, Antony had one last successful fling, discomforting Caesar, though Plutarch conveys a sense of the insignificance of this event before going on to recount a number of other incidents used by the dramatist, including the strange noises which occurred during the night:

> the selfe same night within litle of midnight, when all the citie was quiet, full of feare and sorrowe thinking what would be the issue and ende of this warre: it is said that sodainly they heard a marvelous sweete har-monie of sundrie sortes of instrumentes of musicke, with the crie of a multitude of people, as they had bene dauncing, and had song as they use in Bacchus feastes, with movinges and turninges after the maner of the Satyres: and it seemed that this daunce went through the city unto the gate that opened to the enemies, and that all the troupe that made this noise they heard, went out of the city at that gate. Now, such as in reason sought the depth of the interpretacion of this wonder, thought that it was the god unto whom Antonius bare singular devotion to counterfeate and resemble him, that did forsake them.[56]

The small details are worth noting. Shakespeare incorporates the incident of the soldier who fought bravely and received a generous reward from Cleopatra, but makes no use of the ironical situation of the soldier desert-ing immediately after receiving the reward. Why? Is it because the lovers need building up rather than deflating at this point? Or is it simply that Shakespeare ruthlessly excises fascinating points of detail where they might encumber or distract from the lines he is pursuing at that point in the play? What we have is celebration and munificence:

CLEOPATRA I'll give thee, friend,
    An armour all of gold; it was a king's.
ANTONY He has deserv'd it, were it carbuncled
    Like holy Phoebus' car.
                        (IV.viii.26–9)

Again, it is intriguing to observe the way in which Shakespeare picks up a fact and gives it power by a few words. Plutarch recounts Antony's second challenge to Caesar along with the latter's comment that he had 'many other ways to dye'. The dramatist uses those words but Octavius prefaces them with the dismissive comment 'let the old ruffian know', and the speech concludes with the lines, 'Laugh at his challenge' (IV.i.4–6). Caesar closes the scene with the phrase, 'Poor Antony!' (IV.i.16). In so doing he 'places' Antony from the perspective of both his adversaries and the audience. It seems as if a single line or phrase in Plutarch acts as a catalyst for creating a mood and conjuring lines from Shakespeare's mind. The subsequent descriptions of Antony making his servants and officers weep, and the strange sounds interpreted as the departure of Antony's god, are followed closely, though wonderful little touches are added such as Enobarbus' insistent plea that Antony desist:

> What mean you, sir,
> To give them this discomfort? Look, they weep,
> And I, an ass, am onion-ey'd; for shame,
> Transform us not to women.
>
> (IV.ii.33–6)

That description is followed by a rueful reflection by Antony on his present situation compared with his former glory. Thus, the potent visual image of the two fleets joining, acts as an effective induction to a speech which has at its centre a more complex and abstract imagery:

> The hearts
> That spaniel'd me at heels, to whom I gave
> Their wishes, do discandy, melt their sweets
> On blossoming Caesar: and this pine is bark'd,
> That overtopp'd them all.
>
> (IV.xii.20–4)

The description of Eros' suicide again brings out Antony's capacity to attract love and loyalty, and underlines the strangely enigmatic quality of a man who could behave so savagely to Cicero. In Plutarch such contrasting incidents continually recur. Shakespeare's audience has no such nagging reflections to distance feeling from Antony. The Antony of the play is guilty only of bad judgment, primarily through his love of Cleopatra. Pity for Antony is the dominant emotion. As Plutarch says when describing the way in which the dying Antony is hauled up to the monument, 'They that were present to behold it, said they never saw so pitiefull a sight'.[57] A significant omission from Plutarch's account of Cleopatra's response to the sight of the dying Antony is that 'she rent her garments upon him, clapping her brest, and scratching her face and stomake'.[58] Antony consoled himself with past glories and his Roman death – elements that receive powerful representation in the play.

One vital piece of reinterpretation by Shakespeare relates to Plutarch's description of Caesar bursting into tears when he receives Antony's bloodied sword, but soon emerging from his tent to show the letters that had passed between them in order to justify his own conduct.

Shakespeare's treatment is more ambiguous. When Agrippa says 'Caesar is touch'd' Maecenas responds,

> When such a spacious mirror's set before him,
> He needs must see himself.
>
> (V.i.34–5)

Here the tears are interpreted, not in terms of sorrow for Antony, but as recognition that there is an end of all great men, including Caesar. But, the question must be posed, would this reflection provoke this kind of emotional response, or is Maecenas attempting to put a gloss on crocodile tears, given that Caesar has previously exhibited no sentimental attachment to Antony? Octavius then embarks on a wonderful speech, lamenting,

> That thou my brother, my competitor,
> In top of all design; my mate in empire,
> Friend and companion in the front of war,
> The arm of mine own body, and the heart
> Where mine his thoughts did kindle; – that our stars,
> Unreconcilable, should divide
> Our equalness to this.
>
> (V.i.42–8)

Yet, as soon as a messenger appears, Octavius stops in mid-stream to deal with urgent business which includes the capture of Cleopatra. Only then does Octavius take everyone off to his tent to inspect the correspondence. From a few lines in Plutarch Shakespeare has taken some key points of substance, transforming the straightforward narrative into an ambiguous scene – one that at the very least provokes in the audience a questioning of Octavius' sincerity and an awareness of the nature of political window-dressing.

One of the ironies that Shakespeare takes up from Plutarch is Antony's advice to trust only Proculeius. He is, however, absolutely loyal to Caesar and is the very man who creeps into the monument to take Cleopatra by surprise, and then lies to her about Caesar's intention. Thus, even with his dying words, Antony miscalculates.

Caesar gave Cleopatra a free hand in the burial of Antony, 'who did sumptously and royally burie him with her owne handes, whom Caesar suffred to take as much as she would to bestow upon his funeralls'.[59] But he was desperately anxious to prevent her committing suicide, an anxiety accentuated by her condition:

> Now was she altogether overcome with sorow and passion of minde, for she had knocked her brest so pitiefully, that she had martired it, and in divers places had raised ulsers and inflamacions, so that she fell

into a fever withal: whereof she was very glad, hoping thereby to have good colour to absteine from meate, and that so she might have dyed easely without any trouble.[60]

Caesar's chief weapon was Cleopatra's children. He threatened to put them 'to shameful death' should she allow herself to die. This threat was effective in promoting her recovery, but even when Octavius arrived to talk to her she was a pitiful sight:

Cleopatra being layed upon a litle low bed in poore estate, when she sawe Caesar come in to her chamber, she sodainly rose up, naked in her smocke, and fell downe at his feete marvelously disfigured: both for that she had plucked her heare from her head, as also for that she had martired all her face with her nailes, and besides, her voyce was small and trembling, her eyes sonke into her heade with continuall blubbering: and moreover, they might see the most parte of her stomake torne in sunder. To be short, her bodie was not much better then her minde: yet her good grace and comelynes, and the force of her beawtie was not altogether defaced.[61]

(This portrayal was interestingly incorporated by Helen Mirren in the Stratford production of 1982/3.)

Plutarch then recounts a key incident which Shakespeare uses – having omitted all references to Cleopatra's disfigurement, etc. – and which has caused considerable dispute among critics:

But not withstanding this ougly and pitiefull state of hers, yet she showed her selfe within, by her outward lookes and countenance. When Caesar had made her lye downe againe and sate by her beddes side: Cleopatra began to cleere and excuse her selfe for that she had done, laying all to the feare she had of Antonius. Caesar, in contrarie maner, reproved her in every poynt. Then she sodainly altered her speache, and prayed him to pardon her, as though she were affrayed to dye, and desirous to live. At length, she gave him a breefe and memoriall of all the readie money and treasure she had. But by chaunce there stoode Seleucus by, one of her Treasorers, who to seeme a good servant, came straight to Caesar to disprove Cleopatra, that she had not set in al, but kept many things back of purpose. Cleopatra was in such a rage with him, that she flew upon him, and tooke him by the heare of the head, and boxed him wellfavoredly. Caesar fell a laughing, and parted the fray. Alas, said she, O Caesar: is not this a great shame and reproche, that thou having vouchesaved to take the peines to come unto me, and hast done me this honor, poore wretche, and caitife creature, brought into this pitiefull and miserable estate: and that mine owne servaunts should come now to accuse me, though it may be I have reserved some juells and trifles meete for women, but not for me (poore soule) to set out my selfe withall, but meaning to geve some pretie presents and gifts unto Octavia and Livia, that they making meanes and intercession for me to thee, thou mightest yet extend thy favor and mercie upon me? Caesar was glad to heare her say so, perswading him selfe thereby that she had yet a desire to save her life. So he made her answer, that he did not only geve her that to dispose of at her pleasure, which she had kept backe, but further promised to use her more honorably and bountifully then she would thinke for: and so he tooke his leave of her, supposing he had deceived her, but in deede he was deceived him selfe.[62]

The point at issue is whether, in the play, Shakespeare intends the incident as an example of Cleopatra being caught out while trying to conceal half her wealth (and thereby at that stage intending to live) or whether it is a ploy designed to deceive Octavius about her true intention (to commit suicide). What the last line of the quotation makes clear is that Plutarch's narrative supports the second interpretation. This in itself does not, however, resolve the matter, as it has already been seen that Shakespeare frequently reinterprets an incident recounted by Plutarch.

Immediately after this event Plutarch recounts the arrival of Dolabella, who tells Cleopatra the truth about Octavius' intentions. In response to this information Cleopatra (who has only three days before her forced departure) promptly takes action to arrange her suicide. First, she visits Antony's tomb and gives vent to a long complaint, which includes two significant fears:

Whilest we lived together, nothing could sever our companies: but now at our death, I feare me they will make us chaunge our contries. For as thou being a Romane, hast bene buried in Ægypt: even so wretched creature I, an Ægyptian, shall be buried in Italie . . . For though my griefes and miseries be infinite, yet none hath grieved me more, nor that I could lesse beare withall: then this small time, which I have bene driven to live alone without thee.[63]

Having bathed and eaten she prepares for death. Before dispatching a plea to Caesar to be buried alongside Antony she receives a visit from 'contriemen' bearing a basket of figs. The only hint for Shakespeare's comic character is to be found in the lines,

The souldiers that warded at the gates, asked him straight what he had in his basket. He opened the basket, and tooke out the leaves that covered the figges, and shewed them that they were figges he brought. They all of them marvelled to see so goodly figges. The contrieman laughed to heare them, and bad them take some if they would. They believed he told them truely, and so bad him carie them in.[64]

The description of Caesar hastening to the monument, and the scene which confronted him, is followed closely by Shakespeare:

> Her death was very sodaine. For those whom Caesar sent unto her ran thither in all hast possible, and found the souldiers standing at the gate, mistrusting nothing, nor understanding of her death. But when they had opened the dores, they founde Cleopatra starke dead, layed upon a bed of gold, attired and araied in her royall robes, and one of her two women, which was called Iras, dead at her feete: and her other woman called Charmion halfe dead, and trembling, trimming the Diademe which Cleopatra ware upon her head. One of the souldiers seeing her, angrily sayd unto her: Is that well done Charmion? Verie well sayd she againe, and meete for a Princes discended from the race of so many noble kings. She sayd no more, but fell downe dead hard by the bed. Some report that this Aspicke was brought unto her in the basket with figs, and that she had commaunded them to hide it under the figge leaves.[65]

Plutarch then reports that Caesar acted magnanimously in response to her courage:

> Now Caesar, though he was marvelous sorie for the death of Cleopatra, yet he wondred at her noble minde and corage, and therefore commaunded she should be nobly buried, and layed by Antonius: and willed also that her two women shoulde have honorable buriall.[66]

Shakespeare, however, is more penetrating: he conveys a sense of Caesar's frustration at being thwarted, but also reveals an awareness of Octavius' professionalism – his ability to make the best of a situation, appearing generous once he has been outmanoeuvred. His less than generous nature was revealed by his order to murder Caesarion, Cleopatra's son by Julius Caesar, and the wholesale destruction of Antony's statues. He desisted from dealing out the same treatment to the statues of Cleopatra in response to a payment of 1,000 talents by her friend Archibus. Antony's eldest son, Antyllus, was murdered by soldiers (though whether this was on the instructions of Octavius is not clear). The rest of Antony's offspring (he had seven children by three wives) were all brought up by Octavia, including a daughter named Cleopatra. They married well and gained positions of influence. One of Antony's daughters married a man by the name of Domitius Enobarbus – perhaps giving Shakespeare the name for his largely invented character who is always referred to by Plutarch as Domitius.

In her discussion of the play, *The Common Liar: An Essay on 'Antony and Cleopatra'*, Janet Adelman highlights its tendency to 'frame' characters and incidents and to provide multiple perspectives.[67] Shakespeare is not attempting to present a tragedy along the lines of *Hamlet*, *Othello*,

King Lear or *Macbeth*, where the landscape of the mind dominates the social universe inhabited by the central characters. In *Antony and Cleopatra* the social universe is vivid and palpable. Frequently Antony and Cleopatra appear in close-up, but any attempt to keep the lovers at the dramatic centre of the action results in a distortion of the play. The potency of the political and historical forces which animate the action enhance the play's richness and variety, but reduce Antony and Cleopatra. Octavius Caesar is the embodiment of these political and historical forces. He obliges us to see life from the standpoint of politics and history. The contrasts are not simply between the private and the public worlds or between Rome and Egypt. Whereas Antony responds to events, Octavius Caesar shapes them. He assesses, calculates, manoeuvres and is future-orientated. It is significant that Shakespeare makes him colder and less attractive than the character who appears in Plutarch's account. The dramatist also omits what Plutarch perceived as one of Octavius' failings: his tendency to womanize. Shakespeare's Octavius is clearly disdainful of all women except his sister whom he genuinely loves. Octavia, who has been deprived of her warm attractive features by Shakespeare, is precisely the kind of woman for whom Octavius can feel real affection, but even she is expendable in the political game. For Octavius life *is* politics. There is no suggestion that he feels any qualms in using his sister to further his political ends. Antony, in contrast, agrees to marry Octavia even though there is no advantage of any kind to be gained from the alliance other than the achievement of immediate improvement in relations with Octavius. Ironically, Antony has no need for this reconciliation. It is Octavius who is pressed by Pompey and requires assistance. Antony is evidently reluctant to fight against Pompey, as he later makes clear:

> I did not think to draw my sword 'gainst Pompey,
> For he hath laid strange courtesies and great
> Of late upon me . . .
>
> (II.ii.154–6)

It is evident that Octavius Caesar has carefully prepared the ground for this meeting with Antony. He falsely accuses him of giving at least tacit approval to his brother's rebellion. Antony is outraged by this suggestion and Octavius is far too astute and in control of events not to be aware of the truth of the matter. (Menas, a neutral, clears Antony of complicity – II.i.41–2.) The fabrication is designed to put Antony on the defensive, and the move is followed by Octavius' complaint about Antony's discourteous treatment of his messenger. It is in this context that Agrippa 'spontaneously' puts forward the proposal of marriage. Given the tight control exercised by Octavius over his men it is impossible to believe that such a proposal would be made without prior consultation. Antony displays a degree of political naivety that is breathtaking. It requires neither the benefit of hindsight nor the peculiar advantage of the detached observer to be fully aware of this naivety. Soon after the agreement has been reached, Enobarbus predicts that 'the band that seems to tie their friendship together will be the very strangler of their amity', adding that Antony 'will to his Egyptian dish again: then shall the sighs of Octavia blow the fire up in Caesar' (II.vi.117–24).

Janet Adelman sees this as one of the puzzles of the play, where we are unable to be sure of Octavius' intentions. In order for that view to be tenable it is necessary to accept that Enobarbus is more prescient than Octavius. It is worth noting the cue that Octavius provides for Agrippa. He says of Antony,

> Yet, if I knew
> What hoop should hold us staunch from edge to edge
> O'the world, I would pursue it.
> (II.ii.114–16)

Agrippa in taking up the cue even adopts the same imagery (indeed, all the imagery relating to this marriage is in the form of binding or strangling):

> To hold you in perpetual amity,
> To make you brothers, and to knit your hearts
> With an unslipping knot, take Antony
> Octavia to his wife;
> (II.ii.125–8)

What Antony is being offered is guaranteed friendship. In future, Agrippa promises,

> truths would be tales,
> Where now half tales be truths . . .
> (II.ii.134–5)

A moment of reflection by Antony would alert him to the fact that Caesar has deliberately concocted accusations against him. Antony has already enquired of those who fought with Caesar and they willingly acknowledged that Antony's brother opposed both Octavius and Antony. Given this awareness of Octavius' deviousness it is a really naive individual who falls into the trap.

The framing of Antony and Cleopatra and the contrast between their values and those of the Roman world occur as early as the opening scene of the play. The soldier Philo is scathing in his assessment of the lovers. He makes a clear distinction between the Antony of the past and the Antony of the present:

> Nay, but this dotage of our general's
> O'erflows the measure: those his goodly eyes,

That o'er the files and musters of the war
Have glow'd like plated Mars, now bend, now turn
The office and devotion of their view
Upon a tawny front: his captain's heart,
Which in the scuffles of great fights hath burst
The buckles on his breast, reneges all temper,
And is become the bellows and the fan
To cool a gipsy's lust. Look, where they come:
Take but good note, and you shall see in him
The triple pillar of the world transform'd
Into a strumpet's fool: behold and see.

(I.i.1–13)

The brief dialogue that ensues between the lovers reveals Antony's absorption into a new social world:

CLEOPATRA If it be love indeed, tell me how much.
ANTONY There's beggary in the love that can be reckon'd.
CLEOPATRA I'll set a bourn how far to be belov'd.
ANTONY Then must thou needs find out new heaven, new earth.
ATTENDANT News, my good lord, from Rome.
ANTONY   Grates me, the sum.

(I.i.14–18)

Love is boundless and cannot be confined by Roman calculation; but the news from Rome must be abbreviated so that it does not interfere with pleasure. The Antony who will later complain that he is unable to maintain his 'visible shape' (IV.xiv.14) now commits what amounts to blasphemy when he cries, 'Let Rome in Tiber melt' (I.i.33). Here is a man not simply in love, but one who has turned his back on Roman values. Whereas Octavius is constantly associated with speed and uses time to achieve precisely defined objectives, Antony proclaims,

There's not a minute of our lives should stretch
Without some pleasure now. What sport to-night?
(I.i.46–7)

Meanwhile, the messenger Demetrius is left gasping in amazement: 'Is Caesar with Antonius priz'd so slight?' (I.i.56). In response to Philo's apology for Antony's behaviour, Demetrius, in a telling phrase, conveys the picture of an animated Rome in which politicians and people feed off rumour and report in making their assessment of Antony:

I am full sorry
That he approves the common liar, who
Thus speaks of him at Rome . . .
(I.i.59–61)

122

What this opening scene reveals, therefore, is the sharp contrast between world views. In Roman eyes Antony's behaviour is worse than mere foolery, it constitutes a violation of his responsibilities: he has no right to the luxury of a private world with Cleopatra; his life is wholly public and is evaluated from the standpoint of Rome. The vision of Rome conjured up by Demetrius' few lines is, of course, in striking contrast to the image of Egypt: attractively feminine, playful and indolent. The contrast is succinctly summed up by Cleopatra when she says of Antony:

> He was dispos'd to mirth; but on the sudden
> A Roman thought hath struck him.
>
> (I.ii.79–80)

Here is the division not only between two cultures but within Antony himself. As he is confronted with bad news from Rome and the triumphs of the Parthians, Antony adopts a Roman stance, first insisting on his stoicism, then chastising himself for slackness, and finally acknowledging the inconsistency between living like an Egyptian while attempting to control a third of the Roman Empire:

> These strong Egyptian fetters I must break,
> Or lose myself in dotage.
>
> (I.ii.113–14)

Antony assesses himself in the terms adopted by the Roman soldier in the opening lines of the play. The sense of being in thrall to Cleopatra is reiterated by Antony, but he is also aware of the contrast between the idleness that characterizes Egypt and the action that informs a Roman view of the world:

> I must from this enchanting queen break off,
> Ten thousand harms, more than the ills I know,
> My idleness doth hatch.
>
> (I.ii.125–7)

These lines convey an intense sense of Antony's feeling of being left behind by the course of events, of being marginalized and pushed to the very edge of the political stage. Here is an Antony at the crossroads, seeming to opt for the Roman way. The Roman perspective is reinforced when Antony gives his instructions to Enobarbus to prepare for a 'quick remove' (I.ii.194), and in his observation to Cleopatra,

> But that your royalty
> Holds idleness your subject, I should take you
> For idleness itself.
>
> (I.iii.91–3)

Ironically, it is at the very moment that he is leaving Egypt with a new sense of urgency that Shakespeare presents a scene in which Antony is seen through the eyes of Octavius. The speech says more about Octavius than it does about Antony, but it also powerfully evokes the contrast between Roman and Egyptian values:

> From Alexandria
> This is the news: he fishes, drinks, and wastes
> The lamps of night in revel; is not more manlike
> Than Cleopatra; nor the queen of Ptolemy
> More womanly than he: hardly gave audience, or
> Vouchsaf'd to think he had partners. You shall find there
> A man who is the abstract of all faults
> That all men follow.
>
> (I.iv.3–10)

Here is a wonderful sense of Octavius' contempt for Antony's pleasures. There is a clear feeling of the abstemious man's disdain of the voluptuary – and also the dismissal of a man who puts indulgence before business. Lepidus' gentle defence of Antony merely gives Octavius the opportunity to express his distaste for sex and his fastidious patrician contempt for associating with common men:

> You are too indulgent. Let's grant it is not
> Amiss to tumble on the bed of Ptolemy,
> To give a kingdom for a mirth, to sit
> And keep the turn of tippling with a slave,
> To reel the streets at noon, and stand the buffet
> With knaves that smell of sweat: say this becomes him, –
> As his composure must be rare indeed
> Whom these things cannot blemish, – yet must Antony
> No way excuse his foils, when we do bear
> So great weight in his lightness. If he fill'd
> His vacancy with his voluptuousness,
> Full surfeits, and the dryness of his bones
> Call on him for't. But to confound such time,
> That drums him from his sport, and speaks as loud
> As his own state, and ours, – 'tis to be chid:
> As we rate boys, who being mature in knowledge,
> Pawn their experience to their present pleasure,
> And so rebel to judgement.
>
> (I.iv.16–33)

Although Octavius gives vent to his personal attitudes towards the activities enjoyed by Antony, he maintains the discipline to encapsulate them within an accusation of dereliction of duty. Hence these speeches operate at three levels: Caesar's character is revealed as prim and puritanical; a sharp contrast is drawn between Roman and Egyptian values; a picture is presented of Egypt which reveals something of the essential texture of the society: indisciplined, indolent, pleasure-seeking and tactile, which though intended by Octavius to be seen in a bad light, acts as an attractive counterbalance to Octavius' implied picture of an ideal Rome.

At the end of Octavius' condemnation of Antony a messenger bursts in. Again, the urgency of his entry contrasts sharply with the indolence of Egypt:

> Thy biddings have been done, and every hour,
> Most noble Caesar, shalt thou have report
> How 'tis abroad.

> (I.iv.34–6)

The rest of his speech vividly imparts a sense of the political bustle of Rome as Pompey gains both public sympathy and the support of those whose political fortunes have not flourished under Octavius. Within the confines of a small speech by a messenger Shakespeare creates a feeling of the political situation with its mixture of opportunism, genuine conflict and the mystical value of a name like Pompey. Octavius' response is merely to pour scorn on the vacillating multitude. He does not for one second afford any credence to the opposition:

> I should have known no less;
> It hath been taught us from the primal state
> That he which is was wish'd, until he were;
> And the ebb'd man, ne'er lov'd till ne'er worth love,
> Comes dear'd, by being lack'd. This common body,
> Like to a vagabond flag upon the stream,
> Goes to, and back, lackeying the varying tide,
> To rot itself with motion.

> (I.iv.40–7)

As yet more news arrives of Pompey's growing strength, Octavius is pushed into a longing for the old Antony, the warrior who saved the day at Philippi. Significantly, though, Shakespeare does not have Octavius touch upon that crucial historical moment at all (he gives his character convenient amnesia on that issue, leaving Antony to raise the matter much later). Octavius' speech, which is very close to a passage in Plutarch describing Antony's capacity to endure despite his comfortable upbringing, focuses on the image of the *ideal Roman*. It is ironic that the Antony of the past is the man who is the embodiment of this ideal, when the Antony of the present has only moments before been described by Octavius as a voluptuary:

> Antony,
> Leave thy lascivious wassails. When thou once

Was beaten from Modena, where thou slew'st
Hirtius and Pansa, consuls, at thy heel
Did famine follow, whom thou fought'st against,
Though daintily brought up, with patience more
Than savages could suffer. Thou didst drink
The stale of horses, and the gilded puddle
Which beasts would cough at: thy palate then did deign
The roughest berry, on the rudest hedge;
Yea, like the stag, when snow the pasture sheets,
The barks of trees thou browsed. On the Alps
It is reported thou didst eat strange flesh,
Which some did die to look on: and all this –
It wounds thine honour that I speak it now –
Was borne so like a soldier, that thy cheek
So much as lank'd not.

(I.iv.55–71)

Characteristically, Octavius is able to turn Antony's former greatness against him. In praising Antony, he denounces him. Lepidus' response is ''Tis pity of him' (I.iv.71). This recollection has a powerful resonance, for those in the audience with some knowledge of the historical events would know that the incident in question occurred at a time when Antony and Octavius were fighting each other. Octavius was the victor on that occasion and Antony survived as a political force only through the support of Lepidus. Having both extolled and criticized Antony, Octavius allows himself no further reflections. He prepares for the conflict with words of self-criticism that are astonishing: 'Pompey/Thrives in our idleness' (I.iv.75–6). It is the only time that the word 'idleness' is used in association with Octavius. Before Lepidus takes his leave, however, he has to ask that Octavius keep him abreast of events. Both the tone of Lepidus' request and Octavius' cold response –

Doubt not, sir,
I know it for my bond.
(I.iv.83–4)

indicates a lack of trust and the dominance of Octavius. Here is a scene, then, which is crammed with political life and establishes Rome itself and Octavius as the political centre of gravity. The next scene reveals the flow of love letters between Antony and Cleopatra. In contrast to Octavius' calculated action the Queen of Egypt calls for mandragora and longs to sleep out the time that she is separated from Antony. Unlike Rome's public, political world, the sense of Egypt as the plaything of Cleopatra is suggested by her avowal that either Antony shall receive a letter every day 'Or I'll unpeople Egypt' (I.v.78).

The contrast between the texture of the two societies has been high-lighted recently by Alexander Leggatt in *Shakespeare's Political Drama*:

> This enjoyment of the thing itself is the key to the way in which Shakespeare dramatizes Egypt. The local colour his audience would have expected is all there: the wealth and feasting, for which Egypt was famous: the pyramids, the serpents, the insects; and above all the mysterious, fertile river, breeding monsters generated by the sun . . . In Egypt, as in Shallow's Gloucestershire, the routines of life go on: music, billiards, drinking, fishing, and making love. The Roman scenes are full of information and business, but in Egypt there is a more palpable texture, a stronger sense of felt life. The politicians talk of ruling the world, but a few place-names and a couple of disparaging references to the fickle people do not add up to a world that one can see, much less a world that sounds worth ruling. Rome itself, a palpable city in *Julius Caesar* and *Coriolanus*, complete with streets, shops, public places, houses, famous hills, and a great river, is here as neutral and unatmospheric as a committee room. Its entire political structure seems to consist of Caesar and his entourage. If we recall the formula *Senatus Populusque Romanus*, we notice that the people are a distant rumour and the Senate has vanished completely.[68]

Perceptive as this comment is, pointing up the contrast in the expressive quality of Egypt when set against Rome, there is a misrepresentation of the vision of the Roman world contained within the play. Rome is not as 'unatmospheric as a committee room' nor is it 'just empty scenery'. The reduction of Rome is a function of the political dominance of Octavius. The atrophy of Roman political life and the sapping of the vitality of the Roman ethos conveys a sense of hollowness at the heart of the society, but there is no diminution of the sense of a Roman world with its own physicality which is manifested on the stage through Roman uniforms, and is invoked through references to soldiers, battles, and the Roman crowds, so clearly visualized by Cleopatra in anticipation of the humiliation which awaits her in Rome (V.ii.207–20). Moreover, Octavius in his description of the old Antony as the epitome of Roman virtue invokes a sense of the Roman heritage which contrasts powerfully with the Egyptian world view. Leggatt, commenting on this crucial passage (I.iv.56–71), suggests that Octavius'

> admiration of Antony is genuine; but, where Cleopatra's dream-Antony overflows with power and generosity, Caesar's is grotesquely degraded. He pictures Antony in defeat, and his own imagination lingers over foul images, taking the speech in a direction very different from his overt intention.[69]

But the whole point of this speech is that Antony was the embodiment of

Roman fortitude. Octavius genuinely longs for the aid of such an Antony but does not feel threatened by this elevation of his antagonist because he has so manifestly relinquished those qualities in exchange for Egyptian values which Octavius disdains. The 'foul images' contained in the speech, far from degrading Antony, extol him. What Leggatt perceives as the intangibility of Rome, 'just empty scenery', is rather a reflection of the decline in Roman public life. Rome is neither shadowy, empty nor unatmospheric: it is very different from the Rome of *Julius Caesar* or *Coriolanus* because it is politically less alive. The political life of Rome – and Leggatt quite rightly emphasizes that 'The play's political scenes have a remarkable quality of sharp, close observation'[70] – is precisely encapsulated in the conference between Pompey and the triumvirate (II.vi). But that scene is carefully prepared for by an earlier scene which reveals the character of Pompey and delineates the contrast between the social worlds of Rome and Egypt.

The first view of Pompey suggests a man who is capable and confident, but his miscalculation is soon in evidence:

> I shall do well:
> The people love me, and the sea is mine;
> My powers are crescent, and my auguring hope
> Says it will come to the full. Mark Antony
> In Egypt sits at dinner, and will make
> No wars without doors. Caesar gets money where
> He loses hearts: Lepidus flatters both,
> Of both is flatter'd: but he neither loves,
> Nor either cares for him.
>
> (II.i.8–16)

For all his awareness of opposition to Caesar and the questionable strength of the political link between Lepidus and his associates, Pompey is taken completely by surprise. In refusing to believe that Antony has arrived in Rome, he provides one of the finest visions of Egypt in the play:

> all the charms of love,
> Salt Cleopatra, soften thy wan'd lip!
> Let witchcraft join with beauty, lust with both,
> Tie up the libertine in a field of feasts,
> Keep his brain fuming; Epicurean cooks
> Sharpen with cloyless sauce his appetite,
> That sleep and feeding may prorogue his honour,
> Even till a Lethe'd dulness . . .
>
> (II.i.20–7)

Here is the image of luxury, indulgence, excess and indolence. It is what Egypt means to the Romans. When he finally accepts that Antony's arrival in Rome is imminent, Pompey reveals that he is living in the past. He believes that Antony's soldiership 'Is twice the other twain' (II.i.35) – something Antony signally fails to demonstrate in the play. Moreover, he shows a Hotspur-like capacity for rationalization by suggesting that the arrival of Antony bears testimony to his strength.

When they meet, Pompey airs his personal grievances against Antony, who duly acknowledges his obligations. They interact as men in a scene dominated by the impersonal political control of Octavius. The latter immediately takes the initiative, demanding a reply to the triumvirate's proposal and warning him of the consequences of refusal. Pompey's response contains a number of elements: first, he makes a formal opening which emphasizes his power; second, he recounts history: the assassination of Caesar with an implied defence of Brutus and Cassius on the grounds that they sought to preserve democracy; thirdly, he portrays himself as merely taking up their cause, and also refers to his intention of avenging his father:

> To scourge the ingratitude that despiteful Rome
> Cast on my noble father.
>
> (II.vi.22–3)

What is significant about this speech is that Pompey feels driven to justify his action in broad political terms. The feeling Shakespeare conveys is one of political opportunism, but politicians can never openly confess to such motives (even to themselves?). Octavius' response is telling – 'Take your time' (II.vi.23) – as it implies an invitation to Pompey to elaborate motives to his heart's content so long as he eventually complies with the offer that has been made. In other words, his terse comment exposes Pompey's speech for what it is: political rhetoric. This pre-battle confrontation is characteristic of Shakespeare and this particular meeting is reminiscent of Worcester and Henry in *Henry IV Part I*, where the King similarly (though at greater length) devalues the Earl of Worcester's grievances.

Antony's assertion of the triumvirate's military superiority precipitates a personal response from Pompey. They interact as men, whereas the relationship between Octavius, Lepidus and Pompey is purely political. Indeed Lepidus interrupts the personal wrangle:

> Be pleas'd to tell us –
> For this is from the present – how you take
> The offers we have sent you.
>
> (II.vi.29–31)

Octavius, in supporting Lepidus, is even more brief: 'There's the point' (II.vi.31). These short stabbing comments are characteristic of Octavius in this scene. Once Pompey has agreed terms and suggests ratification Caesar replies: 'That's the next to do' (II.vi.59). He makes only one personal observation in the scene (though his political comments are brief he manifestly controls that arena), and that is both striking and surprising. He comments to Pompey:

> Since I saw you last,
> There is a change upon you.
>
> (II.vi.52–3)

What makes him say this? Is this one of Shakespeare's famous brush strokes where he is revealing the keen awareness of Octavius to changes in a man's physical appearance, with its potential for influencing his spirit or morale – which in turn has possible political consequences? As the tensions diminish and the atmosphere becomes more relaxed and personal, a natural rapport between Pompey and Enobarbus is apparent and contrasts with the absence of friendly interchange between Octavius and Enobarbus. But even as the political tension subsides, awareness of political consequences remains. Pompey's summary of the agreement conveys a feeling that the triumvirate has driven a very hard bargain (probably based on an awareness of their respective military strengths). But Menas' aside ('Thy father, Pompey, would ne'er have made this treaty' (II.vi.82–3)) suggests that it is so harsh from Pompey's standpoint as to be totally unacceptable. It is a delicate cue from Shakespeare to reinforce the feeling of Pompey's maladroitness. Menas openly expresses his annoyance with Pompey when he tells Enobarbus:

> For my part, I am sorry it has turned to a drinking.
> Pompey doth this day laugh away his fortune.
>
> (II.vi.102–3)

Enobarbus' reply underlines the critical nature of decision-making: 'If he do, sure he cannot weep't back again' (II.vi.104). If, however, Pompey is guilty of a major political blunder, the ensuing dialogue between Menas and Enobarbus implies a political miscalculation of even greater magnitude by Antony. When Menas receives the surprising news of Antony's marriage to Octavia his response suggests wistfulness and despondency: 'Then is Caesar and he for ever knit together' (II.vi.112). Enobarbus quickly concedes the political nature of the marriage but, adopting and inverting the image of binding, retorts: 'But you shall find the band that seems to tie their friendship together will be the very strangler of their amity' (II.vi.117–19). Thus the captains see much further than their generals. Lepidus has already been revealed as a political make-weight, and will be more brutally exposed in the next scene where, after his child-like questions about crocodiles, he is carried out totally drunk. Enobarbus gives a clear line to the future when he confidently predicts that Antony 'will to his Egyptian dish again', so 'that which is the strength of their amity shall prove the immediate author of their variance' (II.vi.123–7). Octavius escapes censure: significantly, his captains never engage in an assessment of his personal or political judgments; only the naive could believe that Agrippa's suggestion of the marriage alliance between Antony and Octavia is not pre-arranged. Octavius' captains are disciplined civil servants of a very different kind from Enobarbus and Menas (both of whom desert through disillusionment). As Leggatt puts it, 'There is no discernible affection between him and his associates, but they work together easily'.[71]

The scene on Pompey's barge provides a new angle of vision. Here the great men are seen at their ease. Sharp contrasts soon emerge. Part of the conversation between Antony and Octavius to which the audience is privy is remarkable:

ANTONY Thus do they, sir: they take the flow o'the Nile
    By certain scales i'the pyramid; they know,
    By the height, the lowness, or the mean, if dearth
    Or foison follow. The higher Nilus swells,
    The more it promises: as it ebbs, the seedsman
    Upon the slime and ooze scatters his grain,
    And shortly comes to harvest.
                     (II.vii.17–23)

This response reveals the nature of Octavius' interest in Egypt: how does the economy operate? In explaining the techniques of the Egyptians, Antony conveys a sense of a scientific approach to agriculture and creates a vision of natural fecundity which seems to remove back-breaking labour. The audience is simultaneously made aware of Roman curiosity, allied with a desire for knowledge, and the serious nature of Octavius' interests – even when he is at leisure. In sharp contrast, Lepidus' area of interest in the exotic is confined to crocodiles. While he descends into drunkenness the audience is given another opportunity of eavesdropping as Menas almost drags Pompey to one side to suggest murdering the triumvirate:

MENAS These three world-sharers, these competitors,
    Are in thy vessel. Let me cut the cable,
    And when we are put off, fall to their throats:
    All there is thine.
POMPEY   Ah, this thou shouldst have done,
    And not have spoke on't! In me 'tis villainy,
    In thee, 't had been good service. Thou must know,
    'Tis not my profit that does lead mine honour;
    Mine honour, it. Repent that e'er thy tongue
    Hath so betray'd thine act. Being done unknown,
    I should have found it afterwards well done,
    But must condemn it now. Desist, and drink.
                     (II.vii.69–79)

Pompey would gladly be the beneficiary of this treacherous act but is unwilling to sanction it. His reason is contained in the formula "Tis not my profit that does lead mine honour;/Mine honour, it' (II.vii.75–6). But this does not really express the truth. Pompey fears his reputation will be tarnished. Thus the restraint is not strictly moral, but social. Ironically, when the time is ripe he is outmanoeuvred by Octavius and is killed by Antony's officer, who acts without permission – just as Pompey says Menas should have acted. Lepidus, too, is swiftly despatched. News of their removal is given at the same time, thereby accentuating the feeling that Octavius is both subtle and ruthless. He disposes of his enemies while preserving his reputation.

The remainder of the scene aboard Pompey's barge deepens the sense of contrast between the leading political characters and also conveys a feeling of the difference between an Egyptian Bacchanal and a Roman one. Pompey, in attempting to enliven the proceedings, says, 'This is not yet an Alexandrian feast', to which Antony replies: 'It ripens towards it'. Caesar, however, feels that things have gone too far already. He only reluctantly agrees to join in the toast proposed to him, complaining, 'It's monstrous labour when I wash my brain/And it grow fouler'. Antony's plea to Caesar to join the spirit of things is expressed in a way which makes for perhaps the finest example of dramatic irony in the whole of Shakespeare: 'Be a child o'the time' (II.vii.94–8). Caesar is quintessentially the 'child o'the time'. The character for whom life is politics joins in the festivity as a matter of political necessity rather than for pleasure. When Octavius complains,

> But I had rather fast from all, four days,
> Than drink so much in one.
>
> (II.vii.100–1)

Antony's response is:

> Come, let's all take hands,
> Till that the conquering wine hath steep'd our sense
> In soft and delicate Lethe.
>
> (II.vii.104–6)

Two things are particularly striking: first, it is impossible to imagine Octavius making such a reference to the river of forgetfulness: here is a man for whom political life is all-embracing; whereas Antony loves the relaxation, fellowship and abandon associated with feasting, for Octavius it represents a distraction and an abuse of time. Second, it is hard to imagine Octavius joining in the dancing with anything other than distaste. Shakespeare has created a character who finds physical contact unpleasant; what is natural to Antony is repulsive to him; he feels alienated in this

situation. It is Caesar who brings proceedings to a premature close as
soon as the song and dance is over:

> What would you more? Pompey, good-night. Good brother,
> Let me request you off: our graver business
> Frowns at this levity. Gentle lords, let's part,
> You see we have burnt our cheeks. Strong Enobarb
> Is weaker than the wine, and mine own tongue
> Splits what it speaks: the wild disguise hath almost
> Antick'd us all. What needs more words? Good night.
> Good Antony, your hand.
>
> (II.vii.117–24)

Whereas Antony and Pompey are glad of an excuse for a party, Octavius
views it as a tradition requiring the giving and receiving of hospitality as
part of the confirmation of an agreement. His obligation fulfilled, he asks
simply and directly, 'What would you more?' (II.vii.117).

Significantly, attention is drawn to the contrast between a Roman and
an Egyptian bacchanal. The difference is not merely one of less abundance
and abandonment than the Egyptian counterpart; this Roman feast is
overwhelmingly masculine. No Egyptian banquet is presented on stage,
but the portrayal of Egypt is essentially feminine: none of the Egyptian
males possesses Roman masculinity: we have a soothsayer, a treasurer
and a eunuch. At least at the level of the subconscious there is an awareness that Egyptian feasts abound in women and that the texture of such
affairs is entirely different from that which takes place on Pompey's barge.

As the scene of confrontation with Pompey and the scene on his barge
both serve to highlight contrasts between Octavius and Antony and to
interrogate the process of political decision-making, so too do the council-
of-war scenes in Rome and Egypt throw these contrasts into sharp relief.
Octavius expresses to Agrippa and Maecenas his disgust at Antony's
behaviour:

> Contemning Rome he has done all this, and more
> In Alexandria: here's the manner of't:
> I'the market-place, on a tribunal silver'd,
> Cleopatra and himself in chairs of gold
> Were publicly enthron'd: at the feet sat
> Caesarion, whom they call my father's son,
> And all the unlawful issue that their lust
> Since then hath made between them. Unto her
> He gave the stablishment of Egypt, made her
> Of Lower Syria, Cyprus, Lydia,
> Absolute queen.
>
> (III.vi.1–11)

Although Octavius is glad of a pretext for denouncing Antony, his contempt for the actions, the splendour and the elevation of Cleopatra is clearly genuine. Here is an image which is anathema to the Romans:

MAECENAS   This in the public eye?
CAESAR I'the common show-place, where they exercise.
    His sons he there proclaim'd the kings of kings;
    Great Media, Parthia, and Armenia,
    He gave to Alexander; to Ptolemy he assign'd
    Syria, Cilicia, and Phoenicia: she
    In the habiliments of the goddess Isis
    That day appear'd, and oft before gave audience,
    As 'tis reported so.
MAECENAS   Let Rome be thus inform'd.
AGRIPPA Who, queasy with his insolence already,
    Will their good thoughts call from him.
                                    (III.vi.11–21)

Antony has alienated his remaining support in Rome and given Octavius the initiative. After Octavius has outlined Antony's complaints against him, Agrippa calls for action: 'Sir, this should be answer'd' (III.vi.30), only to be informed that the action has already been taken. Significantly, Octavius' account of recent events (including the removal of Lepidus) is at variance with that of Eros in the previous scene:

Caesar, having made use of him in the wars 'gainst Pompey, presently denied him rivality, would not let him partake in the glory of the action, and not resting here, accuses him of letters he had formerly wrote to Pompey; upon his own appeal, seizes him; so the poor third is up, till death enlarge his confine.

                                        (III.v.6–12)

Here, Shakespeare provides an ideal opportunity for the audience to observe the way in which politicians choose to present their actions and to make judgments about the probable course of events. Octavia arrives in the middle of this meeting to be informed by Octavius of Antony's flight to Egypt, using language that reveals his awareness of his adversary's every move:

                        I have eyes upon him,
And his affairs come to me on the wind.
                            (III.vi.62–3)

The political manipulator who is constantly ahead of his opponents hypocritically asserts that he has been tardy in responding to Antony's preparations out of tender respect for his sister's pleas:

> Welcome hither:
> Your letters did withhold our breaking forth
> Till we perceiv'd both how you were wrong led,
> And we in negligent danger. Cheer your heart . . .
>
> (III.vi.78–81)

The contrast between this scene and the parallel scene in Egypt could not be more stark. First, Enobarbus attempts to dissuade Cleopatra from active participation in the war:

> Your presence needs must puzzle Antony,
> Take from his heart, take from his brain, from's time,
> What should not then be spar'd. He is already
> Traduc'd for levity, and 'tis said in Rome
> That Photinus, an eunuch, and your maids
> Manage this war.
>
> (III.vii.10–15)

Then Antony expresses amazement at the speed of Octavius' advance:

> Is it not strange, Canidius,
> That from Tarentum, and Brundusium
> He could so quickly cut the Ionian sea,
> And take in Toryne? You have heard on't sweet?
>
> (III.vii.20–3)

Next, there is a dispute in which Enobarbus and Canidius vigorously proclaim the folly of fighting by sea, but Antony submits to Cleopatra's whim:

ANTONY   Canidius, we
   Will fight with him by sea.
CLEOPATRA   By sea, what else?
CANIDIUS Why will my lord do so?
ANTONY   For that he dares us to't.
ENOBARBUS So hath my lord dar'd him to single fight.
CANIDIUS Ay, and to wage this battle at Pharsalia,
   Where Caesar fought with Pompey. But these offers,
   Which serve not for his vantage, he shakes off,
   And so should you.
ENOBARBUS   Your ships are not well mann'd,
   Your mariners are muleters, reapers, people
   Ingross'd by swift impress. In Caesar's fleet
   Are those that often have 'gainst Pompey fought,
   Their ships are yare, yours heavy; no disgrace
   Shall fall you for refusing him at sea,
   Being prepar'd for land.

ANTONY   By sea, by sea.
ENOBARBUS Most worthy sir, you therein throw away
    The absolute soldiership you have by land,
    Distract your army, which doth most consist
    Of war-mark'd footmen, leave unexecuted
    Your own renowned knowledge, quite forgo
    The way which promises assurance, and
    Give up yourself merely to chance and hazard,
    From firm security.
ANTONY   I'll fight at sea.
                                        (III.vii.27–48)

The scene not only indicates Antony's folly and weakness, but also reveals the way in which Octavius has manoeuvred to ensure that the battle is fought where and how he pleases. Enobarbus' reference to 'chance and hazard' immediately triggers a recollection of Antony's admission that in all matters of chance Octavius wins even against the odds (II.iii.31–7). The entrance of the messenger announcing Octavius' arrival in Toryne and Antony's disbelieving response accentuates the sense of the disparity between his fumbling and Octavius' breathtaking speed. Finally, even a soldier approaches Antony and pleads that the battle be fought on land. At the end of this scene Antony's disastrous subservience to Cleopatra is aptly summarized by Canidius:

                so our leader's led,
    And we are women's men.
                                (III.vii.69–70)

The contrast is not simply between ruthless efficiency and mismanagement: it is also one of atmosphere. Even Octavius' right-hand man Agrippa can't keep up with him; in Antony's camp even a common soldier has a better grasp of the situation and takes the liberty of speaking out. The scene closes with Canidius again expressing amazement at Caesar's progress – 'This speed of Caesar's/Carries beyond belief' (III.vii.74–5) – a soldier's account of Octavius' cunning and secretive departure from Rome, and, in sharp contrast with the political exchanges, an image which conveys a sense of the historical significance of these movements and decisions:

    With news the time's in labour, and throws forth,
    Each minute, some.
                                (III.vii.80–1)

If the preparations for Actium reveal Octavius in a much more favourable light than Antony, the preliminaries to the final battle set the latter's warmth and generosity against the former's niggardliness. Octavius' rewards are meagre in spirit and substance:

> And feast the army; we have store to do't,
> And they have earn'd the waste. Poor Antony!
> (IV.i.15–16)

Antony instructs Cleopatra:

> Call forth my household servants, let's to-night
> Be bounteous at our meal.
> (IV.ii.9–10)

and employs a figure that epitomizes his delight in the physical proximity of his men before reducing them to tears:

> I wish I could be made so many men,
> And all of you clapp'd up together in
> An Antony; that I might do you service,
> So good as you have done.
> (IV.ii.16–19)

Later he gives vent to this emotion by proclaiming:

> Had our great palace the capacity
> To camp this host, we all would sup together,
> And drink carouses to the next day's fate.
> (IV.viii.32–4)

Octavius, anticipating the closing phase of the conflict – 'The time of universal peace is near' (IV.vi.5) – gives instructions to Agrippa,

> Plant those that have revolted in the vant,
> That Antony may seem to spend his fury
> Upon himself.
> (IV.vi.9–11)

Enobarbus recounts how Alexas deserted Antony to join Octavius and 'for this pains,/Caesar hath hang'd him' (IV.vi.15–16). As he concludes the account, he receives news that Antony has sent his treasure after him with 'His bounty overplus' (IV.vi.22). The 'mine of bounty' (IV.vi.32) rewards the deserter and apologizes to him; the great conqueror Octavius is devious and ruthless to the last. Antony, however, remains incompetent to the end. He cautions Cleopatra to trust only Proculeius (who remains firmly loyal to Octavius). He is not even capable of dispatching himself cleanly. Thus although the soldier and leader secures only one momentary flush of success in the entire play, his warmth of spirit is powerfully presented.

The closing phase of the play continues to develop issues of political calculation, and the process of creating history and myth, just as surely as it builds up the love affair from the image of Cleopatra as cold scraps –

I found you a morsel, cold upon
Dead Caesar's trencher: nay, you were a fragment
Of Gnaeus Pompey's,

(III.xiii.116–18)

to the vision of the god-like Antony and his magnetic queen:

Noblest of men, woo't die?
Hast thou no care of me, shall I abide
In this dull world, which in thy absence is
No better than a sty? O, see, my women:
The crown o'the earth doth melt. [Antony dies]
                    My lord?
O, wither'd is the garland of the war,
The soldier's pole is fall'n: young boys and girls
Are level now with men: the odds is gone,
And there is nothing left remarkable
Beneath the visiting moon.

(IV.xv.59–68)

As Antony asserts with his dying breath that he is 'a Roman, by a Roman/
Valiantly vanquish'd' (IV.xv.57–8) so Cleopatra insists that after Antony
has been buried she too will die 'after the high Roman fashion' (IV.xv.87).

The change of tone at the beginning of Act V is abrupt. As Cleopatra
anticipates her departure from the world, Octavius Caesar is busily arrang-
ing her capture. He is shocked to hear that Antony is dead, but it is his
sense of the historic moment and his role in history that shapes his feelings.
He is transformed from the busy civil servant to historian and icono-
grapher. Shakespeare's character perceives the events of the moment as
history:

The breaking of so great a thing should make
A greater crack. The round world
Should have shook lions into civil streets,
And citizens to their dens. The death of Antony
Is not a single doom, in the name lay
A moiety of the world.

(V.i.14–19)

This is not something as simple as insincerity: it is the dramatist's presentation of the character's awareness of the requirements of his role and his
position on the stage of history. Shakespeare not only makes the audience
aware that they are observing the re-creation of historical events, but
conveys a sense of the participants in the original events being aware of
their special location in the historical process and their sensitivity to the
needs of the moment. As Caesar sheds a few tears, Agrippa accounts for

them not in terms of compassion for Antony but as a recognition of his own mortality:

> When such a spacious mirror's set before him,
> He needs must see himself.
>
> (V.i.34–5)

Octavius, however, seizes the moment to deliver an encomium on Antony. It is formally generous but devoid of the spontaneous feeling that animated Antony's speech over the body of Brutus:

> O Antony,
> I have follow'd thee to this, but we do launch
> Diseases in our bodies. I must perforce
> Have shown to thee such a declining day,
> Or look on thine: we could not stall together,
> In the whole world. But yet let me lament
> With tears as sovereign as the blood of hearts,
> That thou my brother, my competitor,
> In top of all design; my mate in empire,
> Friend and companion in the front of war,
> The arm of mine own body, and the heart
> Where mine his thoughts did kindle; – that our stars,
> Unreconciliable, should divide
> Our equalness to this. Hear me, good friends . . .
>
> (V.i.35–48)

Just as he reaches the climax, Octavius, aware of the urgency in the messenger's face, breaks off to attend to the business in hand. This historic moment when time slows almost to a halt is passed, and Octavius is unwilling to risk further losses for the sake of completing his speech. His first task is to ensure the capture of Cleopatra:

> Lest, in her greatness, by some mortal stroke
> She do defeat us. For her life in Rome
> Would be eternal in our triumph . . .
>
> (V.i.64–6)

His instructions delivered on the matter, Octavius Caesar can then direct his attention to establishing the historical record:

> Go with me to my tent, where you shall see
> How hardly I was drawn into this war,
> How calm and gentle I proceeded still
> In all my writings. Go with me, and see
> What I can show in this.
>
> (V.i.73–7)

Whereas earlier in the play Shakespeare has juxtaposed Octavius' interpretation of events with the interpretations of others, here there is no alternative view. Octavius has won and Shakespeare shows this ever-precise character establishing the historical record – free from contrary views. Shakespeare, reading the historical writings of Plutarch, Hall and Holinshed, not to mention scores of quasi-historical sources such as the stories of the Trojan war, was acutely aware of the gaps and contradictions in the varying accounts. Octavius is about to present his associates with the best documentary evidence. The audience does not see it, but the selectivity of the file can hardly be in doubt. The key figures in the drama of history recognize themselves as such and attempt to shape the way history will judge them. Shakespeare, by generating doubts and uncertainties, obliges the audience to think imaginatively about these dramatized historical matters and, by implication, about all 'historical' presentations.

The probing of history does not, of course, end there. There is the question of the relationship between history and myth: real and imagined characters grow beyond the bounds of actuality, leaving future generations to make judgments while simultaneously being excited by myth. This process is seen in Cleopatra's revelation of Antony in her dialogue with Dolabella:

CLEOPATRA I dreamt there was an Emperor Antony.
    O such another sleep, that I might see
    But such another man!
DOLABELLA   If it might please ye, –
CLEOPATRA His face was as the heavens, and therein stuck
    A sun and moon, which kept their course, and lighted
    The little O, the earth.
DOLABELLA   Most sovereign creature, –
CLEOPATRA His legs bestrid the ocean, his rear'd arm
    Crested the world: his voice was propertied
    As all the tuned spheres, and that to friends:
    But when he meant to quail, and shake the orb,
    He was as rattling thunder. For his bounty,
    There was no winter in't: an autumn 'twas
    That grew the more by reaping: his delights
    Were dolphin-like, they show'd his back above
    The element they lived in: in his livery
    Walk'd crowns and crownets: realms and islands were
    As plates dropp'd from his pocket.
DOLABELLA   Cleopatra!
CLEOPATRA Think you there was, or might be such a man
    As this I dreamt of?
DOLABELLA   Gentle madam, no.

CLEOPATRA You lie up to the hearing of the gods.
　But if there be, or ever were one such,
　It's past the size of dreaming: nature wants stuff
　To vie strange forms with fancy, yet to imagine
　An Antony were nature's piece, 'gainst fancy,
　Condemning shadows quite.

(V.ii.76–100)

Here the audience is challenged to relate the Antony observed on the stage to Cleopatra's vision. Certainly the Antony of the play falls far short of Cleopatra's demi-god. But did the historical Antony possess qualities accessible only to Cleopatra, so that everyone else fails to be fully touched by that magic? Or is Cleopatra re-making her life and elevating the disastrous love affair to a plane which transcends the sordid judgments of the everyday world? These and other possible interpretations inevitably permeate the consciousness as the sublime music and images of Cleopatra's vision take hold of the imagination.

Even at this point, however, there is a sudden fall from the heights of imagination as Cleopatra inveigles the truth about her destiny from Dolabella, and is then confronted by Octavius himself – 'Sole sir o'the world' (V.ii.119) as she aptly calls him. The manoeuvring goes on. Cleopatra seeks to counter Octavius' false assurances by persuading him that she intends to live. Her device is to call her treasurer, Seleucus, to verify her inventory of treasure, and then have him reveal that half has been excluded from the list. This is sometimes cited as one of the incidents where it is impossible for the audience to know whether Seleucus is playing his part in a pre-arranged plot with Cleopatra or betraying her. Whereas in Plutarch he happens to be present, in the play he has to be sent for. Moreover, the historical Octavius desperately wanted both the treasure and Cleopatra; here he is dismissive of the treasure:

Caesar's no merchant, to make prize with you
Of things that merchants sold. Therefore be cheer'd,

(V.ii.182–3)

In addition, Cleopatra has already been informed by Dolabella of Caesar's plans. Her only hope is for an opportunity to commit suicide. All the evidence, therefore, points strongly towards an arrangement having been made between Cleopatra and Seleucus. Her horror at the thought of being put on display in Rome is clearly articulated to Iras.

CLEOPATRA　　　　　　　Now, Iras, what think'st thou?
　Thou, an Egyptian puppet shall be shown
　In Rome as well as I: mechanic slaves
　With greasy aprons, rules, and hammers shall
　Uplift us to the view. In their thick breaths,

> Rank of gross diet, shall we be enclouded,
> And forc'd to drink their vapour.
> IRAS   The gods forbid!
> CLEOPATRA   Nay, 'tis most certain, Iras: saucy lictors
> Will catch at us like strumpets, and scald rhymers
> Ballad us out o'tune. The quick comedians
> Extemporally will stage us, and present
> Our Alexandrian revels: Antony
> Shall be brought drunken forth, and I shall see
> Some squeaking Cleopatra boy my greatness
> I'the posture of a whore.
>
>   (V.ii.206–20)

One fascinating feature of this play is the way in which Rome is frequently visualized in Egypt (Antony, for instance, tells Eros how he will be 'windowed' in Rome while his master is humiliated in the street) invariably in a prosaic way: dusty streets and dirty citizens. It possesses none of the colour, luxury or magnificence of Egypt. Nevertheless, the Roman ethos of *gravitas* exerts a powerful hold over the imagination: so much so that Cleopatra in preparing for death – bidding farewell to both the manoeuvring and the pleasures of earthly existence – absorbs the central Roman value of constancy.

> My resolution's plac'd, and I have nothing
> Of woman in me: now from head to foot
> I am marble-constant: now the fleeting moon
> No planet is of mine.
>
>   (V.ii.237–40)

Octavius, having reflected on the Seleucus affair, becomes suspicious too late. His sense of history once more is much stronger than his grievance at being deceived, for he affords the lovers an appropriate funeral and monument. After giving instructions he concludes, 'And then to Rome' (V.ii.363), thus generating a feeling of movement and activity – of history moving on, leaving the lovers to the imagination. Time does not stop as it does in the four great tragedies: there is a powerful sense of tragedy but those four words – 'And then to Rome' – have an effect totally unlike anything at the end of *Hamlet*, *Othello*, *King Lear* or *Macbeth*. Part of our imaginative energies are absorbed by Octavius Caesar and the Roman world, forcing contemplation of Antony's and Cleopatra's actions in the unfolding historical process as well as seeing them as tragic figures who rise above historical judgments.

A good deal of attention has been devoted to the deaths of Antony and Cleopatra, especially our feelings towards these events. The view seems to be widespread that the deaths do not generate the same sense of pain or suffering that characterize other Shakespearian tragedies. Why is this? At least part of the answer for many commentators resides in what they perceive to be the elevation of the lovers and their love above the miserably prosaic – turning Caesar's triumph into a hollow victory – a world reduced and devoid of grandeur. When full allowance has been made for the magnificence of the poetry which undoubtedly elevates Antony and Cleopatra, there is a deficiency to be accounted for. The nature of this gap between the sublime and the experience which precedes the deaths of the lovers has been touched on by A.H. Mason, for example, who comments on Antony:

> We are *told* I don't know how many times that he was a supreme specimen of humanity, so lofty indeed that to indicate the scale it was necessary to suppose that his nature partook of the divine. The Antony who is presented dramatically never makes us believe in these reports . . . I cannot believe that Shakespeare tried very hard to make us feel, feel intimately, what he so often talks about. He has not made us know what it is for a man to be like Mars, nor has he brought us near knowing what it would be for a man to be like Bacchus. We do not get near enough to the root and springs of action that could make a life of lovemaking and drinking and general jollity seem the expression of a force of nature.[72]

In contrast, John Middleton Murry gives expression to a total acceptance of Cleopatra's vision of Antony:

> In those lines, simply and strangely, Antony is made incorporate with Nature, with the riches of harvest, and the golden splendour of a stubble-field; but no less than with this quiet opulence, incorporate also with the gleam and flash and strong impetuosity of the dolphin. And all this we feel to be true. This is Antony. It is as though his essence had been made plain, his secret revealed to Cleopatra in her vision. And this again is true to the deeps of human experience: we do know those we have loved better after their death than we knew them while they lived; and sometimes the deepening of knowledge is so profound that we could almost say that, in comparison with the knowledge we now possess, our former knowledge was ignorance. The difference between us and Shakespeare is that Shakespeare can express the kind of knowledge which remains unutterable and unuttered in the hearts of us ordinary folk.

And he completes this picture by discerning a transformation in Cleopatra and the attainment of a supreme love which transports the lovers and dwarfs the dungy earth:

> Now in very deed, Cleopatra loves Antony: now she discerns his royalty,

and loyalty surges up in her to meet it. Now we feel that her wrangling with Caesar and her Treasurer which follows is all external to her – as it were a part which she is still condemned to play 'in this vile world': a mere interruption, an alien interlude, while the travail of fusion between the order of imagination and love, and the order of existence and act, is being accomplished: till the flame of perfect purpose breaks forth:

> Now Charmian!
> Show me, my women, like a queen: go fetch
> My best attires: I am again for Cydnus,
> To meet Mark Antony.
>
> (V.ii.226–9)

No, not *again* for Cydnus: but now for the first time, indeed. For that old Cydnus, where the wonder pageant was, was but a symbol and prefiguration of this. That was an event in time; this is an event in eternity. And those royal robes were then only lovely garments of the body, now they are the integument of a soul. They must show her like a queen, now, because she *is* a queen, as she never was before.[73]

For very many critics there is, therefore, no sense of incongruity between the failures and indignities experienced by the lovers and their final elevation or triumph. They become themselves most truly in their final moments. This feeling produces a co-mingling of sadness at the death of two vibrant spirits and the splendour and magnificence which they embodied, and a joy at their spiritual attainment (which may be interpreted either in terms of Antony's vision of their wandering in the Elysian fields or in terms of their place in history). This view accounts for the contrast between the feeling generated by this play and the sense of pain and waste which is experienced at the end of *Hamlet*, *Othello*, *King Lear* and *Macbeth*. Nevertheless, it is incomplete in that many theatregoers as well as readers of the play perceive a sense of incongruity between the elevation of the lovers and their actions prior to the concluding phase of the play – and even within that phase – which incorporates the near absurd elements of Antony's botched suicide and his being hauled up to the monument. What seems present throughout the play, right to the end, is an intermingling of splendour and vitality with incompetence, folly and self-deception. Something which is as intensely realized as the magnificent vision of the Antony of Cleopatra's imagination is the visualization of the captive dragged through the streets of Rome and ridiculed by the actors.

If it is not possible to succumb to a wholehearted acceptance of Cleopatra's vision, it is not because of a failure by Shakespeare, but because the duality of vision is maintained to the end. What these characters do is to recognize their historical reality: the tawdry and ignoble is a perfectly acceptable aspect of living in a world where they manoeuvre for power (power not as an end but as a means to enable them to enjoy the variety and abundance that a third of the world can give them), but the baser elements have to be purged in forging a *historical* identity. When Antony's sword proves inadequate to 'earn our chronicle' (III.xiii.175) it has to be sought through the transforming power of the imagination. What the audience experiences is the creation of myth. The process of observation is not, however, wholly objective: the observers are seduced by the creators as the creators seduce themselves. The power of Shakespeare's poetry is such that it is possible to believe that Cleopatra is revealing an inner reality, the essence of the experience of the lovers. But the poetry is not intended to overwhelm entirely a sense of detachment which enables the auditor or reader to understand and objectify the process while simultaneously enjoying it. At a lower level this process is seen at work in Octavius' generous encomium on Antony and the choric approval of Agrippa and Maecenas. Octavius sees the present as history and makes the scene accordingly. His generosity does not, however, extend as far as accepting part of the responsibility for the conflict. On the contrary, he seeks to document his own innocence. Unlike the big four tragedies, this play does not end on a note which makes the surrounding historical events irrelevant. Antony and Cleopatra win their place in history and myth – their names reverberate with magnificence and splendour – but Octavius' words 'And then to Rome' (V.ii.363) possess a potency and significance which remain after the burial of Antony and Cleopatra: even while they occupy centre stage they are placed historically. Left behind as the current of political and historical events continue to flow, they are also left above history in a way that the recording of their failures cannot tarnish. Shakespeare enables us to understand the objective analysis of these historical characters and the events which they influenced, while simultaneously affording us the pleasure of partaking of the myth – something which is not simply unreality but which is an aspect of reality.

These contrasting perceptions are articulated in a variety of ways, but it is essential to comment on the way in which imagery is employed as a vitalizing means of expressing the fundamental dualities that characterize the play. The most persistent images relate to growth, food, binding, water and dissolution, and the planets. Antony's sword functions as symbol: he is stripped of it by Cleopatra when he is taken to bed drunk; he recognizes that Cleopatra has deprived him of his martial prowess by reference to his sword:

> O, thy vile lady!
> She has robb'd me of my sword.
> (IV.xiv.22–3)

and

My sword, made weak by my affection . . .
(III.xi.67)

His inability to use it is revealed by his botched suicide; and finally his sword is handed to Octavius Caesar by Decretas, thereby symbolizing the transfer of power of the last third of the world. Maurice Charney has linked this image to two other elements to suggest the way in which the interweaving of verbal and physical features combine to create a structure which has a powerful thematic significance:

> These movements in the fate of Antony grow out of the tragic conflict between the values of Egypt and Rome and may be illustrated in three image themes: sword and armor, vertical dimension, and dissolution. The sword and armor Antony wears are the visible signs of his soldiership and empire; but as the play progresses, the power of Antony's sword is undercut by his association with Cleopatra, and his unarming is a formal dumbshow for his renunciation of Rome. This pattern of Antony's tragedy is also reflected in images of lowness and height and in a very characteristic imagery of dissolution. Out of many possible themes, these three express the fate of Antony with most significance and originality.[74]

Charney also draws attention to the way in which the sword is transformed 'from a military to a procreative term'[75] when, for instance, Agrippa says of Cleopatra,

> She made great Caesar lay his sword to bed;
> He plough'd her, and she cropp'd.
(II.ii.228–9)

For the most part, however, Charney focuses on the visual imagery – which is evident in performance but much less so on the page.

Perhaps the most striking and intriguing aspect of the imagery of the play is the way in which each image is used both in a positive and a negative way. The abundant images of binding, for instance, illustrate the point well (my italics):

ANTONY These strong Egyptian *fetters* I must break.
(I.ii.113)

POMPEY   but how the fear of us
    May *cement* their divisions, and *bind up*
    The petty difference, we yet not know.
(II.i.47–9)

ANTONY And then when poisoned hours had *bound me up*
    From mine own knowledge . . .
(II.ii.90–1)

OCTAVIUS   Yet, if I knew

146

What *hoop* should *hold us staunch* from *edge to edge*
O'the world, I would pursue it.

$$(\text{II.ii.114–6})$$

AGRIPPA   and to *knit* your hearts
With an *unslipping knot* . . .

$$(\text{II.ii.126–7})$$

MENAS Then is Caesar and he for ever *knit* together . . .
ENOBARBUS But you shall find the *band* that seems to *tie* their friendship
together will be the very *strangler* of their amity.

$$(\text{II.vi.112–19})$$

OCTAVIUS Let not the piece of virtue which is set
Betwixt us, as the *cement* of our love
To keep it builded, be the ram to batter
The fortress of it . . .

$$(\text{III.ii.28–31})$$

CLEOPATRA With thy sharp teeth this *knot intrinsicate*
Of life at once *untie* . . .

$$(\text{V.ii.303–4})$$

OCTAVIUS   Most meet
That first we come to words, and therefore have we
Our written purposes before us sent,
Which if thou hast considered, let us know
If 'twill *tie up* thy discontented sword . . .

$$(\text{II.vi.2–6})$$

Likewise, food can be various and delectable, excessive, scraps or something fought over by voracious dogs:

CLEOPATRA   Now I *feed* myself
With most *delicious poison* . . .
                I was
A *morsel* for a monarch . . .

$$(\text{I.v.26–31})$$

POMPEY Tie up the libertine in a *field of feasts*,
Keep his brain fuming; *epicurean cooks*
Sharpen with *cloyless sauce* his *appetite*,
That sleep and *feeding* may prorogue his honour,
Even till a Lethe'd dulness . . .

$$(\text{II.i.23–7})$$

LEPIDUS   'Tis not a time
For private *stomaching* . . .

$$(\text{II.ii.8–9})$$

LEPIDUS Touch you the *sourest* points with *sweetest* terms.
(II.ii.24)

ENOBARBUS   Our courteous Antony . . .
    Being barber'd ten times o'er, goes to the *feast*;
    And for his *ordinary*, pays his heart,
    For what his *eyes eat* only.
(II.ii.222–6)

ENOBARBUS Age cannot wither her, nor custom *stale*
    Her infinite variety: other women *cloy*
    The *appetites* they *feed*, but she makes *hungry*,
    Where most she *satisfies*.
(II.ii.235–8)

ENOBARBUS He will to his Egyptian *dish* again.
(II.vi.123)

ENOBARBUS Then, world, thou hast a pair of *chaps*, no more,
    And throw between them all the *food* thou hast,
    They'll *grind* the one the other.
[chaps = jaws] (III.v.13–15)

ANTONY I found you as a *morsel*, cold upon
    Dead Caesar's *trencher*: nay, you were a *fragment*
    Of Gnaeus Pompey's . . .
(III.xiii.116–18)

ENOBARBUS A diminution in our captain's brain
    Restores his heart; when valour *preys* on reason,
    It *eats* the sword it fights with . . .
(III.xiii.198–200)

ANTONY   but please your thoughts
    In *feeding* them with those my former fortunes
    Wherein I liv'd: the greatest prince o'the world . . .
(IV.xv.52–4)

CLEOPATRA   in their thick breaths,
    Rank of *gross diet*, shall we be enclouded,
    And forc'd to *drink* their vapour.
(V.ii.210–12)

CLOWN You must not think I am so simple but I know the devil himself
    will not *eat* a woman: I know that a woman is a *dish* for the gods,
    if the devil *dress* her not.
(V.ii.271–4)

Water may have the delicacy of the 'morn-dew on the myrtle-leaf', it can

148

be as magnificent as the ocean which Antony and Cleopatra visualize as his natural element, or it can be as bitter and distasteful as the horses' urine which Antony drinks on his retreat over the Alps:

OCTAVIUS The *stale* of horses, and the gilded *puddle*.
(I.iv.62)

OCTAVIUS And the *ebb'd* man, ne'er lov'd till ne'er worth love,
Comes dear'd, by being lack'd. This common body,
Like to a vagabond flag upon the *stream*,
Goes to, and back, lackying the varying *tide*,
To rot itself with motion.
(I.iv.43–7)

ENOBARBUS . . . the *tears* live in an onion, that should *water* this sorrow.
(I.ii.167–8)

CLEOPATRA I'll set thee in a *shower* of gold, and *hail*
Rich pearls upon thee.
(II.v.45–6)

AMBASSADOR Such as I am, I come from Antony:
I was of late as petty to his ends,
As is the *morn-dew* on the myrtle-leaf
To his grand *sea*.
(III.xii.7–10)

ENOBARBUS   thou art so *leaky*
That we must leave thee to thy *sinking* for
Thy dearest quit thee.
(III.xiii.63–5)

ANTONY   I, that with my sword
Quarter'd the world, and o'er *green Neptune's back*
With ships made cities, condemn myself, to lack
The courage of a woman . . .
(IV.xiv.57–60)

CLEOPATRA   his delights
Were *dolphin-like*, they show'd his back above
The *element* they lived in . . .
(V.ii.88–90)

Water takes on a special form when it becomes part of the process of dissolution which Antony experiences as authority and vitality 'melt' from him. The general who can, in the opening scene, dismiss all that Rome symbolizes is later distressed to lose all sense of fixity and form until he dissolves.

149

ANTONY Let Rome in Tiber *melt*.
(I.i.33)

CLEOPATRA *Melt* Egypt into Nile!
(II.v.78)

ANTONY Authority *melts* from me . . .
(III.xiii.90)

CLEOPATRA *Dissolve* my life . . .
By the *discandying* of this pelleted storm.
(III.xiii.162–5)

ENOBARBUS The *poisonous damp* of night *disponge* upon me . . .
(IV.ix.13)

ANTONY   The hearts
That spaniel'd me at heels, to whom I gave
Their wishes, do *discandy*, *melt* their sweets
On blossoming Caesar: and this pine is bark'd,
That overtopp'd them all.
(IV.xii.20–4)

ANTONY Sometime we see a *cloud* that's dragonish,
A *vapour* sometime, like a bear, or lion . . .
That which is now a horse, even with a thought
The *rack dislimns*, and makes it *indistinct*
As water is in water . . .
                          here I am Antony,
Yet *cannot hold this visible shape*, my knave.
(IV.xiv.2–14)

CLEOPATRA The crown o'the earth doth *melt*.
(IV.xv.63)

CHARMIAN *Dissolve*, *thick cloud*, and *rain*, that I may say,
The gods themselves do *weep*!
(V.ii.298–9)

'Disponge' and 'discandy' appear to be Shakespeare's coinages, so that the dramatist 'seems to be creating his own vocabulary to establish the feeling of disintegration in the Roman world'.[76] If anything, the sense of dissolution is even stronger than this, becoming cosmic in significance, and is associated with the planetary imagery. The image of Antony undergoes a metamorphosis, from dissolution to elevation.

ANTONY When my good *stars*, that were my former guides,
Have empty left their *orbs*, and shot their fires

Into the abysm of hell.
>(III.xiii.145–7)

ANTONY   Alack, our terrene *moon*
Is now *eclips'd*, and it portends alone
The fall of Antony!
>(III.xiii.153–5)

SECOND GUARD   The *star* is fall'n.
>(IV.xiv.106)

OCTAVIUS   that our *stars*,
Unreconciliable, should divide
Our equalness to this.
>(V.i.46–8)

CLEOPATRA His face was as the *heavens*, and therein stuck
A *sun* and *moon*, which kept their course, and lighted
The little O, the *earth* . . .
His legs bestrid the ocean, his rear'd arm
Crested the *world*: his voice was propertied
As all the tuned *spheres*, and that to friends:
But when he meant to quail and shake the *orb*,
He was as rattling thunder.
>(V.ii.79–86)

CLEOPATRA I am marble-constant: now the fleeting *moon*
No *planet* is of mine.
>(V.ii.239–40)

CHARMIAN   O *eastern star*!
>(V.ii.307)

The growth imagery proceeds from a sense of the relationship between inadequate husbandry and its consequences, through the perception of fecundity and over-ripeness, to a retrospective vision of Antony as a tree that towered over his rivals:

ANTONY   O then we bring forth *weeds*,
When our quick minds lie still, and our ills told us
Is as our *earing* [ploughing].
>(I.ii.106–8)

AGRIPPA She made great Caesar lay his sword to bed;
He *plough'd* her, and she *cropp'd*.
>(II.ii.227–8)

CLEOPATRA Ram thou thy *fruitful* tidings in mine ears,
That long time have been *barren*.
>(II.v.24–5)

FIRST SERVANT   Some o'their *plants* are *ill-rooted* already,
   the least wind i'the world will blow them down.

                                        (II.vii.1–3)

ANTONY   tell him he wears the *rose*
   Of youth upon him . . .

                    (III.xiii.20–1)

CLEOPATRA What, no more ceremony? See, my women,
   Against the *blown rose* may they stop their nose,
   That kneel'd unto the *buds*.

                              (III.xiii.38–40)

ANTONY You were *half blasted* ere I knew you . . .
                    (III.xiii.105)

OCTAVIUS *Plant* those that have revolted in the vant . . .
                              (IV.vi.9)

CLEOPATRA   For his bounty,
   There was no *winter* in't: an *autumn* 'twas
   That *grew* the more by *reaping*.

                         (V.ii.86–8)

CLEOPATRA   a grief that smites
   My very heart at *root*.

                    (V.ii.104–5)

ANTONY   if I lose mine honour,
   I lose myself: better I were not yours
   Than yours so *branchless*.

                         (III.iv.22–4)

ANTONY   melt their sweets
   On *blossoming* Caesar: and this *pine* is *bark'd*
   That *overtopp'd* them all.

                         (IV.xii.22–4)

Significantly, the endlessly bountiful Antony belongs to Cleopatra's vision:
whereas the earthly Antony brought forth weeds through his inaction, the
Antony of memory and myth, the recreated Antony, is free of such petty
blemishes.

Set against the images of Antony's munificence is the sense of Octavius
as master of the world. The character encouraged by Antony to 'Be a
child o'the time' (II.vii.98) is precisely that. He both understands and
controls the world. Cleopatra's delicate irony cannot diminish the substance of her description of Caesar as 'Sole sir o'the world' (V.ii.119). As
Thidias asserts, Octavius really is 'The universal landlord' (III.xiii.72).

Consideration of the imagery of this play, therefore, should not stop at contrasting the Roman and Egyptian world or the Egyptianization of Antony with its consequences for his political failure and his attainment of greatness in death, but calls for a wider awareness. The 'blossoming' Caesar has his triumph too; bonds can stifle as well as strengthen; the sense of fate or destiny as exemplified by the Soothsayer and the various auguries, Antony's unlucky stars or the desertion of his god, Hercules, have to be set against decisions and deeds that precipitate disaster. There are significant juxtapositions in the imagery which sets Roman austerity against Egyptian indulgence, or political calculation against sensuality and generosity; but there is also a juxtaposition between the prosaic or earth-bound and the imaginative or cosmic. The imagery delineates and illuminates contrasts in values between the worlds of Rome and Egypt (see, for example, Susan Snyder's 'Patterns of motion in *Antony and Cleopatra*'[77]) but also projects a contrast within the theatre: there are those who willingly surrender to the cosmic and sublime and those who wish to contemplate the lower depths as well as the stars. *Antony and Cleopatra* disconcerts because it explores the guile and folly of reality along with the attainment of immortality and the *process* of the creation of myth. Life is politics, life is history and life is something else. The something else may be the joy of watching Cleopatra hop forty paces through the street, or attempting to imagine a more magnificent and permanent existence. Shakespeare, by continually changing the focus, affords a sense of all these realities and imaginings.

4

SOUNDS, WORDS, GESTURES AND DEEDS IN *CORIOLANUS*

> from face to foot
> He was a thing of blood, whose every motion
> Was tim'd with dying cries . . .
> > (II.ii.108–10)

> before him he
> Carries noise, and behind him he leaves tears:
> Death, that dark spirit, in's nervy arm doth lie,
> Which, being advanc'd, declines, and then men die.
> > (II.i.157–60)

> I have seen the dumb men throng to see him, and
> The blind to hear him speak . . .
> > the nobles bended
> As to Jove's statue, and the commons made
> A shower and thunder with their caps and shouts . . .
> > (II.i.260–5)

Plutarch begins his account of the life of Caius Martius Coriolanus by commenting on his noble origins and drawing attention to a salient fact: 'being left an orphan' he was brought up by his mother. The historian considers this to have been a great misfortune:

> For this Martius naturall wit and great harte dyd marvelously sturre up his corage, to doe and attempt noble actes. But on the other side for lacke of education, he was so chollericke and impacient, that he would yeld to no living creature: which made him churlishe, uncivill, and altogether unfit for any mans conversation. Yet men marveling much at his constancy, that he was never overcome with pleasure, nor money, and howe he would endure easely all manner of paynes and travailles: thereupon they well liked and commended his stowtnes and temperancie. But for all that, they could not be acquainted with him, as one cittizen useth to be with another in the cittie. His behaviour was so unpleasaunt to them, by reason of a certaine insolent and sterne manner he had, which bicause it was to lordly, was disliked.[1]

154

Unlike Shakespeare's character, this man lacks the ability to establish comfortable relationships with his peers: socially, he is something of a misfit. The rough side of Shakespeare's character emerges only in his relationship with the plebeians: his assertiveness does not arise from a sense of personal superiority but from his deeply ingrained belief in the superiority of his class. He has absorbed the patrician contempt for the plebeians without any accompanying guile or hypocrisy.

Although there is a wide divergence between Shakespeare and Plutarch in this crucial area, they both emphasize Coriolanus' martial qualities and the role of physical courage in the society. Shakespeare's Cominius says:

> It is held
> That valour is the chiefest virtue and
> Most dignifies the haver . . .
>   (II.ii.83–5)

Plutarch specifies the principle and the hero's dedication to physical prowess:

> Now in those dayes, valliantnes was honoured in Rome above all other vertues: which they called *virtus*, by the name of vertue selfe, as including in that generall name, all other speciall vertues besides. So that *virtus* in the Latin, was asmuche as valliantnes. But Martius being more inclined to the warres, then any other gentleman of his time: beganne from his Childehood to geve him self to handle weapons, and daylie dyd exercise him selfe therein. And outward he esteemed armour to no purpose, unles one were naturally armed within. Moreover he dyd so exercise his bodie to hardnes, and all kynde of activitie, that he was very swift in ronning, strong in wrestling, and mightie in griping, so that no man could ever cast him.[2]

In his very first battle, Plutarch records, Martius saved a fallen Roman soldier by standing astride him and killing his enemy. This action, undertaken before the eyes of the Roman Dictator, led to Martius being awarded the garland of oaken boughs. However, there is no mention of Martius striking the Tarquin on the knee as in Shakespeare. In recounting the subsequent battles in which Martius fought, and won honours on every occasion, Plutarch insists that Martius differed from all other soldiers in one crucial respect:

> the only thing that made him to love honour, was the joye he sawe his mother dyd take of him. For he thought nothing made him so happie and honorable, as that his mother might heare every bodie praise and commend him, that she might allwayes see him returne with a crowne upon his head, and that she might still embrace him with teares ronning downe her cheekes for joye.

155

This desire to please his mother was not confined to military exploits, but encompassed all aspects of his life:

> But Martius thinking all due to his mother, that had bene also due to his father if he had lived: dyd not only content him selfe to rejoyce and honour her, but at her desire tooke a wife also, by whom he had two children, and yet never left his mothers house.[3]

The two children are reduced to one by the dramatist, but the enormous influence of Martius' mother is powerfully felt in the play, and the view is ventilated that the courageous deeds are undertaken to please her rather than out of any desire to serve his country (I.i.37–8).

The first major social conflict recounted by Plutarch – something which is merely alluded to by Shakespeare – grew out of the severe oppression of the commonality by the rich, who exploited them by means of high interest rates backed up by harsh penalties. Before their successful battle against the Sabines, the Senate had promised the common soldiers protection from usury and more respectful treatment. Once victory was secured the Senate reneged on their promises thereby provoking open rebellion. This in turn led to fresh assaults on Rome and the emergence of a political crisis in which opinions were divided between adopting a conciliatory policy and using all the force available to beat the plebeians into submission. Coriolanus favoured the latter approach, believing that concessions led to disobedience and anarchy. The Senate failed to reach a decision after days of deliberation, so the plebeians responded not with violence but by means of an orderly withdrawal from the city. They encamped on a nearby hill. Their sense of grievance, and awareness of being an exploited class, is clearly articulated by Plutarch:

> they sayed, to dwell at Rome was nothing els but to be slaine, or hurte with continuall warres, and fighting for defence of the riche mens goodes.[4]

Here is a society in which class antagonism has reached the point where it threatens total breakdown. The Senators responded to the crisis by sending Menenius as emissary. He succeeded partly as a consequence of his persuasiveness, employing the fable of the belly, and partly because of the willingness of the Senate to make important constitutional concessions:

> These persuasions pacified the people, conditionally, that the Senate would graunte there should be yerely chosen five magistrates, which they now call *Tribuni Plebis*, whose office should be to defend the poore people from violence and oppression. So Junius Brutus, and Sicinius Vellutus, were the first Tribunes of the people that were chosen, who had only bene the causers and procurers of this sedition. Hereupon the cittie being growen againe to good quiet and unitie, the people immedi-

atly went to the warres, shewing that they had a good will to doe better then ever they dyd, and to be very willing to obey the magistrates in that they would commaund, concerning the warres.[5]

It is worth noting at this point that in Livy's account (translated by Philemon Holland in 1600 and believed to have been known by Shakespeare) Menenius owes his credit with the plebeians to being one of them by birth. He is described by Livy as 'a faire spoken and eloquent man, gratious withall and wellbeloved among the commons, for that he was from them descended'.[6] He later goes on to add that Menenius was

> a man all his life time before beloved indifferently of the Senatours and the Commons: but after the insurrection, much more deere unto the Commons than before. This truchman, this mediator for civile attonement, this Embassadour and messenger from the Senatours to the commons, this reconciler and reducer of the commons home againe into the cittie, had not at his death sufficient to defray the charges of his funerals: the commons therefore made a purse and a contribution of a Sextant by the poll, and were at the cost to interre and burie him worshipfully.[7]

Here, Shakespeare's 'shaping' of character and structure can be seen very clearly. His Menenius is certainly *not* a man of plebeian origins: he is valuable in oiling the political wheels, and possesses a diction and style which persuades the common people that he is sympathetic towards them, but he has no more genuine regard for them than Coriolanus. He is an authentic patrician who enjoys the good life:

> I am known to be a humorous patrician, and one that loves a cup of hot wine, with not a drop of allaying Tiber in't . . . one that converses more with the buttock of the night than with the forehead of the morning.
>
> (II.i.46–52)

It is hard to imagine this Menenius dying penniless.

Shakespeare, of course, transfers the fable of the belly and Menenius' key role to the political crisis which occurred three years after the retreat to the Sacred Mount. The Menenius of history was already dead by then. Here is an example of Shakespeare drawing on a character, detecting his vital role in society and creating for him a language and style which enable him to carry out this necessary function. Shakespeare's Menenius is essentially hypocritical – but his kind of hypocrisy is needed to prevent social tensions becoming explosive, something which Coriolanus never understands.

In his account of the constitutional change, Plutarch draws attention to the manipulative qualities of the tribunes Brutus and Sicinius (a feature developed by Shakespeare): they only had 'bene the causers and procurers of this sedition'.[8] Livy provides no hint that those chosen as tribunes played any such role. On the contrary, he suggests that Sicinius, rather than resorting to violence, formulated the policy of what would now be referred to as passive resistance. The immediate response of Martius was to stir the patricians into demonstrating their superiority over the plebeians in terms of fighting prowess. The necessity for this appeal suggests that for those at the top, wealth had become a greater indicator or guarantee of status than martial prowess.

There is also a significant discrepancy between Plutarch and Livy in describing the capture of Corioles by Martius. Shakespeare adheres closely to Plutarch's description of the initial retreat of the Romans and their subsequent assault on the city:

> he dyd encorage his fellowes with *wordes* and *dedes* [my emphases], crying out to them, that fortune had opened the gates of the cittie, more for the followers, then the flyers. But all this notwithstanding, fewe had the hartes to followe him. Howbeit Martius being in the throng emong the enemies, thrust him selfe into the gates of the cittie . . . But he looking about him, and seeing he was entred the cittie with very fewe men to helpe him, and perceyving he was environned by his enemies that gathered round about to set apon him: dyd things then as it is written, wonderfull and incredible, aswell for the force of his hande, as also for the agillitie of his bodie, and with a wonderfull corage and valliantnes, he made a lane through the middest of them, and overthrewe also those he layed at . . . By this meanes, Lartius that was gotten out, had some leysure to bring the Romaines with more safety into the cittie. The cittie being taken in this sorte, the most parte of the souldiers beganne incontinently to spoyle, to carie awaye, and to looke up the bootie they had wonne. But Martius was marvelous angry with them, and cried out on them, that it was no time now to looke after spoyle, and to ronne straggling here and there to enriche them selves, whilest the other Consul and their fellowe cittizens peradventure were fighting with their enemies . . . Wherefore taking those that willingly offered them selves to followe him, he went out of the cittie, and tooke his waye towards that parte, where he understoode the rest of the armie was . . .[9]

In Livy's account Martius makes use of brands of fire to set some buildings alight once he is inside the gates, but Shakespeare ignores this realistic detail and instead provides a scene in which Martius enters the city *alone*. Plutarch's magnificent warrior (who enters the city with a few men) becomes in the play superhuman – and isolated.

One aspect of the narrative account which becomes a vital element in the play is the focus on 'words and deeds'. Plutarch recounts how Martius, having taken Corioles, leads a force against the most fierce of the enemy bands (the Antiates). Once more he fights like a man possessed, refusing to retire even when fainting with exhaustion, until the military triumph is complete. Thus the dramatist differs from the historian only in one crucial respect: his Martius enters the city of Corioles alone. For the rest he does no more than dramatize Plutarch's narrative. Though Shakespeare invents the fight between Martius and Aufidius, Plutarch recounts how Cominius commended Martius 'beyond the moone' before offering him a tenth of all the spoils. The dramatist once more follows the historian closely in that Martius rejects the reward, accepting only 'a goodly horse with a capparison, and all furniture to him' and requesting the release of a former host:

and as for his other offer, which was rather a mercenary reward, then an honorable recompence, he would none of it, but was contented to have his equall parte with other souldiers. Only, this grace (sayed he) I crave, and beseeche you to graunt me. Among the Volsces there is an olde friende and hoste of mine, an honest wealthie man and now a prisoner, who living before in great wealth in his owne countrie, liveth now a poore prisoner in the handes of his enemies: and yet notwithstanding all this his miserie and misfortune, it would doe me great pleasure if I could save him from this one daunger: to keepe him from being solde as a slave. The souldiers hearing Martius wordes, made a marvelous great showte among them: and they were moe that wondred at his great contentation and abstinence, when they sawe so litle covetousnes in him, then they were that highely praised and extolled his valliantnes.[10]

Shakespeare picks up the word 'mercenary' from this account but makes one or two small but significant changes. The prisoner on whose behalf Martius appeals is a poor man in the play, and suffering from the exhaustion of battle Martius forgets his name. Cominius, recognizing that Martius is adamant in his refusal of special rewards, then announces that henceforth he shall be called Coriolanus.

It is at this point in Plutarch's narrative that the problem of the dearth of corn arises (as a consequence of the refusal of the plebeians to work the land the previous year). Shakespeare has made effective dramatic use of this material by placing it at the beginning of the play; the political crisis gathers greater immediacy and resonance by being about food and starving people rather than interest rates. Plutarch makes clear his antagonism towards the common people and applauds the Senators for their wisdom in dispatching one group to Velitres to repopulate a city recently ravaged by plague (selecting, incidentally, those considered most subversive or vociferous in pressing the claims of the plebeians) and sending another group to fight the Volsces 'hoping by means of forreine warre, to pacifie their sedition at home'.[11] Not surprisingly Sicinius and Brutus attack the policy of colonization on the grounds that many will be sent to their deaths. Despite the soundness of this protest Plutarch refers to them as 'two seditious Tribunes'.[12] At this point Martius intervenes:

> Martius then, who was now growen to great credit, and a stowte man besides, and of great reputation with the noblest men of Rome, rose up, and openly spake against these flattering Tribunes. And for the replenishing of the cittie of Velitres, he dyd compell those that were chosen, to goe thither, and to departe the cittie, apon great penalties to him that should disobey: but to the warres, the people by no meanes would be brought or constrained. So Martius taking his friendes and followers with him, and such as he could by fayer wordes intreate to goe with him, dyd ronne certen forreyes into the dominion of the Antiates, where he met with great plenty of corne, and had a marvelous great spoyle, aswell of cattell, as of men he had taken prisoners, whom he brought awaye with him, and reserved nothing for him selfe. Afterwardes having brought backe againe all his men that went out with him, safe and sounde to Rome, and every man riche and loden with spoyle: then the hometarriers and housedoves that kept Rome still, beganne to repent them that it was not their happe to goe with him, and so envied both them that had sped so well in this jorney, and also of malice to Martius, they spited to see his credit and estimation increase still more and more, bicause they accompted him to be a great hinderer of the people.[13]

This whole incident receives only brief and retrospective mention in the play. Into this 'space' Shakespeare inserts the marvellous scene of Martius' triumphant return to Rome, followed by his reluctant agreement, in response to his mother's pleading, to stand for Consul. Describing Martius' stand for office, Plutarch makes the telling point that 'the common people favored his sute, thinking it would be a shame to them to denie, and refuse, the chiefest noble man of bloude, and most worthie persone of Rome, and specially him that had done so great service and good to the common wealth'.[14] Shakespeare vivifies this point in a dialogue between two common men who realize that refusal would constitute ingratitude.

Then comes a major difference between the dramatist and the narrator. Plutarch explains,

> For the custome of Rome was at that time, that suche as dyd sue for any office, should for certen dayes before be in the market place, only with a poore gowne on their backes, and without any coate underneath, to praye the cittizens to remember them at the daye of election: which was thus devised, either to move the people the more, by requesting them in suche meane apparell, or els bicause they might shewe them their woundes they had gotten in the warres in the service of the

160

common wealth, as manifest markes and testimonie of their valliantnes.[15]

Shakespeare's character finds this unbearable. Unable to bring himself to show his wounds, he treats the plebeians with contempt. Plutarch's hero has no such qualms and initially gains popular support without difficulty – only to lose it just as quickly:

> Now Martius following this custome, shewed many woundes and cuttes apon his bodie, which he had receyved in seventeene yeres service at the warres, and in many sundrie battells, being ever the formest man that dyd set out feete to fight. So that there was not a man emong the people, but was ashamed of him selfe, to refuse so valliant a man: and one of them sayed to another, We must needes chuse him Consul, there is no remedie. But when the daye of election was come, and that Martius came to the market place with great pompe, accompanied with all the Senate, and the whole Nobilitie of the cittie about him, who sought to make him Consul, with the greatest instance and intreatie they could, or ever attempted for any man or matter: then the love and good will of the common people, turned straight to an hate and envie toward him, fearing to put this office of soveraine authoritie into his handes, being a man somewhat partiall toward the nobilitie, and of great credit and authoritie amongest the Patricians, and as one they might doubt would take away alltogether the libertie from the people. Whereupon for these considerations, they refused Martius in the ende, and made two others that were suters, Consuls.[16]

In the play it takes the wiles of the tribunes to persuade the plebeians to change their minds. Thus, Shakespeare's hero is more unyielding and his plebeians more generous than their counterparts in the narrative. Plutarch, although contemptuous of the tribunes, allocates them no role in stirring up antagonism against Martius at this point. Shakespeare makes them a crucial element. Although Martius is outraged by the behaviour of the plebeians in Plutarch, he is spurred on by the young noblemen who looked upon him as 'their captaine and leader to the warres, that taught them all marshall discipline, and stirred up in them a noble emulation of honour and valliantnes'.[17] Shakespeare, emphasizing his isolation throughout the play, gives him no entourage.

There is no immediate upheaval in Plutarch's account. Rather, another element enters the situation when a great abundance of corn is brought to Rome. The common people held that the corn, received as a gift by Rome, should be distributed freely, while the rest should be sold at a low price. The majority of the Senate also inclined towards this viewpoint until Martius made a powerful speech, opposing such lenity, which received a great deal of support, especially among the younger Senators. Plutarch recounts Martius' long vehement speech. One fascinating example of Shakespeare adopting and adapting a phrase from North occurs when Martius warned the nobility that 'they nourrished against them selves, the naughty seede and cockle, of insolencie and sedition'.[18] In the play, Martius talks of nourishing the

> cockle of rebellion, insolence, sedition,
> Which we ourselves have plough'd for, sow'd and scatter'd . . .
>
> (III.i.69–70)

This outburst constituted a two-fold attack on the plebeians, who were enraged when they received the reports of Martius' speech. The antagonism directed against the Senate was diverted towards Martius by the tribunes, who sent their officers to arrest him. The patricians physically protected Martius from arrest by driving back the tribunes and their officers, the aediles. However, when they found the city in uproar on the following morning the consuls sought to appease their anger with soothing words and the promise of cheap corn. The tempest abated, but the tribunes insisted that Martius stand trial. Plutarch enumerates the charges brought against him (that he sought to deprive the people of their political rights and effectively incited civil war), and the motive of his accusers, namely, to neutralize him, or better still to ensure that he would never gain popular support. At this point in the play Martius' mother and Menenius appeal to him to adopt a conciliatory tone. Martius realizes that he is unable to do so but promises his best endeavours. He only bursts forth into violent abuse after the tribunes have, with deft calculation, denounced him as a traitor. Such calculation is not required in Plutarch's account:

> So Martius came, and presented him selfe, to aunswer their accusations against him, and the people held their peace, and gave attentive eare, to heare what he would saye. But where they thought to have heard very humble and lowly wordes come from him, he beganne not only to use his wonted boldnes of speaking (which of it selfe was very rough and unpleasaunt, and dyd more aggravate his accusation, then purge his innocencie) but also gave him selfe in his wordes to thunder, and looke therewithall so grimly, as though he made no reckoning of the matter. This stirred coales emong the people, who were in wondefull furie at it, and their hate and malice grewe so toward him, that they could holde no lenger, beare, nor indure his bravery and careles boldnes. Whereupon Sicinius, the cruellest and stowtest of the Tribunes, after he had whispered a litle with his companions, dyd openly pronounce in the face of all the people, Martius as condemned by the Tribunes to dye. Then presently he commaunded the Aediles to apprehend him, and carie him straight to the rocke Tarpeian, and to cast him hedlong downe the same. When the Aediles came to laye handes upon

Martius to doe that they were commaunded, divers of the people them selves thought it to cruell, and violent a dede. The noble men also being muche troubled to see such force and rigour used, beganne to crie alowde, Helpe Martius . . . the tumulte and hurly burley was so great, untill suche time as the Tribunes owne friendes and kinsemen weying with them selves the impossiblenes to convey Martius to execution, without great slaughter and murder of the nobilitie: dyd persuade and advise not to proceede in so violent and extraordinary a sorte, as to put such a man to death, without lawfull processe in lawe, but that they should referre the sentence of his death, to the free voyce of the people.[19]

What is abundantly clear from this account is that politically Rome is on a knife-edge. In the new constitutional situation Martius is unable to get away with his customary abuse of the people. He is living in the past and the nobles have to choose between saving him and risking civil war. At this point even Martius is aware of the precariousness of the situation and of the fierce contention that it has provoked in the Senate. Consequently, to alleviate the political tensions he makes a conciliatory gesture:

Martius seeing the Senate in great doubt how to resolve, partely for the love and good will the nobilitie dyd beare him, and partely for the feare they stoode in of the people: asked alowde of the Tribunes, what matter they would burden him with? The Tribunes aunswered him, that they would shewe howe he dyd aspire to be King, and would prove that all his actions tended to usurpe tyrannicall power over Rome. Martius with that, rising up on his feete, sayed: that thereupon he dyd willingly offer him self to the people, to be tried apon that accusation. And that if it were proved by him, he had so muche as once thought of any suche matter, that he would then refuse no kinde of punishment they would offer him: conditionally (quoth he) that you charge me with nothing els besides, and that ye doe not also abuse the Senate. They promised they would not. Under these conditions the judgement was agreed upon, and the people assembled.[20]

Despite adopting a voting procedure which placed Martius at a distinct disadvantage, the tribunes failed to make their case. Shakespeare omits any reference to this political nicety but absorbs fully the deviousness which the tribunes evince at this point in the narrative:

And then when the Tribunes sawe they could not prove he went about to make him self King: they beganne to broache a freshe the former wordes that Martius had spoken in the Senate, in hindering the distri-bution of the corne at meane price unto the common people, and persuading also to take the office of Tribuneshippe from them. And for the third, they charged him a newe, that he had not made the common distribution of the spoyle he had gotten in the invading the territories of the Antiates: but had of his owne authoritie devided it among them, who were with him in that jorney. But this matter was most straunge of all to Martius, looking least to have bene burdened with that, as with any matter of offence. Whereupon being burdened on the sodaine, and having no ready excuse to make even at that instant: he beganne to fall a praising of the souldiers that had served with him in that journey. But those that were not with him, being the greater number, cried out so lowde, and made suche a noyse, that he could not be heard.[21]

Shakespeare's Martius whips the crowd into a fury by his denunciation of them (a response triggered by the tribunes' calculated accusation of 'traitor'); here, he is simply shouted down as he attempts to make his case. Plutarch then describes his reaction to the sentence of banishment:

he only of all other gentlemen that were angrie at his fortune, dyd outwardly shewe no manner of passion, nor care at all of him selfe. Not that he dyd paciently beare and temper his good happe, in respect of any reason he had, or by his quiet condition: but bicause he was so caried awaye with the vehemencie of anger, and desire of revenge, that he had no sence nor feeling of the hard state he was in . . .[22]

This description of Martius is much more akin to Shakespeare's portrayal of him when he becomes leader of the Volsces:

He is their god. He leads them like a thing
Made by some other deity than nature,
That shapes man better . . .
                    (IV.vi.91–3)

The desire for revenge is then white hot; he is implacable, seemingly inhuman. As Cominius says,

                    'Coriolanus'
He would not answer to; forbad all names:
He was a kind of nothing, titleless,
Till he had forg'd himself a name o'th'fire
Of burning Rome.
                    (V.i.11–15)

Shakespeare's clear sense of character and purpose is vividly apparent in the contrast between his treatment of Martius' departure from the city and Plutarch's. The latter provides the following description:

he went immediatly to the gate of the cittie, accompanied with a great number of Patricians that brought him thither, from whence he went on his waye with three or foure of his friendes only, taking nothing with him, nor requesting any thing of any man. So he remained a fewe dayes

164

in the countrie at his houses, turmoyled with sundry sortes and kynde of thoughtes, suche as the fyer of his choller dyd sturre up. In the ende, seeing he could resolve no waye, to take a profitable or honorable course, but only was pricked forward still to be revenged of the Romaines: he thought to raise up some great warres against them, by their neerest neighbours.[23]

Shakespeare's Martius is accompanied to the gates by his family and a few friends. Cominius makes a half-hearted offer to accompany him for a month but Martius declines and, in sharp contrast to Plutarch's character, goes *alone*. Shakespeare's Martius endures the baiting of the plebeians, being, as he later describes it, 'Whoop'd out of Rome' (IV.v.79). He has no 'great number of Patricians' with him: guilt or embarrassment keeps them away. Finally, Shakespeare's hero may be bitter, but he also possesses a misplaced confidence: 'I shall be lov'd when I am lack'd' (IV.i.15). He fails to understand that he is totally unnecessary in time of peace. Indeed, he does not even have a productive *political* role to play (far less an economic one). His total inability to comprehend the nature of social control, change and adjustment, the political dynamics of society, ensures that he is a liability. Coriolanus never reveals the slightest indication of knowing what an economy is. Interestingly, just before he makes his assertion that he will soon be missed, Volumnia utters a curse which reminds the audience of the existence of economic life:

Now the red pestilence strike all trades in Rome,
And occupations perish!

(IV.i.13–14)

As he departs, Martius gives his wife and mother an assurance which Shakespeare infuses with dramatic irony:

While I remain above the ground you shall
Hear from me still, and never of me aught
But what is like me formerly.

(IV.i.51–3)

What he says is the literal truth: he has only two aspects: a loved son, husband and friend; and a terrifyingly potent war machine to be feared. This richness, intensity and range of suggestion does not arise from the contrast between drama and narrative: it is the result of Shakespeare animating and vitalizing a fascinating narrative account with his insight and vision. A key psychological difference is that Plutarch's Martius determines immediately to effect revenge on Rome. Shakespeare's hero embarks on such a policy only when he feels utterly desolate – when he understands that a man cannot exist outside society.

Only at this point in the narrative does Plutarch first mention Aufidius, though the nature of this opening comment on the great warrior is such that it is little wonder that Shakespeare presents him very early in the play:

> Now in the cittie of Antium, there was one called Tullus Aufidius, who for his riches, as also for his nobilitie and valliantnes, was honoured emong the Volsces as a King. Martius knewe very well, that Tullus dyd more malice and envie him, then he dyd all the Romaines besides: Bicause that many times in battells where they met, they were ever at the encounter one against another, like lustie coragious youthes, striving in all emulation of honour, and had encountered many times together. In so muche, as besides the common quarrell betweene them, there was bred a marvelous private hate one against another.[24]

The historian provides a vivid account of the disguised Martius making his way to Aufidius' house, entering and taking a place at the 'chimney harthe', before making a simple but significant point:

> They of the house spying him, wondered what he should be, and yet they durst not byd him rise. For ill favoredly muffled and disguised as he was, yet there appeared a certaine majestie in his countenance, and in his silence . . .[25]

In contrast, Shakespeare creates a quasi-comic scene in which the servants are not impressed by the ragged, uninvited guest and even threaten him. It is only after his true identity has been revealed that they claim to have noticed something special about him. Shakespeare's device also creates the opportunity for revealing the inevitability of conflict between the two great warriors: servants make invidious comparisons which will be made later by the more formidable soldiers.

Among the complaints that Martius enumerates to Aufidius is that he has been stripped of everything but his name by the 'envie and crueltie of the people' whose malice has been allowed 'by the sufferance of the dastardly nobilitie and magistrates' who have 'forsaken' him.[26] Shakespeare uses the term 'dastard nobles' (IV.v.76) and gives a burning intensity to this sense of betrayal by Martius' own class – a feeling powerfully generated by North's 'forsaken'. Having accepted Martius' promise to fight 'with better good will for all you, then ever I dyd when I was against you' they feast together but do not until 'a fewe days after'[27] discuss the means of attacking Rome. And at this point Shakespeare makes a significant departure from Plutarch. The former presents a picture of peace and concord in Rome with even Menenius being defensive in his support of Martius – 'All's well, and might have been much better if/He could have temporiz'd' (IV.vi.16–17). Plutarch portrays an entirely different situation:

> the cittie of Rome was in marvelous uprore, and discord, the nobilitie

against the communaltie, and chiefly for Martius condemnation and banishment. Moreover the priestes, the Soothesayers, and private men also, came and declared to the Senate certaine sightes and wonders in the ayer, which they had seene.[28]

The point of contrast is startling and significant. Shakespeare presents a Rome which is better off without Martius – unless they find themselves in a war. He also changes the perception of the situation among the Volsces. In Plutarch they are reluctant to fight against Rome without good reason:

Now Tullus and Martius had secret conference with the greatest personages of the cittie of Antium, declaring unto them, that now they had good time offered them to make warre with the Romaines, while they were in dissention one with another. They aunswered them, they were ashamed to breake the league, considering that they were sworne to keepe peace for two yeres. Howbeit shortely after, the Romaines gave them great occasion to make warre with them. For on a holy daye common playes being kept in Rome, apon some suspition, or false reporte, they made proclamation by sound of trumpet, that all the Volsces should avoyde out of Rome before sunne set. Some thincke this was a crafte and deceipt of Martius, who sent one to Rome to the Consuls, to accuse the Volsces falsely, advertising them howe they had made a conspiracie to set apon them, whilest they were busie in seeing these games, and also to set their cittie a fyre. This open proclamation made all the Volsces more offended with the Romaines then ever they were before . . .[29]

Clearly, this presentation of Martius' guile runs totally counter to Shakespeare's character. Moreover, the dramatist secures far greater force and economy by eliminating the debates and goings on in Antium. Once Aufidius has embraced Coriolanus, the next time we encounter the hero he is in the field terrifying the Romans. There are other important changes made by Shakespeare at this point. First, the joint commanders go together to attack Roman territory, whereas in Plutarch, Aufidius remains at home to take charge of the defences. Second, Plutarch describes another wile of Martius that Shakespeare omits:

Howbeit the gayne of the spoyle and the hurte they dyd to the Romaines in this invasion, was the least parte of his intent. For his chiefest purpose was, to increase still the malice and dissention betweene the nobilitie, and the communaltie: and to drawe that on, he was very carefull to keepe the noble mens landes and goods safe from harme and burning, but spoyled all the whole countrie besides, and would suffer no man to take or hurte any thing of the noble mens. This made greater sturre and broyle betweene the nobilitie and people then was before.[30]

167

Meanwhile, the Volsces grew in confidence as Martius returned triumphant from his first assault on Roman territory – losing not one man in the fighting. In his second assault (the two invasions are conflated by Shakespeare to a single campaign) Martius, for the most part, exercises restraint and mercy, but also proves capable of great savagery. He is so successful that there is a scramble to join him:

> Afterwards, he tooke the cittie of Boles by assault . . . where he had a marvelous great spoyle, and put every man to the sword that was able to carie weapon. The other Volsces that were appointed to remaine in garrison for defence of their countrie, hearing this good newes would tary no lenger at home, but armed them selves, and ranne to Martius campe, saying they dyd acknowledge no other captaine but him.[31]

Here are the seeds of discord which Shakespeare introduces only when Martius is camped outside the gates of Rome. Shakespeare's Aufidius has been with Martius all along but is unofficially relegated to the position of second-in-command.

The picture inside the Rome of the play is one of dissension. The patricians denounce the plebeians while the latter attempt to encourage embassies and endeavour to deny any responsibility for the situation. This is very different from Plutarch's account of the contrasting attitudes of the two social groups when Coriolanus is besieging the sacred town of Lavinium:

> Then fell there out a marvelous sodain chaunge of minde amonge the people, and farre more straunge and contrarie in the nobilitie. For the people thought good to repeale the condemnation and exile of Martius. The Senate assembled upon it, would in no case yeld to that.[32]

Shakespeare omits this ironical situation of the plebeians pleading on behalf of Martius for amnesty while the Senators refuse! However, the situation changes when Martius, receiving news of the Senate's resolution, sets off in a rage to besiege Rome. When they see his camp five miles from Rome, 'they all agreed together to send ambassadours unto him, to let him understand howe his countrymen dyd call him home againe, and restored him to all his goodes, and besought him to deliver them from this warre'.[33]

The first embassy consisted of Martius' friends, who were soon shocked to encounter him seated in his 'chayer of state, with a marvelous and an unspeakable majestie'.[34] Although they responded immediately to the atmosphere and humbled themselves, Martius was unyielding:

> When they had done their message: for the injurie they had done him, he aunswered them very hottely, and in great choller. But as generall of the Volsces, he willed them to restore unto the Volsces, all their

landes and citties they had taken from them in former warres: and moreover, that they should geve them the like honour and freedome of Rome, as they had before geven to the Latines. For otherwise they had no other meane to ende this warre, if they dyd not graunte these honest and just conditions of peace. Thereupon he gave them thirtie dayes respit to make him aunswer. So the ambassadours returned straight to Rome, and Martius forthwith departed with his armie out of the territories of the Romaines. This was the first matter wherewith the Volsces (that most envied Martius glorie and authoritie) dyd charge Martius with. Among those, Tullus was chief: who though he had receyved no private injurie or displeasure of Martius, yet the common faulte and imperfection of mans nature wrought in him, and it grieved him to see his owne reputation bleamished, through Martius great fame and honour, and so him selfe to be lesse esteemed of the Volsces, then he was before.[35]

Evidently, although Martius' resolution was frightening to his former friends, it failed to satisfy the Volsces. There are a number of interesting points in this passage which must have fired Shakespeare's imagination. A small verbal point is the word 'injurie' in the first line of the quotation, which Shakespeare draws into his phrase 'his injury/The gaoler to his pity' (V.i.64–5). More important is the antagonism felt by Aufidius because he is being overshadowed. Plutarch is explicit in insisting that Aufidius 'receyved no private injurie or displeasure of Martius'. In Shakespeare he complains of having been treated as a subordinate. Does this reflect the truth, or is the dramatist giving an example of a rationalization by Aufidius designed to provide some justification (to his associates and himself) for his plans to revenge himself on Martius? The latter appears to be the more plausible explanation.

While Rome itself enjoyed a respite of thirty days Martius went on the rampage, capturing seven Roman cities. When the time expired the Romans sent a second embassy, claiming that they would be reasonable provided the Volsces withdrew. Martius' response was to reiterate his (very reasonable) conditions. He gave them a further three days for deliberation. Despite Martius' injunction to the contrary they sent a third embassy to him, consisting this time of praetors, augurers and soothsayers. They were unceremoniously bundled out of the camp.

The fourth embassy arose as a consequence of the divine inspiration of Valeria, 'Publicolaes owne sister',[36] a woman renowned for her modesty and virtue ('chaste as the icicle' (V.iii.65)). She appealed to Martius' wife and mother who immediately consented to join her and other ladies as ambassadors of Rome. (There is no equivalent in the narrative of the earlier scene in the play of the three women together (I.iii).) Plutarch provides a vivid picture of their entry to the Volsces camp and Martius' response:

> they went in troupe together unto the Volsces campe: whome when they sawe, they of them selves did both pitie and reverence her, and there was not a man amonge them that once durst say a worde unto her. Nowe was Martius set then in his chayer of state, with all the honours of a generall, and when he had spied the women comming a farre of, he marveled what the matter ment: but afterwardes knowing his wife which came formest, he determined at the first to persist in his obstinate and inflexible rancker. But overcomen in the ende with naturall affection, and being altogether altered to see them: his harte would not serve him to tarie their comming to his chayer, but comming downe in hast, he went to meete them, and first he kissed his mother, and imbraced her a pretie while, then his wife and litle children. And nature so wrought with him, that the teares fell from his eyes, and he coulde not keepe him selfe from making much of them, but yeelded to the affection of his bloode, as if he had bene violently caried with the furie of a most swift running streame. After he had thus lovingly received them, and perceiving that his mother Volumnia would beginne to speake to him, he called the chiefest of the counsell of the Volsces to heare what she would say.[37]

Here is a description of the emotional movement which Shakespeare captures and elaborates. As Volumnia develops her appeal she gives expression to the anguish of her situation:

> we can not (alas) together pray, both for victorie, for our countrie, and for safety of thy life also: but a worlde of grievous curses, yea more then any mortall enemie can heape uppon us, are forcibly wrapt up in our prayers. For the bitter soppe of most harde choyce is offered thy wife and children, to forgoe the one of the two: either to lose the persone of thy selfe, or the nurse of their native contrie.

Shakespeare incorporates that last phrase as he does the next resonant expression that is employed by Volumnia:

> thou shalt no soner marche forward to assault thy countrie, but thy foote shall treade upon thy *mothers wombe* [my italics], that brought thee first into this world.

Volumnia goes on to admit that her son seems to be caught between a choice of betraying the Volsces or destroying his 'naturall countrie', but insists that there is a middle way which offers mutual benefit of reconciliation. Having placed this 'opportunity' before him she then makes a threat which is followed closely in the play:

> But if it faile, and fall out contrarie: thy selfe alone deservedly shall

carie the shamefull reproche and burden of either partie. So, though the ende of warre be uncertaine, yet this notwithstanding is most certaine: that if it be thy chaunce to conquer, this benefit shalt thou reape of thy goodly conquest, to be chronicled the plague and destroyer of thy countrie. And if fortune also overthrowe thee, then the world will saye, that through desire to revenge thy private injuries, thou hast for ever undone thy good friendes, who dyd most lovingly and curteously receyve thee.

Martius is silent for so long that Volumnia once more appeals to his duty to honour his parent, employing a phrase that registered immediately with Shakespeare: 'No man living is more bounde to shewe him selfe thankfull in all partes and respects, then thy selfe'. She adds another phrase from which Shakespeare wrings a great deal of emotional pressure: 'besides, thou has not hitherto shewed thy poore mother any curtesie'. Shakespeare has 'Thou hast never in thy life/Show'd thy dear mother any courtesy' (V.iii.160–1). Finally she falls to her knees and gains an immediate response:

But since by reason I cannot persuade thee to it, to what purpose doe I deferre my last hope? And with these wordes, her selfe, his wife and children, fell downe upon their knees before him. Martius seeing that, could refraine no lenger, but went straight and lifte her up, crying out: Oh mother, what have you done to me? And holding her hard by the right hande, oh mother, sayed he, you have wonne a happy victorie for your countrie, but mortall and unhappy for your sonne: for I see my self vanquished by you alone.[38]

Here is a fascinating crux for Shakespeare, because at this point Livy records that the Volsces were so shocked by the unnatural sight of the mother kneeling to her son that they turned away. Shakespeare inverts the situation. Clearly remembering Livy's comment, he has Martius appeal to Aufidius with the remark,

> Now, good Aufidius,
> Were you in my stead, would you have heard
> A mother less? or granted less, Aufidius?
> (V.iii.191–3)

The reply which he receives is terse and ambiguous: 'I was mov'd withal' (V.iii.194). This provides a fine example of Shakespeare following his source material closely at one level of his mind while at another level a variety of emotional and dramatic possibilities are being evaluated. He is never so enthralled by the rich narrative in front of him that he ceases to be actively analytical in contemplating the options available.

The Volsces quite naturally have divided feelings about the decision.

However, 'no man contraried his departure, but all obeyed his commaundement, more for respect of his worthines and valiancie, then for feare of his authoritie'.[39] The Romans experience a celebratory release of tension and set up a temple to the women. It is clear from their sense of relief that the Romans expected to be overwhelmed by Martius. In the circumstances, the Volsces had every reason to feel betrayed, as the terms which Martius had previously offered the Romans were perfectly reasonable. Nevertheless, Martius was held in such favour among the Volsces that he could have ridden out the storm but for the malice of Aufidius. Plutarch provides a comprehensive but economical account of what happened from the moment of their return to Antium to the final defeat of the Volsces:

Now when Martius was returned againe into the cittie of Antium from his voyage, Tullus that hated and could no lenger abide him for the feare he had of his authoritie: sought divers meanes to make him out of the waye, thinking that if he let slippe that present time, he should never recover the like and fit occasion againe . . . The people hereupon called a common counsaill, in which assembly there were certen oratours appointed, that stirred up the common people against him: and when they had tolde their tales, Martius rose up to make them aunswer. Now, notwithstanding the mutinous people made a marvelous great noyse, yet when they sawe him, for the reverence they bare unto his valliantnes, they quieted them selves, and gave still audience to alledge with leysure what he could for his purgation. Moreover, the honestest men of the Antiates, and who most rejoyced in peace, shewed by their coun-tenaunce that they would heare him willingly, and judge also according to their conscience. Whereupon Tullus fearing that if he dyd let him speake, he would prove his innocencie to the people, bicause emongest other things he had an eloquent tongue, besides that the first good service he had done to the people of the Volsces, dyd winne him more favour, then these last accusations could purchase him displeasure. . . . For these causes Tullus thought he might no lenger delaye his pretence and enterprise, neither to tarie for the mutining and rising of the common people against him: wherefore, those that were of the conspira-cie, beganne to crie out that he was not to be heard, nor that they would not suffer a traytour to usurpe tyrannicall power over the tribe of the Volsces, who would not yeld up his estate and authoritie. And in saying these wordes, they all fell upon him, and killed him in the market place, none of the people once offering to rescue him. Howbeit it is a clere case, that this murder was not generally consented unto, of the most parte of the Volsces: for men came out of all partes to honour his bodie, and dyd honorably burie him, setting out his tombe with great store of armour and spoyles, as the tombe of a worthie persone and great captaine. The Romaines understanding of his death, shewed no other honour or malice, saving that they graunted the ladyes the request they made: that they might mourne tenne moneths for him . . . Now Martius being dead, the whole state of the Volsces hartely wished him alive againe. For first of all they fell out with the Aeques . . . After that, the Romaines overcame them in battell, in which Tullus was slaine in the field, and the flower of all their force was put to the sworde: so that they were compelled to accept most shamefull conditions of peace, in yelding them selves subject unto the conquerers, and promising to be obedient at their commandement.[40]

The most intriguing element in this description is Aufidius' manoeuvre to ensure that Martius does not have the opportunity to speak in his own defence 'bicause emongest other things he had an eloquent tongue'. Shakespeare's treatment is dramatically much more powerful and psychologically more telling. Aufidius, just like the tribunes in the earlier 'trial' scene, knows full well that the best way to defeat Martius is to have him condemn himself out of his own mouth. In Rome the taunt that he could not endure was 'traitor'; in Corioles the trigger is 'boy of tears'. To have his manhood questioned, especially by Aufidius whom he has beaten so often, is unendurable. This is a master stroke from the character who saw Martius weep and said, 'I was mov'd withal' (V.iii.194). Martius' response is immediate, devastating and suicidal. To recall his feat of taking Corioles single-handed – 'like an eagle in a dove-cote' (V.vi.114) – is enough to cause a wave of anger that permits Aufidius and his accomplices to kill him. The outburst is sufficient only to effect the murder. The recoil is instantaneous. The First Lord denounces Aufidius with the comment, 'Thou hast done a deed whereat valour will weep' (V.vi.132). Aufidius himself is therefore obliged to deliver a final encomium acknowledging the greatness of his adversary and rival:

> Beat thou the drum that it speak mournfully;
> Trail your steel pikes. Though in this city he
> Hath widow'd and unchilded many a one,
> Which to this hour bewail the injury,
> Yet he shall have a noble memory.
>
> (V.vi.149–53)

Interestingly, Livy has a less comprehensive account of Martius' fate and one which is also less certain:

When he had withdrawne the legions out of the territorie of Rome, he gat himselfe, men said, such hatred and displeasure for this action, that it cost him his life; and murdered he was, some report one way, some another. But I find in *Fabius* a most ancient writer, that he lived untill he was an old man: who reporteth this of him: That oftentimes in his latter daies he used to utter this speech, *A heavie case and most wretched, for an aged man to live banisht.*[41]

The alternative ending of Coriolanus' life possesses as much poignancy as the one indicated by Plutarch, but it has much less dramatic power. One significant point from the standpoint of the present study is that a distinguished Roman historian admits he does not know which account is true. Shakespeare frequently encountered this kind of statement in his historical researches, which must have encouraged his natural scepticism towards 'historical facts'. The dramatist was able to perceive very clearly the way in which historical accounts were shaped by parties with vested interests, such as Octavius Caesar, or by 'partial' historians or romantics. This awareness must have fortified his natural proclivity for sifting, re-evaluating and reshaping 'historical' details such as the murder of Hector by Achilles in *Troilus and Cressida*.

In his summing up of Martius' character Plutarch praises him for his incorruptibility but criticizes him for behaving contemptuously towards the common people and then being angered by their refusal to honour him:

> For as it is an evill thing to flatter the common people to winne credit: even so is it besides dishonesty, and injustice also, to atteine to credit and authoritie, for one to make him selfe terrible to the people, by offering them wrong and violence . . . For he that disdaineth to make much of the people, and to have their favour, shoulde much more scorne to seeke to be revenged, when he is repulsed. For, to take a repulse and deniall of honour, so inwardly to the hart: commeth of no other cause, but that he did too earnestly desire it.[42]

Here is a contrast between Shakespeare's interpretation of Coriolanus and Plutarch's. Although the dramatist creates a dialogue in which one officer protests that although it is a virtue not to flatter the common people it is a vice to deliberately scorn them (II.ii.16–23), Shakespeare's hero does not feel wounded by their failure to honour him. What makes him bitter is betrayal by the patricians. His idea of service to the state does not include the plebeians: conceptually, for him, they are outside the society. As he says when protesting about showing his battle scars to the people:

> To brag unto them, thus I did, and thus,
> Show them th'unaching scars which I should hide,
> As if I had receiv'd them for the hire
> Of their breath only!

> (II.ii.147–50)

Plutarch's Martius does not possess this insulation from plebeian ingratitude. He is not as consistent as Shakespeare's. The historian's criticism does not apply to Shakespeare's hero. The historian's Coriolanus also suffers a further disability which is not shared by the hero of the play, namely, a lack of affability within his own peer group. In the play Coriolanus is betrayed or sacrificed by the patricians simply as an act of political expediency. The warrior who keeps the enemy from the gates provokes a crisis of such magnitude that the choice for the patricians lies between sanctioning his exile or countenancing civil war. Another criticism made by Plutarch is that Coriolanus used dishonest means to provoke the war between the Volsces and the Romans:

> And Martius, as Dionysius the historiographer writeth: dyd by craft and deceipt bring the Romaines into warres against the Volsces, causing the Volsces maliciously, and wrongfully to be suspected, that went to Rome to see the games played.[43]

Shakespeare's hero is devoid of this characteristic: he never exhibits guile or mendacity – though interestingly Livy attributes this quality to him as well, claiming that Aufidius and Martius 'laid their heads together and complotted to make warre upon the Romanes'.[44] Finally, Plutarch denounces Coriolanus for rejecting the official embassies from Rome but succumbing to the pleas of his mother:

> yet he had no reason for the love of his mother to pardone his contrie, but rather he should in pardoning his contrie, have spared his mother, bicause his mother and wife were members of the bodie of his contrie and city, which he did beseige . . . For he withdrew his army, not at the request of the Romaines, against whom he made warre: nor with their consent, at whose charge the warre was made . . . So by this dede of his, he tooke not away the enmity that was betwene both people: but leaving warre still betwene them, he made the Volsces (of whome he was generall) to lose the oportunity of noble victory.[45]

Here again is a difference of emphasis between the historian and the dramatist, because in the play the focus of Volumnia's appeal is Martius' duty to Rome. What is clear from the narrative is that the Romans are unwilling to settle matters on a reasonable basis. They invite their own destruction by their intransigence. Failure to follow through the attack is, therefore, a total betrayal of the Volsces. The situation is different in the play: it appears that Coriolanus' aim is not to put the Volsces on a new footing with Rome, one much closer to equality, but a passionate desire to destroy Rome as an act of revenge. Why the Volsces can feel betrayed in the play is that they have been deprived of the opportunity of annihilating their enemies after suffering so many humiliating defeats at their hands.

The central difference between Plutarch and Shakespeare, however, is that the dramatist locates the source of the tragedy in the ethos of the society. The hero is the embodiment of the central value of his social universe: he is not an aberration but the epitome of the value system. Coriolanus absorbs the values with peculiar force by means of the special relationship he has with his mother and because he possesses remarkable integrity. All this would be perceived by the patricians as admirable in the social world which precedes the action of the play; at this juncture in history it is fatal. The play focuses on a collision of social forces at a time when the common people are acquiring a new sense of their place in the social universe. 'Rome' is no longer the aristocracy. The society is experiencing a metamorphosis: the aristocratic element can adapt and adjust; the political Machiavellians belonging to lower orders and the aristocratic lubricator of the system, Menenius, will manoeuvre for the best position circumstances will allow, and both will manipulate the people in the process. But as the earth moves in this social world there can be nothing but disaster for the man of fixed principles and powerful emotions. Constancy is now a fatal flaw; this is a world for the temporizer.

That *Coriolanus* is Shakespeare's most political play has been widely recognized. Indeed, Maurice Charney goes so far as to suggest that 'Our interpretation of *Coriolanus* depends, of course, on our own moral values.'[46] There can be no 'of course' about it, but a brief survey of the contrasting attitudes to the play reveals that many critics have responded in terms of their values and perceptions of the dramatist's sympathies. Coleridge writes of 'The wonderful philosophic impartiality in Shakespeare's politics',[47] whereas Hazlitt comes to an entirely different conclusion:

> The whole dramatic moral of *Coriolanus* is that those who have little shall have less, and that those who have much shall take all that others have left. The people are poor; therefore they ought to be starved. They are slaves; therefore they ought to be beaten.[48]

Swinburne, writing sixty years later, felt able to dismiss such a view of the play as irrelevant:

> It is from first to last, for all its turmoil of battle and clamour of contentious factions, rather a private and domestic than a public or historical tragedy . . . the whole force of the final impression is not that of a conflict between patrician and plebeian, but solely that of a match of passions played out for life and death between a mother and a son.[49]

Likewise, Dowden maintains that 'The subject of *Coriolanus* is the ruin of a noble life through the sin of pride'. For him, politics are marginalized in the play:

> the central and vivifying element in the play is not a political problem, but an individual character and life. The tragic struggle of the play is

not that of patricians with plebeians, but of Coriolanus with his own self. It is not the Roman people who bring about his destruction; it is the patrician haughtiness and passionate self-will of Coriolanus himself.[50]

For Dowden, Coriolanus' pride emanates from two sources, 'a passionate self-esteem which is essentially egoistic; and secondly a passionate prejudice of class'.[51] What Dowden fails to recognize is the way in which the former is forged by the latter. 'Politics' is not confined to the matter of conflict between patricians and plebians; Shakespeare explores the transmission and articulation of values, which is a profoundly socio-political act. Coriolanus' pride, if that is the best word to describe it, arises out of his conception of *service to the society*. Hence his feeling of total outrage at being called 'traitor'. Similarly, as valour is the supreme value in this culture he gasps in disbelief as he is called 'boy of tears' by Aufidius. When, therefore, critics claim that the play is essentially about the personal tragedy of Coriolanus, with politics relegated to a subordinate position, they are failing to recognize Shakespeare's powerful grasp of the relationship between the process of socialization, which is highly politicized in this state, and the individual personality. Coriolanus is an instrument perfectly fashioned by the values of his society; he is the embodiment of its ethos. When he exclaims 'I banish you!' (III.iii.123) this is something much more than churlish bravado, or a rejection of his society. At that moment he sees himself as the embodiment of the society in its uncorrupted state. The society which he leaves behind him, in which the common people are granted a place in the commonwealth, nominally as equals, is something abhorrent and totally alien to him. The personal tragedy of Coriolanus arises not out of some temperamental inability to be tactful. It is the consequence of being moulded in a society which has very clearly defined and limited values. Here is the idealist who has absorbed through his mother the values of his society in the most pure and undiluted form. This upbringing or socialization is effective in producing the perfect representation of a true Roman, and one who would be deified in any earlier historical epoch. The tragedy arises because the perfect Roman finds himself active in a society that is experiencing change. This transition can be handled by those who dilute their values with a good deal of 'allaying' (to use Menenius' word) hypocrisy. The play is not *primarily* political through its display of political intrigue and class warfare; but it is *essentially* political in that the personal tragedy of *Coriolanus* arises out of the highly political nature of the social universe into which Caius Martius is born, lives and dies. The hero dies not because he is irascible, but because he is pure. We can be deeply moved by his situation and his defeat while being contemptuous of his values. Coriolanus did not make the values; he simply absorbed them. In portraying this tragedy of a great individual, Shakespeare simultaneously portrays the mechanics of social change.

Coriolanus is the only idealist in the play; those most at home in the political sphere are manipulative and cynical, including Menenius and the tribunes. Paradoxically, change is effected through the manoeuvres of the politically adept responding to the pressures from below. As such adjustments work their way through, even the value-system is gradually transformed. Only in *Coriolanus* is valour the 'chiefest virtue'. Rome retains its claims on its children throughout the Roman plays, but in *Julius Caesar* service to the society is conceived in terms other than valour, while in *Antony and Cleopatra* the supreme opportunist and individualist, Octavius Caesar, reveals no commitment to Roman values, though he finds it convenient to expound them (as when he provides his magnificent description of the Antony that was – the man who embodied endurance and constancy).

Many of the commentators who have emphasized the political dimension of the play have argued for its contemporary significance and its ideological bias. This is one of the few occasions where there is widespread feeling that Shakespeare is expressing his personal antagonism to democratic ideas and giving vent to his fear of the many-headed multitude. O.J. Campbell, for instance, claims that,

> Though Shakespeare is not in this play showing his contempt for the common man, he is nevertheless expressing his vigorous disapproval of democracy. In common with all political theorists of his age, he regarded it as the absence of all government – a form of organized disorder.[52]

Rossiter puts his case at somewhat greater length but with similar firmness:

> In considering what Shakespeare gave Coriolanus to think right, we cannot overlook the fact that in May 1607 there was an insurrection which began in Northamptonshire and soon spread to other counties. It was a peasant insurrection; and partly about corn – anyway, about food. It was mainly against enclosures; but the engrossing of corn was a simultaneous grievance: an endemic economic evil of the day. The insurrection of the *Romans*, as told by Plutarch, was about *usurers* (they get a line at I.i.79; but nobody would see it unless told to look for it). I wish no emphasis on Shakespeare's role as investor in malt. I only say: There were these risings, they kept happening in Elizabethan times; and if you ask what is his fear of the mob and disorder, it is answered at once in Marcius's mouth:

> my soul aches
> To know, when two authorities are up,
> Neither supreme, how soon confusion
> May enter 'twixt the gap of both, and take
> The one by th'other.
>
> (III.i.107–11)

Taking that with what we find elsewhere, in this and other plays, I cannot doubt that those lines are heart-felt. They are (for once) what William Shakespeare also thought – in 1607. It follows that we must swallow our democracy, and, if we would grasp the play, accept it that the political convictions of Marcius are *right*.[53]

Hence this most astute of critics identifies Martius' views with those of the dramatist and insists on their rightness in terms of Elizabethan and Jacobean England. Reuben Brower likewise draws attention to contemporary events and insists on their significance:

> That Shakespeare takes the famine as the principal cause for the plebeians' complaints, rather than as in Plutarch 'the sore oppression of usurers', is almost certainly traceable to the unrest in England, more especially to the Midlands revolt of 1607. The extensive emphasis in the play – as compared with the *Life* – on the body–state metaphor is probably to be explained in part by the contemporary concern with the dangers of insurrection.[54]

Finally, Willard Farnham adopts a similar line of argument, concluding with a significant critical point:

> common people were unfit to have ruling power in a state, not only because they were many-minded and had no stability, but also because they were shortsighted and had no power to see the interests of any other group than their own. A democratic government, then, was an evil government, and it might upon very good authority be called no true government at all but only a perversion of government . . . The arisocratic government presented in *Coriolanus* is obviously an imperfect one, and the common people who rebel against it are shown to have grievances. But it is significant that although, as the drama develops, we are often invited to sympathize with individual ordinary citizens, we are rarely if ever invited to sympathise with the tribunes, who are the means by which the citizens as a body are becoming a political power and challenging the authority of the patricians – the means, in other words, by which Rome is bringing democracy into being.[55]

This last point reveals a weakness in the argument. The tribunes are unquestionably unattractive – they are political manipulators – but that fact cannot be used to demonstrate Shakespeare's antagonism to *democratic institutions*. Throughout the Roman plays, and the English histories, Shakespeare reveals a firm grasp of political realities, including the manipulative propensities of those attracted to the political arena. But just because the people's representatives are charlatans and are likely to be so in the future, this by no means suggests that representative government is a bad thing. It does imply that the people are unlikely to gain direct access to the decision-making process and will be subject to manipulation by those in power. This does not imply that the political leverage of the people is the same in all circumstances; on the contrary, it would appear from the action of the play that the people are in desperate need of representation. The aristocratic perspective is bankrupt and Rome is already moving into a period where political skills and effective social organization will be more important than the simple inculcation of military values. This is a society in a stage of transition and Coriolanus is the physical embodiment of the tension that reaches breaking point.

Interestingly, Brower draws attention to the way in which Martius appears integrated in his adopted society:

> The last scene of the play begins as an ironic repetition of the scene in which he had 'mildly' given in to his mother's advice. At that time he had not been able to sustain the part; but now he 'bows his nature' and comes 'marching' in, *The commoners being with him*'. In contrast to the usual isolation of his figure from the plebeians, Coriolanus is seen *with* the people, and we catch another ironic reflection from the past: Menenius's easy companionship with the lower orders. Coriolanus seems for once to 'belong', and he cries happily, 'I am return'd your soldier,/No more infected with my country's love . . .' (V.vi.71–2). What was once his health is now disease, and loyalty to the enemies of Rome is his 'cure'. He is so terribly unaware of what he has been doing that he responds with dreamlike deafness to Aufidius's cry of 'traitor' – the exact echo of the Tribunes' earlier ''Has spoken like a traitor . . .' (III.i.162).[56]

There is a good deal of truth in this argument but also some confusion. Clearly, Martius does not apply the Roman autocratic values in this society. Perhaps that is why Shakespeare deviated from Plutarch in making the Volscian who calls forth Martius' compassion a 'poor man' rather than a rich one. Released from his Roman world, he can think of the common man as something other than sub-human. He has not learnt to play the hypocrite, as Brower implies, or as Aufidius disingenuously claims (V.vi.21–6). One of the significant points usually missed by critics is that this society *feels* distinctly different from that of Rome: it feels more tribal, less hierarchical (for an elaboration of this point see Anne Barton, 'Livy, Machiavelli, and Shakespeare's *Coriolanus*'[57]). The Volscians appear to lack Rome's sense of mission. Their society is less brittle. Likewise, the term 'traitor' cannot hurt Martius nearly as much here as he has not spent his entire life serving this state. His status and his relationship to the social organism is very different from that which prevailed in Rome. Martius has entered a new world: he has acted primarily out of self-interest and the Volscians have a right to question his actions without causing him to feel a sense of outrage at their ingratitude. What they are not free to question is his manhood – hence the explosive response to Aufidius' carefully calculated insult, 'boy of tears'.

What is clear, then, is that Shakespeare establishes two sharply delineated social worlds. The connections between character, values, social classes and political institutions are so tightly forged that any interpretation of the play in terms of psychology or character or class conflict must of necessity provide a partial and distorting perspective. Neither human psychology nor political institutions can be given primacy: the power and fascination of the play resides in their complex interaction. Likewise, it is a mistake to see the most detached and impartial of writers giving expression to his political sympathies in this play. The energy, vitality and intense conflicts which animate the play create an immediate awareness of class antagonisms and quickly trigger individual prejudice, but only the most bigoted member of the audience can remain impervious to the distortions or excesses of 'their' side.

The opening scene is the most tumultuous in the whole of Shakespeare. It embodies a tremendous physicality and vigour. The citizens are in a rage. Immediately, the dichotomies and ironies that are so central to an understanding of the play are brought to the surface. The very first utterance, for instance, draws the distinction between words and actions. The First Citizen says, 'Before we *proceed* any further, hear me *speak*' [my italics]. The mutinous citizens are, of course, armed with staves and clubs and are poised for action. Nevertheless, their response is not to dismiss mere talk; they cry in unison 'Speak, speak'. The First Citizen then poses a question which reveals the desperate nature of the situation: 'You are all resolved rather to die than to famish'. Their commitment to action seems unequivocal as they reply, 'Resolved, resolved'. The next move by the First Citizen is to focus the elemental force which awaits direction: 'First, you know Caius Martius is chief enemy to the people'. Once more assent is swift and emphatic, with the now familiar pattern of repetition: 'We know't, we know't'. Agreement is then sought by the First Citizen on the action which is to be taken: 'Let us kill him, and we'll have corn at our own price. Is't a verdict?' It seems that there is once more unanimity: 'No more *talking* on't; let it be *done*. Away, away!' [my italics]. Words have paved the way for action and now give way to action – almost. For at this moment there is a voice of dissent in the form of the Second Citizen, who requests 'One word, good citizens'. This creates the opportunity for the First Citizen to broaden his attack to encompass a whole social class and to play on the contrast between starvation and superabundance:

We are accounted poor citizens, the patricians good. What authority surfeits on would relieve us. If they would yield us but the superfluity

while it were wholesome, we might guess they relieved us humanely;
but they think we are too dear: the leanness that afflicts us, the object
of our misery, is as an inventory to particularize their abundance; our
sufferance is a gain to them.

(I.i.14–21)

This is not a matter of a relative shift of resources to achieve a greater
degree of equality, rather there is an insistence on an intensity of class
antagonism directed at the plebeians which is positively malicious. Hunger
is not perceived as being accidental; it is the consequence of deliberate
policy.

Given the magnitude of class division in this society and the desperation
engendered by hunger, it is surprising that action gives way to further
words – words that diminish the clarity of the conflict. The Second Citizen
comes to the defence of Martius in particular, rather than the patricians
as a class, by insisting on his service to the society *as a whole*: 'Consider
you what services he has done for his country?' (I.i.29–30). Interestingly,
the First Citizen does not deny that they have all benefited from this
action, but rather casts doubt on his motives. This immediately creates an
awareness of an ambiguity. The plebeians have a commitment to their
country as well as to their class. Though irate at being neglected they
implicitly recognize their attachment to the community as a whole. This
is precisely the foundation upon which Menenius is able to base his case
in defence of the patricians. The Second Citizen's defence of Caius Martius
also reveals the capacity of the plebeians to be generous spirited even
when they are on the brink of riot. Before employing his famous fable of
the belly, which is used to emphasize the organic nature of the society,
Menenius sets about insinuating an identity of interests, both by his
employment of the term 'my countrymen' (I.i.53), and by the simplicity
and homeliness of his diction – epitomized by his second speech:

Why masters, my good friends, mine honest neighbours,
Will you undo yourselves?

(I.i.61–2)

Menenius is positively audacious in his assertion that the patricians care
for the plebeians 'like fathers' (I.i.76), but his initial line of argument
contains two other elements. First, that the dearth is not the fault of any
human agency; and second, that no matter how vociferous or violent the
plebeians are in their protest they cannot hope to exert a serious influence
on events because the Roman state is an all-powerful, impersonal machine:

For your wants,
Your suffering in this dearth, you may as well
Strike at the heaven with your staves, as lift them
Against the Roman state, whose course will on

The way it takes, cracking ten thousand curbs
Of more strong link asunder than can ever
Appear in your impediment.

(I.i.65–71)

The riposte of the First Citizen focuses on the question of the paternalism of the patricians. In rejecting Menenius' claim he uses words which possess an intensity that proclaim the antagonistic and parasitic nature of the patricians:

> Care for us? True indeed! They ne'er cared for us yet. *Suffer us to famish*, and their storehouses *crammed* with grain; make *edicts for usury*, to support usurers; repeal daily any *wholesome* act established against the rich, and provide more *piercing* statutes daily, to *chain up* and *restrain* the poor. If the wars *eat us not up*, they will; and there's all the love they bear us.

(I.i.78–85; my italics)

The plausibility of the plebeians' claim is accentuated by their simplicity, which is comic, while the potency of the threat they represent is simultaneously diminished. These simple and sincere men are no match for Menenius, who easily manoeuvres them into the position where they relinquish action in order to digest his words. The submission of the ringleader to Menenius' offer of delivering an illuminating tale is both touching and comic:

> FIRST CITIZEN Well, I'll hear it, sir; yet you must not think to fob off
> our disgrace with a tale; but, and't please you, deliver.

(I.i.92–4)

Despite the patent inadequacy of the fable of the belly as a means of demonstrating the worth of the patricians – after all, the plebeians are being starved so the 'belly' is not disbursing its vital substance throughout the social organism – Menenius is confident that it has been successful because he feels free to bait the First Citizen and to chastize the rest as soon as his moral tale has been delivered. Indeed, as seduction gives way to scolding he implicitly rejects his conception of society as an organism and presents a vision of contending forces:

> But make you ready your stiff bats and clubs;
> Rome and her rats are at the point of battle;
> The one side must have bale.

(I.i.160–2)

The image is telling: 'Rome' means patricians only; the plebeians are parasites. Later, the tribunes assert that 'The people are the city' (III.i.198). For them the patricians are the parasites. The conflict in this

183

society is not simply the result of a quest for political supremacy: it represents a profound class antagonism based on a conception of worthiness versus the parasitic. For the patricians worthiness emanates from noble blood; the dignity arising from political decision-making and authority; and from military prowess. The relationship of the plebeians to Rome is not even equivalent to the beast of burden to the farmer: the patricians despise the plebeians for having pretensions, for asserting rights arising from their common humanity. The plebeians for their part accept a status of inferiority, but as the producers of food, the very basis of life, they are unable to consider themselves worthless. On the contrary, their leaders go so far as to invert the accepted relationship between the two classes, implying the superiority of the producers of food.

While the raw nature of class antagonism is clearly felt by the audience, Martius arrives on the scene to provide a new intensity to the conflict. He reveals a depth of contempt for the plebeians which is breathtaking:

> What's the matter, you dissentious rogues
> That, rubbing the poor itch of your opinion,
> Make yourselves scabs?

> (I.i.163–5)

The basis of his contempt is twofold: the plebeians lack courage in battle and they are inconstant:

> What would you have, you curs,
> That like nor peace nor war? The one affrights you,
> The other makes you proud. He that trusts to you,
> Where he should find you lions, finds you hares;
> Where foxes, geese: you are no surer, no,
> Than is the coal of fire upon the ice,
> Or hailstone in the sun . . .
>   . . . Trust ye?
> With every minute you do change a mind,
> And call him noble that was now your hate,
> Him vile that was your garland. What's the matter,
> That in these several places of the city,
> You cry against the noble Senate, who
> (Under the gods) keep you in awe, which else
> Would feed on one another?

> (I.i.167–87)

His concluding lines provide a justification for the authority of the patricians: they are the factors or stewards of the gods; without their firm rule the plebeians would create a state of anarchy: they would devour each other. In a play which has a great deal to do with hunger, the numerous references to eating are wolvish or savage rather than domestic.

They relate to unbridled wantonness rather than to satisfying the necessary requirements of the body. Likewise, references to food point up the extremes of dearth or abundance, and this dichotomy is accentuated by the use of these words even when food is not the issue. Menenius claims that the plebeians 'abundantly . . . lack discretion' (I.i.201); Coriolanus narrates how the protesters claimed 'That meat was made for mouths' (I.i.206), suggesting something elemental if not savage. Again, on receiving news that the Volscians are in arms he expresses his delight by claiming 'then we shall ha'means to *vent*/Our musty superfluity' (I.i.224–5; my italics): lines which bring together the idea of surplus people – best disposed of – and the question of the stored surplus/actual shortage of corn; 'vent' brings together the meaning 'cast out' and 'vend', 'to sell', like marketing musty corn.

Thus, as early as the opening scene Shakespeare has created an awareness of a divided society. There is a bifurcation between the noble and the ignoble; the lower orders are viewed with contempt; they riot only when they are pushed to the point of starvation, and then they are almost fobbed off. The plebeians are not viewed as citizens by the patricians. They fulfil a vital economic role, but economic activity is perceived as the very lowest of human functions. The roles which are esteemed are political and military. The plebeians fulfil a military function, but they are not professional soldiers – they lack the steely courage and competence of their social superiors. For their part the plebeians accept a position of inferiority (and are more than willing to admire Caius Martius for his martial qualities), but because they live on the edge of subsistence they are incapable of seeing their economic function, the provision of food, as trivial. Only those who never go hungry can adopt an attitude of contempt to production of food. Despite the passion and desperation of the group of plebeians who are outmanoeuvred by Menenius, it is difficult to imagine them being a major threat to the stability of society. The news that another such group has forced a constitutional innovation, the right to elect their own representatives to speak for them in the Senate, suggests a greater intensity of violence or a higher calibre of leadership. Evidently this society is riven with a degree of class conflict which borders on revolution. The tension is diminished first through political compromise and second through the advent of war, which creates a form of unity. Even so, Martius, like Menenius earlier, refers to the plebeians as rats (employing the pervasive animal imagery):

The Volsces have much corn: take these rats thither,
To gnaw their garners.

(I.i.248–9)

In contrast, Titus Lartius, who expresses his determination to fight despite his injuries or disabilities, draws from Martius the admiring response, 'Oh, true-bred!' (I.i.242).

Before the opening scene is over, the audience has the opportunity of assessing the representatives of the people. Unlike their followers they are neither gullible nor naive. Brutus and Sicinius paint a telling picture of Martius' behaviour when they were elected tribunes, but these devious men completely fail to comprehend the nature of his integrity. They advance subtle reasons for his willingness to serve under Cominius because they can't understand him. Thus the opening scene closes with an awareness of the simplicity of the plebeians – tinged with generosity; Martius' unbending contempt for the people and total belief in the worth of the patricians; the subtlety of Menenius, which makes him an effective go-between: the cement that holds together antagonistic social classes; and the subtlety and guile of the tribunes, who exhibit a very limited understanding of their chief adversary.

The following brief scene, set in Corioles, is characterized by the analytical nature of a discussion between Aufidius and the Senators as they evaluate the consequences of Rome's premature discovery of their war preparations. One of the key facts set out by Aufidius is that 'The dearth is great' (I.ii.10). Perhaps surprisingly, Aufidius adds the parenthetical comment about Martius, 'Who is of Rome worse hated than of you' (I.ii.13), implying that Rome means not the patricians but the people. The dialogue also reveals Aufidius as no mere fighting machine (though his comments, like those of Martius in the previous scene, build up the heroic conflict between the two super-warriors) but a highly respected colleague in the decision-making process.

Having exhibited the social division within Rome and contrasted it fleetingly with another society, Shakespeare digs deeper in the exploration of Roman values. A striking feature of Act I scene iii is the juxtaposition of tenderness and violence. The process begins with Volumnia chastising Virgilia for her natural anxiety:

I pray you, daughter, sing, or express yourself in a more comfortable sort. If my son were my husband I should freelier rejoice in that absence wherein he won honour, than in the embracements of his bed, where he would show most love. When yet he was but tender-bodied, and the only son of my womb; when youth with comeliness plucked all gaze his way; when for a day of kings' entreaties, a mother should not sell him an hour from her beholding; I, considering how honour would become such a person – that it was no better than picture-like to hang by th'wall, if renown made it not stir – was pleased to let him seek danger where he was like to find fame. To a cruel war I sent him, from whence he returned, his brows bound with oak. I tell thee, daughter, I sprang not more in joy at first hearing he was a man-child, than now in first seeing he had proved himself a man.

(I.iii.1–18)

Volumnia elevates the glories of war above the pleasures of the marriage bed (the first of three occasions in the play when this comparison is made) and expresses the enthusiasm with which she released her 'tender-bodied' child and 'only son' of her 'womb' to the hazards of 'cruel' war. When Virgilia attempts to puncture what she takes for bravado with the question, 'But had he died in the business, madam, how then?' Volumnia's reply is immediate and unequivocal:

> Then his good report should have been my son, I therein would have found issue. Hear me profess sincerely: had I a dozen sons, each in my love alike, and none less dear than thine and my good Martius, I had rather had eleven die nobly for their country, than one voluptuously surfeit out of action.

(I.iii.20–5)

Here is an emphatic statement of what it means to be a Roman. Total dedication to the society is the supreme value. To have a loved one die on the battlefield is cause for celebration rather than mourning. Moreover, a real cause for sorrow would be to have 'one voluptuously surfeit out of action'. Here is a very clear sense of the value of abstinence: in this society the prize for being successful does not consist in acquiring wealth and 'living well' – the reward is recognition of service. Given the deep inculcation of these values it is hardly surprising that Martius dedicates himself to war and spurns the booty as 'The common muck of the world' (II.ii.126).

The ideal of energy and endurance is expressed by means of a strange and surprising simile in Volumnia's next speech. In describing her son's passage through the enemy ranks she compares the warrior with the farmer:

> His bloody brow
> With his mail'd hand then wiping, forth he goes
> Like to a harvest man that's task'd to mow
> Or all, or lose his hire.

(I.iii.34–7)

This simile is surprising because Volumnia feels such contempt for the sweat and effort involved in the mundane task of producing food. It is strange because of the contrast between the life-enhancing activity of the farmer and the life-destroying actions of the warrior. Awareness of the incongruity, even if only partially registered by the audience, casts an unattractive shadow over the glories of the battlefield. Moreover,

187

Shakespeare may be conveying the feeling that there is a part of the
patrician consciousness that recognizes the worth of common work. The
creative/destructive, fragile/violent dichotomies are further underlined
when Volumnia insists:

> The breasts of Hecuba
> When she did suckle Hector, look'd not lovelier
> Than Hector's forehead when it spit forth blood
> At Grecian sword contemning.
>
> (I.iii.40–3)

Virgilia is horrified by the sentiment and the image: 'Heavens bless my
lord from fell Aufidius!' Volumnia's riposte involves direct reference to
body parts in a way which emphasizes strength and sinewy toughness:

> He'll beat Aufidius' head below his knee,
> And tread upon his neck.
>
> (I.iii.46–7)

Valeria's description of Martius' son playing with a butterfly and tearing
it to pieces with his teeth provokes Volumnia's laconic comment 'One
on's father's moods', to which Valeria adds, 'Indeed, la, 'tis a noble child'
(I.iii.66–7). This extolling of violence creates a sense of imbalance in life
engendered by the worship of martial honour.

After sitting by the very hearthside where Martius imbibed his values,
the audience is fully prepared for the warrior's magnificent feats on the
battlefield. In the battle for Corioles, Martius denounces the soldiers with
a torrent of invective for having allowed themselves to be beaten back to
their trenches. He then leads them into a desperate assault on the city.
As he enters the gates his followers hang back believing Martius is too
foolhardy. However, they quickly come to his aid when he emerges bleeding, and take the city. Martius again pours scorn on them as they fall to
spoil before galvanising his force to support Cominius:

> See here these movers, that do prize their hours
> At a crack'd drachma! Cushions, leaden spoons,
> Irons of a doit, doublets that hangmen would
> Bury with those that wore them, these base slaves,
> Ere yet the fight be done, pack up. Down with them!
> And hark, what noise the general makes! To him!
> There is the man of my soul's hate, Aufidius,
> Piercing our Romans. Then, valiant Titus, take
> Convenient numbers to make good the city,
> Whilst I, with those that have the spirit, will haste
> To help Cominius.
>
> (I.v.4–14)

188

The line 'And hark, what noise the general makes! To him!' provides a precise division of the speech: the noise of battle acts as a catalyst to propel Martius into further action; the phrase 'piercing our Romans' is vivid and urgent. When Titus Lartius suggests that Martius has done enough, he responds,

> Sir, praise me not;
> My work hath yet not warm'd me. Fare you well.
> The blood I drop is rather physical
> Than dangerous to me.
>
> (I.v.16–19)

Surprisingly, when we encounter Martius' admired colleague, Cominius, in the next scene, we discover that he and his men are taking a breather after retreating. He employs a formula that it is impossible to imagine coming from the lips of Martius:

> Breathe you, my friends; well fought; we are come off
> Like Romans, neither foolish in our stands
> Nor cowardly in retire.
>
> (I.vi.1–3)

Martius greets Cominius in terms that equate the joys of the battlefield with the sweetest hours of love:

> Oh! let me clip ye
> In arms as sound as when I woo'd; in heart
> As merry as when our nuptial day was done,
> And tapers burn'd to bedward.
>
> (I.vi.29–32)

The greeting over, he expresses amazement that they are not fighting when the battle has yet to be won:

> Where is the enemy? Are you lords o'th'field?
> If not, why cease you till you are so?
>
> (I.vi.47–8)

Within seconds Martius has secured volunteers to join him in an attack on the hardiest of the enemy forces, and leads them into battle with the cry: 'O me alone! Make you a sword of me!' (I.vi.76), subconsciously giving expression to his role as a weapon of war (the Arden editor, Philip Brockbank, allocates this line to the soldiers). In sharp contrast to the vituperation which Martius characteristically directs at his men, Cominius encourages them by conveying a sense of fellowship and promising a division of the spoils or honour that ensues:

> March on, my fellows:
> Make good this ostentation, and you shall

189

Divide in all with us.

(I.vi.85–7)

Martius has no sympathy with men who do not automatically give their all in fighting for their country; Cominius has a wider range of sympathy and understanding. The greater warrior is the lesser man. The more thorough, comprehensive and undiluted is the ethic of service through martial prowess, the narrower is the basis of the society. Even though these scenes show Martius in a comfortable relationship with Cominius and Titus Lartius, they also reveal his isolation.

When he finally catches up with Aufidius, his arch rival, Martius again emphasizes his aloneness, not to boast, but to stir his enemy to more violence:

> Within these three hours, Tullus,
> *Alone* I fought in your Corioles walls . . .
> (I.viii.7–8; my italics)

Despite this awareness of his singularity, Martius cannot endure to have his praises sung in public. Cominius can hardly wait to praise him publicly and takes pleasure in the thought that even the plebeians will feel impelled to extol his virtue:

> where the dull tribunes,
> That with the fusty plebeians hate thine honours,
> Shall say against their hearts, 'We thank the gods
> Our Rome hath such a soldier'.
> (I.ix.6–9)

Martius' embarrassed reply is:

> Pray now, no more. My mother,
> Who has a charter to extol her blood,
> When she does praise me, grieves me. I have done
> As you have done, that's what I can; induc'd
> As you have been, that's for my country.
> He that has but effected his good will
> Hath overta'en mine act.
> (I.ix.13–19)

Cominius nevertheless insists:

> Rome must know
> The *value* of her own.
> (I.ix.20–1; my italics)

When offered a tenth of the plunder Martius refuses anything more than an equal share, responding courteously, but in a language that underscores his feeling towards his society:

190

> I thank you, general;
> But cannot make my heart consent to take
> A *bribe* to *pay* my sword . . .
>
> (I.ix.36–8; my italics)

Whereas the common men scrambled for trifles, he sees battle exclusively in terms of *service*.

Throughout this scene there is a tension between deeds and words. When Martius claims that his wounds smart 'To hear themselves remember'd', Cominius replies

> Should they not,
> Well might they fester 'gainst ingratitude,
> And tent themselves with death.
>
> (I.ix.29–31)

Service, Cominius insists, must be recognized, and proper recognition requires that deeds be embodied in words. Martius' obvious embarrassment reveals that he is not proud in the sense of possessing a conceit which relishes praise. Indeed, taking up the food imagery employed by Cominius in describing Martius' second military triumph of the day –

> Yet cam'st thou to a morsel of this feast,
> Having fully din'd before.
>
> (I.ix.10–11)

he makes the seemingly perverse protest,

> you shout me forth
> In acclamations hyperbolical,
> As if I lov'd my little should be dieted
> In praises sauc'd with lies.
>
> (I.ix.49–52)

For the man who is constantly denounced as proud, his modesty is breathtaking. His pride arises from his sense of being a true Roman, of belonging to that class which is unsullied by petty concerns of daily life, but are manifestly dedicated to the achievement of military prowess and guaranteeing the strength and integrity of Rome.

There is another striking and ambiguous development in this scene. Having rejected the reward of ten per cent of the spoils Martius begs the enfranchisement of a Volscian prisoner, a poor man who formerly assisted him. This is the only time that Martius shows any concern for a *poor* man. In Plutarch's account the man is rich. Is Shakespeare implying that Martius has the capacity to be sympathetic to a poor individual so long as he does not perceive him as a member of an inferior social class? Is his conception of a sharp social division between the noble and ignoble confined to

191

Rome? Or is there some other explanation? Certainly, if Shakespeare momentarily broadens Martius' range of sympathies he soon narrows them again. Martius explains how he failed to save the man during the battle:

> He cried to me. I saw him prisoner.
> But then Aufidius was within my view,
> And wrath o'erwhelm'd my pity.
>
> (I.ix.82–4)

He also forgets the man's name. Does this imply a limitation, or the loss of memory arising from sheer exhaustion, as he claims? Whatever his limitations, Martius possesses a clear sense of his own integrity. The reward of service is the doing of it. His commitment to being the supreme warrior permits no deviation. But the counterpart of his unquenchable spirit on the battlefield is an appallingly limited social vision and an inflexible sense of a code of right living. He is incapable of the kind of 'adjustment' that Aufidius evinces after being beaten once more:

> Five times, Martius,
> I have fought with thee; so often hast thou beat me;
> And wouldst do so, I think, should we encounter
> As often as we eat. By th'elements,
> If e'er again I meet him beard to beard,
> He's mine, or I am his. Mine emulation
> Hath not that honour in't it had: for where
> I thought to crush him in an equal force,
> True sword to sword, I'll potch at him some way,
> Or wrath or craft may get him.
>
> (I.x.7–16)

The near perfect warrior lacks Martius' integrity but possesses the facility for adapting himself in a slippery world.

Martius' welcome home, his seemingly successful election to the consulship, and the last-minute manipulation by the tribunes, is portrayed in masterful detail by Shakespeare. Special significance is attached to key concepts such as value and worth, saying and doing, or words and actions, in all their manifestations, epitomized by Martius' conception of hypocrisy:

> I will, sir, flatter my sworn brother the people, to earn a dearer esti-
> mation of them; 'tis a condition they account gentle; and since the
> wisdom of their choice is rather to have my hat than my heart, I will
> practise the insinuating nod, and be off to them most counterfeitly; that
> is, sir, I will counterfeit the bewitchment of some popular man, and
> give it bountiful to the desirers. Therefore, beseech you, I may be
> consul.
>
> (II.iii.94–102)

The movement and countermovement of sympathy is carefully structured, commencing with the dialogue between Menenius on the one side and Brutus and Sicinius on the other as they anticipate Martius' return. Before descending to the level of personal abuse they evaluate Martius (employing words like 'abundance' and 'poor' which run through the play like a leitmotif),

> MENENIUS In what enormity is Martius poor in, that you two have not
> in abundance?
> BRUTUS He's poor in no one fault, but stored with all.
> SICINIUS Especially in pride.
> BRUTUS And topping all others in boasting.
>
> (II.i.15–19)

There is no question of the tribunes giving Martius his due, and they are either malicious or obtuse in ascribing personal conceit or boasting to him – which his inability to stay to hear his deeds recounted before the Senators demonstrates:

> Your honours' pardon:
> I had rather have my wounds to heal again
> Than hear say how I got them.
> (II.ii.68–70)

Indeed, he plays down his actions, insisting that he cannot stay 'To hear my nothings monster'd' (II.ii.77). The ways in which news of his actions percolate through the city, and the unrestrained response, are carefully delineated, beginning with the excitement of Volumnia, Menenius and Virgilia. The former emphasizes the magnitude of Martius' achievements:

> The senate has letters from the general, wherein he gives my son the
> whole name of the war: he hath in this action outdone his former deeds
> doubly.
>
> (II.i.132–5)

She recounts to Menenius Martius' former achievements and victories, before celebrating his qualities with a chilling statement that checks audience enthusiasm for the hero:

> before him he
> Carries noise, and behind him he leaves tears:
> Death, that dark spirit, in's nervy arm doth lie,
> Which, being advanc'd, declines, and then men die.
> (II.i.157–60)

Martius enters to the sound of trumpets, the Herald's praise and the unrestrained welcome of the crowd (once more noise or sounds constitute a vital shaping force), to which he responds with great dignity and an acute sense of embarrassment:

No more of this; it does offend my heart.
Pray now, no more.

(II.i.167–8)

Noise gives way to stillness. On meeting his family he first kneels to his mother before turning to comfort his wife who is crying with joy:

My gracious silence, hail!
Wouldst thou have laugh'd had I come coffin'd home,
That weepst to see me triumph? Ah, my dear,
Such eyes the widows in Corioles wear,
And mothers that lack sons.

(II.i.174–8)

Here is one of the most telling speeches in the play: the grammatical shift in 'coffin'd' and the striking simile of eyes worn like ornaments hold the attention. The holding-up process, the jerking of consciousness, is calculated. The audience has partly surrendered to the relief of Virgilia on the safe return of Coriolanus, but Shakespeare deflects attention to the camp of the defeated: there the tears are of sorrow; there are the newly made widows and mothers without sons. And so it always is in war: for every victor there is a victim. The very values of war are laid open to question.

If the tribunes are wide of the mark in attributing boastfulness to Coriolanus, they are accurate with regard to his desire to please his mother. It is all the more remarkable, therefore, that when she expresses her wish that he be made consul for the fulfilment of her ambitions, he responds with great self-perception and without equivocation:

Know, good mother,
I had rather be their servant in my way
Than sway with them in theirs.

(II.i.200–2)

This is a critical juncture: Martius becomes vulnerable to the tribunes only when he enters the political arena. It is the moment when Martius is at the height of his prestige that the tribunes plan his downfall. Brutus provides a colourful picture, tinged with malice, of the whole of Rome pouring out to see him (and his very expressions reveal the tribunes' contempt for the common people):

Your prattling nurse
Into a rapture lets her baby cry
While she chats him. The kitchen malkin pins

194

Her richest lockram 'bout her rechy neck,
Clamb'ring the walls to eye him . . .
(II.i.204–8)

Brutus recognizes that if Martius gains the consulship their influence will count for nothing. However, Sicinius insists that Martius lacks the temperament to retain his office and that the common people will quickly forget his services when they are reminded of his antagonism towards them. Brutus takes comfort that Martius has sworn not to undertake the tradition of exposing his wounds to the populace to gain their support:

Nor showing (as the manner is) his wounds
To th'people, beg their stinking breaths.
(II.i.233–4)

And he goes on to reiterate Coriolanus' view of the people:

holding them,
In human action and capacity,
Of no more soul nor fitness for the world
Than camels in their war, who have their provand
Only for bearing burthens, and sore blows
For sinking under them.
(II.i.246–51)

After further reports of the hero-worship of Coriolanus, by nobility and people alike, Brutus and Sicinius decide to go to the Capitol,

And carry with us ears and eyes for th'time,
But hearts for the event.
(II.i.267–8)

Their comment provides one of the best examples of Shakespeare's continued play on eyes, ears, heart and tongues – the interplay between perceiving, feeling and speaking. What their dialogue highlights is concern with their personal offices: they exhibit no concern for the people whom they represent. Indeed, they show a positive contempt for the people, which spills out in their description of the 'kitchen malkin' with her 'rechy neck'. (Note Hamlet's contempt for a 'pair of rechy kisses' (III.iv.186).) Their natural facility for contriving contrasts with the exchange of the officers, who weigh up Martius' virtues and vices with complete honesty:

FIRST OFFICER That's a brave fellow; but he's vengeance proud, and loves not the common people.
SECOND OFFICER 'Faith, there hath been many great men that have flattered the people, who ne'er loved them; and there be many that they have loved, they know not wherefore: so that if they love they know not why, they hate upon no better a ground. Therefore, for

195

Coriolanus neither to care whether they love or hate him manifests the true knowledge he has in their disposition, and out of his noble carelessness lets them plainly see't.

FIRST OFFICER If he did not care whether he had their love or no, he waved indifferently 'twixt doing them neither good nor harm; but he seeks their hate with greater devotion than they can render it him, and leaves nothing undone that may fully discover him their opposite. Now to seem to affect the malice and displeasure of the people is as bad as that which he dislikes, to flatter them for their love.

SECOND OFFICER He hath *deserved worthily* of his country; and his *ascent* is not by such *easy degrees* as those who, having been *supple* and *courteous* to the people, *bonneted*, without any further *deed* to have them at all into their *estimation* and *report*; but he hath so *planted* his *honours* in their *eyes* and his *actions* in their *hearts*, that for their *tongues* to be *silent* and not confess so much were a kind of *ingrateful injury*. To report otherwise were a malice that, giving itself the lie, would pluck reproof and rebuke from every *ear* that *heard* it.

(II.ii.5–34; my italics)

Shakespeare here conveys a sense of the depth of the social universe, a feeling that issues and characters are discussed throughout the society, and frequently the greatest clarity of thought and expression comes from relatively minor characters who, untouched by political ambition or narrow factional advantage, are more dispassionate. The references to eyes, hearts, tongues and ears reinforce a feeling of animated discussion, disputation and assessment. The officers also contrast acheivement gained through insinuation and flattery with that gained by action. This is not to say that these minor characters are always right or that the truth is only to be found in such crevices: the Second Officer, for instance, is quite mistaken in his view that Martius consciously sets out to antagonize the people: he fails to understand that Martius can't help himself. In speaking his mind he merely articulates what his fellow patricians feel. Unlike them he has not learnt that it is impolitic always to speak what is felt. For him, not saying what he feels as forcefully as he can constitutes hypocrisy. What the First Officer perceives as a kind of perverseness has an explanation that he can't be expected to understand, but his failure does not arise from prejudice. In contrast, the tribunes have no interest in understanding Martius. They are prepared to place the worst interpretation on all his actions and flaws which make him vulnerable to their machinations. Audience sympathy for Martius, therefore, arises partly from the contempt felt for his political adversaries, the tribunes, rather than through any lack of sympathy with the people. On the contrary, in the interaction between

Martius and those whose voices he seeks it is difficult not to wince at his contemptuous behaviour towards common men, who are astonishingly generous in the face of continued provocation. The Third Citizen, while recognizing their power of veto, insists that in the light of Martius' service to the state they are morally obliged to support his bid for consulship:

> We have power in ourselves to do it, but it is a power that we have no power to do. For, if he show us his wounds and tell us his deeds, we are to put our tongues into those wounds and speak for them. So if he tell us his noble deeds, we must also tell him our noble acceptance of them. Ingratitude is monstrous, and for the multitude to be ingrateful, were to make a monster of the multitude; of the which we being members, should bring ourselves to be monstrous members.
>
> (II.iii.4–13)

But to make the customary appeal to these people is seen by Martius as a kind of hypocrisy that he will 'blush in acting':

> To brag unto them, thus I did, and thus,
> Show them th'unaching scars which I should hide,
> As if I had receiv'd them for the hire
> Of their breath only!
>
> (II.ii.145–50)

He is absolutely right. The last phrase perfectly conveys his evaluation of them and the absurdity of the required action. For him they are not *Romans*, and he has not fought on their behalf even though he fought alongside them. In fact, the hypocrisy is doubled as far as he is concerned by virtue of the fact that they failed to fight like Romans. As he expresses the point:

> What must I say? –
> 'I pray, sir,' – Plague upon't! I cannot bring
> My tongue to such a pace. 'Look, sir, my wounds!
> I got them in my country's service, when
> Some certain of your brethren roar'd and ran
> From th'noise of our own drums.'
>
> (II.iii.51–6)

Running right through these exchanges is a contrast between words, deeds and values: Martius cannot market his wounds like a merchant. When requested by Menenius to address them in 'wholesome manner' his riposte is characteristic: 'Bid them wash their faces,/And keep their teeth clean' (II.iii.62–3). Embodied in these lines is all the aristocratic sense of superiority and arrogance that pervades Shakespeare's Roman worlds. By viewing the lower orders as contemptible (and their dirtiness is a fundamental expression of their inferiority) there is no need to feel uncomfortable about the disparity in resources, privileges and opportunities enjoyed by these groups. Significantly, Martius has to descend to the market place to seek the support of the plebeians (he also suffers the indignity of being put to death in the market place of an alien country). Perceiving such a place as bereft of honourable actions, he talks in terms of impersonal and tainted transactions: 'Well then, I pray, your *price* o'th' consulship?' The reply is a total denial of his implied evaluation of the people and tilts the balance of audience sympathy sharply in their favour: 'The price is, to ask it kindly.' (II.iii.74–5). Even after Martius' contemptuous behaviour the plebeians give him their support and withdraw it only after the persistent and calculating manipulation of the tribunes.

Although he is brutally callous and unfeeling in his behaviour towards the plebeians, Martius retains some audience sympathy, which had previously been built up by his demeanour in the Senate and by Cominius' powerful description of his service to Rome:

> For this last,
> Before and in Corioles, let me say
> I cannot speak him home. He stopp'd the fliers,
> And by his rare example made the coward
> Turn terror into sport; as weeds before
> A vessel under sail, so men obey'd
> And fell below his stem: his sword, death's stamp,
> Where it did mark, it took; from face to foot
> He was a thing of blood, whose every motion
> Was tim'd with dying cries: alone he enter'd
> The mortal gate of th'city, which he painted
> With shunless destiny, aidless came off,
> And with a sudden reinforcement struck
> Corioles like a planet. Now all's his;
> When by and by the din of war gan pierce
> His ready sense, then straight his doubled spirit
> Requicken'd what in flesh was fatigate,
> And to the battle came he, where he did
> Run reeking o'er the lives of men, as if
> 'Twere a perpetual spoil; and till we call'd
> Both field and city ours, he never stood
> To ease his breast with panting.

$$\text{(II.ii.101–22)}$$

Here is the image of the superhuman, the embodiment of the supreme Roman value of physical courage and fortitude. Cominius generously acknowledges that Martius is a man apart, he entered the enemy city 'alone', he was a 'thing' and struck the city 'like a planet'; his 'every motion/Was tim'd with dying cries' is a terrifying image; his actions are redoubled in response to 'the din of war'. Moreover, his actions, Cominius claims, constitute pure service, without any thought for reward. His description conveys a clear sense of Martius towering above the petty aspirations of ordinary mortals. It is an assertion of his integrity:

> Our spoils he kick'd at,
> And look'd upon things precious as they were
> The common muck of the world. He covets less
> Than misery itself would give, rewards
> His deeds with doing them, and is content
> To spend the time to end it.
>
> (II.ii.124–9)

It is the *action* of Martius, his *doing*, which contrasts so vividly with the mean-spirited tribunes who work with words to control the actions of others – who, it is felt, would cram their pockets with spoils, and are ruthless in their quest for political power.

The contrast between the persistent, calculating guile of the tribunes and Martius' open contempt for the people is brought into sharp focus in Act III scene i. Here, where there is a great emphasis on speech – 'words', 'voices', 'tongues', 'mouths' – Martius is unstinting in denigrating the people and their tribunes. The mere sight of Sicinius and Brutus causes him to denounce them as the 'tongues o'th'common mouth' (III.i.22). Once Martius is informed that the support which he received from the people has been withdrawn, his contempt is mingled with indignation so that, with the careful manoeuvring of the tribunes, he builds up to a tempest of rage:

> Are these your herd?
> Must these have voices, that can yield them now
> And straight disclaim their tongues? What are your offices?
> You being their mouths, why rule you not their teeth?
> Have you not set them on?
>
> (III.i.32–6)

The plebeians are reduced to the level of beasts, their inconstancy invoked to show that they are unfit to have a voice in decision-making. Even when Martius suspects that they are being manipulated by the tribunes he still sees them as dogs that have been 'set on'. Despite Menenius' repeated attempts to calm him and to make him desist from speaking, Martius eagerly takes the bait offered by Brutus:

> For the mutable, rank-scented meinie, let them
> Regard me as I do not flatter, and
> Therein behold themselves. I say again,
> In soothing them, we nourish 'gainst our senate

The cockle of rebellion, insolence, sedition,
Which we ourselves have plough'd for, sow'd and scatter'd,
By mingling them with us, the honour'd number
Who lack not virtue, no, nor power, but that
Which they have given to beggars.

(III.i.65–73)

One of the surprising features of this speech, in which Martius moves from a justification of his own bluntness to direct opposition to constitutional reforms, is that he employs a metaphor drawn from agriculture. Why does Shakespeare do this? Is it in order to show that at one level of his consciousness the great warrior recognizes the worth of agricultural activity but cannot consciously accept that evaluation because it would constitute a severe challenge to his conception of society and the relative merits of labour and fighting? Martius cannot be dismissed as a fool or knave. He displays a devastatingly powerful logic within the confines of his social vision and the ethos which he has absorbed. None of his family or his associates ever attempt to tell him he is wrong. They only say that he should not speak his mind. After the speech just quoted Menenius says, 'Well, no more', and is supported by the First Senator who adds, 'No more words, we beseech you' (III.i.73–4). But so sure is Martius of his rightness that his indignation swells even higher, employing the disease imagery which is so potent in this scene. For once, the response of Brutus seems spontaneous rather than a calculated gibe:

You speak o'th'people
As if you were a god to punish, not
A man of their infirmity.

(III.i.79–81)

Menenius' attempt to pass off Martius' speech as merely 'choler' drives him to intensify his attack. Sicinius' assertion of authority leaves him gasping in disbelief:

SICINIUS   It is a mind
That shall remain a poison where it is,
Not poison any further.
CORIOLANUS   Shall remain!
Hear you this Triton of the minnows? Mark you
His absolute 'shall'?

(III.i.85–9)

Taking up Sicinius' reference to poison, Martius continues his spiral of invective in a speech which insists on the folly of shared power. His most vivid expression compacts references to the contemptible nature of the multitude, speaking (the quality that ought to be reserved for the noble as opposed to the beastly), eating and disease:

> at once pluck out
> The multitudinous tongue: let them not lick
> The sweet which is their poison.
>   (III.i.154–6)

In a scene in which the patricians have struggled in vain to stop Martius speaking, it is the tribunes who feel able to insist that he "Has said enough'. The point has been reached where they can legitimately make the ultimate charge against him: he is a 'traitor' (III.i.160–1). From this point on, words give way to actions as an attempt is made to arrest Martius. The balance of power shifts dramatically. In the middle of the uproar it is the tribunites who are bid by the plebeians to 'Speak, speak, speak!' (III.i.191). Sicinius' rhetorical question 'What is the city but the people?' receives immediate affirmation by the plebeians: 'True,/The people are the city' (III.i.197–8). The question is no longer one of whether the common people should have a voice in the government of the city, but rather there is an assertion that the people constitute the *essence* of the society. It is the patricians who are peripheral. Only minutes later Martius continues to insist that they are not truly Romans, but a sort of bastard citizenry (simultaneously giving expression to his sense of them as animal rather than human):

> I would they were barbarians – as they are,
> Though in Rome litter'd; not Romans – as they are not,
> Though calv'd i'th'porch o'th'Capitol.
>   (III.i.236–8)

Even at this point in the crisis he has no sense of political reality. The desperate Menenius recognizes that 'this must be patch'd/With cloth of any colour', while a patrician recognizes that the issue now is one of saving Rome, not Martius: 'This man has marr'd his fortune' (III.i.250–2). That single line carries within it all the political awareness and personal detachment of the ruling group. Martius is expendable. Menenius, perhaps equally astute, is not as detached and can only try to exculpate his 'son':

> His nature is too noble for the world:
> He would not flatter Neptune for his trident,
> Or Jove for's power to thunder. His heart's his mouth:
> What his breast forges, that his tongue must vent;
> And being angry, does forget that ever
> He heard the name of death.
>   (III.i.253–8)

Even Menenius, however, gives way to anger at Martius' inability to

play the hypocrite: 'What the vengeance,/Could he not speak 'em fair?'
(III.i.260–1). Moreover, the character who was able to restrain and control
the angry mob by means of the fable of the belly in the opening scene of
the play is now reduced to the position where he has to 'crave a word or
two' (III.i.280) and later to plead for 'One word more, one word'
(III.i.308). Likewise, he is drawn into acceptance of Sicinius' description
of Martius' diseased state:

> SICINIUS He's a disease that must be cut away.
> MENENIUS Oh, he's a limb that has but a disease:
>   Mortal, to cut it off; to cure it, easy.
> (III.i.292–4)

The metaphor of disease is continued in their ensuing dialogue but switches
to food when Sicinius complains,

> Have we not had a taste of his obedience?
> Our aediles smote? ourselves resisted? Come.
> (III.i.315–16)

Menenius' feeble response is to insist that Martius, being merely a soldier,
virtually from his cradle, misrepresents himself because he

>   is ill school'd
> In bolted language; meal and bran together
> He throws without distinction.
> (III.i.318–20)

The concession he secures is a postponement of any action against Martius
until he appears to defend himself in the 'market-place' – the venue that
is so alien to the aristocratic warrior and is the setting for his disgrace in
Rome and his murder in Corioles.

As the political temperature rises Martius is confronted by his mother,
his friends and a Senator, all pleading with him to defuse the political
crisis by pretending to be repentant and conciliatory. Volumnia goes so
far as to coach her son in handling the plebeians:

>   I prithee now, my son,
> Go to them, with this bonnet in thy hand,
> And thus far having stretch'd it – here be with them –
> Thy knee bussing the stones – for in such business
> Action is eloquence, and the eyes of th' ignorant
> More learned than the ears – waving thy head,
> Which often, thus, correcting thy stout heart,
> Now humble as the ripest mulberry
> That will not hold the handling; or say to them,
> Thou art their soldier, and being bred in broils,

202

Hast not the soft way which, thou dost confess,
Were fit for thee to use, as they to claim,
In asking their good loves; but thou wilt frame
Thyself, forsooth, hereafter theirs, so far
As thou hast power and person.

(III.ii.72–86)

Her description shows Volumnia to be a consummate politician as she emphasizes the significance of gesture and employs the wonderful simile of the 'ripest mulberry' to reveal that delicacy of touch which is the hallmark of the *political* manipulator. Menenius is confident of a favourable outcome if Martius can follow the directions precisely, because he recognizes the 'good' qualities of the common people – their naivety and generosity of spirit which leave them open to exploitation:

This but done,
Even as she speaks, why, their hearts were yours:
For they have pardons, being ask'd, as free
As words to little purpose.

(III.ii.86–9)

Before this point has been reached, however, Martius has already criticized his mother for not supporting his recalcitrant position. In a crucial speech he conveys a clear picture of his upbringing. His contempt for the plebeians has been *learnt*; his class pride has been *absorbed* from his mother:

I muse my mother
Does not approve me further, who was wont
To call them woollen vassals, things created
To buy and sell with groats, to show bare heads
In congregations, to yawn, be still, and wonder,
When one but of my ordinance stood up
To speak of peace or war. I talk of you.
Why did you wish me milder? Would you have me
False to my nature? Rather say I play
The man I am.

(III.ii.7–16)

In the face of this perfectly justified complaint the best Volumnia can do is to make a belated attempt to inculcate hypocrisy. Such hypocrisy is justified, she claims, when the existence of a whole social order is at stake. Her appeal to Martius is not merely to play the hypocrite but to play the patriotic hypocrite:

Because that now it lies you on to speak
To th'people; not by your own instruction,

203

Nor by th'matter which your heart prompts you,
But with such words that are but roted in
Your tongue, though but bastards and syllables
Of no allowance to your bosom's truth . . .
I would dissemble with my nature where
My fortunes and my friends at stake requir'd
I should do so in honour. I am in this
Your wife, your son, these senators, the nobles . . .

(III.ii.52–65)

There is a disjunction between words and meaning, heart and tongue: the warrior must display the skills of the actor. When Martius reacts to Menenius' request that he 'Repent what you have spoke' with the revealing phrase, 'For them? I cannot do it to the gods' (III.ii.37–8), it is clear that no amount of persuasion would be effective. Volumnia achieves a seeming victory not by persuasion, but by the withdrawal of her love. Before he submits, however, Martius perceptively protests:

You have put me now to such a part which never
I shall discharge to th'life.

(III.ii.105–6)

Moreover, he reveals an intuitive awareness of the connection between his sense of social superiority and singularity and his potency as a fighter:

I will not do't,
Lest I surcease to honour mine own truth,
And by my body's action teach my mind
A most inherent baseness.

(III.ii.120–3)

Whereas for Volumnia gesture can be employed as a potent weapon against the simple-minded, Martius perceives it as spiritually corrupting. Having placed her son in an impossible position by persuading him to stand for Consul, Volumnia now attempts to go against a lifetime of training in order to rescue the political situation. The final denunciation of her son, which brings about his attempted compliance, is a falsehood:

Thy valiantness was mine, thou suck'st it from me,
But owe thy pride thyself.

(III.ii.129–30)

She claims too much and too little. She *created* the man-child-warrior through the inculcation of singlemindedness and narrowly confined values. The training created the supreme warrior but left him fatally vulnerable in the wider society and especially in the political arena. The hero of Rome is simultaneously the enemy of the people. His conception of society and social worth is so narrow that his creativity has been crushed. Here is a powerful suggestion of an incompatibility between the training of the warrior and the education of a human being. It is not only Volumnia but her whole social class who are found wanting. Their political adjustment is confined to hypocrisy and manoeuvring. They show no sign of responding creatively to the demands of the plebeians. They practise expediency not compassion.

If Martius is the victim of his upbringing, the plebeians are victims of their newly acquired tribunes. Brutus and Sicinius plan every move in advance and manipulate the people they represent. They clearly have little choice but to neutralize Martius politically because he represents a fundamental opposition to their retention of political rights, but they exceed that aim by a wide margin and revel in the defeat and humiliation of their old adversary. Their cynicism in the preparation of Martius' 'trial' and their orchestration of the plebeians is wholly repugnant. Set against these vile politicians Martius' integrity shines like a star.

In setting out accusations against Martius, Brutus resorts to a charge that is patently false and another that is dredged up (the audience has heard nothing of this matter previously):

> In this point charge him home, that he affects
> Tyrannical power. If he evade us there,
> Enforce him with his envy to the people,
> And that the spoil got on the Antiates
> Was ne'er distributed.
>
> (III.iii.1–5)

Brutus makes 'assurance double sure' by advising his associates to 'Put him to choler straight', knowing that

> Being once chaf'd, he cannot
> Be rein'd again to temperance; then he speaks
> What's in his heart, and that is there which looks
> With us to break his neck.
>
> (III.iii.27–30)

In the event the charges are not seriously debated. As the body imagery so effectively conveys, once Brutus denounces Martius as 'traitor', he achieves the very outburst he desires. When his friends try to restrain him, Martius, employing the imagery of the market place, brushes aside their plea, insisting, 'I would not buy/Their mercy at the price of one fair word' (III.iii.90–1). His final speech of the scene possesses the force and sting of a whiplash:

> You common cry of curs! whose breath I hate
> As reek o'th'rotten fens, whose loves I prize

As the dead carcasses of unburied men
That do corrupt my air: I banish you!
(III.iii.120–3)

That final phrase epitomizes his conception of his singleness, his aloneness: he is no mere citizen of Rome: he is the planet and Rome the satellite because he alone is the complete embodiment of Roman values. As he turns his back on the city he genuinely believes that 'There is a world elsewhere!' (III.iii.135). What the desolation of exile does is to show him that even he is not the world unto himself and that there is no social universe waiting to attach itself to him. He has to creep into the enemy city like a beggar and offer his services – and this is not at all what he imagines when he makes his defiant cry. Nor does it seem that he is merely attempting to cheer up his friends and family when he assures them 'I shall be lov'd when I am lack'd' (IV.i.15). The warrior is not required and therefore not missed until there is war or the danger of war. Intuitively he senses something of the isolation he is to endure, and expresses it in a powerful and revealing image:

I go alone,
Like to a lonely dragon that his fen
Makes fear'd and talk'd of more than seen . . .
(IV.i.29–31)

It is one of the ironies of the play that the man who is the embodiment of Roman values and aristocratic pride is also an outsider. In battle his singularity is manifest – he is courageous beyond all reason; in peace this singularity constitutes a threat to his own social class and to the social unity of Rome because of his inability to accept and display the commonplace hypocrisies of his society. If, however, he were able to act out the subtle social subterfuges which come so naturally to Menenius he would not be the superman on the battlefield. The supreme warrior must possess a purity of spirit, a belief that he embodies and incarnates the very best that his society stands for. Martius' little aside in comforting his mother reveals a great deal about the way in which he has absorbed precepts and principles from the cradle:

You were us'd to load me
With precepts that would make invincible
The heart that conn'd them.
(IV.i.9–11)

When Martius fails to stoop it is not because he is obdurate but because, as he says – 'Lest I surcease to honour mine own truth' (III.ii.121) – it will corrupt him. His social vision does not allow him to seek the favours of the plebeians. His social limitation is the concomitant of his heroic stature. When it becomes a matter of preserving the society, and the place of the patricians in it, the hero must be sacrificed. It is this sense of betrayal as much as the pain of social ostracism that leads Martius to a burning desire for revenge. Recognition of the integrated nature of the society is given expression both by Sicinius and Martius. The former replies to Volumnia's verbal assault by claiming that,

> I would he had continued to his country
> As he began, and not unknit himself
> The noble knot he made.
>
> (IV.ii.30–2)

while the latter bewails the strange twist of circumstances that disjoins long-established friendships and turns enemies to 'dear friends/And inter-join their issues' (IV.iv.21–2).

The whole movement of the action from Martius' entry to Antium (IV.v) and his embracement by Aufidius, to the latter's secret denunciation of him (IV.vii) displays a fascinating process of new alliances, embryonic tensions and dissolutions. Aufidius has to ask Martius his name six times before he discovers the identity of the stranger. In accounting for his presence at Aufidius' hearth Martius provides a vivid description of his sense of betrayal by his 'thankless country' which has deprived him of everything but the name Coriolanus:

> Only that name remains.
> The cruelty and envy of the people,
> Permitted by our dastard nobles, who
> Have all forsook me, hath devour'd the rest;
> And suffer'd me by th'voice of slaves to be
> Whoop'd out of Rome.
>
> (IV.v.74–9)

The sense of betrayal by the 'dastard nobles' and defilement by being 'Whoop'd out of Rome' gather up into a hatred of his 'canker'd country' so that he is ready to fight on behalf of those from whom he has 'Drawn tuns of blood'. He has bled for Rome and has bled the Volsces: now he will reverse the process, 'pouring war/Into the bowels of ungrateful Rome' (IV.v.91–131), as Aufidius expresses it. The latter recalls fighting with Coriolanus in his dreams:

> Thou hast beat me out
> Twelve several times, and I have nightly since
> Dreamt of encounters 'twixt thyself and me –
> We have been down together in my sleep,
> Unbuckling helms, fisting each other's throat –
> And wak'd half dead with nothing.
>
> (IV.v.122–7)

But now, astonishingly, he describes a love for his ancient enemy that equals the greatest emotion he has ever felt (drawing on a comparison previously used by Martius and Volumnia):

> I lov'd the maid I married; never man
> Sigh'd truer breath; but that I see thee here,
> Thou noble thing, more dances my rapt heart
> Than when I first my wedded mistress saw
> Bestride my threshold. Why, thou Mars!
> (IV.v.115–19)

Concluding his speech with the glowing lines:

> A thousand welcomes!
> And more a friend than e'er an enemy –
> Yet, Martius, that was much! Your hand: most welcome!
> (IV.v.146–8)

The serving men in reporting the news immediately indulge in comparisons between the warriors – and are unequivocal in pronouncing the superiority of Coriolanus:

SECOND SERVANT He is simply the rarest man i'th'world.
FIRST SERVANT I think he is: but a greater soldier than he, you wot on.
SECOND SERVANT Who? my master?
FIRST SERVANT Nay, it's no matter for that.
SECOND SERVANT Worth six on him.
FIRST SERVANT Nay, not so neither: but I take him to be the greater
    soldier.
> (IV.v.163–71)

Even while the new alliance is being forged in Antium, future rivalry and conflict is suggested. In Rome there is calm, and a surprising binding of factions, which is revealed in the dialogue between the tribunes and Menenius. On observing the approach of the latter Sicinius turns to his colleague with a comment,

SICINIUS 'Tis he, 'tis he. Oh, he is grown most kind
    Of late. Hail, sir!
MENENIUS   Hail to you both!
SICINIUS Your Coriolanus is not much miss'd
    But with his friends: the commonwealth doth stand,
    And so would do, were he more angry at it.
MENENIUS All's well, and might have been much better if
    He could have temporiz'd.
> (IV.vi.11–17)

The last comment is just, but savours of betrayal, for it involves an implicit condemnation of Martius – especially as the one quality he lacks, the ability to temporize, is the very quality which would have prevented him becoming the supreme warrior. Martius is not exclusively to blame. There is a fatal flaw in the body politic which creates a military superman and then fails to confine him to that sphere. This dialogue is immediately followed by a scene of social harmony and tranquillity, which indicates that a new political equilibrium has been achieved. Yet the tribunes feel a need to present an account of recent history which is false:

> BRUTUS   Caius Martius was
> A worthy officer i'th'war, but insolent,
> O'ercome with pride, ambitious past all thinking,
> Self-loving.
> SICINIUS   And affecting one sole throne,
> Without assistance.

Menenius knows this to be untrue but he merely responds: 'I think not so' (IV.vi.29–33). Evidently, he does not wish to disrupt the accommodation that has been achieved. This brief exchange in itself reveals Shakespeare's awareness of the questionable nature of historical accounts: rigorous pursuit of the truth gives way to political expediency.

The new accord quickly disintegrates as news arrives of Martius' impending assault on Rome. Indeed, Cominius' insistence that the consequence of the tribunes' action will be 'To melt the city leads upon your pates' embodies a sense of physical dissolution – which he reinforces in his prediction of the 'temples burned in their cement' (IV.vi.83 and 86). When Menenius implies some doubt about the veracity of the news Cominius provides a picture of Coriolanus at the head of his new army which is terrifying in its solidity and power:

> He is their god. He leads them like a thing
> Made by some other deity than nature,
> That shapes man better; and they follow him
> Against us brats, with no less confidence
> Than boys pursuing summer butterflies,
> Or butchers killing flies.
>   (IV.vi.91–6)

This is enough to smash the infant alliance and to produce an explosion of recriminations starting with Menenius who gives full vent to his patrician contempt for the people:

>   You have made good work,
> You, and your apron-men; you that stood so much

Upon the voice of occupation and
The breath of garlic-eaters!
(IV.vi.96–9)

As Cominius draws a vivid picture of the impending destruction of 'trembling' Rome, Menenius grows ever more animated in his denunciation of the 'beasts' and 'clusters', reaching a climax with language that would do credit to Coriolanus himself:

You are they
That made the air unwholesome when you cast
Your stinking greasy caps in hooting at
Coriolanus' exile.
(IV.vi.130–3)

In responding to the news and a verbal lashing the plebeians reveal their innate tendency to change their minds, doing so in a way which reveals their naivety as well as their lack of constancy:

FIRST CITIZEN   For mine own part,
　　When I said banish him, I said 'twas pity.
SECOND CITIZEN And so did I.
THIRD CITIZEN And so did I; and, to say the truth, so did very many of
　　us. That we did we did for the best, and though we willingly
　　consented to his banishment, yet it was against our will.
(IV.vi.140–6)

Ironically, one of Cominius' comments designed to indicate the awesome power of Coriolanus also exposes a potential weakness in that alliance:

Tullus Aufidius,
The second name of men, obeys his points
As if he were his officer.
(IV.vi.125–7)

This 'problem' is fully articulated in the next scene where Aufidius' Lieutenant warns:

Your soldiers use him as the grace 'fore meat,
Their talk at table and their thanks at end;
And you are darken'd in this action, sir,
Even by your own.
(IV.vii.3–6)

Aufidius recognizes the necessity of keeping Coriolanus at the head of affairs but states unequivocally that he is already planning the downfall of his new ally:

I understand thee well, and be thou sure
When he shall come to his account, he knows not
What I can urge against him. Although it seems,
And so he thinks, and is no less apparent
To th'vulgar eye, that he bears all things fairly
And shows good husbandry for the Volscian state,
Fights dragon-like, and does achieve as soon
As draw his sword: yet he hath left undone
That which shall break his neck or hazard mine
Whene'er we come to our account.

                              (IV.vii.17–26)

And here Shakespeare presents a sharp contrast between the two warriors.
Aufidius is reflective, introspective and politically aware; Coriolanus is
intuitive and devoid of political insight or guile. After an assessment of
the situation in Rome, Aufidius predicts the outcome of the conflict and
attempts to analyse the reasons for Martius' 'failure':

              I think he'll be to Rome
As is the osprey to the fish, who takes it
By sovereignty of nature. First, he was
A noble servant to them, but he could not
Carry his honours even. Whether 'twas pride,
Which out of daily fortune ever taints
The happy man; whether defect of judgement,
To fail in the disposing of those chances
Which he was lord of; or whether nature,
Not to be other than one thing, not moving
From th'casque to th'cushion, but commanding peace
Even with the same austerity and garb
As he controll'd the war; but one of these –
As he hath spices of them all, not all,
For I dare so far free him – made him fear'd,
So hated, and so banish'd: but he has a merit
To choke it in the utt'rance. So our virtues
Lie in th'interpretation of the time,

                              (IV.vii.33–50)

Aufidius is perplexed, but unlike the tribunes is genuinely seeking to
understand why Coriolanus found himself in such sharp conflict with his
own countrymen. He doesn't have the answer but his suggestions impinge
on significant aspects of the problem. His final comment, however, reveals
a major contrast between himself and Coriolanus: Aufidius can interpret
the time; he can think himself into the political situation and manoeuvre
accordingly. He has the mix of qualities that equip him for the battlefield

and the political arena. Nevertheless, he lacks the enormous potency and energy of Martius, and his integrity, too.

The smallness of Aufidius' stature in comparison with Martius is brought out clearly in the closing scene of the play. As he enters his native city Aufidius gives instructions for the denunciation and murder of Martius in the market-place. In this discussion with the three senators Aufidius recognizes that he can regain prominence only by bringing down his rival. He then sets out the case against Martius – the essence of which is that he treated his former enemy with the generosity of a friend only to have his own men seduced by Martius' wiles; he was himself relegated to the status of a mercenary; and finally, victory over the Romans was snatched away at the last moment. No sooner have these plausible complaints been rehearsed than Martius enters the city to the thunderous approval of the people (as happened earlier in Rome), provoking the First Consul to comment:

> Your native town you enter'd like a post,
> And had no welcomes home; but he returns
> Splitting the air with noise.
>
> (V.vi.50–2)

Aufidius opens his assault on Martius by denouncing him as 'traitor' (just as the tribunes had done in Rome). He then drives his adversary into a fury by ridiculing the tearful submission to his mother so that 'pages blush'd at him'. Martius gasps with disbelief, uttering the words 'Hear'st thou, Mars?' Aufidius then makes the vital thrust: 'Name not the god, thou boy of tears!' (V.vi.99–101). The gibe, which challenges Martius' manhood, drives him into a frenzy which causes him to remind his auditors of the dreadful carnage he has inflicted on them:

> Cut me to pieces, Volsces, men and lads,
> Stain all your edges on me. Boy! False hound!
> If you have writ your annals true, 'tis there,
> That like an eagle in a dove-cote, I
> Flutter'd your Volscians in Corioles.
> Alone I did it. Boy!
>
> (V.vi.111–16)

As it was in Rome, the defeat of Martius is prearranged. Aufidius' allies and co-conspirators set up the cry, 'Kill, kill, kill, kill, kill him!' (V.vi.130). After the murder the Second Lord expresses what seems to be the majority feeling when he upbraids Aufidius with the words 'Thou hast done a deed whereat valour will weep' (V.vi.132). Aufidius responds to the chastisement with apparent humility and sorrow, striking precisely the right note to re-establish his position of prominence:

> My rage is gone,
> And I am struck with sorrow. Take him up.
> Help, three o'th'chiefest soldiers. I'll be one.
> Beat thou the drum that it speak mournfully;
> Trail your steel pikes. Though in this city he
> Hath widow'd and unchilded many a one,
> Which to this hour bewail the injury,
> Yet he shall have a noble memory.
>
> (V.vi.146–53)

Whereas Plutarch's Aufidius ensures that Coriolanus does not have the opportunity of addressing the people lest he persuade them to support him, Shakespeare's Aufidius provokes him into an outburst which produces an explosion of anger and facilitates the murder. The brutal deed accomplished, Aufidius accepts the gown of humility and leads the funeral procession. A.C. Bradley's response is:

> the unspeakable baseness of his sneer at the hero's tears is an injury to the final effect. Such an emotion as mere disgust is out of place in a tragic close; but I confess I feel nothing but disgust as Aufidius speaks the last words, except some indignation with the poet who allowed him to speak them, and an unregenerate desire to see the head and body of the speaker lying on opposite sides of the stage.[58]

Bradley, who makes many insightful comments on the play, evidently feels that Shakespeare disrupts the mood appropriate to the climax of tragedy. In making this objection he is trying to fit this play into his conception of the essential nature of Shakespearian tragedy. However, this 'defect' is crucial because Shakespeare is showing the triumph of the temporizer, the rationalizer, the near superman who is endowed with those very qualities which Coriolanus lacks. Coriolanus' greatness finds a reflection in Aufidius' smallness, a character who is much more sympathetic than Bradley allows. Aufidius is a great warrior but is not possessed by a passion that causes him to stretch every sinew of his body on behalf of his society. He has a wider perspective, he is a man of the world; here is an outstanding leader, but not one who will achieve immortality – or tragic stature. If Bradley was misguided in seeking a different kind of tragedy from the one Shakespeare provides, O.J. Campbell is surely much more wrongheaded in his assessment when he claims:

> Shakespeare did not attempt to give *Coriolanus* the structure of a conventional tragedy. Neither in his presentation of the central figure nor in his construction of the plot does he follow orthodox tragic principles. Instead of enlisting our sympathy for Coriolanus, he deliberately alienates it. Indeed he makes the figure partly an object of scorn. Instead of ennobling Coriolanus through his fall and death, he mocks and

ridicules him to the end. In brief, he fills the tragedy so full of the spirit of derision that the play can be understood only if it be recognised as perhaps the most successful of Shakespeare's satiric plays.[59]

One of the key questions that is intimately related to this issue of genre is that of why Caius Martius Coriolanus succumbs to the pleas of his family. Is it love of family or love of Rome? Alexander Leggatt argues that

In surrendering to his family, Coriolanus is confronting and admitting the truth of his own nature. The ultimate appeal has been, I think, not to his capacity to love but to his honesty, his refusal to play a part. We saw that honesty shaken in the political scenes, and in his first reaction to the family we see him fighting against it. It is worth noting that in all of Volumnia's long speech the barb that finally sticks is

This fellow had a Volscian to his mother;
His wife is in Corioles, and his child
Like him by chance.

(V.iii.178–80)

'His child/Like him by chance', with its sarcastic double reality, exposes what the rest of the passage makes implicit: that Coriolanus is living a lie.[60]

Given that Martius is undergoing an inner conflict from the moment he sets eyes on his approaching family it is difficult to be sure precisely which feeling finally sways him. But Leggatt is surely right in suggesting that Martius ultimately perceives the falsity of his position. The thirst for revenge is assuaged during the course of Volumnia's appeal, and he sees himself as a potential murderer of his literal mother, Volumnia, and his spiritual mother, Rome. Rome has failed its greatest warrior but he recognizes the impiety of 'tearing/His country's bowels out' (V.iii.102–3). The patriot, the loving son, husband and father is in a false position, and he is not capable of being false to his nature – that nature which is tough and inflexible, but has been nurtured in the crucible of Rome – a society that is supremely sure of its worth and unrelenting in its articulation and transmission of values. Coriolanus is the supreme product of this culture, the physical embodiment of *romanitas*. His tragedy is that he attains greatness at the very moment the society is experiencing the process of change. Thus only by recognizing the powerful political and historical dimensions of the play is it possible to comprehend its tragic power.

The inability to recognize that Coriolanus is a victim of his culture has led many critics to suggest that he fails to attract sympathy and even that the play itself is a failure. Maurice Charney comments that the play 'has not only not attracted critics, but it has seemed to represent an exhaustion

of Shakespeare's powers', and goes on to add, 'Coriolanus is an unreflec-
tive man of action. His tragedy is massive and overwhelming, almost like
fate, and it does not touch us very personally'.[61] Willard Farnham argues
that 'He is monstrously deficient as a human being, and his deficiency is
the more unfortunate because it tends not to foster pity for him but to
destroy any that we might give him'. He also connects this withdrawal of
sympathy to a weakness in the play, 'The deeply flawed Coriolanus who
repels pity is too deeply flawed for Shakespeare's tragic purposes'. He
concludes, '*Coriolanus* is a magnificent failure in which Shakespeare seems
to have brought his tragic inspiration to an end by taking tragedy into an
area of paradox beyond the effective reach of merely human pity'.[62] In
the light of the foregoing analysis it is difficult to accept these judgments or
the more trenchantly expressed view of Günter Grass in the introduction to
his own play, *The Plebeians Rehearse the Uprising*:

> It is not the all too familiar ambiguity of the hero that has stood in the
> way of this play from the first; rather it is his brutal outrightness that
> sets him between plebeian and patrician and prevents him from arousing
> the faintest sympathy or applause in either a proletarian or a conserva-
> tive audience. What even a monster like Richard III succeeds in making
> us believe – namely, that his daemon drives him to give us the shudders
> and so entertain us – the earthly and unintellectual Coriolanus fails to
> accomplish in a single scene. And even his few virtues, such as his
> modesty, his unwillingness to show the plebeians his wounds and scars,
> his selfless bravery, are obscured by his compulsion, whenever he
> encounters a plebeian, to proclaim his truth.[63]

During the course of this discussion some attention has been devoted
to such fundamental dichotomies as words/deeds, speech/gesture, tender-
ness/violence, moral worth/market value, and to the imagery of body
parts, food, animals and disease. It is necessary to emphasize, however,
that throughout the play there is a complex interplay between sounds,
gestures, words and deeds, speech and action. The opening scene reverberates with the sound of rebellion; the play closes to the sound of the dead
march as the hero's body is borne off. In between, Coriolanus is constantly
surrounded by noise: in battle (Cominius describes how 'the din of war
gan pierce/His ready sense' (II.ii.115–16)), in triumph as the trumpets
announce his return to Rome, and in the riots which attend his appearances before the people and culminate in him being 'Whoop'd out of
Rome' (IV.v.79); in parallel scenes he steals silently into Antium but
enters his adopted city in the final scene to a welcome that splits 'the air
with noise' (V.vi.52) – only to be struck down moments later to the shouts
of 'Tear him to pieces!' and 'Kill, kill, kill, kill, kill him!' (V.vi.120–30).
During the brief interlude after his banishment, while his friends and
family 'Hear nothing from him' the tradesmen are 'singing in their shops'

(IV.vi.8–19). The women are greeted, on returning to Rome, by a tremendous cacophony:

> The trumpets, sackbuts, psalteries and fifes,
> Tabors and cymbals and the shouting Romans
> Make the sun dance.
>
> (V.iv.50–2)

They are welcomed home with the words, 'Unshout the noise that banish'd Martius' (V.v.4).

The silences are as pronounced as the noises, reaching a climax with the stage direction 'Holds her by the hand silent' (V.iii.182) as Coriolanus succumbs to his mother's appeal. Here silence and gesture are intimately connected. Likewise the man of action can't endure to hear his praises spoken. The waves of noise and eddies of silence form a vital part of the landscape of the play. Perhaps the inspiration for this perception came from Plutarch's description of Martius in battle:

> For he was even such another, as Cato would have a souldier and a captaine to be: not only terrible, and fierce to laye about him, but to make the enemie afeard with the sounde of his voyce, and grimnes of his countenaunce.[64]

If so, this little acorn certainly produced a giant oak, because noise pervades the play in the form of shouts and instruments, and through suggestions such as the reference to Martius' son, who prefers to 'hear a drum, than look upon his schoolmaster' (I.iii.55–6). However, the speech which most effectively brings together the sense of the significance of sound and its relationship to gesture is delivered by Coriolanus when he contemplates bowing his nature in accordance with his mother's request:

> Well, I must do't.
> Away my disposition, and possess me
> Some harlot's spirit! My throat of war be turn'd
> Which choired with my drum, into a pipe
> Small as an eunuch, or the virgin voice
> That babies lull asleep! The smiles of knaves
> Tent in my cheeks, and schoolboys' tears take up
> The glasses of my sight! A beggar's tongue
> Make motion through my lips, and my arm'd knees
> Who bow'd but in my stirrup, bend like his
> That hath receiv'd an alms! I will not do't,
> Lest I surcease to honour mine own truth,
> And by my body's action teach my mind
> A most inherent baseness.
>
> (III.ii.110–23)

The process of metamorphosis is comprehensively visualized by Coriolanus; it disgusts him and he recoils from it. Martius can be transformed
'from man to dragon' (V.iv.13) but not from warrior to an actor or a
politician. As Joyce Van Dyke has commented in 'Making a scene: language, style and gesture in *Coriolanus*', 'This catalogue of disjunct entities
– harlot, eunuch, virgin, knaves, schoolboys, beggar – demonstrates the
complete confusion of identity which acting entails for him.'[65]

The man who is incapable of practising the 'insinuating nod' can, however, almost desist from language altogether. One fascinating feature of
the last act relates to speaking and non-speaking. Cominius describes his
failed appeal and Martius' response:

> 'Coriolanus'
> He would not answer to; forbad all names:
> He was a kind of nothing, titleless,
> Till he had forg'd himself a name o'th'fire
> Of burning Rome.
>
> (V.i.11–15)

As Menenius departs on his mission, Cominius insists 'he'll never hear
him', before going on to add:

> I tell you, he does sit in gold, his eye
> Red as 'twould burn Rome; and his injury
> The gaoler to his pity. I kneel'd before him:
> 'Twas very faintly he said 'Rise', dismiss'd me
> Thus, with his speechless hand.
>
> (V.i.63–7)

Menenius is dismissed with the words: 'I will not hear thee speak' (V.ii.90),
while Aufidius praises Martius for having 'stopp'd' his ears against the
pleas of the Romans, never allowing even 'A private whisper' (V.iii.5–7).
But as Martius braces himself to reject his mother, wife and son he is
reduced to unintentional silence:

> Like a dull actor now
> I have forgot my part and I am out,
> Even to a full disgrace.
>
> (V.iii.40–2)

Volumnia's great plea is punctuated by the words, 'Speak to me, son',
'Why dost not speak?', 'Daughter, speak you', 'Speak thou, boy'
(V.iii.148–56). They kneel before him, and this gesture precipitates the
surrender of the war-god who sought to deny 'instinct'

> but stand
> As if a man were author of himself

217

And knew no other kin.

(V.iii.35–7)

Volumnia, who gloried in the vision of her son's violent impregnability –
'He'll beat Aufidius' head below his knee,/And tread upon his neck'
(I.iii.46–7); 'before him he carries noise, and behind him he leaves tears'
(II.i.157–8) – is now grateful for being able to reach the man/boy inside
the god of war. Gesture succeeds where words fail. Just as Cominius feared
words would be inadequate to describe Coriolanus' deeds, so Virgilia is
left speechless in her relief as Coriolanus' safe return draws forth the
welcome from her husband 'My gracious silence, hail!' (II.i.174). Words
may be inadequate or ineffective. They may also be an unsound currency:
as Coriolanus returns to Rome in triumph 'All tongues speak of him'
(II.i.203), but most of them later proclaim his banishment; the 'god' is
cheered into Corioles in the final scene only to be denounced when he
responds to Aufidius' jibe. When he surrenders to his mother he promises
that she shall 'bear/A better witness back than words' (V.iii.203–4).

Throughout the play the dominant images and concepts are opposed in
such a way as to emphasize conflict: shouts either acclaim or denounce;
words can be used to flatter or denigrate, to lie or 'vouch' – Coriolanus
is accused of seeking to 'purge himself with words' (V.vi.8). Food is either
wholesome or unwholesome, abundant or scarce, consisting of a 'musty
superfluity', 'shreds', 'cold bits' or 'fragments'. The 'breasts of Hecuba'
and the 'mother's womb' contrast with the 'bloody brow' and 'mail'd
hand'. The vigour of the tiger, the prowess of the osprey, the uncontroll-
able speed of 'wild horses' contrasts with the sly snarling of dogs and the
gnawing of rats, the courage of the lion with the cowardice of the hare.
The 'gusts', 'mutinous winds', 'blown tide', 'flood' and 'interrupted waters'
are set against 'a few drops of women's rheum' (V.vi.46), and the unaccustomed gesture of Coriolanus who, according to Aufidius, 'water'd his new
plants with dews of flattery' (V.vi.23); 'deed achieving honour', 'dear
estimation', 'renown' and 'gratitude' are set in sharp opposition, to 'ingrate
forgetfulness' and tears that are 'as cheap as lies'; Aufidius is 'wag'd' by
Coriolanus' 'countenance' as if he had been 'mercenary' (V.vi.40–1);
'hire', 'bribe' and 'crack'd drachma' relate to the dubious transactions of
the market place. Aufidius claims that he helped Coriolanus 'reap' his
fame; he in turn insists that if the Volscians 'have writ their annals true'
his deeds cannot be denied, while his mother threatens that if he destroys
Rome, Coriolanus will 'reap' curses and receive a 'chronicle' of destroyer
of his country. The hero, accused of excessive pride, insists that his wounds
'smart/To hear themselves remember'd' (I.ix.28–9) but is nevertheless
perceived as a disease, 'gangren'd' in a world of widespread decay, corruption and infection; Coriolanus in turn refuses to 'beg' the 'stinking breaths'
of the people (II.i.234) even though he has 'planted his honours in their

eyes and his actions in their hearts', so that their 'tongues' must acclaim him or be guilty of 'ingrateful injury' (II.ii.29–32).

Although Coriolanus despises the 'multitudinous tongue' and the 'tongues o'th'common mouth' (III.i.22) the tribunes are able to outmanoeuvre him because they can keep 'ears and eyes for th'time,/But hearts for the event' (II.i.267–8), whereas his 'heart's his mouth:/What his breast forges that his tongue must vent' (III.i.255–6). Rome 'devour'd' everything of Martius apart from the name Coriolanus: 'A name unmusical to the Volscians' ears' (IV.v.59) – and one which Aufidius insists is 'stol'n' (V.vi.89). Whereas a Senator fears that the words of the tribunes will 'unbuild the city' (III.i.196), Menenius denounces them for bringing a 'trembling upon Rome', and Cominius predicts the temples will be 'burned in their cement' (IV.vi.86), Coriolanus tells the successful emissaries, 'Ladies, you deserve/To have a temple built you' (V.iii.206–7). The city which is on the brink of destruction stands firm at the end of the play.

The social universe of *Coriolanus* is characterized by conflict between Romans and Volscians and within Rome itself. This violence finds expression in noise, words, deeds and the imagery of tempests, dissolution, disease, body parts, animals, food and plants. At the heart of the play lies the question of values. Coriolanus is unable to speak 'mildly' to the people or to appear in the 'market-place' and 'beg their stinking breaths' (II.i.234); he has no filter between his heart and his mouth; unable to temporize or to comprehend a world in which the 'breath of garlic-eaters' (IV.vi.99) has 'voices' he is driven first to banishment and then to death (in both cases in the market places) when he is accused of failing to adhere to the values which he holds most dear – service to his country through martial prowess: 'traitor' and 'boy of tears' are the words which drive him to a frenzy of vituperation. Between these events he succumbs to a gesture, the kneeling of his mother, so that his eyes 'sweat compassion' (V.iii.196). The character who is incapable of 'bussing the stones' (III.ii.75) with his knee or practising the 'insinuating nod' (II.iii.99), is described by Menenius as 'able to pierce a corslet with his eye, talks like a knell and his hum is a battery' (V.iv.20–1). *Coriolanus* reverberates with noise; Rome is riven with a conflict over values. Politicians adapt to the new situation; the quintessential Roman cannot. The hero, separated from his home and divided within himself finally surrenders to 'instinct', recognizing that he is unable to act 'As if man were author of himself' (V.iii.36).

5

CONCLUSION

So our virtues
Lie in th'interpretation of the time
(*Coriolanus*, IV.vii.49–50)

The shaping conception of this study has been the conviction that the Roman plays are characterized by a distinctive perspective: here, as nowhere else, Shakespeare sets out to explore the interrelationship between character and society in a context where the social values are intensely felt and powerfully articulated. Nowhere else in the Shakespearean canon has the dramatist set out to convey such a palpable sense of place and values as in the Roman plays. Rome is never mere city or even empire: it is a pulsating, vibrant, social universe laden with history and driven by a sense of mission. In this social world men cannot simultaneously be themselves and participate in the shaping of the society – except Octavius Caesar. Rome imposes severe demands: wholehearted service is insufficient. The service has to be suited to the time. Titus' sacrifice of twenty-two of his twenty-five sons is not enough: he must display judgment: when he fails to do so he is destroyed. Proud Rome becomes 'a wilderness of tigers', but only after Titus has approved the burning alive of an enemy as part of a holy sacrifice and has killed his son in defence of what he conceives to be his Roman honour. Ironically Rome secures the opportunity of establishing a new beginning through the assistance of the barbarian Goths. The fragments of the Andronici, Titus' brother, son, and grandson, are left to learn the lessons and renew the vision of Rome.

Shakespeare ended his exploration of Roman worlds as he began, with a primitive Rome. Caius Martius Coriolanus, like Titus, was born into a Rome where valour was 'the chiefest virtue', and thrived accordingly – until the world changed. The supreme Roman became the 'enemy of the people'. Unable to interpret the time, far less to respond to it, he is deserted by an ideal and idealized world, and driven by a feeling of ingratitude to destroy the society – or its false representation – that shaped him. The flawless Roman is exiled because Rome becomes flawed: the voice of the people begins to be heard. Words carry more weight than action; the skills of the actor and the orator and the politician's supple knee are more in demand than the warrior's stretched sinews and clarion voice in this new world. The sound of drums, trumpets and clanging steel gives way to 'voices'. The people, wholesome in their influence but never distinctly heard in *Titus*, become, in *Coriolanus*, the 'multitudinous tongue', manoeuvred and manipulated by their tribunes. Starved, beaten, mocked and ridiculed, as individuals they behave with commendable generosity of spirit. As a crowd they are never better than comic; at worst their inconstancy is channelled into the denunciation of the hero they cheered to the rooftops.

The people of the Roman plays are denigrated chiefly because they exhibit an intolerable vice: inconstancy. To be inconstant is to be a living denial of the central Roman value. Ironically, the most powerful articulation of this value comes from Octavius Caesar in his description of Mark Antony. The Antony of his vision is a man who no longer exists: the character who drank the 'stale of horses' and whose cheek 'so much as lank'd not' has become, in *Antony and Cleopatra*, a mature voluptuary. He is an Egyptianized Roman who can cry 'Let Rome in Tiber melt' (I.i.33). He is later distressed to find himself swept from the centre stage of history, and is left complaining 'authority melts from me' (III.xiii.90). *Antony and Cleopatra* exhibits a breathtaking richness of contrasts between two cultures: Egypt embodies abundance, luxury, indolence, mystery, enchantment and feeling; Rome is no longer even a pulsating city: it is an administrative centre. The streets are not seen directly; the sight and smell of Rome's mechanics come to the audience only through the eyes of Antony and Cleopatra. Although no longer heroic, neither is Rome effete: compared with Egypt it is a tough political entity. Political life has atrophied, but it retains a world-view and a self-perception of superiority. Realism, order and austerity are potent features of a culture and vision that despises all that Egypt represents.

If the perception of the social universe in *Titus* and *Coriolanus* is of a primitive Rome (in each case moving towards a dilution of values with a more complex culture), the world of *Julius Caesar* is one in which there is a tension between achievement embodied in a great man, and an ideal of shared power and responsibility. Julius Caesar and Brutus represent antithetical strains: each sees himself as the repository of Roman values and greatness. Julius Caesar perceives his own conquests and constancy ('as constant as the northern star' (III.i.60)) as the quintessence of *romanitas*; Brutus seeks the supreme garland of service to his country, and in his quest to achieve this goal is prepared to subordinate all personal considerations. To make his service all the more pure, the assassination of his benefactor is transformed into a sacrifice, a blood ritual. When Titus gives permission for the mutilation and burning of Alarbus, the ritual provokes a shudder, but it is perceived as the product of a primitive

221

society. When Brutus describes the killing of Julius Caesar as a sacrifice the audience recoils as the sophisticated man of integrity manages to blind himself by a rationalization that makes 'butchery' appear 'sacrifice'. The tension between savagery and compassion is highlighted by Antony's soliloquy over the body of Caesar and in his forum speech: in the former he feels pity yet thirsts for revenge; in the latter he wrings compassion from the crowd but cynically exults in the violence he releases. Master of the Roman crowd, he knows how to play upon the sense of ingratitude – that vice so powerfully despised in a culture founded on a belief in service and its concomitant, gratitude.

The characters in the Roman plays bring to the world their own traits but they are shaped by the social universe into which they are born, its values and its history: they imbibe ideals and seek to live up to them in order to validate themselves. They also seek to satisfy personal ambitions. In *Julius Caesar* men live in a world of images: Caesar and Brutus succumb to them in a quest to embody their differing visions of Roman ideals; Antony and Cassius are driven more by personal impulses and passions; Octavius, the detached observer, is the new man who, burning with ambition, senses the future intuitively. Of all the characters in the Roman plays only he is totally in tune with the time. In *Julius Caesar* he is aware of a new era opening before him; in *Antony and Cleopatra* he sweeps aside the last Roman hero and the heroic conception. Antony, the man who wishes to determine events by means of personal combat, is no longer a hero but an embarrassment. What could be further from Titus, or Caius Martius Coriolanus, or Julius Caesar, than Octavius Caesar, the political chessplayer and organization man? Only Octavius Caesar is just right for the social world which he inhabits: the removal of Pompey (albeit a figure whose potency derives exclusively from his name) and Mark Antony draws an epoch to a close.

Throughout these plays there is a tremendous sense of characters seeing themselves as part of the process of history, and the action is frequently framed so that they are perceived as such: the audience sees the actions as emanating from a collision of aspirations, ambitions, beliefs and judgments. In these plays the characters never move in a social and political vacuum: they are greatly influenced by mother Rome and seek to embody what they perceive to be its essence, or to shape it. Ironically, the greatest success is the character most free of Roman ideals – except for a narrow abstemiousness which is puritanical and even frigid. Titus the man is distorted by his limited social perception; Coriolanus, the greatest warrior, is the man possessed of the greatest integrity – he absorbs the ethos of his class so thoroughly that he is both superhuman and inhuman; his circle of compassion extends no further than his family and his class. He is a tragic figure because he is not to blame: he has been constricted by the values he has absorbed with his mother's milk, and is betrayed by those

222

who know how to practise the 'insinuating nod'. Brutus is a tragic figure too, because he also stands for a Roman purity. Like Coriolanus his idealism shines out in comparison with the opportunism displayed by those around him. Ironically this thinker fails to probe deeply enough to perceive his own flaw, and continually fails in the practical decision-making that is the heart of political life. His dying words place him, and underline his limitations, his failure to recognize his own betrayal and his equivocal place in history. Mark Antony serves him better, putting a gloss on what is also the essential Brutus.

As he explored his chief source, Plutarch, Shakespeare encountered a series of enigmas. He did not remove them. He bodied forth characters and events from the narrative but preserved ambiguities. His intention seems not to have been to resolve the uncertainties and inconsistencies, but to vitalize and dramatize the conflicts and mysteries. He sought to retain the fascinating interplay between the personal, historical and political: frequently characters and events are framed, the action stopped so that they become, momentarily, icons. The magnificence of Cleopatra's barge inhabits the same world as Pompey's: a barely believable picture is juxtaposed with the all too believable scene of cut-throats and drunkards. Mighty Caesar falls victim to his self-image, before he falls victim to the daggers of friends, flatterers and enemies. The supremely fashioned war machine, Coriolanus, who so despises the inhabitants of the mundane world, suffers the indignity of defeat in the market place of Rome and death in the market place of an alien society. The world moves on and the heroes are struck down. But always in the Roman plays there is a forced contemplation of the dynamics of social organization and the values which animate the societies: an attempt to visualize the society which is emerging at the end of the play. There is also a forced consideration of history: the role of character, chance and fate in determining events – and the presentation and interpretation of history by participants and observers, 'So our virtues/Lie in th' interpretation of the time'.

NOTES

1 SHAKESPEARE'S ROMAN WORLDS

1 Plutarch, *Lives of the Noble Grecians and Romans*, translated by Sir Thomas North (1579), in Geoffrey Bullough (ed.), *Narrative and Dramatic Sources of Shakespeare* (8 vols, Routledge & Kegan Paul, London, 1966), vol. V, p. 13.
2 Kenneth Muir, *The Sources of Shakespeare's Plays* (Methuen, London, 1977).
3 M.W. MacCallum, *Shakespeare's Roman Plays and their Background* (Macmillan, London, 1910).
4 T.J.B. Spencer, 'Shakespeare and the Elizabethan Romans', *Shakespeare Survey*, vol. 10 (1957), p. 27.
5 Ibid., p. 27.
6 Cited by Spencer, ibid., pp. 27–8.
7 Ibid., p. 29.
8 Cited by Spencer, ibid., pp. 29–30.
9 Cited by Spencer, ibid., p. 30.
10 Cited by Spencer, ibid., p. 30.
11 Ibid., p. 31.
12 Ibid., p. 32.
13 Ibid., p. 33.
14 Ibid., p. 33.
15 Paul A. Cantor, *Shakespeare's Rome: Republic and Empire* (Cornell University Press, Ithaca, NY and London, 1976), p. 16.
16 Ibid., pp. 13 and 15.
17 Janet Adelman, *The Common Liar: An Essay on 'Antony and Cleopatra'* (Yale University Press, New Haven, CT and London, 1973), p. 58.
18 John Wilders, *The Lost Garden: A View of Shakespeare's English and Roman History Plays* (Macmillan, London, 1978), p. 1.
19 Ibid., pp. 5–6.
20 Robert S. Miola, *Shakespeare's Rome* (Cambridge University Press, Cambridge, 1983), p. 17.
21 Ibid., p. 17.
22 Cantor, *Shakespeare's Rome: Republic and Empire*, p. 37.
23 Ibid., p. 38.
24 Ibid., pp. 21–5.
25 Ibid., pp. 50–1.
26 Cited by Miola, *Shakespeare's Rome*, p. 192.
27 T.J.B. Spencer, 'Shakespeare and the Elizabethan Romans', *Shakespeare Survey*, vol. 10, p. 32.
28 Ibid., p. 32.
29 Miola, *Shakespeare's Rome*, p. 42.
30 Ibid., p. 75.
31 Nicholas Brooke, *Shakespeare's Early Tragedies* (Methuen, London, 1968), p. 22.

32 Bullough (ed.), 'Titus Andronicus', Narrative and Dramatic Sources of Shakespeare (8 vols, Routledge & Kegan Paul, London, 1966), vol. VI, p. 23.

33 J.C. Maxwell (ed.), introduction to the New Arden edition of Titus Andronicus (Methuen, London, 1953), p. xxviii.

34 Stanley Wells, introduction to Titus Andronicus (RSC Publications, 1987), p. 14.

35 G.R. Hibbard, 'Titus Andronicus and Romeo and Juliet' in Stanley Wells (ed.), Shakespeare: Select Bibliographical Guides (Oxford University Press, Oxford, 1973), p. 135.

36 E.K. Chambers, The Disintegration of Shakespeare (Oxford University Press, Oxford, 1924).

37 Hereward T. Price, 'The authorship of Titus Andronicus' (Journal of English and Germanic Philology, vol. 47 (1943)), partially reprinted in A. Harbage (ed.), Shakespeare: The Tragedies (Prentice-Hall, Englewood Cliffs, NJ, 1964).

38 John Dover Wilson (ed.), introduction to the New Cambridge Shakespeare edition of Titus Andronicus (Cambridge University Press, Cambridge, 1948).

39 Bullough (ed.), 'Titus Andronicus', Narrative and Dramatic Sources of Shakespeare, vol. VI, p. 32.

40 J.C. Maxwell (ed.), introduction to the New Arden edition of Titus Andronicus, p. xxxiv–vii.

41 Sylvan Barnet (ed.), introduction to the Signet edition of Titus Andronicus (Oxford University Press, Oxford, 1963).

42 E.M. Waith (ed.), introduction to the Oxford Shakespeare edition of Titus Andronicus (Oxford University Press, Oxford, 1984).

43 Stanley Wells, introduction to Titus Andronicus (RSC Publications), p. 15.

44 Ibid., pp. 15–16.

45 J.C. Maxwell (ed.), introduction to the New Arden edition of Titus Andronicus, pp. xxvii–viii.

46 E.M. Waith, 'The Metamorphosis of Violence in Titus Andronicus', Shakespeare Survey, vol. 10 (1957), p. 40.

47 Emrys Jones, The Origins of Shakespeare (Clarendon Press, Oxford, 1977), pp. 91–7.

48 Bullough (ed.), 'Titus Andronicus', Narrative and Dramatic Sources of Shakespeare, vol. VI, p. 31.

49 M.C. Bradbrook, Themes and Conventions of Elizabethan Tragedy (Cambridge University Press, Cambridge, 1935), p. 99.

50 Bullough (ed.), 'Titus Andronicus', Narrative and Dramatic Sources of Shakespeare, vol. VI, p. 31.

51 Robert B. Heilman, 'To know himself: an aspect of tragic structure' in Leonard F. Dean (ed.), Twentieth Century Interpretations of 'Julius Caesar': A Collection of Critical Essays (Prentice Hall, Englewood Cliffs, NJ, 1968), p. 83.

52 Miola, Shakespeare's Rome, p. 69.

2 IMAGES AND SELF-IMAGES IN JULIUS CAESAR

1 Plutarch, Lives of the Noble Grecians and Romans, translated by Sir Thomas North (1579), in Geoffrey Bullough (ed.), Narrative and Dramatic Sources of Shakespeare (8 vols, Routledge & Kegan Paul, London, 1966), vol. V, p. 44.

2 Ibid., p. 63.

3 Ibid., p. 63.

4 Ibid., p. 66.
5 Ibid., p. 66.
6 Ibid., p. 77.
7 Ibid., p. 78.
8 Ibid., p. 78.
9 Ibid., p. 80.
10 Ibid., p. 81.
11 Ibid., p. 81.
12 Ibid., pp. 82–3.
13 Ibid., p. 84.
14 Ibid., p. 83.
15 Ibid., p. 83.
16 Ibid., p. 84.
17 Ibid., p. 85.
18 Ibid., p. 85.
19 Ibid., p. 85.
20 Ibid., pp. 85–6.
21 Ibid., p. 90.
22 Ibid., p. 91.
23 Ibid., p. 91.
24 Ibid., p. 92.
25 Ibid., p. 92.
26 Ibid., p. 93.
27 Ibid., p. 93.
28 Ibid., p. 93.
29 Ibid., p. 94.
30 Ibid., p. 94.
31 Ibid., p. 94.
32 Ibid., p. 94.
33 Ibid., p. 94.
34 Ibid., p. 94.
35 Ibid., p. 95.
36 Ibid., p. 95.
37 Ibid., p. 95.
38 Ibid., p. 97.
39 Ibid., p. 98.
40 Ibid., pp. 98–9.
41 Ibid., p. 101.
42 Ibid., p. 101.
43 Ibid., p. 102.
44 Ibid., p. 102.
45 Ibid., p. 103.
46 Ibid., p. 104.
47 Ibid., p. 105.
48 Ibid., p. 105.
49 Ibid., p. 105.
50 Ibid., p. 88.
51 Ibid., p. 106.
52 Ibid., p. 106.
53 Ibid., p. 106.

54 Ibid., p. 108.
55 Ibid., p. 109.
56 Ibid., p. 110.
57 Ibid., p. 89.
58 Ibid., p. 118.
59 Ibid., p. 119.
60 Ibid., pp. 119–20.
61 Ibid., p. 122.
62 Ibid., p. 123.
63 Ibid., p. 123.
64 Ibid., p. 123.
65 Ibid., p. 124.
66 Ibid., p. 125.
67 Ibid., p. 127.
68 Ibid., p. 127.
69 Ibid., p. 128.
70 Ibid., p. 129.
71 Ibid., pp. 130–1.
72 Ibid., p. 131.
73 Ibid., p. 131.
74 Ibid., p. 131.
75 Ibid., pp. 131–2.
76 Ibid., p. 133.
77 Ibid., p. 133.
78 Ibid., p. 134.
79 Ibid., p. 135.
80 Ibid., p. 135.
81 Ibid., p. 139.
82 Ibid., p. 140.
83 Ibid., pp. 147–8.
84 Ibid., p. 148.
85 Ibid., pp. 148–9.
86 Ibid., p. 149.
87 Ibid., p. 154.
88 Ibid., pp. 150–1.
89 Ibid., pp. 157–8.
90 Ibid., p. 158.
91 Ibid., p. 158.
92 Ibid., p. 159.
93 William and Barbara Rosen, 'Julius Caesar: the speciality of rule', in Leonard F. Dean (ed.), Twentieth Century Interpretations of 'Julius Caesar': A Collection of Critical Essays (Prentice-Hall, Englewood Cliffs, NJ, 1968), p. 111.
94 Adrian Bonjour, The Structure of 'Julius Caesar' (University of Liverpool Press, Liverpool, 1958).
95 Geoffrey Bullough (ed.), Narrative and Dramatic Sources of Shakespeare, introduction to Plutarch's Lives of the Noble Grecians and Romans, vol. V, p. 54.
96 W. Warde Fowler, from Roman Essays and Interpretations, in P. Ure (ed.), Shakespeare: 'Julius Caesar' (Casebook Series, Macmillan, London, 1969), p. 47.

97 Willard Farnham, from *Shakespeare's Tragic Frontier*, in Ure (ed.), *'Julius Caesar'*, p. 65.

98 Ernest Schanzer, from *Shakespeare's Problem Plays*, in Ure (ed.), *'Julius Caesar'*, p. 193.

99 Norman Rabkin, 'Structure, convention and meaning in *Julius Caesar*', in Ure (ed.), *'Julius Caesar'*, p. 105.

100 Hugh M. Richmond, 'Brutus and the end of the play' from *Shakespeare's Political Plays*, in Dean (ed.), *Julius Caesar*, p. 103.

101 L.C. Knights, 'Personality and politics in *Julius Caesar*' from *Further explorations*, in Ure (ed.), *'Julius Caesar'*, pp. 125–6.

102 R.A. Foakes, 'Language and action' from 'An approach to *Julius Caesar*', in Dean (ed.), *Julius Caesar*, pp. 60–3.

103 Alexander Leggatt, *Shakespeare's Political Drama: The History Plays and the Roman Plays* (Routledge, London and New York, 1988), p. 140.

104 R.A.G. Carson, 'The Ides of March', in Ure (ed.), *'Julius Caesar'*, p. 71.

105 R.G. Moulton, from *Shakespeare as a Dramatic Artist*, in Ure (ed.), *'Julius Caesar'*, pp. 36–7.

106 Ernest Schanzer, from *Shakespeare's Problem Plays*, in Ure (ed.), *'Julius Caesar'*, p. 193.

107 Edward Dowden, from *Shakespere: A Critical Study of his Mind and Art*, in Ure (ed.), *'Julius Caesar'*, p. 33.

108 John Palmer, from *Political Characters of Shakespeare*, in Ure (ed.), *'Julius Caesar'*, p. 229.

109 Alexander Leggatt, *Shakespeare's Political Drama*, p. 156.

110 Brents Stirling, from *Unity in Shakespearian Tragedy*, in Ure (ed.), *'Julius Caesar'*, p. 168.

111 William Hazlitt, from *Characters of Shakespeare's Plays*, in Ure (ed.), *'Julius Caesar'*, p. 32.

112 Dowden, from *Shakespere: A Critical Study of his Mind and Art'*, in Ure (ed.), *'Julius Caesar'*, p. 34.

113 Alexander Leggatt, *Shakespeare's Political Drama*, p. 150.

3 REALITIES AND IMAGININGS IN *ANTONY AND CLEOPATRA*

1 Plutarch, *Lives of the Noble Grecians and Romans*, translated by Sir Thomas North (1579); in Geoffrey Bullough (ed.), *Narrative and Dramatic Sources of Shakespeare* (8 vols, Routledge & Kegan Paul, London, 1966), vol. V, p. 219.

2 Ibid., p. 257.

3 Ibid., p. 257.

4 Ibid., p. 257.

5 Ibid., pp. 286–7.

6 Ibid., p. 269.

7 Ibid., p. 320.

8 Ibid., p. 140.

9 Ibid., p. 288.

10 Ibid., p. 290.

11 Ibid., p. 293.

12 Ibid., p. 319.

13 Ibid., p. 321.

14 Ibid., p. 321.

15 Ibid., p. 320.
16 Ibid., p. 321.
17 Ibid., p. 273.
18 Ibid., p. 273.
19 Ibid., p. 275.
20 Ibid., p. 276.
21 Ibid., p. 274.
22 Ibid., p. 276.
23 Ibid., pp. 331–2.
24 Ibid., p. 342.
25 Ibid., p. 343.
26 Ibid., p. 321.
27 Ibid., p. 322.
28 Ibid., p. 322.
29 Ibid., p. 322.
30 Ibid., p. 323.
31 Ibid., p. 323.
32 Ibid., pp. 281–2.
33 Ibid., p. 293.
34 Ibid., p. 283.
35 Ibid., pp. 291–2.
36 Ibid., p. 292.
37 Ibid., p. 293.
38 Ibid., p. 297.
39 Ibid., pp. 295–6.
40 Ibid., pp. 296–7.
41 Ibid., p. 298.
42 Ibid., p. 298.
43 Ibid., p. 299.
44 Ibid., p. 299.
45 Ibid., p. 301.
46 Ibid., p. 302.
47 Ibid., p. 302.
48 Ibid., pp. 302–3.
49 Ibid., pp. 304–5.
50 Ibid., p. 305.
51 Ibid., p. 305.
52 Ibid., p. 306.
53 Ibid., p. 306.
54 Ibid., p. 306.
55 Ibid., p. 308.
56 Ibid., p. 308.
57 Ibid., p. 309.
58 Ibid., p. 310.
59 Ibid., p. 313.
60 Ibid., p. 313.
61 Ibid., pp. 313–14.
62 Ibid., p. 314.
63 Ibid., p. 315.
64 Ibid., p. 315.

65 Ibid., p. 316.
66 Ibid., p. 317.
67 Janet Adelman, *The Common Liar: An Essay on 'Antony and Cleopatra'* (Yale University Press, New Haven, CT, 1973), p. 40.
68 Alexander Leggatt, *Shakespeare's Political Drama: The History Plays and the Roman Plays* (Routledge, London, 1988), pp. 175–6.
69 Ibid., p. 166.
70 Ibid., p. 169.
71 Ibid., p. 170.
72 A.H. Mason, '*Antony and Cleopatra*: telling versus showing', in John Russell Brown (ed.), *Shakespeare: 'Antony and Cleopatra'* (Casebook Series, Macmillan, London, 1968), p. 208.
73 John Middleton Murry, '*Antony and Cleopatra*' from *Shakespeare*, in Brown (ed.), '*Antony and Cleopatra*', p. 131.
74 Maurice Charney, 'The imagery of *Antony and Cleopatra*' from *Shakespeare's Roman Plays*, in Brown (ed.), '*Antony and Cleopatra*', p. 158.
75 Ibid., p. 161.
76 Ibid., p. 169.
77 Susan Snyder, 'Patterns of motion in *Antony and Cleopatra*', *Shakespeare Survey*, vol. 33 (1980), pp. 113–22.

4 SOUNDS, WORDS, GESTURES AND DEEDS IN *CORIOLANUS*

1 Plutarch's *Lives of the Noble Grecians and Romans*, translated by Sir Thomas North (1579); in Geoffrey Bullough (ed.), *Narrative and Dramatic Sources of Shakespeare* (8 vols, Routledge & Kegan Paul, London, 1966), vol. V, pp. 505–6.
2 Ibid., p. 506.
3 Ibid., p. 508.
4 Ibid., p. 510.
5 Ibid., p. 511.
6 *The Romane History of T. Livy*, translated by Philemon Holland (1600); in Geoffrey Bullough (ed.), *Narrative and Dramatic Sources of Shakespeare*, vol. V, p. 497.
7 Ibid., p. 499.
8 Plutarch's *Lives of the Noble Grecians and Romans*, in Bullough (ed.), *Narrative and Dramatic Sources of Shakespeare*, vol. V, p. 511.
9 Ibid., pp. 512–13.
10 Ibid., pp. 514–15.
11 Ibid., p. 516.
12 Ibid., p. 516.
13 Ibid., p. 517.
14 Ibid., pp. 517–18.
15 Ibid., p. 518.
16 Ibid., p. 518.
17 Ibid., p. 519.
18 Ibid., p. 520.
19 Ibid., pp. 522–3.
20 Ibid., p. 524.
21 Ibid., p. 525.

22 Ibid., pp. 525–6.
23 Ibid., p. 526.
24 Ibid., pp. 526–7.
25 Ibid., p. 527.
26 Ibid., p. 528.
27 Ibid., p. 528.
28 Ibid., p. 528.
29 Ibid., p. 530.
30 Ibid., p. 531.
31 Ibid., p. 532.
32 Ibid., p. 533.
33 Ibid., p. 533.
34 Ibid., p. 534.
35 Ibid., p. 534.
36 Ibid., p. 537.
37 Ibid., pp. 538–9.
38 Ibid., pp. 539–41.
39 Ibid., p. 541.
40 Ibid., pp. 543–4.
41 *The Romane History of T. Livy*, translated by Philemon Holland (1600); in Bullough (ed.), *Narrative and Dramatic Sources of Shakespeare*, vol. V, p. 505.
42 Plutarch's *Lives of the Noble Grecians and Romans*, translated by Sir Thomas North (1579); in Bullough (ed.), *Narrative and Dramatic Sources of Shakespeare*, vol. V, pp. 545–8.
43 Ibid., p. 545.
44 *The Romane History of T. Livy*, translated by Philemon Holland (1600); in Bullough (ed.), *Narrative and Dramatic Sources of Shakespeare*, vol. V, p. 502.
45 Plutarch's *Lives of the Noble Grecians and Romans*, translated by Sir Thomas North (1579); in Bullough (ed.), *Narrative and Dramatic Sources of Shakespeare*, vol. V, pp. 547–8.
46 Maurice Charney, '*Coriolanus* and *Timon of Athens*', in Stanley Wells (ed.), *Shakespeare: Select Bibliographical Guides* (Oxford University Press, Oxford, 1973), p. 218.
47 S.T. Coleridge, 'Marginalia and notebooks', from *Shakespearean Criticism* in B.A. Brockman (ed.), *Shakespeare: 'Coriolanus'* (Casebook Series, Macmillan, London, 1968), p. 31.
48 William Hazlitt, from *Characters of Shakespeare's Plays*, in Brockman (ed.), '*Coriolanus*', p. 29.
49 A.C. Swinburne, from *A Study of Shakespeare*, in Brockman (ed.), '*Coriolanus*', p. 41.
50 Edward Dowden, from *Shakespeare: A Critical Study of his Mind and Art*, in Brockman (ed.), '*Coriolanus*', p. 33.
51 Ibid., p. 34.
52 O.J. Campbell, 'Experiment in tragical satire', from *Shakespeare's Satire*, in Brockman (ed.), '*Coriolanus*', p. 77.
53 A.P. Rossiter, 'Political tragedy' from *Angel with Horns*, in Brockman (ed.), '*Coriolanus*', pp. 152–3.
54 Reuben A. Brower, 'The deeds of *Coriolanus*', from *Hero and Saint*, in Brockman (ed.), '*Coriolanus*', p. 217.

55 Willard Farnham, 'Tragic pride' from *Shakespeare's Tragic Frontier*, in Brockman (ed.), *'Coriolanus'*, p. 98.
56 Reuben A. Brower, 'The deeds of Coriolanus', from *Hero and Saint*, in Brockman (ed.), *'Coriolanus'*, p. 212.
57 Anne Barton, 'Livy, Machiavelli and Shakespeare's *Coriolanus*', *Shakespeare Survey*, vol. 38 (1985), pp. 115–29 (esp. pp. 124–5).
58 A.C. Bradley, 'Character and the imaginative appeal of tragedy in *Coriolanus*', from *A Miscellany*, in Brockman (ed.), *'Coriolanus'*, p. 68.
59 O.J. Campbell, 'Experiment in tragical satire', from *Shakespeare's Satire'*, in Brockman (ed.), *'Coriolanus'*, pp. 73–4.
60 Alexander Leggatt, *Shakespeare's Political Drama: The History Plays and the Roman Plays* (Routledge, London and New York, 1988), p. 208.
61 Maurice Charney, 'Style in the Roman plays', from *Shakespeare's Roman Plays*, in Brockman (ed.), *'Coriolanus'*, pp. 118–19.
62 Willard Farnham, 'Tragic pride', from *Shakespeare's Tragic Frontier*, in Brockman (ed.), *'Coriolanus'*, pp. 106–7.
63 Günter Grass, Introduction to *The Plebeians Rehearse the Uprising*, translated by Ralph Manheim (Penguin Books, Harmondsworth, 1972), p. 13.
64 Plutarch's *Lives of the Noble Grecians and Romans*, in Bullough (ed.), *Narrative and Dramatic Sources of Shakespeare*, vol. V, p. 512.
65 Joyce Van Dyke, 'Making a scene: language and gesture in *Coriolanus*', *Shakespeare Survey*, vol. 30 (1977), p. 143.

BIBLIOGRAPHY

Adelman, J. *The Common Liar: An Essay on 'Antony and Cleopatra'* (Yale University Press, New Haven and London, 1973)

Allen, J.W. *A History of Political Thought in England* (Methuen, London, 1957)

Alvis, J. and West, T.G. (eds) *Shakespeare as a Political Thinker* (Carolina Academic Press, Durham, NC, 1981)

Baker, H. *Induction to Tragedy: A Study in a Development of Form in 'Gorboduc', 'The Spanish Tragedy' and 'Titus Andronicus'* (University of Louisiana Press, Baton Rouge, LA, 1939: re-issued by Russell and Russell, New York, 1965)

Baldwin, T.W. *William Shakespeare's Small Latine and Lesse Greeke* (University of Illinois Press, Urbana, IL, 1944)

Barkan, L. *Nature's Work of Art: The Human Body as the Image of the World* (Yale University Press, New Haven and London, CT, 1975)

_____ *The Gods Made Flesh: Metamorphosis and the Pursuit of Paganism* (Yale University Press, New Haven, CT, 1986)

Barnet, S. (ed.) the Signet edition of *Titus Andronicus* (Oxford University Press, Oxford, 1963)

Barroll, J.L. *Artificial Persons: The Formation of Character in the Tragedies of Shakespeare* (University of South Carolina Press, Columbia, SC, 1974)

_____ *Shakespearian Tragedy, Genre, Tradition and Change in 'Antony and Cleopatra'* (Folger Books, Associated University Presses, London and Toronto, 1984)

Battenhouse, R. *Shakespearian Tragedy: Its Art and its Christian Premises* (Indiana University Press, Bloomington, IN, 1969)

Baxter, J. *Shakespeare's Poetic Styles* (Routledge & Kegan Paul, London, 1980)

Bayley, J. *Shakespeare and Tragedy* (Routledge & Kegan Paul, London, 1981)

Berry, R. *Changing Styles in Shakespeare* (Allen & Unwin, London, 1981)

_____ *Shakespeare and Social Class* (Humanities Press International, Atlantic Highlands, NJ, 1988)

Bevington, D. and Halio, J. (eds) *Shakespeare: Pattern of Excelling Nature* (University of Delaware Press, Newark, DE, 1978)

Bliss, L. *The World's Perspective: John Webster and the Jacobean Drama* (Harvester Press, Brighton, 1983)

Boardman, J., Griffin, J. and Murray, O. (eds) *The Oxford History of the Classical World* (Oxford University Press, Oxford, 1986)

Bolgar, R.R. *The Classical Heritage and its Beneficiaries* (Cambridge University Press, Cambridge, 1954)

Bonjour, A. *The Structure of 'Julius Caesar'* (University of Liverpool Press, Liverpool, 1958)

Boorman, S.C. *Human Conflict in Shakespeare* (Routledge & Kegan Paul, London and New York, 1987)

Bradbrook, M.C. *Themes and Conventions of Elizabethan Tragedy* (Cambridge University Press, Cambridge, 1935)
—— *Shakespeare and Elizabethan Poetry* (Chatto & Windus, London, 1951)
—— *Shakespeare the Craftsman: The Clark Lectures, 1968* (Chatto & Windus, London, 1969)
Bradbury, M. and Palmer, D. (eds) *Shakespearean Tragedy*, Stratford-upon-Avon Studies, 20 (Edward Arnold, London, 1984)
Bradley, A.C. *Shakespearean Tragedy* (Macmillan, London, 1904: reprinted Macmillan, London, 1964)
—— *Oxford Lectures on Poetry* (Macmillan, London, 1909)
—— *A Miscellany* (Macmillan, London, 1929) [contains '*Coriolanus*: British Academy Lecture 1912']
Bradshaw, G. *Shakespeare's Scepticism* (Harvester Press, Brighton, 1987)
Bristol, M.D. *Carnival and Theatre: Plebeian Culture and the Structure of Authority in Renaissance England* (Methuen, London and New York, 1985)
Brockbank, P. (ed.) the New Arden Shakespeare, *Coriolanus* (Methuen, London, 1976)
Brockman, B.A. (ed.) *Shakespeare: 'Coriolanus'* (Casebook Series, Macmillan, London, 1977)
Brooke, N. *Shakespeare's Early Tragedies* (Methuen, London, 1968)
—— *Horrid Laughter in Jacobean Tragedy* (Open Books, London, 1979)
Brower, R.A. *Hero and Saint: Shakespeare and the Graeco-Roman Heroic Tradition* (Oxford University Press, Oxford, 1971)
Brown, J.R. (ed.) *Shakespeare: 'Antony and Cleopatra'* (Casebook Series, Macmillan, London, 1968)
—— *Shakespeare's Dramatic Style* (Heinemann, London, 1970)
Brown, J.R. and Harris, B. (eds) *Later Shakespeare*, Stratford-upon-Avon Studies, 8 (Edward Arnold, London, 1966)
Bullough, G. (ed.) *Narrative and Dramatic Sources of Shakespeare*, vol. V, *The Roman Plays* (Macmillan, London, 1964)
—— *Narrative and Dramatic Sources of Shakespeare*, vol. VI, *Other 'Classical' Plays* (Macmillan, London, 1966)
—— *Narrative and Dramatic Sources of Shakespeare*, 8 vols (Routledge & Kegan Paul, London, 1966)
Bulman, J.C. *The Heroic Idiom of Shakespearian Tragedy* (University of Delaware Press, Newark, DE, Associated University Presses, London and Toronto, 1985)
Burckhardt, S. *Shakespearean Meanings* (Princeton University Press, Princeton, NJ, 1968)
Burke, K. *Language as Symbolic Action* (University of California Press, Berkeley, CA, 1966)
Campbell, O.J. *Shakespeare's Satire* (Oxford University Press, London and New York, 1943)
Cantor, P.A. *Shakespeare's Rome: Republic and Empire* (Cornell University Press, Ithaca, NY and London, 1976)
Cavell, S. *Disowning Knowledge in Six Plays of Shakespeare* (Cambridge University Press, Cambridge, 1987)
Chambers, E.K. *The Disintegration of Shakespeare* (Oxford University Press, Oxford, 1924)
Champion, L.S. *Shakespeare's Tragic Perspective* (University of Georgia Press, Athens, GA, 1976)

Charney, M. *Shakespeare's Roman Plays: The Function of Imagery in the Drama* (Harvard University Press, Cambridge, MA., 1961)

Charney, M. (ed.) *Discussions of Shakespeare's Roman Plays* (Harvard University Press, Boston, MA., 1964)

—— *Titus Andronicus* (Harvester Press, Brighton, 1989)

Chaudhuri, S. *Infirm Glory: Shakespeare and the Renaissance Image of Man* (Clarendon Press, Oxford, 1981)

Clarke, M.L. *The Noblest Roman: Marcus Brutus and his Reputation* (Thames & Hudson, London, 1981)

Clemen, W.H. *The Development of Shakespeare's Imagery*, 2nd edn (Methuen, London, 1977)

Coleridge, S.T. *Shakespearean Criticism*, edited by Raysor, T.M., 2 vols (Harvard University Press, Cambridge, MA., 1930)

Colie, R. *The Resources of Kind: Genre Theory in the Renaissance* (University of California Press, Berkeley and Los Angeles, CA, 1973)

Conti, G.B. *The Rhetoric of Imitation*, translated Segal, C. (Cornell University Press, Ithaca, NY, 1986)

'Coriolan', théâtre et politique (Travaux de l'Université de Telouse-le Mirail, Série B, Tome 5, 1984)

Cowper, J.M. (ed.) *A Supplication of the Poore Commons (1546)* (Early English Text Society, London, 1871)

Cox, C.B. and Palmer, D.J. (eds) *Shakespeare's Wide and Universal Stage* (Manchester University Press, Manchester, 1984)

Crutwell, P. *The Shakespearean Moment* (Chatto & Windus, London, 1954)

Daiches, D. *Modern Literary Essays* (University of Chicago Press, Chicago, 1956)

—— *Shakespeare: 'Julius Caesar'* Studies in English Literature No. 65 (Edward Arnold, London, 1976)

Danby, J.F. *Poets on Fortune's Hill* (Faber & Faber, London, 1952)

David, R. *Shakespeare in the Theatre* (Cambridge University Press, Cambridge, 1978)

Dean, L.F. (ed.) *Shakespeare: Modern Essays in Criticism*, 3rd revised edn (Oxford University Press, Oxford, London and New York, 1967)

—— *Twentieth Century Interpretations of 'Julius Caesar'* (Prentice-Hall, Englewood Cliffs, NJ, 1968)

Dessen, A.C. *Elizabethan Drama and the Viewers' Eye* (University of North Carolina Press, Chapel Hill, NC, 1977)

Dickey, F. *Not Wisely but Too Well* (Huntington Library, San Marino, CA, 1957)

Dollimore, J. *Radical Tragedy: Religion, Ideology and Power in the Drama of Shakespeare and his Contemporaries* (Harvester Press, Brighton, 1984)

Dollimore, J. and Sinfield, A. (eds) *Political Shakespeare: New Essays in Cultural Materialism* (Manchester University Press, Manchester, 1985)

Doran, M. *Endeavours of Art: A Study of Form in Elizabethan Drama* (University of Wisconsin Press, Madison, WI, 1954)

—— *Shakespeare's Dramatic Language* (University of Wisconsin Press, Madison, WI and London, 1976)

Dorsch, T.S. (ed.) the New Arden Shakespeare, *Julius Caesar* (Methuen, London, 1965)

Dowden, E. *Shakespeare: A Critical Study of his Mind and Art* (Routledge & Kegan Paul, London, 1875)

Drakakis, J. (ed.) *Alternative Shakespeares* (Routledge & Kegan Paul, London, 1985)

Duthie, G.I. (ed.) *Papers Mainly Shakespearean*, University of Aberdeen Studies 147 (Oliver & Boyd, Edinburgh, 1964)

Eagleton, T. *Shakespeare and Society: Critical Studies in Shakespearean Drama* (Chatto & Windus, London, 1970)

Edwards, P., Ewbank, I.S. and Hunter, G.K. (eds) *Shakespeare's Styles: Essays in Honour of Kenneth Muir* (Cambridge University Press, Cambridge, 1980)

Ellis-Fermor, U. *Shakespeare's Drama*, ed. by Kenneth Muir (Methuen, London and New York, 1980)

Enright, D.J. *The Apothecary's Shop* (R. West, London, 1957)

Erskine-Hill, H. *The Idea of Augustus in English Literature* (Edward Arnold, London, 1983)

Evans, B. *Shakespeare's Tragic Practice* (Clarendon Press, Oxford, 1979)

Faas, E. *Shakespeare's Poetics* (Cambridge University Press, Cambridge, 1986)

Farnham, W. *Shakespeare's Tragic Frontier* (University of California Press, Berkeley, CA., 1950)

―――― *The Medieval Heritage of Elizabethan Tragedy* (Basil Blackwell, Oxford, 1936; reprinted 1970)

Felperin, H. *Shakespearean Representation: Mimesis and Modernity in Elizabethan Tragedy* (Princeton University Press, Princeton, NJ, 1977)

Foreman Jr, W.C. *The Music of the Close: The Final Scenes of Shakespeare's Tragedies* (University Press of Kentucky, Lexington, KT, 1978)

Fowler, W.W. *Roman Essays and Interpretations* (Clarendon Press, Oxford, 1920)

Frye, R.M. *Shakespeare and Christian Doctrine* (Princeton University Press, Princeton, NJ, 1963)

Frye, N. *Fools of Time: Studies in Shakespearean Tragedy* (University of Toronto Press, Toronto, 1967)

Gardner, H. *Religion and Literature* (Faber & Faber, London, 1971)

Goddard, H.C. *The Meaning of Shakespeare* (University of Chicago Press, Chicago, 1951)

Goldberg, J. *James I and the Politics of Literature* (Johns Hopkins University Press, Baltimore, MD, 1983)

Goldman, M. *Shakespeare and the Energies of Drama* (Princeton University Press, Princeton, NJ, 1972)

―――― *Acting and Action in Shakespearean Tragedy* (Princeton University Press, Princeton, NJ, 1985)

Granville-Barker, H. *Prefaces to Shakespeare*, new edn, vols 2, 3 and 6 (Batsford, London, 1982)

Grass, G. *The Plebeians Rehearse the Uprising*, translated by Ralph Manheim (Penguin Books, Harmondsworth, 1972)

Gray, J.C. (ed.) *Mirror up to Shakespeare* (University of Toronto Press, Toronto, Buffalo and London, 1984)

Greenblatt, S.J. *Renaissance Self-Fashioning from More to Shakespeare* (University of Chicago Press, Chicago, 1980)

Greenblatt, S.J. (ed.) *Forms of Power and the Power of Forms in the Renaissance* (Pilgrim Books, Norman, OK, 1982)

Gregson, J.M. *Public and Private Man in Shakespeare* (Croom Helm, London, Barnes & Noble Books, Totowa, NJ, 1983)

Hale, D.G. *The Body Politic: A Political Metaphor in the Renaissance* (Mouton, The Hague and Paris, 1971)

Hamilton, A.C. *The Early Shakespeare* (Huntington Library, San Marino, CA, 1967)

Harbage, A. (ed.) *Shakespeare: The Tragedies* (Prentice-Hall, Englewood Cliffs, NJ, 1964)

Hazlitt, W. *Characters of Shakespeare's Plays* (World's Classics, Oxford University Press, London, New York, Toronto, 1917)

Highfill Jr, P.H. (ed.) *Shakespeare's Craft* (Southern Illinois University Press, Carbondale, IL, 1982)

Holloway, J. *The Story of the Night* (Routledge & Kegan Paul, London, 1961)

Honigmann, E.A.J. *Shakespeare: Seven Tragedies: The Dramatist's Manipulation of Response* (Macmillan, London, 1976)

Honigmann, E.A.J. (ed.) *Shakespeare and his Contemporaries: Essays in Comparison* (Revels Plays Companion Library, Manchester University Press, Manchester, 1986)

Houston, J.P. *Shakespearean Sentences: A Study in Style and Syntax* (Louisiana State University Press, Baton Rouge, LA and London, 1988)

Howard, J.E. and O'Connor, M.F. (eds) *Shakespeare Reproduced: The Text in History and Ideology* (Methuen, New York and London, 1987)

Huffman, C.C. *'Coriolanus' in Context* (Bucknell University Press, Lewisburg, PA, 1971)

Hussey, S.S. *The Literary Language of Shakespeare* (Longman, London and New York, 1982)

Ide, R. *Possessed with Greatness: The Heroic Tragedies of Chapman and Shakespeare* (Scolar Press, London, 1980)

Johnson, S. *Johnson on Shakespeare*, ed. Arthur Sherbo, vol. viii of the Yale Johnson (Yale University Press, New Haven, CT., 1968)

Jones, E. *Othello's Countrymen: The African in English Renaissance Drama* (Oxford University Press, London, 1965)

Jones, E. *Scenic Form in Shakespeare* (Clarendon Press, Oxford, 1971)

—— *The Origins of Shakespeare* (Clarendon Press, Oxford, 1977)

Jorgensen, P.A. *Shakespeare's Military World* (University of California Press, Berkeley, CA, 1956)

—— *William Shakespeare: The Tragedies* (University of California Press, Los Angeles, CA, Twayne Publishers, Boston, MA, 1985)

Kettle, A. (ed.) *Shakespeare in a Changing World* (Lawrence & Wishart, London, 1964)

Kiefer, F. *Fortune and Elizabethan Tragedy* (Huntington Library, San Marino, CA, 1983)

Knight, G.W. *The Imperial Theme*, 3rd edn (Methuen, London, 1951)

—— *The Wheel of Fire: Interpretations of Shakespearian Tragedy*, 4th edn (Methuen, London, 1949)

—— *Shakespearian Dimensions* (Harvester Press, Brighton, Barnes & Noble, Totowa, NJ, 1984)

Knights, L.C. *Some Shakespearean Themes* (Chatto & Windus, London, 1959)

—— *Further Explorations* (Chatto & Windus, London, Stanford University Press, Stanford, CA, 1965)

Kott, J. *Shakespeare Our Contemporary*, 2nd edn revised (Methuen, London, 1967)

Krook, D. *Elements of Tragedy* (Yale University Press, New Haven, CT., 1969)

Lee, R. *Shakespeare: 'Antony and Cleopatra'*, Studies in English Literature, No. 44 (Edward Arnold, London, 1971)

Leech, C. (ed.) *Shakespeare: The Tragedies: A Collection of Critical Essays* (University of Chicago Press, Chicago and London, 1965)

Leggatt, A. *Shakespeare's Political Drama: The History Plays and the Roman Plays* (Routledge, London, 1988)

Lerner, L. (ed.) *Shakespeare's Tragedies: An Anthology of Modern Criticism*, 4th edn (Penguin Books, Harmondsworth, Middlesex, 1970)

Long, M. *The Unnatural Scene: A Study in Shakespearean Tragedy* (Methuen, London, 1976)

MacCallum, M.W. *Shakespeare's Roman Plays and their Background* (Macmillan, 1910; new edn, introduced by T.J.B. Spencer, 1967)

Mahood, M.M. *Shakespeare's Wordplay* (Methuen, London and New York, 1957)

Margeson, J.M.R. *The Origins of Shakespeare's Tragedies* (Clarendon Press, Oxford, 1967)

Markels, J. *The Pillar of the World* (Ohio State University Press, Columbus, OH, 1968)

Martindale, C. (ed.) *Ovid Renewed* (Cambridge University Press, Cambridge, 1988)

Maxwell, J.C. (ed.) the New Arden Shakespeare, *Titus Andronicus* (Methuen, London, 1953)

McNeir, W.F. *Shakespeare's 'Julius Caesar': A Tragedy Without a Hero* (Wiesbaden: Akademie der Wissenschaften, Mainz, 1971)

Mehl, D. *Shakespeare's Tragedies: An Introduction* (Cambridge University Press, Cambridge, 1987)

Mills, L.J. *The Tragedies of Shakespeare's 'Antony and Cleopatra'* (Indiana University Press, Bloomington, IN, 1964)

Miola, R.S. *Shakespeare's Rome* (Cambridge University Press, Cambridge and New York, 1983)

Montano, R. *Shakespeare's Concept of Tragedy: The Bard as Anti Elizabethan* (Gateway Editions, Chicago, 1985)

Morris, C. *Political Thought in England: Tyndale to Hooker* (Oxford University Press, London, New York and Toronto, 1953)

Moulton, R.G. *Shakespeare as a Dramatic Artist* (Clarendon Press, Oxford, 1885)

Muir, K. *The Sources of Shakespeare's Plays* (Methuen, London, 1977)

—— *The Singularity of Shakespeare and other Essays* (Liverpool University Press, Liverpool, 1977)

Murray, J.M. *Countries of the Mind* (Dutton, New York, 1922)

—— *Shakespeare* (Jonathan Cape, London, 1936)

Nicolet, C. *The World of the Citizen in Republican Rome*, transl. by P.S. Falla (University of California Press, Berkeley, CA, 1980)

Nicoll, A. (ed.) *Shakespeare Survey*, vol. 10 (Cambridge University Press, Cambridge, 1957)

Nuttall, A.D. *A New Mimesis: Shakespeare and the Representation of Reality* (Methuen, London, 1983)

Orgel, S. *The Illusion of Power: Political Theatre in the English Renaissance* (University of California Press, Berkeley, CA, 1975)

—— *The Renaissance Imagination: Essays and Lectures by D.J. Gordon* (University of California Press, Berkeley, CA, and London, 1975)

Palmer, J. *Political Characters of Shakespeare* (Macmillan, London, 1945)

Parker, P. and Hartman, G. (eds) *Shakespeare and the Question of Theory* (Methuen, London, 1985)

Phillips, J.E. *The State in Shakespeare's Greek and Roman Plays* (Columbia University Press, New York, 1940)

Phillips, J.E. (ed.) *Twentieth Century Interpretations of 'Coriolanus': A Collection of Critical Essays* (Prentice-Hall, Englewood Cliffs, NJ, 1970)

Platt, M. *Rome and Romans According to Shakespeare* (Universität Salzburg, 1976)

Poole, A. *Coriolanus* (Harvester Press, Brighton, 1988)

Proser, M. *The Heroic Image in Five Shakespeare Tragedies* (Princeton University Press, Princeton, NJ, 1965)

Rabkin, N. *Shakespeare and the Common Understanding* (Free Press, New York, 1967)

Raleigh, W. (ed.) *Dr. Johnson on Shakespeare* (Oxford University Press, London, 1908)

Ribner, I. *Patterns in Shakespearean Tragedy* (Methuen, London, 1960)

Richmond, H. *Shakespeare's Political Plays* (Random House, New York, 1967)

Ridley, M.R. (ed.) the New Arden Shakespeare, *Antony and Cleopatra* (Methuen, London, 1965)

Riemer, A.P. *A Reading of Shakespeare's 'Antony and Cleopatra'* (Sydney University Press, Sydney, 1968)

Ripley, J. *'Julius Caesar' on Stage in England and America 1599–1973* (Cambridge University Press, Cambridge, 1980)

Root, R.K. *Classical Mythology in Shakespeare* (Gordian Press Inc., New York, 1965)

Rosen, W. *Shakespeare and the Craft of Tragedy* (Harvard University Press, Cambridge, MA, 1960)

Rossiter, A.P. *Angel with Horns* ed. by G. Storey (Longman, London, 1961)

Sanders, W. *The Dramatist and the Received Idea: Studies in the Plays of Marlowe and Shakespeare* (Cambridge University Press, Cambridge, 1968)

Schanzer, E. *The Problem Plays of Shakespeare* (Routledge & Kegan Paul, London, 1963)

Scullard, H.H. *A History of the Roman World from 753 to 146 BC* (Methuen, London, 1935)

Schwartz, M. and Khan, C. (eds) *Representing Shakespeare* (Johns Hopkins University Press, Baltimore, MD, 1980)

Sewell, A. *Character and Society in Shakespeare*, 2nd edn (Oxford University Press, Oxford, 1961)

Shackford, M.H. *Plutarch in Renaissance England with Special Reference to Shakespeare* (Wellesley College, 1929)

Sharp, B. *In Contempt of all Authority: Rural Artisans and Riots in the West of England, 1586–1660* (University of California Press, Berkeley, CA, 1980)

Shaw, G.B. *Shaw on Shakespeare*, ed. by E. Wilson (Penguin Books, Harmondsworth, Middlesex, 1969)

Simmons, J.L. *Shakespeare's Pagan World: The Roman Tragedies* (University Press of Virginia, Charlottesville, VA, 1973)

Smith, A.J. *Literary Love* (Edward Arnold, London, 1983)

Spencer, T.J.B. 'Shakespeare and the Elizabethan Romans', *Shakespeare Survey*, vol. 10 (1957)

—— *William Shakespeare: The Roman Plays*, Writers and their Work No. 157 (Longman, London, 1963)

—— *(ed.) Shakespeare's Plutarch* (Penguin Books, Harmondsworth, 1964)

Spencer, T. *Shakespeare and the Nature of Man* (Macmillan, New York, 1942)

Spurgeon, C.F.E. *Shakespeare's Imagery: And What It Tells Us* (Cambridge University Press, Cambridge, 1935)

Stauffer, D.A. *Shakespeare's World of Images: The Development of his Moral Ideas*, 2nd edn (Indiana University Press, Bloomington, IN and London, 1973)

Stewart, J.I.M. *Character and Motive in Shakespeare* (Longman, London, 1949)

Stirling, B. *The Populace in Shakespeare* (Columbia University Press, New York, 1949)

—— *Unity in Shakespearian Tragedy: The Interplay of Theme and Character* (Columbia University Press, New York, 1956)

Summers, J.H. *Dreams of Love and Power: On Shakespeare's Plays* (Clarendon Press, Oxford, 1984)

Sutherland, J. and Hurstfield, J. (eds) *Shakespeare's World* (Edward Arnold, London, 1964)

Talbert, E.W. *The Problem of Order: Elizabethan Political Commonplaces and an Example of Shakespeare's Art* (University of North Carolina Press, Chapel Hill, NC, 1962)

Thomas, K. *Religion and the Decline of Magic: Studies in Popular Beliefs in 16th and 17th Century England* (Weidenfeld & Nicolson, London, 1971)

Thomson, J.A.K. *Shakespeare and the Classics* (Allen & Unwin, London, 1952)

Tillyard, E.M.W. *Shakespeare's History Plays*, 8th edn (Chatto & Windus, London, 1969)

Tobias, R.C. and Zolbrod, P.G. (eds) *Shakespeare's Late Plays: Essays in Honour of Charles Crow* (Ohio University Press, Athens, Ohio, 1974)

Tomlinson, T.B. *A Study of Elizabethan and Jacobean Tragedy* (Cambridge University Press, Cambridge, Melbourne University Press, Melbourne, 1964)

Traci, P.J. *The Love Play of 'Antony and Cleopatra'* (The Hague, 1970)

Traversi, D.A. *An Approach to Shakespeare*, 2 vols, 3rd edn (Hollis & Carter, London, Sydney and Toronto, 1969)

—— *The Roman Plays* (Hollis & Carter, London, 1963)

Ure, P. (ed.) *Shakespeare: 'Julius Caesar'* (Casebook Series, Macmillan, London, 1969)

Van Doren, M. *Shakespeare* (Holt, Rinehart & Winston Inc., London and New York, 1939)

Van Laan, T.F. *Role-Playing in Shakespeare* (University of Toronto Press, Toronto, 1978)

Velz, J.W. *Shakespeare and the Classical Tradition: A Critical Guide to Commentary, 1660–1960* (University of Minnesota Press, Minneapolis, MN, 1968)

Vickers, B. *Shakespeare: Coriolanus*, Studies in English Literature, No. 58 (Edward Arnold, London, 1966)

Waith, E.M. *The Herculean Hero* (Columbia University Press, New York, 1962)

—— The Oxford Shakespeare edition of *Titus Andronicus* (Oxford University Press, Oxford, 1984)

Wells, R.H. *Shakespeare, Politics and the State* (Macmillan, Basingstoke, 1986)

Wells, S. (ed.) *Shakespeare: Select Bibliographical Guides* (Oxford University Press, Oxford, 1973; revised edition 1990)

—— *The Cambridge Companion to Shakespeare Studies* (Cambridge University Press, Cambridge, 1986)

—— *Shakespeare and the Classical World, Shakespeare Survey* 31 (Cambridge University Press, Cambridge, 1979)

—— Commentary on Royal Shakespeare Company Programme/Text of *Titus Andronicus* (RSC Publications, 1987)

Whitaker, V.K. *Shakespeare's Use of Learning* (Huntington Library, San Marino, CA, 1953)

—— *The Mirror up to Nature: The Technique of Shakespeare's Tragedies* (Huntington Library, San Marino, CA, 1965)

Wikander, M.H. *The Play of Truth and State: Historical Drama from Shakespeare to Brecht* (Johns Hopkins University Press, Baltimore, MD and London, 1986)

Wilders, J. *The Lost Garden: A View of Shakespeare's English and Roman History Plays* (Macmillan, London, 1978)

—— *New Prefaces to Shakespeare* (Blackwell, Oxford, 1988)

Williamson, M.L. *Infinite Variety: 'Antony and Cleopatra' in Renaissance Drama and Earlier Tradition* (Lawrence Verry, Mystic, CT, 1974)

Wilson, J.D. *The Essential Shakespeare* (Cambridge University Press, Cambridge, 1932)

—— New Cambridge Shakespeare, *Titus Andronicus* (Cambridge University Press, Cambridge, 1948)

Wilson, H.S. *On the Design of Shakespearian Tragedy* (University of Toronto, Toronto, and Oxford University Press, Oxford and London, 1957)

Wrightson, K. *English Society 1580–1680* (Hutchinson, London, 1982)

INDEX

Adelman, J. 8–9, 119, 121
Alexander 42
Allam, R. 75, 89
Amyot, Jacques 3
Andronicus, Comnenus 24
Appian 6, 62, 64–6
Aristotle 67

Baker, Sean 80
Barnet, S. 26
Barton, A. 180
Barton, J. 26
Bonjour, A. 67
Bradbrook, M. C. 36
Bradley, A. C. 213
Brockbank, P. 189
Brook, Peter 23, 26
Brooke, N. 23–4, 38
Brower, R. 179–80
Brutus, Lucius Junius 19, 47, 156
Bullough, G. 2, 24, 36, 64, 67, 93

Campbell, O. J. 178, 213
Cantor, P. A. 7–8, 10–12, 22
Carson, R. A. G. 69
Cato, Marcus 19, 51, 59, 216
Chambers, E. K. 26
Charney, M. 146, 176, 214–15
Coleridge, S. T. 176
Cox, Brian 23
Crassus 42

Deeds of Caesar, The 102
Dennis 5
Dowden, E. 85, 90, 176–7
Dryden, J. 5

Euripides 28

Farnham, W. 67, 179, 215
feast of Lupercal 4, 40, 44
Flavius, Josephus 101
Foakes, R. A. 68
Fowler, W. W. 67
Fulbecke, W. 6

Grass, G. 215

Hall 3, 140
Hamlet 8, 10, 67, 119, 142, 144, 195
Hazlitt, W. 89, 176
Heilman, R. B. 38
Henry IV Part I 129
Henry VIII 10
Hibbard, G. R. 26
Holinshed 3, 140
Holland, Philemon 62, 157

James, Emrys 77, 90
Jones, E. 28

King John 10
King Lear 8, 10, 24–6, 31, 33, 37, 39,
    67, 120, 142, 144
Knights, L. C. 68
Kyd, T. 5–6, 23, 38, 67

Leggatt, A. 69, 85, 90, 127–8, 131, 214
Livy 5, 157–9, 171, 173–5, 180
Lodge, T. 101

Macbeth 10, 24, 67, 120, 142, 144
MacCallum, M. W. 3

242

Machiavelli 180
Mason, A. H. 143
Maxwell, J. C. 26
Meres, Francis 26
Miola, R. S. 10–11, 38
Mirren, Helen 117
Montaigne 6
Moulton, R. G. 80
Muir, K. 3
Murry, J. Middleton 143

Old Vic 26
Olivier, Sir Laurence 23, 26
Othello 26, 67, 119, 142, 144
Ovid 36

Palmer, J. 85
Parthian campaign 4, 94, 104–5
Peele 26
Percy's *Reliques* 28
Pharos, Isle of 41, 112
Pharsalia 43, 48
Philippics 62, 94
Pope, A. 5
Price, H. T. 26

Rabkin, N. 67
Ravenscroft, E. 25
Reynolds, R. 6
Richard II 9
Richard III 9
Richmond, H. M. 67

Rosen, B. and W. 66
Rossiter 178–9
Royal Shakespeare Company
    productions 23, 26–7, 35–8, 75, 77,
    80, 89–90, 117
Rymer, T. 5

Samos, Isle of 96, 108
Schanzer, E. 67, 84
Seneca 28
Snyder, S. 153
Spencer, T. J. B. 5–7, 23
Stationers' Register 6
Stirling, B. 88
Suetonius 6, 62–4
Sumpter, Donald 38
Swinburne, A. C. 176

Tacitus 5–6
Tate, N. 5
Theodosius 24
Troilus and Cressida 33, 174

Ure, P. 9–10

Van Dyke, J. 217

Waith, E. M. 26, 28, 36
Warner, Deborah 23
Wells, S. 25–6
Wilders, J. 9
Wilson, J. D. 26